BUDDHIST SECTS IN INDIA

BUDDHIST SECTS IN INDIA

NALINAKSHA DUTT

MOTILAL BANARSIDASS PUBLISHERS
PRIVATE LIMITED • DELHI

Reprint : Delhi, 1987, 1998, 2007
Second Edition : Delhi, 1978

ISBN : 81-208-0427-9 (Cloth)
ISBN : 81-208-0428-7 (Paper)

MOTILAL BANARSIDASS
41 U.A. Bungalow Road, Jawahar Nagar, Delhi 110 007
8 Mahalaxmi Chamber, 22 Bhulabhai Desai Road, Mumbai 400 026
203 Royapettah High Road, Mylapore, Chennai 600 004
236, 9th Main III Block, Jayanagar, Bangalore 560 011
Sanas Plaza, 1302 Baji Rao Road, Pune 411 002
8 Camac Street, Kolkata 700 017
Ashok Rajpath, Patna 800 004
Chowk, Varanasi 221 001

PRINTED IN INDIA
BY JAINENDRA PRAKASH JAIN AT SHRI JAINENDRA PRESS,
A-45, NARAINA, PHASE-I, NEW DELHI 110 028
AND PUBLISHED BY NARENDRA PRAKASH JAIN FOR
MOTILAL BANARSIDASS PUBLISHERS PRIVATE LIMITED,
BUNGALOW ROAD, DELHI 110 007

INTRODUCTION

It is striking that as far back as 1859, i.e., over a century ago, the attention of European scholars was drawn to the appearance of Buddhist sects in India, mentioning their names without, however, any comment. The earliest article was written by St. Julien, 'Listes diverses des noms des dix-huit sectes du bouddhisme' in the *Journal Asiatique*, 1859. This was followed by M.V. Vassilief in 1860, Drs. Rhys Davids and Oldenberg in 1881, H. Kern in 1884 and I. P. Minayeff in 1884 (vide for details, pages 11-13) of this book.

It was after the publication of the translation of the Chinese version of Vasumitra's treatise on eighteen sects of Buddhism in India by Prof. J. Masuda, who happened to be a Lecturer in the Calcutta University and also a colleague of the present writer, in the *Asia Major*, vol. II (1925) supplemented by the Tibetan texts on the eighteen schools by Bhavya and Vinītadeva entitled *Nikāya-bhedavibhaṅga* and *Samayabhedoparacanacakra* respectively.

It should be noted that Vasumitra's treatise had three Chinese translations:

(i) 'Shi-pa' pu' -lun, ascribed either to Kumārajīva(401-13) or to Paramārtha (546-69).

(ii) Pu'-chi-i-lun, ascribed to Paramārtha. This translation, according to Masuda, appears to be more accurate.

(iii) I-pu'-tsung-lun, ascribed to Hiuen Tsang (662), is regarded by Masuda as the best of the translations.

There were four scholars, bearing the name of Vasumitra:

(i) Vasumitra of Kaniṣka's Council and one of the authors of the Mahāvibhāṣā.

(ii) Vasumitra of the Sautrāntika school.

(iii) Vasumitra, who appeared a thousand years after Buddha's parinibbāna, and

(iv) Vasumitra of the Sarvāstivāda school, from whom Hiuen Tsang learnt the Sarvāstivāda doctrines.

It is curious that none of the books and articles mentioned on pp. 11-13 refers to such an important Pali Abhidhamma text as the *Kathāvatthu* published in 1897 and its commentary in 1889 and the former work's English translation by Mrs. C.A.F. Rhys Davids entitled *Points of Controversy* (1915).

The antiquity of the *Kathāvatthu* traditionally goes back to the days of Emperor Aśoka, under whose auspices the Third Buddhist Council was held with Moggaliputta Tissa as its president. The special features of this book are that

(i) it presents the doctrines of the opponents, i.e., an exposition of the doctrines of a particular non-Theravāda school;

(ii) it allows him to state his arguments as well as

(iii) to quote in their support the statements of Buddha, occurring in the Nikāyas or elsewhere in any Piṭakan text.

After giving full scope to the opponents for the grounds of their views, Moggaliputta Tissa, the president, refuted them from the standpoint of Theravāda by counter-arguments as well as with the help of quotations from the Buddhavacanas.

The contribution of the present author lies not only in making an analytical study of the treatises of Vasumitra, Bhavya and Vinītadeva but also the *Kathāvatthu* and its commentary by Buddhaghoṣa as well as the *Abhidharamakośa-vyākhyā,* an excellent edition of which has been published by Prof. Wogihara of Japan and the *Sammitīya-nikāya śāstra* translated from Chinese by Prof. Venkataraman of the Viśvabhāratī and *The Gilgit Manuscripts*, III, edited and published by the present writer, containing the original Mūlasarvāstivāda Vinaya, and also the Jñānaprasthāna Sūtra partially restored from Chinese by Śānti Bhikṣu also of the Viśvabhāratī.

This book ends with an Epilogue, in which an attempt has been made to show how Mahāyānism developed as a natural consequence of the views of the Mahāsaṅghikas and as a development of the nebulous conception of Bodhisattva and Buddhakāyas in the *Divyāvadāna* and *Avadāna-śataka*, ascribed to the Sarvāstivādins and also as a reaction to the realism of the Sarvāstivādins, and how gradually Mahāyānism surpassed Hīnayānism both in popularity and propagation.

To this book has been added an Appendix containing a synopsis of the ancient geography of India as described by Hiuen Tsang; it also throws light on the dispersal of Buddhist seats in India along with a brief account of the Buddhist sects as given by I-tsing and the localities where these were existing at his time, i. e., half a century after Hiuen Tsang's visit to India.

In fine, I should like to thank my learned friend, Sri K. L. Mukhopadhyay, M.A. for suggesting the appropriate title of the book, which helped me to confine my attention exclusively to the Buddhist Sects in India. I should mention that I have derived much benefit from the *Histoire du Bouddhisme indien* (Louvain, 1956) of Prof. E. Lamotte, who has also published many other valuable works on Mahāyāna Buddhism, utilising exhaustively the Chinese versions of the lost Sanskrit texts. I also thank my student Dr. Miss Ksanika Saha, Ph. D. for preparing the Indexes.

NALINAKSHA DUTT

CONTENTS

Introduction		...	v
Abbreviations		...	xi
I	Political Background from Ajātasatru to Mahāpadma Nanda	...	1
II	Sources and Account of the Second Buddhist Council	...	11
III	Disruptive Forces in the Saṅgha	...	34
IV	Sources and Classification of Sects	...	48
V	The Mahāsāṅghikas	...	57
VI	Doctrines of Group II Schools	...	98
VII	Doctrines of Group III Schools	...	121
VIII	Doctrines of Group IV Schools	...	181
IX	Doctrines of Group V Schools	...	211
	Epilogue	...	218
	Appendix : Hiuen Tsang and I-tsing on the dispersion of Buddhist Sects in India	...	261
INDEX		...	291

ABBREVIATIONS

Aspects—*Aspects of Mahāyāna Buddhism* by N. Dutt (1930)
ASR.—Archaeological Survey Report (Govt. of India)
Aṣṭa.—*Aṣṭasāhasrikā Prajñāpāramitā* (ASB. edition)
Bareau—*Les sectes du Petit Vehicule* (BEFEO. 1956)
E.I. or Ep. Ind—*Epigraphia Indica*
EMB.—*Early Monastic Buddhism* by N. Dutt, 2 vols. (1941)
Fa-hien—James Legge's *Travels of Fa-hien in India & Ceylon.*
H.T —Hiuen Tsang
I-tsing—Takakusu's *Records of the Buddhist Religion in India & Malay Archipelago*
Kośa-vyākhyā or Kośa—Prof. Louis de la Vallée Poussin's French translation
Kvu.—*Kathāvatthu* (P.T.S.)
Masuda—Masuda's Translation of Vasumitra's *Treatise on Buddhist Sects*, published in the Asia Major, II
Mmk.—*Mañjuśrī-mūla-kalpa* (Trivandrum Sanskrit Series)
Mtu—*Mahāvastu*, edited by Prof. E Senart
M. Vṛ.—*Mādhyamika Vṛtti*, edited by Prof. Louis de la Vallée Poussin
Ray Chaudhury—*Political History of Ancient India* by H. C. Ray Chaudhury (3rd edition)
Schiefner—Prof. Schiefner's German translation of the *Tibetan History of Buddhism of Tāranātha*
V.—Vasumitra or Vasubandhu
Watters—Watters' *Yuan Chwang's Travels In India*, 2 vols.
Winternitz—*History of the Buddhist Literature* (Cal. Uni.)

CHAPTER 1

POLITICAL BACKGROUND FROM AJĀTASATTU TO MAHĀPADMA NANDA

The session of the First Buddhist Council took place soon after the mahāparinirvāṇa of Buddha (486 B.C.) in the eighth year of the reign of king Ajātasattu, who ruled for 32 years from 493 B.C. Ajātasattu extended his father's dominion beyond Magadha and ruled over Aṅga, Kāśi and the states of the Vajjian confederacies.[1] The Buddhist traditions are unanimous in stating that Ajātasattu in his early days was not very well-disposed towards Buddha and his religion, but later on, his mind changed and he became a patron of the religion, supporting whole-heartedly the session of the First Council.

In the *Mahāvaṃsa* commentary[2] and the *Mañjuśrimūlakalpa*[3] (henceforth abbreviated as *Mmk.*), Ajātasattu's enthusiasm for rendering service to the new religion, is referred to but there is no evidence to show his interest in the propagation of the religion.

UDĀYIBHADDA (461-445 B.C.)

According to the Buddhist and Jaina traditions, though not according to the *Purāṇas*,[4] Ajātasattu was succeeded by his son Udāyibhadda. He ruled for 16 years 461 B.C.[5] The *Mm*k. says that like his father he was not only enthusiastic about the

---

1. See *Buddhist India*, ch. 1; H.C. Raychaudhuri, *Political History of Ancient India*, 3rd ed., p. 140. *Mañjuśrīmūlakalpa*, p. 604.

2. In the *Vaṃsaṭṭhappakāsinī*, (p. 145), it is pointed out that Ajātasattu repaired the 18 great monasteries of Rājagaha.

3. *Mmk.*, p. 603.

श सनार्थं तु बुद्धानां कारयिष्यति अग्रधीः ।
महाराजाजातविख्यातो मागधेयो नराधिपः ॥

4. Raychaudhuri, *op. cit.*, p. 143.

5. 20 years according to the *Mmk.*, p. 704. Prof. Chattopadhyaya assigns to him a reigning period of 25 years.

religion but also had the sayings of Buddha collected.[1] In the same text[2] again, it is stated that the religion would decline after Buddha's death, the kings would be fighting with one another, and the monks would busy themselves with various secular matters, find fault with one another, and lack in self-restraint. The monks and men would be demoralised, indulge in false disputations, and become jealous of one another. The non-Buddhists would gain the upper hand and the people would revert to Brāhmanism and take to animal killing and similar other evil practices. If these mutually contradictory statements of the *Mmk.* be considered along with the discreet silence of the Ceylonese chronicles about the acvtivities of Udāyibhadda, it seems that the cause of Buddhism found little favour with the king. The text adds that there would, however, be some good men, gods and beings other than human, who would continue to worship the relics, and though the religion would be on the wane, there would be at least eight distinguished monks[3] with Rāhula as the chief to protect it.

Bu-ston[4] writes that the guardianship of Buddhism was entrusted by the Teacher to (Mahā) Kāśyapa, who in turn assigned it

---

Recently Prof. K. Chattopadhyaya has re-examined the question of succession of the kings of Magadha and arrived at the conclusion that *Darśaka* was an alternative name of Udāyi as *Śreṇika* was of Bimbisāra and *Kunika* of Ajātaśatru. (See *Proc. of the Indian History Congress*, Lahore, 1940, pp. 140-7). Prof. Bhandarkar identifies Darśaka with Nāgadāsaka. Cf. *Divyāvadāna*, p. 369.

1. *Mmk.*, p. 604.

तस्यापि सुतो राजा उकाराख्यः प्रकीर्त्तितः ।
भविष्यति तदा क्षिप्रं शासनार्थं च उद्यतः ॥
तदेतत् प्रवचनं शास्तु लिखापयिष्यति विस्तरम् ।
पूजांश्च महतीं कृत्वा दिक् समन्तान् नयिष्यति ॥

2. *Mmk.*, pp. 597-98.

3. The list of monks given in *Mmk.*, p. 64 : is as follows :—

Śāriputra, Maudgalyāyana, Mahākāśyapa, Subhūti, Rāhula, Nanda, Bhadrika, Kaphiṇa.

Ibid., p. 111 : Śāriputra, Maudgalyāyana, Gavāmpati, Piṇḍola Bharadvāja, Pilindavatsa, Rāhula, Mahākāśyapa, Ānanda.

4. Obermiller's *Translation of Bu-ston's History of Buddhism* (henceforth abbreviated as Bu-ston), II, p. 88.

to Ānanda. Both Kāśyapa and Ānanda passed away during the life-time of Ajātasattu, Ānanda charged his disciple Śāṇavāsika to protect the religion after his demise and to ordain, in course of time, Upagupta of Mathurā. He foretold that, according to the prophecy of the Teacher, Upagupta would become a Buddha but not with all the characteristics of a Sambuddha. Just before his demise, Ānanda also ordained 500 Brāhmanical anchorites with Madhyāntika at their head, commissioning to him the propagation of the religion in Kashmir. The episode of Madhyāntika and his activities in Kashmir do not however, find any mention in the Ceylonese chronicles.

ANURUDDHA'S SON MUṆḌA (445-437 B.C.)

Udāyibhadda, after a reign of 16 years (461-445 B.C.), was succeeded by his son Anuruddha, whose period of reign as well as that of his son Muṇḍa was very short, being only 8 years in all, 445-437 B.C. In the *Divyāvadāna*[1] king Muṇḍa is described as the son of Udāyibhadda, and no mention is made of Anuruddha. In the *Aṅguttara Nikāya*,[2] king Muṇḍa is mentioned as approaching-bhikkhu Nārada on the death of his queen Bhaddā. He listened to a discourse of bhikkhu Nārada delivered at Pāṭaliputta on the impermanence of worldly beings and objects. In the Jaina tradition preserved in the *Pariśiṣṭaparvan* (ch. vi), it is stated that a prince in the guise of a Jaina novice killed Udāyin. Prof. Chattopadhyaya surmises that this novice might be king Muṇḍa.[3]

NĀGADĀSAKA (437-413 B.C.)

King Muṇḍa was succeeded by his son Nāgadāsaka, who ruled for 24 years. With Nāgadāsaka ended the rule of the line of kings that commenced with Bimbisāra.[4] In the Ceylonese

1. *Divyāvadāna*, p. 369.
2. *Aṅguttara*, III, pp. 57f.
3. K. Chattopadhyaya, *op. cit.*
4. The *Divyāvadāna* (p. 369) says that Muṇḍa's son was Kākavarṇi. In the *Aśokāvadāna* and *Divyāvadāna*, the line of kings is given as follows :—

Bimbisāra-Ajātaśatru-Udāyibhadra-Muṇḍa-Kākavarṇi-Sahali - Tulakucī-Mahāmaṇḍala-Prasenajit-Nanda-Bindusāra-Susīma-Aśoka.

chronicles, all the successors of Bimbisāra are described as patricidal (*pitughātakavaṃsa*); how far this statement is reliable remains to be examined, but it seems that the Buddhists were not in much favour of these kings, and evidently, as the *Mmk.* says Buddhism was on the wane all along this period of about half a century. Madhyāntika's departure to Kashmir and his attempt to propagate Buddhism far away from Magadha is also an indirect hint at the unpopularity of the religion in the province of its origin.

ŚIŚUNĀGA DYNASTY

The throne of Nāgadāsaka was usurped by his minister, Śiśunāga, who according to the tradition preserved in the *Uttaravihāra-aṭṭhakathā*, was the son of a Licchavi prince of Vaisāli by a courtezan.[1] As he was adopted by a minister, he came to be known as a minister's son. According to a late tradition preserved in the *Mālālaṅkāra-vatthu,* Śiśunāga had his residence at Vaisāli, to which place he later transferred his capital from Rājagaha. He ruled for 18 years (413-395 B.C.) and is said to have humbled the Pradyota dynasty of Avantī.[2] As far as the testimony of the Buddhist texts is concerned, no incident of note ever occurred in the history of Buddhism during his reign.

Śiśunāga was succeeded by his son Kālāśoka (395-367 B.C.) of the Ceylonese chronicles or Kākavarṇin of the *Purāṇas*. Many scholars are of the opinion that the two names are of the same person. The *Aśokāvadāna* places Kākavarṇin after Muṇḍa and makes no mention of Kālāśoka while the *Mañjuśrīmūlakalpa* speaks of Viśoka as the successor of Śiśunāga. Tāranātha has confused the Emperor Aśoka with Kālāśoka and made Viśoka a son of the former. In the *Kathāvatthu-aṭṭhakathā* (p. 2) Kālāśoka is called simply Aśoka. The outstanding event that took place. in the history of Buddhism during his reign is the session of the Second Buddhist Council (*see infra*).

---

1. *Vaṃsaṭṭhappakāsinī* I, p. 155.
2. Raychaudhury, *Political History of Ancient India* (henceforth abbreviated as *PHAI.*) (1932), p. 147.

According to the *Mahābodhivaṃsa,* Kālāśoka was succeeded by his ten sons: Bhadrasena, Koraṇḍavarṇa, Maṅgura, Sabbañjaha, Jālaka, Ubhaka, Sañjaya, Koravya, Nandivardhana, and Pañcamaka, who ruled simultaneously for 22 years (367-345 B.C.) but in the *Purāṇas* only one is mentioned, *viz.*, Nandi-vardhana. This tradition, however, is not corroborated by other Buddhist sources, according to which, Kālāśoka or Viśoka was succeeded by his son Śūrasena, who reigned for 17 years.[1]

Śūrasena supported the bhikṣus of the four quarters for three years and offered a hundred kinds of requisites to all *caityas* existing on the face of the earth.[2] Tāranātha makes Arhat Śāṇavāsika and Arhat Yaśa contemporaries of Śūrasena and refers to the appearance of Mahādeva and his five propositions during his reign.

Śūrasena was succeeded by Nanda, who, according to Tāranātha,[3] was Śūrasena's son. The *Mmk.*[4] says that king Nanda was very powerful, maintained a large army and made Puṣpapura his capital. He, it is said, acquired wealth through magical means. On the basis of the following stanza in the *Mmk.*:

नीचमुख्यसमाख्यातो ततो लोके भविष्यति ।
तद्धनं प्राप्य मन्त्रीरसौ लोके पार्थिवतां गतः ॥

Jayaswal[5] remarks that Nanda was at first a minister of the previous king and that he belonged to a low family but was the leading man of the community. Through unexpected acquisition of wealth he became the king of the country. He entertained the

1. Also called Ugrasena in the *Mahābodhi-vaṃsa*. Cf. *Mmk.*, p. 611.
तस्याप्यनन्तरे राजा शूरसेनः प्रकथ्यते ।

2. Schiefner, *Tāranātha's Geschichte des Buddhismus,* p. 50-51. The restoration from Tibetan may well be Śūrasena instead of Vīrasena. Cf. *Mmk.* p. 611.

तेनापि कारिता शास्तुः कारा सुमहती तदा ।
स्तूपैरलंकृता सर्वा समुद्रान्ता वसुन्धरा ॥

3. Schiefner, *op. cit.*, p. 52. King Nanda came of the Licchavi tribe.
4. *Mmk.*, pp. 611-12.
5. *Imperial History of India*, p. 14.

bhikṣus in Kāśī for many years.[1] King Nanda was surrounded by Brāhmaṇa ministers, on whom also he bestowed wealth. At the instance of his spiritual teacher (*Kalyāṇamitra*), he offered several gifts to the *caityas* built on Buddha's relics.[2] King Nanda ruled for 20 years and died as a true Buddhist at the age of sixty-six.[3]

During the reign of king Nanda. Bhikṣu Nāga spoke highly of the five propositions of Mahādeva, which led to the appearance of four sects.[4] In this connection, reference may be made to the statement of Tāranātha to the effect that during the reign of Aśoka (i.e. Kālāśoka) there appeared a Brāhmaṇa Vatsa in Kashmir, who was learned but very wicked. He took pleasure in preaching the Ātmaka theory, travelled all over the country and made the simple people accept his teaching and caused a dissension in the Saṅgha.[5] It is a well-known fact that the Vātsiputrīyas[6] were one of the four sects, and probably this school came into existence at an earlier date but was recognized as a separate school at the time of king Nanda.

Tāranātha as well as Bu-ston speak of the successor of Nanda as his son Mahāpadma, who, they state, was devoted to Buddhism and furnished the monks at Kusumapura with all the necessaries of life.[7] They further state that Vararuci and Pāṇini, who were his father's ministers, continued to be his ministers, but Vararuci was hated and ultimately killed by him. As an atonement for the sin of killing a Brāhmaṇa, 24 monasteries were erected by him. During his reign, Tāranātha states, Sthiramati, a disciple of Nāga,[8] caused further divisions in the Saṅgha by propagating his teacher's propositions.

Raichaudhury and other scholars place king Nanda after the reign of the sons of Kālāśoka. Jayaswal, on the basis of the

---

1. Schiefner, *op. cit.*, p. 53.
2. *Mmk.*, pp. 611-12.
3. *Mmk.*, p. 612.
4. Schiefner, *op. cit.*
5. *Ibid.*
6. The propounders of the Ātmaka theory maintained that a soul passes from one existence to another. This theory was rejected by Buddha.
7. Schiefner, *op. cit.*, p. 55.
8. See above, p. 5.

Mmk., places Śūrasena after Kālāśoka. It may be that Sūrasena was another name of Bhadrasena, the first son of Kālāśoka. In the history of Buddhism we know that, after the session of the Second Council during the reign of Kālāśoka, dissensions arose in the Buddhist Saṅgha. Mahādeva's five propositions were regarded by Vasumitra and Bhavya as the main cause of the dissensions. Mahādeva was followed by Nāga, who, in his turn, was followed by Sthiramati in the propagation of the five propositions. In view of this succession of teachers, it is quite probable that Kālāśoka was succeeded by Śūrasena, and Śūrasena by Nanda. Bu-ston[1] writes that troubles arose in the Buddhist Saṅgha 137 years after Buddha's *parinibbāna.* This date coincides with the reign of Nanda and therefore his information as also of Tāranātha that Śūrasena intervened between Kālāśoka and Nanda, appears to be authentic. It is quite likely that the Tibetan historians mistook the name Mahāpadma Nanda for the names of two personages, Nanda and Mahāpadma, and made the latter a son of the former. It may be that king Nanda took the appellation Mahāpadma sometime after the commencement of his reign.

The *Mmk.* and the Tibetan historians furnish us with interesting information regarding the time and activities of the famous grammarians Pāṇini and Vararuci. Regarding Pāṇini, the texts mention that he was born at Bhīrukavana in the west (probably north-west) and that though he was a Brāhmaṇa, he was strongly inclined to the Buddhist faith, and that he attained proficiency in grammar (*śabdaśāstra*) through the grace of Avalokiteśvara. He composed the well-known *Pāṇini-vyākaraṇa* and ultimately attained *Śrāvakabodhi.* The date of Pāṇini is placed by Weber, Maxmüller, Keith, and several other scholars between 350 and 300 B.C., and this is precisely the period during which king Nanda reigned, hence the contemporaneity of Nanda and Pāṇini, as stated by Buddhist writers, seems to be correct.

Regarding Vararuci, our information is that he was an erudite scholar and started writing explanatory *śāstras* on Buddha's words. Prof. Belvalkar[2] has collected ample evidence to show

1. Bu-ston, II, p. 76.
2. *Systems of Sanskrit Grammar*, pp. 11, 27, 85.

that Vararuci was another name of Kātyāyana of the Aindra School of grammarians, which school, Tāranātha says, was believed to be earlier than the Paṇinian school. To this school also belongs Kaccāyana's Pāli grammar. Vararuci's interest in writing exegetical literature is also referred to by Belvalkar.[1] In view of all these references, it may be stated that Vararuci was also a contemporary of king Nanda and Pāṇini and that he, like his famous namesake Mahākaccāyana, specialised in writing commentaries on Buddha's enigmatic expressions. From the above account, it may be concluded that dissensions in the Buddhist Saṅgha commenced in the reign of Kālāśoka and multiplied during the reigns of Śūrasena and Mahāpadma Nanda.

Principal Centres of Buddhism

The names of monks and the geographical information furnished by the accounts of the Second Council throw some light on the extent of the area which came under the influence of the Buddhist Church. The leading monks of the time were counted as eight, viz., Sabbakāmī, Sāḷha, Revata, Khujjasobhita, Yasa, Sambhūta Sāṇavāsī, Vāsabhagāmika and Sumana.[2] The first six were disciples of Ānanda, while the remaining two of Anuruddha. Ānanda died during the later part of the reign of Ajātasattu, and so his disciples at the time of the Second Council were well advanced in age. Sabbakāmi was then the Saṅghatthera but Revata was the recognized leader. In the Sanskrit tradition, Sambhūta Sāṇavāsī is given prominence as he, according to this tradition, was selected by Ānanda as the monk to take charge of the religion after him. In the Chinese traditions, he is shown as taking the leading part in the deliberations of the Council. The Vaiśālians were monks of the eastern countries (*pācīnakā*), so also were Sabbakāmī, Sāḷha of

1. *Ibid.*, p. 84.

2. Bu-ston (II, p. 93) gives a slightly different list : Yaśas, Sāḍha, Dhanika, Kubjita, Ajita, Sambhūta, Revata.

Sahajāti,[1] Khujjasobhita and Vāsabhagāmika.[2] In Bu-ston's account, Sabbakāmī is said to have been residing at Vaisāli. Hiuen Tsang states that Khujjasobhita belonged to Paṭaliputra while Sāḷha hailed from Vaisāli. It will be observed that Sāḷha of Sahajāti or Vaisāli was at first in an indecisive mood. King Kālāśoka, also like Sāḷha, was at first in favour of the Vaisālians, but later on, at the intervention of his sister Bhikkhunī Nandā, he became inclined towards the Westerners. In the early history of Buddhism, Vaisāli is described as a town seething with non-Buddhistic thinkers and as a centre of the followers of Nigaṇṭha Nāṭaputta. Hence it is quite in keeping with the traditions of the country that non-orthodox Buddhists should find a footing there.

Yasa, the most active figure in the account and the one who started the commotion, hailed, according to Hiuen Tsang, from Kośala. He left Vaisāli for Kosambī, where he organised a party with sixty monks of Pāvā (Pāveyyakā)[3] and eighty monks of Avantī, all of the Western countries.[4] He proceeded with them first to Sambhūta Sāṇavāsī of Mathurā and met him at Ahogaṅga.[5] Accompanied by him they went to meet Revata, another Westerner, belonging to Kanauj and met him at Soreyya. The fourth Western monk was Sumana. Thus we see that there

---

1. Soṇaka, according to Bu-ston, II, p. 93. Sahajāti is identified with Bhiṭā, 9 miles, S.S.W. from Allahabad. Sir John Marshall identifies Sahajāti with Bhiṭā on the basis of the inscription : 'Māgadhī Sahajātiye nigamaśa'. See N. N. Ghosh, *Early His. of Kausambi*, p. 89.

2. Bu-ston (p. 93) gives the following geographical information :—
   (i) Sarvakāmin of Vaiśālī
   (ii) Yaśas of Dhanika
   (iii) Śāḍha of Soṇaka
   (iv) Dhanika of Sāṃkāśya (in Magadha, see Przyluski, *Le Concīle de Rājagaha*. p. 286)
   (v) Kubjita of Pāṭaliputra
   (vi) Ājita of Śrughna
   (vii) Sambhūta of Māhiṣmatī
   (viii) Revata of Sahajāti

3. Pāṭheyyakā is another reading.

4. *Vaṃsaṭṭhappakāsinī* p. 166 : Pacchimikā yeva Pāveyyakā.

5. Ahogaṅga is a mountain near the sources of the Ganges, Moggaliputta Tissa resided there just before the Third Council, see B.C. Law, *Geog. of Early Buddhism*, p. 40.

was a clear geographical division among the monks. The opposition to the Vaisālian practices was started by Yasa of Kosala, and supported by Revata of Soreyya (Kanauj), Sambhūta Sāṇavāsī of Mathurā, and Sumana, whose native place is not mentioned anywhere. This testifies to the fact that the monks of the western countries, viz. Kauśāmbī,[1] Avantī, Mathurā were more orthodox in their observance of the Vinaya rules as adopted by the Theravādins. In the deliberations of the Council, Sabbakāmī, though the Saṅghatthera, was not given the lead, and this also proves the lack of his whole-hearted support to the agitation started by Yasa. Sāḷha's attitude, as mentioned above, was at first indecisive and similar probably was also the view of Khujjasobhita of Pāṭaliputra.

Prof. Przyluski also has noted the geographical division of monks in his *Concile de Rājagṛha* (pp. 308-09) and remarked that there were definitely three centres, viz., Vaiśālī,[2] Kauśāmbī and Mathurā. Kauśāmbī and all south-western countries became later on the seat of the Theravādins, while Mathurā and the north-western countries of the Sarvāstivādins. The Westerners of this Council were therefore the group of monks who came to be later on known as the Sthavirās and Sarvāstivādins, while the Easterners, who had their seat at Vaiśālī, were the Mahāsaṅghikas and their offshoots. Whatever might have been the differences between the Easterners and the Westerners, it is apparent that Buddhism was prevalent at the time all over the central belt of India from Avantī[3] to Vaiśālī and from Mathurā to Kauśāmbī. The chief centre of Buddhism, it seems, was shifted at that time from Rājagṛha to Pāṭaliputra, which also became the seat of the rulers. The Mahāsaṅghikas also made Pāṭaliputra their chief centre.[4]

---

1. Kauśāmbī is identified with the ruins at Kośam, 38 miles from Allahabad above the Yamunā. Watters, II, p. 75.

In the Sarvāstivāda Vinaya account of the Kauśāmbī dispute, one party is described as Vaisālian and the other Kauśāmbian.

2. Vaiśālī is identified with Besarh in the Muzaffarpur district of Behar.

3. Avantī in ancient times was divided into two parts, the northern part with its capital at Ujjeni is identified with Malwa.

4. See *Infra*.

CHAPTER II

SOURCES OF THE SECOND BUDDHIST COUNCIL

Pāli : Cullavagga XII ; Mahāvaṃsa IV, Dīpavaṃsa IV & V; Samantapāsādikā, Mahābodhivaṃsa, Sāsanavaṃsa.

Sanskrit : Mañjuśrī-mūla-kalpa, p. 597[1]

Sinhalese : Nikāya-saṅgraha

Tibetan ; Dul-va (XI, 323-330 ; Mūlasarvāstivāda Vinaya, translated by W. W. Rockhill ; Bu-ston's History of Buddhism translated by E. Obermiller ; Tāranātha's History of Buddhism translated into German by A. Schiefner.

Chinese : (i) Mahāsaṅghika Vinaya found at Pāṭaliputra by Fa-hien and translated into Chinese by Buddhadatta and Fa-hien in 416 A.D. It does not mention all the ten defections but only the most important ones.

(ii) Mūlasarvāstivāda Vinaya (Kṣudrakavastu) translated by I-tsing in 710 A.D. It mainly preserves the tradition.

(iii) Recitation in four parts : School of the Dharmaguptakas. translated into Chinese by Buddhayaśas and Tchou-fu-nien in the 5th century A.D.

(iv) Recitation of the Mahiśāsaka Vinaya translated by Buddhajīva, a Kashmirian monk, in 424 A.D. Fa-hien came across a copy of the original Vinaya in Sanskrit in Ceylon. It was probably in Pāli, as it closely followed the Cullavagga XII.

---

1. वैशाल्यां च शुभे देशे चैते स्थाने सुशोभने ।
एवम्प्रकारा ह्यनेकाश्च शासनार्थं तु कारणात् ॥
....
छिद्रप्रहारिणो नित्यं सव्रणा दोषदस्तथा ।
भिक्षवो ह्यसंयतास्तत्र मुनिरस्तं गते युगे ॥
स्थापिता रक्षणार्थाय शासनं भुवि मे तदा ।
अष्टौ महर्द्धिका लोके वीतरागा निरास्रवाः ॥

(v) Recitation of Che-song-liu (Vinaya in ten sections Daśādhyāya) of the Sarvīstivāda school, translated by Puṇyatrāta, Kumārajīva, and Vimalākṣa.

It may be mentioned that the Vinaya texts of Sarvāstivāda and Mūlasarvāstivāda are very close to each other, as far as the account of the Second Council is concerned.

It is definite that Ken-pen-chou-yi-tsie-yeou is older than the Daśādhyāya Vinaya. The latter reveals a sectarian spirit, already developed, and the spirit of the expansion of Buddhism when it was far advanced in propagation.

(vi) The account of the Vinaya-mātṛkā-sūtra (Tassho ed. 1463 k. 4, p. 819). This work appertains to the Haimavata sect and is preserved only in Chinese translation of about the end of the fourth and beginning of the fifth century A.D.

(vii) Vasumitra, Bhavya and Vinītadeva, translated by J. Masuda in Asia Major, vol. II. Vasumitra's treatise has one Tibetan and three Chinese translations of Kumārajīva (402-412), Paramārtha (557-569) and Hiuen Tsang (662). Koue-ki, a disciple of Hiuen Tsang, wrote a commentary on Paramārtha's treatise. Paramārtha was the most learned Indian missionary, who went to China to propagate the religion. He was as intelligent as Kumārajīva.

Ki-tsang, a monk of Parthian origin, being the son of a Parthian merchant settled in China, and the Chinese mother of Nan-kin's. He traced the origin of sects from the beginning to the end. He worte a commentary on aramārtha's treatise on Vasumitra.

Modern Works on the Second Council :

W. Wassilief, *Der Buddhismus* (1860) ; T. W. Rhys Davids and H. Oldenberg, *Vinaya Pitaka* (S. B. E.) (1881); H. Kern, *Manual of Buddhism* (1884, 1891); I. P. Minayeff, *Buddizmu* (1884); H. Oldenberg, *Buddhistische Studien in Z.D.M.G.*, LII (1898); S. Beal, *Vinaya of the Dharmaguptakas;* Louis de la Vallée Poussin (1905) in *E.R.E.*, IV, 179-84, and in *Le Muséon*, vi, 30-37 ; Francke, *J.P.T.S.* (1908). W. Geiger, *Introduction to Mahāvaṃsa*; R. C. Majumdar in B. C. Law *Buddhistic Studies*

Volume; Paul Demiéville, *The Origin of Buddhist Sects in Mélanges chinois bouddhiques* vol. I; M. Hofinger, *Étude sur le Concile de Vaiśāli in Le Muséon*, vol. XX (1946); A Bareau, *Les sectes bouddhiques du Petit Vehicule* (1955).

TRADITIONAL ACCOUNT OF THE SECOND BUDDHIST COUNCIL

In the account of the Vinaya texts, the deviations in the disciplinary rules have been discussed, but apart from these deviations, there were a few doctrinal disputes, which are as follows :—

The dissidents challenged the Sthaviravādins' claims that Arhats were perfectly pure in physical and mental activities as well as in the knowledge of the highest Truth, i.e. they were fully emancipated. They asserted that the Arhats had four imperfections with an additional item about the realization of the Truth by an exclamation "Aho". These are known as the five points of Mahādeva. Hence, the reasons for holding the session of the Second Council were two, disciplinary and doctrinal. Both of them are being taken up for consideration in this chapter. The account of *Cullavagga* runs as follows :—

Some of the Vajjian monks of Vaisāli allowed as lawful certain rules, which were not in conformity with the rules of the *Pātimokkha-sutta.* Yasa of Kosambī, while at Vaisāli, happened to notice the deviations and strongly protested against them. At this attitude of Yasa, the Vajjian monks excluded him from the Saṅgha by *ukkhepanīya-kamma* (act of excommunication). Yasa then made an appeal to the laity, but it was of no avail and he had to flee from the country to his native place. From there he attempted to form a group of monks, who supported his views. He sent messengers to the monks of Pāṭheyya and Avantī, and he himself went to Ahogaṅga, the residence of Sambhūta Sāṇavāsī. There he was joined by sixty theras of Pāṭheyya and eighty theras of Avantī, and gradually by several others. They all decided to meet Sthavira Revata of Soreyya, who was then the chief of the Saṅgha. Before they could reach Soreyya, Revata became aware of Yasa's mission and started for Vaisāli and the meeting of Revata with other monks took place at

Sahajāti. The Vaisālian monks, in order to forestall Yasa's plans, approached Revata at Sahajāti with robes and other gifts but failed to win him over to their side. Sāḷha of Sahajāti was at first wavering between the two parties, but ultimately he sided with Yasa. The Vajjian monks, being unsuccessful in this attempt of theirs, approached king Kālāsoka at Pupphapura, and persuaded him to believe that the monks of the western countries were making a sinister move to get possession of the Teacher's Gandhakūṭī in the Mahāvanavihāra at Vaisāli. The king at first took up their cause but later on changed his mind, it is said, at the intervention of his sister who was a *bhikkhunī*. The session of the Council was held at Vaisāli with 700 members, but as there was great uproar during the deliberations it was decided to refer the matter to a body of referees consisting of eight members, four from the western and four from the eastern countries. This was done by *ubbāhikā* (voting) as described in the *Pātimokkha*. The findings of the referees, which were all against the Vaisālian monks, were placed before the larger body constituting the Council and were confirmed.

The Ceylonese chronicles continue the story and write that the findings were not accepted by all the Vaisālian monks, some of whom held another Council and included in it all monks, arhats and non-arhats, and decided matters according to their own light. This assembly was called Mahāsaṅgha or Mahāsaṅgīti.

Time and Site of the Council

All the traditions state that a Council was held about a century (110 or 137 years) after Buddha's death to suppress certain un-Vinayic acts practised by a group of monks of Vaisāli. The Council was held at Vaisāli, but the traditions differ about the name of the monastery where the scene of the session was laid. In Pāli the name of the monastery is given as *Vālukārāma*, and this is corroborated by the Mahāsaṅghika Vinaya.[1] According to Bu-ston, the name of the monastery was *Kusumapura*,[2] but

1. Watters, *op. cit.*, II, p. 73.
2. Bu-ston, II, p. 96.

it is not corroborated by any other text. Bu-ston probably confused the capital of the province with that of the seat of the Council, or it may be that the Mahāsaṅghikas, after their defeat in the Vaisālian Council, held another Council at Paṭaliputra.

No President

A remarkable feature of the Council is that it did not elect any President. By the *ubbāhikā* process a body of referees consisting of eight monks was formed to go into the questions of dispute, and each tradition gave prominence to its favoured monk. Thus, we see that though Sabbakāmī is recognized as the Saṅghatthera, the Pāli tradition accords to Revata, a Westerner, the leadership of the Council,[1] Bu-ston gives prominence to Sabbakāmī and Khujjasobhita (Kubjita). In view of these differences regarding the leading monk, we have to conclude that there was no elected President and the business was carried on by a Committee, with four monks of the western countries and four monks of the eastern regions. Hence, Venerables Sabbakāmī, Sāḷha, Khujjasobhita and Vāsabhagāmika were Easterners, while Venerables Revata, Sambhūta Sāṇavāsī, Yasa and Sumana Westerners.

The ten un-Vinayic acts

All the earlier sources agree in stating that the main business of the Council was to examine the validity of the ten un-Vinayic acts performed by a section of the Vaisālian monks, but there exists a wide divergence of opinion in their interpretations, but it is difficult to decide which of those accessible to us should be accepted. Those that appear more plausible are mentioned here.

The ten un-Vinayic acts with their interpretations, as found in the Pāli texts, are as follows:—

(*i*) *Siṅgiloṇa kappa* or the practice of carrying salt in a horn for use when needed, which contravened, according to the

1. The Dharmaguptakas, Mahisāsakas, Sarvāstivādins follow the Pali tradition.

Theravāda view, the rule against storing of articles of food (*cf. Pācittiya* 38).

(*ii*) *Dvaṅgula kappa* or the practice of taking food after midday, lit. when the shadow (on the sun-dial) is two digits wide (*cf. Pāc.* 37).

(*iii*) *Gāmantara kappa* or the practice of going to a neighbouring village and taking a second meal there the same day, committing thereby the offence of over-eating (*cf. Pāc.* 35).

(*iv*) *Āvāsa kappa* or the practice of observance of *uposathas* in different places within the same parish (*sīmā*) (prohibited in the *Mahāvagga*, II, 8. 3).

(*v*) *Anumati kappa* or the practice of performing an ecclesiastical act and obtaining its sanction afterwards (contrast *Mahāvagga*, IX, 3. 5).

(*vi*) *Āciṇṇa kappa* or the practice of using precedents as authority.

(*vii*) *Amathita kappa* or the practice of drinking milk-whey after meal (against *Pāc.* 35).

(*viii*) *Jalogiṃ pātum* or the practice of drinking palm-juice, which is fermenting but is not yet toddy (against *Pāc.* 51).[1]

(*ix*) *Adasakaṃ nisīdanaṃ* or the practice of using a borderless sheet to sit on (contrary to *Pāc.* 89).

(*x*) *Jātarūparajataṃ* or the practice of accepting gold and silver (prohibited in *Nissagg.* 18).[2]

Bu-ston, on the basis of the tradition preserved in the Mūla-Sarvāstivāda Vinaya, enumerates the undermentioned ten acts. Prof. L. de la Vallée Poussin translated the same from the *Dulva*.

---

1. Cf. *Mūlasarvāstivāda Vinaya* (Gilgit ms.), *Cīvaravastu* p. 142. मद्यं मृष्टयवान् प्रक्षिप्य भूमौ निखातव्यम् । शूक्तत्वे परिणतं परिभोक्तव्यम् । शूक्तत्वानुपयोज्यं तु छोरयितव्यम् । मा भिक्षवः शास्तारमुद्दिशद्भिर्मद्यमदेयमपेयमन्तः कुशाग्रेणापि ।

2. For a discussion on the interpretations of the terms, see Minayeff, *Recherches* etc., I, pp. 44-50.

The first three rules are relaxations made by Buddha of the more stringent rules, regarding the storage of food and eating to suit the conditions created by famine in Vesāli. The people of Vesāli continued to observe the relaxed rules though they were abrogated later by the Theravādins in their *Vinaya*.

The order of enumeration has been changed for the convenience of comparison with the Pāli list.

Both the translations of Obermiller and L. de la Vallée Poussin are reproduced here:—

(*i*) *Using the sacred salt*: (Obermiller) Mixing the salt that is to be kept for life-time with that which is used in general makes it thus an object of use.[1]

(L. V. P.) Mixing salt consecrated for life-time with food appropriate to the moment.[2]

The Dharmaguptas and the Mahīśāsakas offer quite a different interpretation. According to them, the word *siṅgi* is *śṛṅga* (*vera*) = ginger and *loṇa* = salt. Their interpretation is to "mix the food with salt and ginger."[3]

(*ii*) *Taking food with two fingers*: (Obermiller) The food that has been left (from a previous meal) they eat, taking it with two fingers.

(L. V. P.) Eating food of both kinds, not being a remainder, with two fingers.[4]

(*iii*) *Eating on the way:* (Obermiller) The monks, having gone a yojana or a half, assemble and eat on the pretext that they are travelling.

(L. V. P.) Having gone a yojana or a half-yojana, and having eaten food in troop, rendered the meal in troop legal by reason of the journey.

(*iv*) *Admission of a mixture*: (Obermiller) The monks mix a *droṇa* measure of milk with as much sour milk and drink it at undue time.

(L. V. P.) After agitating a full measure (*droṇa*) of milk with a full measure of curd, and then eating the preparation out of time.[5]

---

1. Cf. Gilgit Ms. Vol. III, pt. i, p. xiii : अस्ति आयुष्मन्द्भयां शृङ्गापुटं लवणं यावज्जीवमधिष्ठितम् । *cf. Mv*. vi. 3. 1.

2. *Indian Antiquary*. 1908, pp. 91, 104.

3. *Ibid*., p. 91.

4. Dharmaguptas : "derogation from sobriety as if, for example, a monk after an ample repast, forgetting the rule of good conduct, began to take food with two fingers and to eat the food remaining."

The Mahīśāsakas, say, "to eat a second time after having risen before taking a sufficient meal."

5. The Dharmaguptas and Mahīśāsakas say : "to drink, beyond the time allowed, a mixture of cream, butter, honey and sugar."

(*v*) *Taking intoxicating drink*: (Obermiller) The monks take wine in the manner of a leech that sucks blood and having drunk, excuse it on the ground of illness.

(L. V. P.) Drinking fermented liquor with a sucking action like leeches, rendering it legal by reason of illness.[1]

(*vi*) *Making a new rug:* (Obermiller) Taking a new rug without stitching it by a patch of the so-called Sugata span taken from the old one.

(L. V. P.) Not having patched their new mats with a border, a Sugata's cubit broad, from the old mat.[2]

(*vii*) *Begging gold and silver:* (Obermiller) The monks anoint an alms-bowl with fragrant spices, put it on the head of a Śramaṇa, on a table or a seat, or in a narrow passage at the four cross-roads, and proclaim: "This is a sublime vessel, if you deposit your gifts in it and fill it, you are to reap great merit."

(L. V. P.) Taking alms-bowls such as were round, pure and suitable for ritual, anointing them with perfumes, fumigating them with incense, adorning them with various fragrant flowers, placed on the head of a monk over a cushion went about the highways, streets and cross-roads, crying as follows:—"Here, ye people, who have come from various towns and countries, and ye wise people of Vaiśālī ! this *pātra* is a lucky one, to give in it is to give much, or whoever shall fill it will obtain a great fruit, a great advantage, a great activity, a great development."

[As far as the seven un-Vinayic acts, mentioned above, are concerned, all the Vinaya texts, including those of the Mahīśāsakas and the Dharmaguptas agree, though they have differed in interpretations, which have all been pointed out.][3]

(*viii*) *Digging ground:* (Obermiller) It is considered admissible for monks to live by agriculture. (L. V. P.) They may live by turning up the soil with their own hands.

On this un-Vinayic act, the comment of the Sarvāstivādins stands alone, and this seems to be due to careless Sanskritization

1. According to the Mahīśāsakas, it is a question of intoxicating liquor, which had become fermented.

2. According to the Mahīśāsakas, to make for oneself a mat of undetermined dimensions; there is no question of fringe.

3 According to the Dharmaguptas, the Vajjiputtakas think their conduct may be justified by declaring that "this has been done from time immemorial."

of *āciṇṇa* by *āchinna*, unconsciously changing the root *car* to *chid*. Hence the interpretation offered by the Sarvāstivādins should be left out of account.

(*ix*) *Approving*: (Obermiller) The dissidents perform religious functions, and at the same time persuade the monks in attendance to approve the same.(L. V. P.). The Venerable Ones (absent monks) having approved, do ye count it as approved, caused the resolutions of the incomplete Saṅgha to be approved by the monks of the parish.[1]

Bu-ston or Obermiller was misled by the Tibetan rendering of the Sanskrit word *anumodanā*, which, though derived from the root *mud*, does not carry the meaning of 'rejoice'. *Anumodanā* in Pāli means 'acquiescence to an act done by the Saṅgha in one's absence'. This is also an instance of the anomaly of converting a Prakrit word into Sanskrit. It is not known what the original Prakrit word was, but evidently the Pālists made it *anumati*. In any case, the interpretations offered by the different Vinaya texts are similar, i.e., getting an ecclesiastical act performed in an incomplete assembly and approved later by the absentee members.

The Mahīśāsakas and the Sarvāstivādins have both omitted *āvāsakappa* of the Pāli list. It seems that these schools included all the irregularities committed by the Vajjian monks relating to the performance of ecclesiastical acts in a regular or irregular assembly within *anumodanā kappa,* while the Theravādins (Pāli) and the Dharmaguptas have split it up into two: *anumati* and *āvāsa*. The Dharmaguptas, it will be noted, interpreted *āvāsakappa* slightly differently. They state that "in the *āvāsa*, besides the regular acts, the innovators accomplished others."

(*x*) *Exclamation of astonishment*: (Obermiller) The monks of Vaiśālī perform religious observances and at the same time admit such exclamations as *aho*.

1. The Dharmaguptas support the Pāli interpretation while the Mahīśāsakas say, "In the accomplishment of an ecclesiastical act to call others one by one afterwards to hear the same."

Perhaps in order to keep the number of deviations at ten, the Mahīśāsakas and the Sarvāstivādins borrowed one point from Mahādeva's five and made it the first of their list, viz., "Exclamation of *aho*."

(L. V. P.) The monks of Vaiśālī having rendered legal the exclamation *aho* performed an ecclesiastical act illegally in an incomplete or complete Saṅgha or legally in an incomplete Saṅgha.

The interpretation given in the Vinaya of the Sarvāstivādins is a laboured one and appears more or less a repetition of the previous un-Vinayic act of the Vajjiputtakas.

The exclamation of *aho* has been discussed in the *Kathāvatthu* (xi. 4) under the heading: *'Idaṃ dukkhan ti' vācaṃ bhāsato 'idaṃ dukkhan ti' ñāṇaṃ pavattatī ti.*[1]

A comparison of the two lists (Pāli and Sanskrit) shows that both the traditions have worked on a common original list, which was probably in Prakrit and definitely neither in Pāli nor in Sanskrit. This is stated on the basis of the change noticed in the words: *siṅgiloṇa*, *āciṇṇa* and *anumati*. The anomaly of *āvāsa* cannot be explained. As regards the remaining six items, the interpretations of both the schools are acceptable.

In connection with the ten deviations in the disciplinary rules, it is necessary to recount the tradition preserved in the Mahāsaṅghika Vinaya,[2] translated by M. Hofinger from Chinese into French. It runs as follows:—

The Piṭakas of Buddha's teachings were rehearsed by 700 monks, at Vāluka Saṅghārāma in Vaiśāli. The monks of Vaiśāli used to address the donors (*dānapati*) in these words: "Respected brothers, at the time when Bhagavān Buddha was living, we received two meals in a day, robes, service and adoration. After his *parinirvāṇa*, who will take care of us, we have

---

1. See *Infra*.

2. *Mahāvastu* (ed. of Senart, p. 2) opens with the words that it is the first book of the Vinaya of the Lokottaravādins, a sub-sect of the Mahāsaṅghikas.

Fa-hien (414 A.D.) procured a transcript of the original Mahāsaṅghika Vinaya and translated it into Chinese two years later. *Vide* Takakusu, *Records of the Buddhist Religion by I-tsing*, p. xx.

become orphans, and so we request you to give silver to the Saṅgha. As we are Buddhist friars, you should give to the Saṅgha one, two, up to ten *Kārṣāpaṇas*."

On the day of Uposatha, donors put large sums into the basin placed at the crossing of roads. The monks collected the contents, and after dividing them according to the number of bhikṣus, distributed the same among the monks present. In this way came the turn of the Vinayadhara Yaśa, and he was offered his share. Yaśa enquired, "Wherefrom was this money coming?" They replied, "We received money as well as medicines." Yaśa retorted that it was wrong; it was not permissible. They replied "You are slandering the Saṅgha by these words. You should therefore be excommunicated by *utkṣepanīya karman* (act of excommunication)."

After this was done, Yaśa went to the Venerable Daśabala, who was then residing in Mathura and told him that he had been excommunicated by *utkṣepanīya-karman*. Daśabala said, "Why did you submit to it? There was no reason for your submission." Yaśa said, "The *Vinaya Piṭaka* must be rehearsed, Buddha's law must not be allowed to be destroyed." To the question where the Council should be held, Yaśa replied that it should be held at the place where the deviations had occurred.

Then the Saṅgha of 700 monks assembled from the regions of Mathura, Sāṃkāśya, Kānyakubja, Śrāvastī, Sāketa and other places of Madhyadeśa. The Saṅgha was composed of those who received directly from the mouth of the Teacher one or two sections of the *Vinaya Piṭaka* as also those who heard it from the mouth of his direct disciples, the Śrāvakas. There were also common men (*pṛthagjanas*), *śaikṣas*,[1] *aśaikṣas*,[2] *traividyas*[3] and *ṣaḍbhajñas*[4] *balaprāptas* and *vaśībhūtas* — in all 700 members. They assembled at Vāluka Saṅghārāma in Vaiśāli. At this time

1. Lit. under training.

2. Lit. completed training. i.e., who have become *arhats*.

3. Lit. possessing the three kinds of knowledge viz. (a) Knowledge of duḥkha, anitya and anātman, (b) Knowledge of former births, (c) Knowledge of the destruction of one's own impurities.

4. Lit, Six higher knowledge, or power, viz., divyacakṣu, divyaśrotra, paracittajñāna, pūrvenivāsānusmṛti, ṛddhi, cittaparyāya-jñāna.

Mahākāśyapa, Upāli, Ānanda, etc. were *parinirvṛta*, and so Yaśa became the president of the Council. First, he put the question to the Assembly that who would rehearse the *Vinaya Piṭaka?* The bhikṣus replied that Venerable Daśabala should rehearse it. Then Daśabala said, "Venerables, there are the Sthaviras, who may not like the session of the Council." The bhikṣus replied in the affirmative and said that they were Sthaviras, who were designated by Buddha as *Upādhyāyas* endowed with 14 *dharmas* and the foremost of those as the Vinayadhara." The bhikṣus said, "You have heard the *Vinaya Piṭaka* from the mouth of Buddha, you must therefore rehearse the Piṭaka." Daśabala said, "When you enjoin me to rehearse the Piṭaka, you should approve what conformed to the Law, and if something is discordant, you must interrupt me, We are anxious to show respect to the Law, which conforms to *artha* (sense) and not to that which does not conform to the *artha*." All was then settled and approved.

Then Daśabala began to reflect where the assembly should be held. He came to the conclusion that it should be held within the limits (*sīmā*) of the place where the deviations had occurred. He then pointed out that there were nine precepts, which must be observed. These were:—

(i) Four Pārājikās of the *Prātimokṣa-sūtra.*

(ii) Bhikṣus are permitted to ask for a soup-basin, robes, medicines, if they needed them, but they must not ask for gold and silver.

Five propositions of Mahādeva

Vasumitra, followed by Bhavya and Vinītadeva, writes that on account of the five propositions propounded by Mahādeva, the Saṅgha became divided into two schools, *Mahāsaṅghika* and *Sthaviravāda.* The five propositions are:—

The Arhats

1. are subject to temptation (cf. *Kvu.* II. 1; *Atthi arahato rāgo ti?*)
2. may have residue of ignorance (cf. *Kvu.* II. 2: *Atthi arahato aññāṇan ti?*)

3. may have doubts regarding certain matters (cf. *Kvu.* II, 3: *Atthi arahato kaṅkhā ti?*)
4. gain knowledge through other's help (cf. *Kvu.* II. 4; *Atthi arahato paravitāraṇā ti?*)
5. The Path is attained by an exclamation (as "*aho*" cf. *Kvu.* II. 3 & 4 & XI. 4).

Paramārtha gives an account of the Second Council which has been translated by Paul Demiéville (*Mélanges chinios et bouddhiques,* I):

The Second Council was held at Pāṭaliputra, 116 years after *Mahāparinirvāṇa,* during the reign of Aśoka (perhaps Kālāśoka). The members were all bhikṣus (i.e., not necessarily Arhats). The president of the Council was Bāṣpa (lit. tears). In the Council the controversy provoked by Mahādeva led to the division of the Saṅgha into two schools, Sthavira and Mahāsaṅghika. Mahādeva's heresy was twofold. On the one hand, he wanted to incorporate all the Mahāyāna sūtras into the Tripiṭaka, and on the other he attributed to the Arhats diverse imperfections, such as doubt, certain measure of ignorance, etc. Paramārtha did not condemn the latter entirely, as he recognized the imperfections of Arhats as partially true and partially false. He was inspired by the Mahāyānic moral teachings, which contained in essence more particularly the Vijñānavāda views. He was a fervent supporter of Vijñānavāda.

It is said that Mahādeva fabricated many sūtras and authorized his disciples to compose treatises, as they thought fit, and they should also refute the objections raised by their adversaries, so that the conservatives, i.e., the Sthaviras might be disposed to admit the authenticity of the Mahāyānic tradition. Paramārtha seems to be neutral and sophistic on the point. He had recourse to the expedient of conciliating both the *yānas* and attributed to Buddha three kinds of interpretations. Paramārtha, in order, perhaps, to spare the good name of Emperor Aśoka, said, according to the *Mahāvibhāṣā,* that Mahādeva was supported by the queen of Aśoka, by whom the opponents of Mahādeva were thrown into the Ganges. By their supernatural power they then flew to Kashmir.

It is said that after Mahādeva's death, the two sections of the Saṅgha became united by holding a fresh Council, purifying the scriptures and modifying those introduced by Mahādeva after examining them anew. Paramārtha, however, writes that it produced veritable schism, separating the two schools completely. In the *Vibhāṣā* such rapprochement is not mentioned. After the Second Council, the dissidents moved to the north of Rājagṛha.

It was pointed out at the beginning of this chapter that some of the Chinese translations of the original texts in Sanskrit mention that the cause of the schism of the Saṅgha was not merely the ten deviations in the disciplinary rules but also in the doctrinal matters, relating to the claims of the Sthaviravādins that the Arhats were perfectly emancipated, which were challenged by the Mahāsaṅghikas and their sub-sects. The dissidents held the five views mentioned above.

The Theravādins emphatically deny that an Arhat, who is free from attachment (*vītarāga*), can be subject to temptation. The opponents, as shown in the *Kvu.*, draw a subtle distinction between a *Sa-*(= *Sans. Sva-*) *dhammakusala-arhat* and a *Para-dhammakusala-arhat*, the former, according to the commentator, is a *Paññāvimutta* and the latter an *Ubhatobhāgavimutta*, that is, the knowledge of the former is confined to his own personal attainments while that of the latter is extended to others' attainments besides his own. In the Pāli texts the *Ubhatobhāgavimutta* is not regarded as superior to the *Paññāvimutta;* the only distinction made between the two is that the former has *samathābhinivesa*[1] and realization of eight *vimokkhas,*[2] while the latter has *vipassanābhinivesa*[3] and realization of only four jhānas,[4] but as far as the question of *rāga* or *āsava* is concerned both the classes of Arhats must be regarded as completely free from it. The subtle distinction drawn by the opponents is therefore of no avail according to the Theravādins.

1. *Samatha* leads to concentration of thoughts and eradication of attachment (*rāga*). Cf. *Aṅguttara*, I, p. 61 : *rāgavirāgā cetovimutti.*

2. For the eight *Vimokkhas*, see Appendix.

3. *Vipassanā* leads to knowledge and removal of ignorance. Cf. *Aṅguttara*, I, p. 61 : *avijjāvirāgā paññāvimutti.*

4. Cf. *Aspects*, pp. 250, 276. See *Majjhima*, I, p. 477 and *Manorathapūraṇi*, III, p. 188; *Puggala-paññatti*,14, 72.

The next two points, that an arhat may have ignorance (i.e. *aññāṇa* and not *avijjā*) and doubt (*kaṅkhā* or *vimati*), are also vehemently opposed by the Theravādins on the ground that one cannot be an arhat unless he has got rid of *avijjā* and *vicikicchā* and developed perfect vision free from impurities (*virajam vītamalaṃ dhammacakkhuṃ*) after having dispersed all his doubts (*kaṅkhā vapayanti sabbā*).

The opponents, as presented in the *Kvu.*, in this case also draw a distinction between a Sadhammakusala-arhat and a Paradhammakusala-arhat, saying that both the classes of arhats may not have *avijjā* in regard to the truths, the theory of causation, etc., or *vicikicchā* about Buddha, Dharma and Saṅgha or the absence of soul, but the former may have *aññāṇa* and *kaṅkhā*, say, as regards the name and family of an unknown man or woman or of a tree. It should be noted here that the opponents do not mean *sabbaññutañāṇa* (omniscience) but just *paradhammañāṇa*—an intellectual power attained by the Ubhatobhāgavimutta-arhats, by which power they can know many things outside themselves. Arguing in this way the opponents maintain that a section of the arhats, i.e., the Paññāvimuttas or Sadhammakusala-arhats have ignorance (*aññāṇa*) relating to things or qualities other than those belonging to himself.

The same arguments and counter-arguments are adduced in the next discussion relating to *atthi arahato paravitāraṇā ?* The word *paravitāraṇā* perplexed our translator Mr. Shwe Zan Aung.[1] The discussion in the *Kvu.* reveals that the word means that an arhat develops faith in the Triratna or acquires knowledge of the truths, etc., not by himself but through the instruction of his preceptor, in whom he has firm faith. The Theravādins oppose the contention of the opponents, saying that an arhat is *vītamoha* and is possessed of *dhammacakkhu* and so he does not require *paravitāraṇā*. The opponents contend as before that a Sadhammakusala-arhat requires *paravitāraṇā* while a Para-dhammakusala-arhat does not.

1. "Excelled by others." See *Points of the Controversy*, p. 119. Buddhaghosa writes : yasmā yesaṃ tāni vatthuni pare vitaranti pakāsenti ācikkhanti tasmā tesaṃ atthi paravitāraṇā ti.

Cf, Masuda p. 24 : "gain spiritual perception by the help of others (lit. enlightenment through others)".

Another statement of Vasumitra relating to the Arhats, namely, "one who is kṛtakṛtyaḥ (=Pāli: katakaraṇīyo) does not take any dharma to himself i.e. has no attachment for worldly things" is echoed, I think, in the *Kvu.* (XVII, 1 & XXI. 2) in these terms: *atthi arahato puññopacayo ti?* and *arahā kusalacitto parinibbāyatī ti.* The Theravādins agreeing with the Mahāsaṅghikas contend that the *citta* of Arhats goes beyond *pāpa* and *puṇya*, *kusala* and *akusala, kriyā* and *vipāka*, hence, to speak of them as acquiring merits or demerits is absurd. The opponents, the *Andhakas*, however, contend that the Arhats perform many good deeds, e.g., make gifts, worship caityas and so forth, and remain always self-possessed (*sato sampajāno*) even at the time of his parinibbāna, and so he does collect merits and passes away with *kusalacitta.*

Neither the above discussions in the *Kathāvatthu* nor the terse statements of Vasumitra help us much in finding out the real difference between the Andhakas and the Theravādins about the position of an Arhat. The Mahāyāna Works point out the distinction thus: Arhats, who are perfect Śrāvakas, get rid of only *kleśāvaraṇa*, i.e., the veil of impurities consisting of rāga, doṣa, moha, sīlabbataparāmāsa, and vicikicchā but not of *jñeyāvaraṇa*, i.e., the veil which conceals the Truth — the veil which can only be removed by realizing the Dharmaśūnyatā or Tathatā.[1] It is the Buddha alone, who is perfectly emancipated and who has both *kleśāvaraṇa* and *jñeyāvaraṇa* removed. That the Mahāsaṅghikas appear to be groping to get at this clear distinction will be evident from two other topics discussed in the *Kvu.* but not referred to in Vasumitra's treatise. The topics are, — *atthi kiñci saññojanaṃ appahāya parinibbānan ti?* (XXII. 1) or *arahattappattīti?* (XXI. 3). To these the Mahāsaṅghikas reply in the affirmative, saying that an arhat is *nikkileso* (free from impurities) and does attain parinibbāna or arhatta but as he is not cognizant of all that is *Buddhavisaya* (domain of Buddha's knowledge), it must be admitted that some saññojanas are left in him. This opinion may be taken as a hint that the arhats do not remove the *jñeyāvaraṇa*.

---

1. For details, see *Aspects*, pp. 35ff.

There are a few subsidiary discussions in the *Kathāvatthu* relating to Arhats. These are given here briefly:—

IV. 1. Householders cannot become Arhats — *Theravādins*.
But householders like Yasa, Uttiya, Setu became Arhats — *Uttarāpathakas*.

IV 2. No one is born as Arhat — *Therav*.
But there are Upahacca-(uppajja)-parinibbāyī Arhats — *Uttarāp*.

IV 3. All dharmas of Arhats are not anāsava, e.g. their physical body etc. — *Therav*.
But Arhats are anāsavā (free from āsavas) — *Uttarāp*.

IV 4. In the Arhat stage, only arhattaphala is acquired —*Therav*.
But all the phalas are possessed by the Arhats — *Uttarāp*.

IV. 5. An Arhat is chaḷupekkho (see App.) — *Therav*.
Rather, Arahā chahi upekkhāhi samannāgato — *Uttarāp*.

IV. 10. All saññojanas are gradually destroyed and not by Arhattamagga alone — *Therav*.
But by the destruction of all saññojanas one becomes an Arhat — *Andhakas*.

XVII 2. Arhats may have untimely death as arahatghātaka is mentioned in the Buddhavacanas — *Therav*.
But as one cannot become an Arhat before the karmic effects are exhausted, an Arhat cannot have untimely death — *Rājagirikas* and *Siddhatthīkas*.

XVII 3. Arhats do not die when in imperturbable meditation and devoid of kriyācitta — *Therav*.
But did not Gautama Buddha pass away immediately after arising from the 4th jhāna — *Uttarāp*.

Dr. Bareau (*Les Sectes* etc. p. 64) after studying the Chinese commentary *Kouie-ki* has commented on the five propositions thus:—

(a) *Seduction of Arhats*: An Arhat may discharge semen in sleep on account of dreams caused perhaps by spirits; for such mental weakness for which the Arhat is not responsible, may be treated in the same manner as one treats physical excretions like urine, saliva, etc. In the *Kathāvatthu* (ii. 1) it is stated "*atthi arahato sukkavisaṭṭhī ti*." The Śaila schools, according to Buddhaghoṣa, contend that there are bhikkhus, who claimed arhatship in the belief that they had attained that stage, but actually they had not attained it. Again, there are bhikkhus who claim arhatship falsely.

(b) *Ignorance:* } Ignorance attributed to an Arhat is not
(c) *Doubt:* } nescience (*avidyā*), the first term in the formula of causation (*paṭicca-samuppāaa*). The doubts of an Arhat do not relate to the teachings of Buddha. An Arhat's ignorance or doubt relates to his inability to tell the name and family of a person, or of a tree, or herb and so forth, because he is not omniscient like Buddha (*Kvu. XX*. 3).[1]

(d) *Requiring other's help*: This point is also explained in the above manner, i.e., an Arhat may get himself acquainted with the name of a person, or family, or a tree, or a herb from another person.

(e) *Exclamation "Aho":* This is explained as that it is not unusual for a meditator while developing the first meditation (*jhana = dhyāna*), which is associated with reasoning (*vitakka*) and reflection (*vicāra*) to make an exclamation when he realizes that life is misery (*dukkha*). But, it should be noted that since an Arhat is not in the first stage of meditation, this explanation is far-fetched.

1. *Kvu. Aṭṭhakathā*, p. 189: Arahā sabbaṃ Buddhavisayaṃ na jānāti. Arahato sabbaññuta-ñāṇābhāvena paṭisedho kato na avijjā-vicikicchānaṃ appahānena.

Watters[1] collected some information about the life of Mahādeva from the *Abhidharma-vibhāsā-śāstra* (ch. 99).[1] According to this work, Mahādeva was the son of a Brahmin merchant of Mathura. He had his ordination at Kukkuṭārāma in Pāṭaliputra. By his zeal and abilities, he soon became the head of the Buddhist establishment there. The ruling king was a patron and friend of Mahādeva. With his help he was able to oust the senior orthodox monks and establish his five dogmas as mentioned above. Yuan Chwang records that at the instance of the reigning king, an assembly of monks was summoned. In this assembly the senior brethern, who were Arhats, voted against

1. Watters, *op. cit.*, I, pp. 267-68.

the five dogmas, which, however, were supported by a large number of non-Arhat bhikkhus.

The Chinese pilgrim, it will be observed, mentioned both the five dogmas and the few un-Vinayic acts of the Vaisālian monks as the cause of the Council and cleavage of the Saṅgha. The compiler of the *Kathāvatthu* was aware of the five dogmas, which were attributed by Buddhaghoṣa to the Mahāsaṅghikas. There can be no doubt therefore that the statements of Vasumitra and others were authentic. The *Dīpavaṃsa* also states that the seceders introduced alterations in the doctrines as well.

M. Hofinger,[1] after studying all the Chinese sources dealing with the Second Buddhist Council, arrived at the following conclusion:—

The Council of Vaiśāli is not a fiction. The sources that we have at present are revised and amplified versions of a very old tradition. It may be held that the session of the Council took place at an epoch about a century after Buddha's *parinirvāṇa,* i.e., about 386 B.C., in the tenth year of Kālāśoka's reign. A conflict arose about the disciplinary rules between the religieux residing at Vaiśāli, the Vajjiputtakas; and the rest of the community of Buddhist India. The account of the controversy is identical in all the Vinaya texts and it assumes the existence of a pre-canonical or proto-canonical account very close to the time of occurrence. The exaggerated age of a few Theras and the supernatural events do not discredit the authenticity of the Council. Some accounts created a chronological anomaly by not distinguishing Kālāśoka from Dharmāśoka.

The progressive growth of the tradition may well be divided into two courses, which were independent of each other. The first is represented by the account of the Mahāsaṅghika Vinaya and the second by the accounts in all the other Vinaya texts. The singular original is eastern and the others manifest a common development, i.e., a secession between the easterners and the westerners. The later version, Sthavira-Sarvāstivāda introduces new divergences in their traditions. The agreement of the later versions may be indicated thus:—

1. *Etude sur le concile de Vaiśāli*, p. 249.

Cullavagga XII and Mahīśāsaka Vinaya have direct affinity, similarly have Dharmagupta and Haimavata Vinaya but a little less the Sarvāstivāda Vinaya. It appears strange that the Mūlasarvāstivāda version is less close to the Sarvāstivāda version. It seems that the former is older than the latter. Chronologically, the traditions may be arranged thus:—

Earliest — Mahāsaṅghika and Mūlasarvāstivāda
Earlier — Dharmagupta
Next — Sthavira and Mahīśāsaka
Latest — Sarvāstivāda and Haimavata.

In this connection, it is worth while to recount the countries included in the peregrinations of Buddha. Buddha travelled northwards up to Mathura, and his missionary work was confined mainly to the large territory of the Ganges basin. The Sarvāstivādins preferred Mathura while the Sthaviras and Mahīśāsakas the south western area. In between these two regions was the habitat of the Dharmaguptas.

M. Hofinger has adduced evidences and arguments to establish the authenticity of the session of the Second Buddhist Council. The only addition that can be made to it is that a canonical text like the *Kathāvatthu* discussed the doctrines of the different sects. Still stronger are the evidences furnished by the inscriptions so far discovered.

The question that should be discussed next is whether the schism was due to the divergences in Vinaya rules only or to the five dogmas of Mahādeva or to both. It seems that both the causes were responsible for the schism, because both of them indicate the advent of the broad division of Buddhism into Hīnayāna and Mahāyāna, the latter favouring the Bodhisattva practices even at the sacrifice of Vinaya rules, e.g. fulfilling the wishes of an individual even by sacrificing the Vinaya prohibitions. The Mahāsaṅghikas were the forerunners of the advent of Mahāyānism. In the *Mahāvastu*, the first book of the Vinaya of the Lokottaravādins, a branch of the Mahāsaṅghikas, contains many Mahāyānic traces, to which reference will be made in due course in another chapter.

Now the question that can be raised is: To which of the two causes is the schism mainly due? The second alternative is

Regions and Localities interested in the affairs of the Second Buddhist Council in the traditions of different Sects

Theravāda (Cullavagga)	Mahīśāsaka vinaya	Dharmagupta vinaya	Sarvāstivāda vinaya	Mūlasarvāstivāda vinaya	Mahāsaṇghika vinaya
—	—	—		—	—
Vesālī	Vaiśāli	Vaiśāli	Vaiśāli	Vaiśāli	Vaiśāli
Pāṭheyya	Pāṭheyya	Pāṭheyya	—	—	Śrāvastī, Sāketa
Ahogaṅga	Ahogaṅga	Ahogaṅga		—	—
—	Mathurā	—	Mathura region	—	—
Saṃkassa	—	Sāṃkāṣya	Sāṃkāṣya	Sāṃkāṣya	—
Kaṇṇakujja	—	Kāṇyakubja	—	—	Kāṇyakubja
Udumbara	—	—	—	—	—
Aggalapura	Aggalapura	---	—	—	—
Sahajāti	—	—	Sahajā	Sahajā	—
Avanti	—	—	Dekkhan	—	—
Kosāmbī	Kauśāmbī	—	—	—	—
Dakkhiṇāpatha	—	—	—	—	—
Soreyya	—	—	—	—	—
—	—	Po-ho river	—	—	—
—	—	—	Kośala	—	—
—	Ālavi	—	—	—	—
—	—	Pāṭaliputra	Pāṭaliputra	—	—
			Vāsavagrāmika		
			Srughna		
			Tohoei		
			Sukhavihāra		

Sthaviras of the Western countries, who took part in the Second Buddhist Council

Sthavira	Mahīsasaka	Dharmagupta	Sarvāstivāda	Mūlasarvāstivāda
Revata Sambhūta Sāṇavāsī Yasa Sabbakāmi Sumana Sālha	same	same	same	same
Khujjasobhita	Pou tcho tsong	Pou-tcho-suo-mo	Ki-ichosou mi-lo	Kiungan (Kubjita)
Vāsabhagāmika	P'o-cha-lan	P'o-cheon-ts'uen	P'o-ye.k'ie-mi (?)	P'o-tso (?)
—	Tch'ang fa	—	—	—
—	—	—	—	Ajtai

preferable, as it indicated the advent of Mahāyānic conceptions. The two traditions may be explained thus:

The division of monks began with the differences of opinion regarding the interpretation of the ten Vinaya rules during the reign of Kālāśoka, i.e., some time before the appearance of Mahādeva (or Nāga),[1] i.e. it was about half a century later, Mahādeva or Nāga, propounded the five dogmas during the reign of King Nanda. His disciple Sthiramati propagated it further. As regards the fact that the tradition of the breach of ten rules appears in the Vinaya texts and the Ceylonese chronicles the tradition about Mahādeva's five dogmas appears in the Tibetan and Chinese versions of the treatises of Vasumitra, Paramārtha and other writers on the doctrines of sects. It may therefore be stated that the Vinaya texts, being concerned only with the disciplinary aspect of the religion, passed over the doctrinal differences, while Vasumitra and other writers, being more concerned with doctrinal differences than with disciplinary rules, considered it unnecessary to repeat the ten un-Vinayic acts[2] of the Vaisalian monks. The sources of information for the Ceylonese chronicles, being the Vinaya texts, passed over the doctrinal differences. Yuan Chwang, being an annalist, was interested in both doctrines and disciplinary rules, and so he recorded the divergences in regard to both. It is quite probable that the schism began with disciplinary rules and, in course of time, incorporated matters of doctrines.

It is apparent from the tenor of the ten un-Vinayic rules and the five dogmas of Mahādeva, that the Vaisālians wanted a certain amount of latitude and freedom in the interpretation and observance of the rules and to introduce into their organization and general governance a democratic spirit, which was gradually disappearing from the Saṅgha. The exclusive power and privileges, which the Arhats claimed for themselves, were looked upon

1. In *Tāranātha* (Schiefner) Nāga is described as a disciple of Mahādeva, and Sthiramati as a disciple of Nāga.

2. The Vaisalian monks were called Vajjiputtakas in the Pali texts. In the *Aṅguttara Nikāya* (I, p. 230) it is noticed that a Vajjiputtaka monk approached Buddha telling him that it would be difficult for him to observe the 250 rules of the *Pātimokkha*.

with distrust and disfavour by the Vaisalians, (who preferred a democratic rule to a monarchical government). The claim of the Arhats to become the exclusive members of the important Councils and to arrive at decisions, which were binding on the non-Arhats could not appeal to the Vajjians — a clan imbued with a democratic spirit. The five dogmas of Mahādeva also indicated that the Arhats were not all fully perfect persons as was the view of the orthodox Theravādins, and that the Arhats had a few limitations. The Vaisālians refused to be bound down by the decision of the Arhats, and so they convened a Council of both Arhats and non-Arhats, calling it a Mahāsaṅgīti and agreed to abide by the decisions of the enlarged assembly. This new body believed sincerely that the decisions taken by them were in conformity with the instructions of the Teacher.

Effect on the Saṅgha

Some of the Vaisālian monks separated themselves from the Saṅgha of the Elders or the Orthodox, the Theras or Sthaviras, and organized a new one of their own, calling it a Mahāsaṅgha, from which they came to be known as Mahāsaṅghikas. From this time the cleavage in the Saṅgha became wider and wider, ultimately giving rise to as many as eighteen or more sub-sects. The Thera or Sthaviravādins were split up into eleven sects and remained as Hīnayānic throughout their existence while the Mahāsaṅghikas became divided into seven sub-sects, gradually gave up their Hīnayānic doctrines and paved the way for the appearance of Mahāyānism. Once the disruptive forces were set in motion, the Saṅgha could not remain a single whole. Sect after sect came into existence on slight differences of opinion concerning doctrines, disciplinary rules and even cutting, dyeing and wearing of robes (Cf. Watters, *Yuan Chwang*, i. p. 151).

In view of the general mutual agreement of the different traditions, the session of the Second Council should be taken as authentic.

The only point which requires further evidences is the date of the Council and the name of the king under whose auspices the Synod was held. The Ceylonese chronicles give Kālāsoka as the name of the king. Kālāsoka succeeded Śiśunāga and is identified with Kākavarṇin of the *Purāṇas*. In view of the fact that Śiśunāga transferred his capital to Vaiśāli it is not unlikely that his son should continue to make Vaisali his royal seat and take interest in the affairs of the Saṅgha existing in his capital. If Kālāśoka be accepted as the royal patron of the Synod, the date of the session should be put about a century after Buddha's demise. Kern has questioned the statement of the Ceylonese chronicles about the age of the monks who took a leading part in the deliberations of the Synod, and has pointed out that the names do not include any of the list of teachers given in the fifth chapter of the *Mahāvaṃsa*. Since Kern's apprehensions are not baseless, we should take the statement of the *Mahāvaṃsa* 'that some of the monks lived at the time of the Buddha' with a certain amount of caution. As far as the line of teachers is concerned, Kern overlooks the fact that it is a list of succession of the spiritual teachers of Moggaliputta Tissa and not a list of the succession of the Saṅghattheras. Kern's conclusion that the Second Council "preceded the schism but had no connection with the Mahāsaṅghikas" seems to be his personal conviction and not based on any evidence, and so is his remark that Aśoka was first designated as Kālāśoka, and then with his changed attitude towards Buddhism, he was designated Dharmāśoka. Vasumitra places the session of the Council during the reign of Mahāpadma Nanda. This statement is probably due to the confusion made by Vasumitra that Mahādeva's five propositions were the main and actual cause of the schism.

Chapter III

DISRUPTIVE FORCES IN THE SAṄGHA

I

Though the Order of monks (*Saṅgha*) was organised on a democratic basis, Buddha felt that after his demise there might be discord among the monks. In the *Mahāparinibbānasuttanta* (76-77) Buddha told his disciples that as long as the monks adhered to the practices mentioned below, the Saṅgha would thrive and not decline. These were—

(1) Avoid fruitless talks.
(2) Hold assemblies as frequently as possible.
(3) Perform all ecclesiastical acts in concord (*samaggā*).
(4) Listen and be respectful to the senior monks, particularly to the head of the Saṅgha.

These four instructions implied his anxiety about the well-being of the Saṅgha in future. During his life-time there were two occasions when a split in the Saṅgha became imminent, but he did not regard them as actual dissensions. The first took place when he was at Kosambī on account of a minor difference of opinion between the *Dhammadharas* and the *Vinayadharas*,[1] and the other was the one initiated by Devadatta that the monks should lead a more austere life.[2]

In the Nikāyas and other early texts also, there appear a few references to the possibility of discord in the Saṅgha and the condemnation of *saṅghabheda* as one of the five extreme offences like patricide, matricide, and so forth. In the Vinaya, there are directions as to when a dissension among the monks should be regarded as a regular or an irregular *saṅghabheda*. In the account of the First Council also, a rift is noticeable in the lute in the

1. *Mahāvagga*, X; *Majjhima*, Kosambisutta; *Dhammapadaṭṭhakathā*, Kosambivatthu. In the Gilgit ms. of the *Mūlasarvāstivāda Vinaya*, the story remains substantially the same with slight variations in geographical details.

2. *Cullavagga*, vii. 3. 14; *Jātakas*, I, p. 34.

refusal of Thera Purāṇa of Dakkhiṇāgiri to accept *in toto* the texts adopted by Mahākassapa and his followers as *Buddhavacana.* His insistence on the introduction of a few disciplinary rules clearly shows a lack of unanimity among the monks immediately after Buddha's death (see *infra*, p. 39 n.).

The Tradition of Kosambī

At Kosambī, there were two teachers, one a Dhammadhara and the other a Vinayadhara, both imparting instructions in their respective subjects to two different groups of students. One day the Dhammadhara teacher committed a very light offence through inadvertence and when pointed out, he expressed regret for it, but this was talked about by the Vinayadhara teacher among his students and lay devotees. The students and lay admirers of the Dhammadhara teacher became offended at this provocative attitude of the Vinayadhara teacher and his followers, and there was a sharp cleavage not only between the two groups but also between their respective lay devotees. Buddha intervened, and at first failed to make up the difference, and it was out of sheer disgust that he preferred to retire to the forest to be served by an elephant than by the quarrelling people of the world. At this attitude of the Teacher, the quarrelling teachers, students and lay public came to their senses and settled their dispute. This episode cannot strictly be called a *saṅgha-bheda*, but it shows the possibility of dissension in the Saṅgha.

The episode of Devadatta

The episode of Devadatta is almost a *saṅghabheda* though it is not recognized as such in the Vinaya.[1] Devadatta was an

---

1. Yuan Chwang writes that he saw three Buddhist monasteries in Karṇasuvarṇa, where, in accordance with the teaching of Devadatta, milk-products were not taken as food. Watters, II, pp. 191, 192. I-tsing states that milk is an unlawful food. See Takakusu, *I-tsing*, p. 43 : Milk was not included in Devadatta's menu.

advocate of more austere discipline and requested the Teacher to make the following five rules compulsory for all monks. :—

That the monks

(i) should live in the forest;

(ii) subsist solely on doles collected from door to door;

(iii) dress themselves in rags picked up from dust-heaps;

(iv) dwell always under a tree and never under a roof;

(v) never eat fish or flesh.

Buddha could not agree to Devadatta's proposals. He believed more in person's own initiative than in obligatory rules, and so he left to the monks the option of observing the restrictions. There were the provisions of *dhūtaṅgas* (rigorous practices), but these were not made compulsory for all monks. There were among Buddha's direct disciples some *dhūtavādins* (practisers of dhūtaṅgas). This was too much for Devadatta, who departed to Gayāsīsa with a number of disciples, who supported him. It is said that at the instance of Buddha, Sārīputta and Moggallāna later won them over to Buddha's side.

Apprehensive statements in the Nikāyas

Once Cunda and Ānanda approached Buddha with the news of the death of Nigaṇṭha Nāṭaputta and apprised him of the quarrels that immediately followed his death among his disciples. Buddha assured them that among his disciples there was no disagreement as far as his fundamental teaching, consisting of the 37 *Bodhipakkhiya dhammas*,[1] was concerned. There might be after his death, he said, some differences of opinion relating to abhidhamma (*atireka-dhamma* = subsidiary points of doctrine),[2] *ajjhajīva* (subsidiary rules of livelihood) and *adhi-pātimokkha* (extra rules of discipline) but these should be treated as unimportant (*appamattaka*), but should there be any differences relating to the fruits (*phala*), path (*magga*, *paṭipadā*) or the

1. Viz., (i) four *satipaṭṭhānas;* (ii) four *sammappadhānas*; (iii) four *iddhipādas*; (iv) five *indriyas*; (v) five *balas*; (vi) seven *bojjhaṅgas*; (vii) eightfold path. See *Dīgha*, xvi, 50; *Majjhima*, II, pp. 77, 103, 104; *Lalitavistara* (Bibl. Ind.), pp. 34-37; *Saṅgīti-paryāya* in *JPTS.*, 1904-05, pp. 71, 75. *Mahāvyutpatti*, sv.

2. *Atthasālinī*, p. 2.

congregation (*saṅgha*), it would be a matter of regret and might harm the people.[1] In differences concerning minor matters such as those mentioned above, his instruction was that the erring monks should be politely pointed out that they were putting a different interpretation on a text, and that in the interest of the Saṅgha, they should give it up for practical purposes. He suggested that a sane and reasonable member among the erring monks should be selected for the purpose.[2] In the *Saṅghādisesa* section of the *Pātimokkha*[3] appear similar instructions (*vide* rules 10-11) with the addition that if the erring monk or monks do not change their views, he or they should be treated as guilty of the Saṅghādisesa offence. In the *Aṅguttara*[4] there is a reference to Ānanda complaining to Buddha that Anuruddha's disciple Bāhiyo was in the habit of picking quarrels among the monks and causing dissension in the Saṅgha while his teacher would not say a word to him. Buddha pacified Ānanda by saying that Anuruddha had never interfered in Saṅgha matters, and that all such disputes had so far been settled by himself or Sāriputta and Moggallāna.

Failing to make up differences by polite persuasion Buddha's instruction was to take resort to the seven methods of settlement (*adhikaraṇasamathas*), defined in the *Majjhima Nikāya* and the *Pātimokkha.* Buddha attributed all quarrels to the selfish motives of the monks or their possession of certain wicked qualities. He held out the prospect of a happy and glorious life like that of the god Brahmā to a monk in his after-life as the result of any act of his that would serve to re-unite the groups of monks separated from one another, while he declared that the monk sowing dissension among his brethren, was doomed to perdition for an aeon.[5]

Definition of Saṅghabheda

Every quarrel or difference of opinions among the bhikkhus was not characterized by Buddha as a *saṅghabheda.* It is

1. *Majjhima,* II, p. 245; cf. *Dīgha,* III, p. 117f.
2. *Majjhima,* II, pp. 238-39.
3. *Aṅguttara,* II, p. 239.
4. See the chapter on *Pātimokha.*
5. *Aṅguttara,* V, pp. 73, 75, 78; *Cullavagga,* vii. 5.

described in the *Vinaya* thus : "For not only is a formal putting forward and voting on the false doctrine essential to schism as distinct from mere disagreement, but the offending bhikkhus must also be quite aware that the doctrine so put forth was wrong, or at least doubtful, and also that the schism resulting from his action would be or probably be disastrous to the Dhamma. In other words, the schism must be brought about deliberately by putting forward a doctrine known to be false, or at least doubtful, or with the express intention or object of injuring thereby the Dhamma."[1] This definition obviously represents the opinion of the conservative school, the Theravādins, who usually looked upon all those who differed from them with suspicion and ascribed an evil motive to the holding of dissentient views. It is very likely that the dissenters held an honest opinion that their views were devoid of any evil motive of injuring the Dhamma. It will, therefore, be apparent from a neutral standpoint that evil intention is not an essential factor in *saṅghabheda*. The essentials are :— (1) belief in a dissentient religious view regarding either one or more points of faith or discipline; (2) acceptance of the dissenting view by eight or more fully ordained monks; (3) the division taken among the aforesaid eight or more monks must show a majority on the side of the dissenters. When the disunion is confined to eight monks, it is called *Saṅgharāji*. This restriction as to the number forming the essential of *saṅgharāji* shows that it might at any moment develop into a *saṅghabheda*, by drawing an additional monk into the difference. Of course, *bonafide* belief and the presence of regular monks are necessary requisites.[2]

Differences in the First Council Proceedings

In the proceedings of the First Council it will be observed that Mahākassapa was keen on securing the approval of all the

1. *Mahāvagga*, ch. x; *Vinaya Texts* (*S.B.E.*), pt. iii, p. 271 n.

2. *Cullavagga*, vii, 5,1; *Milindapañha*, p. 108 : "No layman can create a schism, nor a sister of the order, no one under preparatory instruction, nor a novice of either sex. It must be a bhikkhu under no disability, who is in full communion and co-resident" (*S.B.E.*, vol. xxxv, p. 163).

senior monks, particularly of Gavampati and Purāṇa, for the texts settled by his Council as *Buddhavacana*.[1] Gavampati remained neutral, i.e., he did not wholeheartedly accept the proceedings of the Council as final, while Purāṇa expressed his inability to accept the same as the words of the Teacher.[2] He further insisted on the incorporation into the Vinaya of the eight rules relating to food.[3] The Mahīśāsaka Vinaya not only upheld these eight rules as pointed out by Prof. Przyluski[4] but also gave special recognition to Purāṇa as one of the foremost teachers of the time.

All these testimonies clearly indicate that the seeds of dissensions had already been sown in the Saṅgha during Buddha's life-time and that these sprouted forth in full vigour in the second century after Buddha's demise.[5]

II

PROBABLE CAUSES FOR DISSENSIONS IN THE SAṄGHA

In the preceding chapter, it has been shown that disruptive forces were already at work within the Saṅgha during and immediately after Buddha's life-time. On scrutinizing these and the state of the Buddhist Church as presented in the Nikāyas and the Vinaya, we may regard the following facts as the probable causes for dissension in the Saṅgha :—

Absence of the Supreme-head of the Church

Buddha thought that the prescription of heavy punishment for schisms in the Church would check them effectively and that his Dhamma and Vinaya were comprehensive enough to keep

1. See *EMB*, I, ch. xxii.
2. *Cullavagga*, xi, 1.11.
3. The eight rules (as translated by Suzuki from Chinese) are :—

(i) cooking food indoors; (ii) cooking indoors; (iii) cooking food of one's own accord; (iv) taking food of one's own accord; (v) receiving food when rising early in the morning; (vi) carrying food home in compliance with the wish of the giver; (vii) having miscellaneous fruits; and (viii) eating things grown in a pond.

4. Przyluski, *Le Concile de Rājagṛha*
5. See *Infra*, Ch. VII.

intact the religion established by him, obviating thereby the appointment of the supreme religious head. He relied on the unaided strength of *dhamma* and *vinaya,* and directed that his teachings would be the Teacher after his death.[1] Vassakāra asked Ānanda whether any bhikkhu had been specified by Buddha as one who would after his death become the leader of men under whom everybody would seek shelter. Ānanda answered in the negative. He asked again whether any bhikkhu had been selected by the *Saṅgha* as would become their leader, etc. To this also Ānanda answered in the negative. Vassakāra was curious to know the cause of the concord prevailing in the Church in spite of there being no leader (lit. refuge). Ānanda replied, "We are not without a refuge (*appaṭisaraṇā*), *dhamma* is our refuge. There is a treatise called *Pātimokkha* which has been formulated by the omniscient Teacher and which all the monks living in the same parish (*gāmakkhetta*) have to recite in a monastery where they assemble on the *uposatha* days. Should there occur any difference or doubt in the recitation, the bhikkhus present explain them in accordance with the *dhamma* (hence they have *dhamma* as their refuge)."[2] In answer to another question put by Vassakāra, Ānanda explained that though there was no supreme head of the fraternity, yet there was in each parish a qualified head who was respected by the monks under his charge and whose guidance was strong enough to keep the great many parishes remain together in religious concord. This conversation makes it clear that each parish was under the control of the seniormost and the best qualified monk that the parish could afford.[2]

In the Pātimokkha assemblies, the monks interpreted the subtle expressions of the Teacher in different ways and introduced additional materials in the interpretations, and passed them in the name of Buddha. This happened in most of the parishes scattered over the whole of northern India. There was none at that time in the whole of the Buddhist community who could resolve the numberless divergences into one uniform whole and convert the threatening centrifugal forces then at

1. *Dīgha*, II, p. 154 : *Yo mayā dhamma ca vinayo ca desito paññatto so vo mam' accayena Satthā.*
2. *Majjhima*, III, pp. 7ff.

work into centripetal tendencies, conducive to the well-being of the whole Saṅgha.

Mahākassapa made an attempt to remedy this defect of the Saṅgha as a whole by convening a Council, but, as we have shown above, (p. 39n.) he, too, was not fully successful.

System of specialization in different branches of Buddhist literature

The Pali literature is replete with terms like (i) *Suttantikas* or masters of Suttanta (or the Sutta-piṭaka); (ii) *Vinayadharas* or repositories of the rules of discipline (Vinaya-piṭaka), (iii) *Mātikādharas* or those versed in *mātikā* (=*abhidhamma*); (iv) *Dhammakathikas* or the preachers of the Buddhist doctrine.[1] In the Aṭṭhakathā again, appear further terms like *Dīghabhāṇaka* and *Majjhima-bhāṇaka* (reciters of the *Dīgha* and *Majjhima Nikāyas*).[2]

In those days, when writing was hardly used for recording the sayings and discourses of Buddha, the means for preserving and handing them down to posterity was recitation and memorization. This was akin to the method that had been in vogue in India from the earliest Vedic period. Among the Buddhists we find that the memorizing of different portions of the Piṭaka was entrusted to different sets of bodies separated from one another in course of time and bearing names descriptive of their acquisitions.[3]

In the account of the First Council it will be observed that Ānanda was requested to recite the *Suttas* while Upāli the

1. In the *Mahāparinibbāna Suttanta* (*Dīgha*, II, p. 77) it is enjoined upon the bhikkhus that they should offer due respect to the *Saṅghapitara* or *Saṅgha parināyaka* (the head of the parish), who should be a bhikkhu of long standing and experience for the well-being of this Saṅgha. See also *Aṅguttara*, IV, p. 21; V, p. 353.

2. Childers in his *Pāli Dictionary* (s.v. saṅgha) says that a *Saṅghatthera* is usually selected as the President of an assembly. He cites, for instance, Kassapa, the then Saṅghatthera as the President of the First Council. He also points out that a Saṅghatthera is not always the one who is the longest ordained for Sabbakāmin, who was the longest *upasampanna* bhikkhu, was not the President of the Second Council.

3. *Dīgha*, II, p. 125; *Aṅguttara*, I, p. 117.

Vinaya. This would not have been the case if Ānanda or Upāli was not generally famed for proficiency in the particular branches of the Piṭaka. Elements of such specialization can be noticed in the quarrel that took place between the *dhammakathikas* and the *vinayadharas*.[1] Colleagueship in studies gave rise to unity among the *dhammakathikas* on the one side and the *vinayadharas* on the other in such a significant method that each group made the cause of one individual member its common cause and took sides in the dispute.

It is interesting that arrangements of beds and seats were made for the residence of the bhikkhus.[2] Dabba Mallaputta, it is said, made such an arrangement that the bhikkhus, adopting the same course of study (*sabhāgā*), resided at the same place in order that the *Suttantikas* could recite *suttantas* among themselves while the *Vinayadharas* could discuss the rules of discipline with one another, and the *Dhammakathikas* could deal with the matters of doctrine. Instances are not rare of a feeling of rivalry among these bodies, each member of which wished and was pleased to see the body, to which he belonged, take precedence over other bodies in occupying a seat or in taking food, in assemblies or in thanksgiving after a meal.

These separate bodies, which existed for a particular function necessary for the whole Buddhist community, e.g., the preservation of a particular portion of the Piṭaka by regular recitations, imbibed, in course of time, doctrines which could be looked upon as peculiar to the body holding them and in this way, the body developed into a separate religious school of Buddhism. Such instances are found among the Theravādins, who had developed into such a school from the *Vinayadharas*, the

---

1. *Sum Vil.*, I, p. 15; *Papañcasūdanī*, p. 79.

2. *Vinaya*, IV. 15. 4. (*S.B.E.* xiii, p. 339). "On the Pavāraṇā day the greater part of the night has passed away while the bhikkhus were in confusion : the bhikkhus were reciting the Dhamma, those versed in Suttantas were propounding the Suttantas, those versed in Vinaya were discussing the Vinaya, the Dhamma preachers were talking about the Dhamma".

In the *Sum. Vil.*, I. p. 15, it is stated that the memorization of the *Majjhima-nikāya*, *Saṃyutta-nikāya* and *Aṅguttara-nikāya* was entrusted to Sāriputta, Mahākassapa and Anuruddha respectively and their respective di sciples.

Sautrāntikas from the *Suttantas*, the Sarvāstivādins from the Ābhidhammikas and the Vaībhāṣikas from the Vibhāṣās.

Grouping around noted teachers

The crystallization of bodies happened not only for the preservation of literature but also for the grouping of monks around a noted teacher. Buddha gave prominence to some of his disciples by extolling them for their attainment of proficiency in certain branches of the Buddhist dhamma.[1] Of them the following may be mentioned :— (i) Sāriputta, the foremost of the highly wise (*mahāpaññānam*); (ii) Mahāmoggallāna, the foremost of the possessors of miraculous powers (*iddhimantānam*), (iii) Anuruddha, the foremost of the possessors of divine eyes (*dibba-cakkhukānam*); (iv) Mahākassapa, the foremost of the followers of *dhūta* precepts (*dhūtavādānam*); (v) Puṇṇa Mahtāniputta, the foremost of the preachers of *dhamma* (*dhammakathikānam*); (vi) Mahākaccāyana, the foremost of the expositors (*saṅkhittena bhāsitassa vitthārena atthaṃ vibhajantānam*); (vii) Rāhula, the foremost of the students ('*sikkhākāmānam*'); (viii) Revata Khadiravaniya, the foremost of the forest-recluses (*āraññikānām*); (ix) Ānanda, the foremost of the vastly learned (*bahussutānam*); and (x) Upāli, the foremost of the masters of Vinaya (*vinayadharānam*).

Buddha indirectly pointed out to his new disciples the preceptor most suited to each in view of his particular mental leanings. This practice led to the grouping of students around a teacher or his direct disciples, hence the remark *dhātuso sattā saṃsandanti samenti*[2] on the principle that like draws like. In the *Saṃyutta Nikāya*,[3] we read of ten chief theras, viz., Sāriputta, Moggallāna, Mahākoṭṭhita, etc., each having ten to forty disciples under his tutelage. Buddha on a certain occasion pointed out that the group of bhikkhus formed around each of these *theras* was possessed of the same special qualifications as those that characterised the *thera* himself. Thus the bhikkhus under Sāriputta's tutelage were *mahāpaññāvantā*, those under Mahā-

1. *Vinaya*, II, pp. 75, 76.
2. *Saṃyutta*, II, p. 157.
3. *Saṃyutta*, II, pp. 155, 156.

moggallāna's were *mahiddhikā*, those under Mahākassapa's were *dhūtavādā*, the founders of the Kāśyapīya sect.

Yuan Chwang noticed about a thousand years later that on auspicious days the Ābhidhammikas worshipped Śāriputra, the Vinayists Upāli, the Śrāmaṇeras Rāhula, the Sūtraists Pūrṇa Maitrāyaṇīputra, the Samādhists Mahāmoggallāna, the bhikkhuṇīs Ānanda, the Mahāyānists Mañjuśrī and other Bodhisattvas.[1]

In the first four classes of bhikkhus, the aforesaid affinity between them and their leaders is obvious. In the next three classes, the affinity existed all the same, though it may not be apparent on the face of it. For the Samādhists followed Mahāmoggallāna because he was the master of *iddhi par excellence*, which could be obtained only through *samādhi*, and the bhikkhuṇīs followed Ānanda because to him the order of nuns owed its origin.

The principal points of resemblance between the followers and their preceptors were the ties that bound them together, but these were the points which constituted the features by which the chief qualities of the preceptors were distinguished. These distinctions among them did not lie in any differences of doctrines, which they professed but in the degrees of proficiency attained by each, in particular aspects of Buddhistic *sādhanā.* But the divisions, though not proceeding from radical differences in doctrine, grew stereotyped in course of time, and fusion between them later became an impossibility due to the centrifugal tendencies they naturally developed as separate bodies. Thus the division which had originated without any doctrinal differences gradually gave rise to the latter and grew into full-fledged schools.

Latitude allowed in Discipline

It has already been mentioned in connection with the episode of Devadatta[2] that Buddha allowed a certain amount of latitude to his disciples in the observance of Vinaya rules. He laid more

1. Watters, *Yuan Chwang*, I, p. 302.
2. See above, p. 35-36.

Mahadevas 5 dogmas
Buddhist Studies Dr. B. M. Barua

D.-L. other Bud schools, from Sarvastivada
p 99 Madhyamaka on down

Reification making real
Soteriology Salvation Doctrine
Pericope Extract
Salvic
gnosis
Mahavastu
5 vimuttis?
DOCETICALLY

emphasis on mental than on physical discipline. In his discussion with Upāli, a lay disciple of Nigaṇṭha Nāṭaputta, he pointed out that he considered *manodaṇḍa* as more important than *kāyadaṇḍa* in spiritual culture.[1] In the *Mahāparinibbānasutta*, his direction regarding the abrogation of minor disciplinary rules clearly revealed his viewpoint in regard to external discipline.[2] In short, in his estimation, *paññā* and *citta* practices were far more important than *sīla* observances.[3] He realized the value of the latter for the new adepts, but that was not the be-all and the end-all of his scheme of culture. From the history of the growth of the Vinaya code[4] it will be observed how he made concession after concession for the physical comforts of his disciples. His code was not a hard-and-fast one. He made exceptions in favour of the bhikkhus, who were placed at a disadvantage by reason of the locality in which they resided. In the border countries (*paccantima janapada*) such as Avantī, the converts were few and intractable, hence, Buddha at the request of Kaccāyana and Puṇṇa Mantānīputta made some exceptions in their favour in regard to the rules for formation of an assembly for ordaining monks and the use of leather-made shoes and other articles prohibited to the bhikkhus dwelling in the Middle country.[5]

Particularly noticeable is his reply to the Vajjiputtaka monk who expressed his difficulty in observing all the 250 rules of the *Pātimokkha*. Buddha said that he would be satisfied if the bhikkhu would practise the three Śikṣās,[6] viz., *adhisīla*, *adhicitta* and *adhipaññā*, by which he meant the minute observance of the discipline envisaged in the *aṭṭhaṅgikamagga*.

Austerities made optional

From his personal experiences Buddha recommended to his disciples the middle path which eschewed austerities as a means

1. *Majjhima*, I, p. 372f.
2. *Dīgha*, II, p. 154.
3. See, *EMB.*, ch. VI.
4. *EMB.*, I, ch. XVI.
5. For boundaries, see B.C. Law, *Geography of Early Buddhism; Vinaya* I, pp. 197-98; *Divyāvadāna*, p. 21.
6. *Majjhima*, II, p. 8, p, 9. Cf. *DhA.*, I, p. 334 : Sekho ti adhisīlasikkhā adhicittasikkhā adhipaññāsikkhā ti imā tisso sikkhā sikkhaṇato sotāpattimaggaṭṭhaṃ ādiṃ katvā yāva arahattamaggaṭṭhā sattavidho sekho . . .

of attaining the goal. Buddha, who himself led a life of severe austerity was convinced that austerities alone could never fulfil his mission.[1] For this reason, austere practices do not figure in his disciplinary code[2] but there is ample evidence to show that Buddha praised those ascetics who took to the *dhūta* precepts.[3] He yielded to the strong tendency of those disciples, who believed in the efficacy of austerities and could not be satisfied with a religion barren of such practices. Mahākassapa, one of his most favourite disciples, was an advocate of austerities, and it was difficult for the Teacher not to comply with the wishes of disciples like him. The system of living a forest-life, therefore, came into vogue in the early days of Buddhism, and so there are in the Vinaya special rules for the *āraññakas* who were required to attend the fortnightly *Pātimokkha* assemblies, though at the same time they were exempted from many formalities.

Faith instead of moral observances

It cannot be exactly determined when firm faith in *Buddha*, *Dhamma* and *Saṅgha* came to be recognized as a means to the attainment of Nirvāṇa. In the *Vatthūpamasutta*, so much emphasis is laid on it that a monk, having firm faith in the *Triratna*, is exempted from observing even the rules of food. This *sutta* further shows that a monk, taking to faith, needs not practise the *sīlas* as recommended for the generality of monks.[4]

In view of what has been stated above, we may conclude that strict observance of the Vinaya rules was not in the Teacher's mind, though after his demise his disciples made the most of the same. In fact, they became more and more ritualistic and failed to use common discretion. A slight deviation from the Vinaya laws made them sinners, though such violations of the law

---

1. *Majjhima*, I, p. 17.
2. *Vinaya*, V, 131, 193.
3. *Aṅguttara*, III, p. 344f.
4. *Majjhima*, I, p. 36.

See also *Buddhistic Studies* (p. 329) for detailed treatment by Dr. B.M. Barua.

mattered little in spiritual advancement. The protest raised by the Mahāsaṅghikas had nothing untoward in it, and the Theravādins, we may say, magnified it. We do not mean to justify laxity in discipline, but when discipline ends in literal and superficial observance of a set of rules, one has the right to examine them on merit.

Chapter IV

SOURCES AND CLASSIFICATION OF SECTS

Dr. Bareau[1] has dealt with the different traditions of thought concerning the origin of sects chronologically, thus :—

I. The first epoch — Sinhalese traditions in the *Dīpavaṃsa* (4th century A.D.). Buddhaghoṣa in his introduction to the commentary on the *Kathāvatthu* added six sects to the list of *Dīpavaṃsa*, viz., Rājagirikas, Siddhatthikas, Pubbaseliyas, Aparaseliyas, Haimavata, and Vājiriya, grouping the first four under the Andhakas. He attributed a number of views to the Uttarāpathakas, Hetuvādins and the Vetullakas. Perhaps the Haimavatas and Vājiriyas were included in the Uttarāpathakas. In the tradition are mentioned Ekabbohārikas, Paññattivādins, and Bahussutiyas of the northern branch of the Cetiyavādins, who belonged to the southern branch of the Mahāsaṅghikas.

II. The second epoch — The Sāṃmitīya tradition of Bhavya placed the Haimavatas under the Sthavira group, and identified Hetuvādins with Sarvāstivādins. It followed the Sinhalese tradition in its conception of the sub-sects of the Mahāsaṅghikas.

III. The third epoch — Kashmirian tradition:—

(a) *Śāriputra-paripṛcchā-sūtra* of the Mahāsaṅghikas. The original text is not available. Its Chinese translation was made between 327 and 420 A.D.

(b) *Samaya-bhedoparacana-cakra* of Vasumitra of the Sarvāstivāda school. It has one Tibetan translation and three Chinese translations of about 400 A.D. In this tradition Haimavata is included in the Sthavira group.

(c) *Mañjuśrī-paripṛcchā-sūtra* available only in Chinese translation made in 518 A.D. by Saṅghapāla. In this text the Haimavatas appear as an offshoot of Sarvāstivāda. This text seems to have many errors if its list be compared with that in the *Mahāvyutpatti*. In this tradition, the sub-divisions of the Mahāsaṅghikas are enlarged by the

1. Bareau, *Les Sectes du Petit Véhicule* (*BEFEO*., 1956), pp. 16f.

addition of Lokottaravāda, Aparaśaila, Pūrvaśaila and Uttaraśaila.[1]

Vinītadeva and the author of the *Bhikṣuvarṣāgrapṛcchā* divided the eighteen sects into five groups, thus:

I. & II. Mahāsaṅghikas comprising Pūrvaśaila, Aparaśaila, Haimavata, Lokottaravāda and Prajñaptivāda.

III. Sarvāstivādins comprising Mūlasarvāstivāda, Kāśyapīya, Mahīśāsaka, Dharmagupta, Bahuśrutīya, Tāmraśāṭīya and a section of the Vibhajyavāda.

IV. Sāṃmitīyas comprising Kaurukullaka, Avantaka and Vātsīputrīya.

V. Sthaviras comprising Jetavanīya, Abhayagirivāsin, and Mahāvihāravāsin.

Vinītadeva's information and classification evidently point to a posterior date. He includes some of the later schools in his enumeration and omits some of the older schools, which were probably extinct by his time, e.g., the Ekavyavahārika, Gokulika, Dharmottarīya, and Bhadrayānika. Particularly noticeable is his inclusion of the Ceylonese sects like Jetavanīya[2] (i.e. Sāgalika of the *Mahāvaṃsa*, v. 13) Abhayagirivāsin[3] (i.e. Dhammarucika of the *Mahāvaṃsa*, v. 13) and the Mahāvihāravāsin. The Jetavanīya, it will be noted, come into existence as late as the reign of Mahāsena (5th century A.D.).

Tāranātha in his 42nd chapter (*Kurze Betrachtung des Sinnes der vier Schulen*)[4] furnishes us with very important identifications of the different names of schools appearing in the lists of Bhavya, Vasumitra, Vinītadeva and others. After reproducing the several lists, he gives the following identifications :

(i) Kāśyapīya = Suvarṣaka.
(ii) Saṃkrāntivādin = Uttarīya = Tāṁraśāṭīya.
(iii) Caityaka = Pūrvaśaila = Schools of Mahādeva.
(iv) Lokottaravāda = Kaukkuṭika.
(v) Ekavyavahārika is a general name of the Mahāsaṅghikas.

---

1. Bareau, *op. cit.*, p. 16f.
2. *Vaṃsaṭṭhappakāsinī*, p. 175; Sāgalikā nāma Mahāsenarañño Jetavanavāsino bhikkhu.
3. *Ibid.* It was founded in Ceylon during the reign of Vaṭṭagāmaṇī.
4. Schiefner, *op. cit.*, pp. 270-74.

(vi) Kaurukullaka, Vātsīputrīya, Dharmottarīya, Bhadrayānīya and Channagarika held almost similar views.[1]

These identifications help us to trace the Uttarāpathakas of the *Kathāvatthu*. This school should be identified with the Uttarīyas of Bhavya and the Saṃkrāntivādins of Vasumitra or Saṃkrāntikas of the Pāli texts. The Saṃkrāntivādins were also known as the Tāmraśāṭīyas probably on account of their copper-coloured robes. Out of these Tāmraśāṭiyas or Uttarāpathakas or Saṃkrāntivādins or Dārṣṭāntikas arose the Sautrāntikas, who are often mentioned in the *Śaṃkarabhāṣya*, *Sarvadarśanasaṅgraha* and similar other works of the Brāhmanic schools of philosophy.

A comparison of the different lists of Schools shows that their groupings quite agree with one another. The Mahāsaṅghika branches may be sub-divided into two groups. The earlier (or the first) group comprised the original Mahāsaṅghikas, Ekavyavahārikas and Caityakas or Lokottaravādins. According to Tāranātha, Ekavyavahārikas and the Mahāsaṅghikas were almost identical. The chief centre of this group was at Pāṭaliputra. The later (or the second) group of Schools came into existence long after the Mahāsaṅghikas. They became widely known as the Śaila Schools or the Andhakas,[2] and made their chief centre at Amarāvatī and Nāgārjunikoṇḍa. With them may be classed the Bahuśrutīya and Prajñaptivādins, as in doctrinal matters the former agreed more with the Śaila Schools than with the Mahāsaṅghikas, while the latter had its origin as a protest against the doctrines of the Bahuśrutīyas.

The third group of Schools is formed by the earlier Mahīśāsakas, and Sarvāstivādins with the later Mahīśāsakas, Dharma-

---

1 Tāranātha tells us further that during the reign of the Pāla king, seven schools only were known. These were :

(i) Sāṃmitīya comprising Vātsīputrīya and Kaurukullaka.

(ii) Mahāsaṃghika comprising Prajñaptivāda and Lokottaravāda.

(iii) Sarvāstivāda comprising Tāmraśāṭīya and Sarvāstivāda. The former became known as Dārṣṭāntika, out of which developed the Sautrāntika School. This corroborates Masuda's remark as against that of Louis de la Vallée Poussin that the Dārṣṭāntikas preceded the Sautrāntikas. See *Asia Major*, p. 67fn.

2 To the Andhakas should be added the Vetulyakas and the Hetuvādins according to the *Kathāvatthu*.

guptakas, Kāśyapīyas, Saṃkrāntikas or Uttarāpathakas,[1] or Tāmraśāṭīyas.

The fourth group comprised the Vajjiputtakas or Vātsīputrīyas with Dharmottarīyas, Bhadrayānikas, Channagarikas, and Sammitīyas, and also Kaurukullakas. In this group, practically all the schools merged in one, *viz.*, the Vātsīputrīyas, otherwise known as the Sāṃmitīyas.

The last, the fifth group but the earliest in origin, was the Theravāda which, as Vinītadeva says, formed a group with the Ceylonese sects, *viz.*, Jetavanīya, Abhayagirivāsins and Mahāvihāravāsins.

Prof. Lamotte in his *Histoire du Bouddhisme Indien* (p. 578) has furnished us with a tabular statement of the geographical distribution of the several schools on the basis of inscriptions discovered so far. According to this statement, the schools, divided into several groups in our scheme, are reproduced here.

Groups I & II

Comprising Mahāsaṅghikas and its sub-sects Pūrvaśaila and Aparaśaila (also known as Caityika), Haimavata, Lokottaravāda and Prajñaptivāda. The Śaila schools are collectively known as the Andhakas, which included Rājagirikas and Siddhatthikas.

I & II Mahāsaṅghika

1. Mahasaghiya (Konow, p. 48) : Lion Capital of Mathura (1st cen. A.D.).
2. Mahasaṃghiga (Ḳonow, p. 170): Wardak Vase, year 51 of Kaṇiṣka (ca. 179 A.D.).
3. Mahāsaghiya (Lüders, 1105) : Karle Cave of the year 18 of Gautamīputra Śātakarṇi (circa 106-130 A.D.).
4. Mahāsaghiya (Lüders, 1106): Karle Cave of the year 24 of Vāśiṣṭiputra Pulomā (ca. 130-159 A.D.).
5. Ayirahaṃgha (*EI.* XX, p. 17): Pillar of Nāgārjunikoṇḍa of the year 6 of Māṭharīputra Vīrapuruṣadatta of the Ikṣvāku dynasty (ca. 250-275 A.D.).

---

1 Vasumitra mentions Sautrāntika as an alternative name for Saṃkrāntikas or Saṃkrāntivāda. See Masuda, *Asia Major*, II, p. 67 fn. The Sautrāntikas are called Uttarāpathakas in the *Kathāvatthu*. See *Infra*.

6. Ayirahagha (*EI*, XX. p. 20) Pillar of Nāgārjunikoṇḍa (ca. 250-275 A.D.).

Pūrvaśaila and Aparaśaila

1. Puva(s)eliya (*EI*, XXIV, p. 259): Pillar with Dharmacakra of Dharaṇikoṭa : probable date of Vāśiṣṭhīputra Pulomā (ca. 130-159).
2. Puvaseliya (*An. Rep. ASI*, 1923-24, p. 93) : Allūru (Kistna dist.).
3. Aparamahāvinaseliya (*EI*, XX, p. 17): Nāgārjunikoṇḍa Pillar of the year 6 of Māṭharīputra Vīrapuruṣadatta (ca. 250-275).
4. Aparamahāvinaseliya (*EI*, p. 19): Pillar of Nāgārjunikoṇḍa of the year 6 of the same king.
5. Aparamahāvinaseliya (*EI*, XX, p. 21): Temple of Nāgārjunikoṇḍa of the year 18 of the same king.
6. (Apa) raseliya (*EI*, XXVII, p. 4): Slab of Ghaṇṭaśālā, formerly, Ukhasirivadhamana = Bardamāna of Ptolemy (VII, I, 93).
7. Aparīsela (Lüders, 1020 with the correction in *IHQ*, XVIII, 1942, p. 60): Kānheri Cave, date as above.
8. Rājagirinivasika (Lüders 1250); Amarāvatī sculpture, date as above.

Caityika or Śailas

1. Cetikiya (Lüders, 1248): Inscribed stone of Amarāvatī of the reign of Vāśiṣṭhiputra Pulomā (ca. 130-159)
2. Cetika (Murti, No. 33, p. 278) : slab of Amarāvatī (date as above)
3. Cetiyavaṃdaka (Lüders, 1223) : sculpture of Amarāvatī (do)
4. Cetiavamdaka (Lüders, 1263) : sculpture of Amarāvatī (do)
5. Cetika of Rājagiri (Lüders, 1250) sculpture of Amarāvatī (do)
6. Jaḍikiya (Lüders, 1244) : Pillar of Amarāvatī (do)

7. Cetika (Lüders, 1130) : Nasik cave (do)
8. Cetiya (Lüders, 1171) : Junnar Cave (do)
9. Seliya (Lüders, 1270) : Pillar of Amarāvatī (do)
10. Mahāvanaseliya (Lüders, 1230) : do (do)
11. Mahāvanasela (Lüders, 1272) : sculpture of Amarāvatī (do)

Haimāvata[1]

1. Hemavata (Lüders, 156) : Crystal casket of Sonāri stūpa of Suṅga epoch, (2nd cent. B.C.)
2. Hemavata (Lüders, 158) : Steatite casket of Sonāri stūpa 2 of Suṅga epoch (2nd cent. B.C.)
3. Hemavata (Lüders, 655); Majumdar, 3 : Steatite casket of Sāñcī stūpa. Suṅga epoch (2nd, cent. B.C.)

Group III Sarvāstivāda

Comprising Mūlasarvāstivāda, Kāśyapīya, Dharmagupta, Bahuśrutīya, Tāmraśāṭiya and a section of Vibhajyavāda.

Sarvāstivāda

1 & 2. Sarvastivatra (Konow, p. 48) : Mathura Lion Capital (1st cent. A.D.).

3. Sarvastivatin (Konow, p. 137) : Shah ji-ki- Ḍheri (Shrine of Kaṇiṣka) (ca. 128-151).

4. Sa[rvasti]vadati (Konow, p. 145) : Zeda Pillar of Kaṇiṣka (circa 128-151).

5. Sarvastivada (Konow, p. 155) : Copper stūpa of Kurram (ca. 128-151).

6. Sarvāstivadin (Konow, p. 176) : Inscribed potsherd of Ḍheri without date.

1 Re. *Haimavatas* : scholars who have dealt with these sects differ in their opinions. While some place the *Haimavatas* as a sub-sect of the *Mahāsaṅghikas*, others include them among the sub-sects of the *Sarvāstivādins*.

7. Sarvāstivādin (Lüders, 918-19) : Buddhist statue of Kāman (no date).
8. Sarvāstivādin (Lüders, 929) : Buddhist balustrade of Sarnath.
9. Savasthidiya (Lüders, 125) : Buddhist statue of Mathura without date.

Kāśyapīya

1. Ka ... (Konow, p. 63) : Inscribed pottery of Takht-i-Bahi (no date).
2. Kaśavia (Konow, p. 88) : Ladle of copper of Taxila, gift of Iśparakka probably Aśpavarma, vassal of Azes II (ca. 5-19 A. D.).
3. Kaṣyaviya (Konow, p. 89) : Copper ladle of Bedadi in the kingdom of Uraśā (no date).
4. Kaṣ(y)aviya (Konow, p. 122) : A jug of Pālāṭū Ḍherī (no date).
5. Kaśśapīya (Lüders, 904) : Buddhist cave of Pabhosā of the year 10: probably the fifth Suṅga.
6. Sovasaka (Lüders, 1106) : Karle Cave of the year 24 of Vāśiṣṭhiputra, Pulomā (ca. 130-159).

Bahuśrutīya

1. Bah (uṣuti) aka (Konow, p. 122) : Jar of Pālaṭu Ḍheri (no date).
2. Bahusutīya (*EI.* XX, p. 24 : Pillar of Nāgārjunikoṇḍa of the reign of Māṭharīputra Vīrapuruṣadatta (ca. 250-275).
3. Bahusutīya (*EI*, XXI, p. 62) : Pillar of Nāgārjunikoṇḍa of the year 2 of Ehuvula Śāntamūla II of the Ikṣvāku dynasty (end of the 3rd century).

Vātsiputriya

1. Vātsīputrika (Lüders, 923) : Buddhist Pillar of Sarnath of the Gupta epoch (4th cen.)

Mahīśāsaka

1. Mahi (sa) saka (*EI*, XX, p. 24) : Pillar of Nāgārjunikoṇḍa of the year 11 of Enuvula Śāntamūla II of the Ikṣvāku dynasty (end of the 3rd cent.).

2. Mahiśāsaka (*EI*, I, p. 238) : Pillar of Kura at Salt Range (Panjab) of the reign of Toramāna Shah Jauvia (end of the 5th cent.).

Sautrāntika

1. Sutaṃtika (Lüders, 797): Pillar of Bharhut of the Suṅga epoch (2nd cent. A.D.).
2. Sutātika (Lüders, 635) : Sāñci of the Suṅga epoch.
3. Sutātikini, Sātātikini (Lüders, 352, 319) : Sāñci of the Suṅga epoch.

Dharmottarīya

1. Dhamutarīya (Lüders, 1094-95) : Gift of two pillars to the Dharmottarīya school of Sūrpāraka (without date).

2. Dhammuttariya (Lüders, 1152) : Junnar Cave (no date).

Bhadrayānīya

1. (Bhādāya)nīya (Lüders, 987) : Kanheri Cave of the reign of Yajñaśrī Śātakarṇi (ca. 174-203).

2. Bhādrajanijja (Lüders, 1018) : Kanheri Cave (without date).

3. Bhadāvanīya (Lüders, 1123) : Nasik Cave of the year 10 of Vāsiṣṭhiputra Pulomā (ca. 130-159).

   Bhadāyaniya (Lüders, 1124): Nasik Cave of the years 19 and 22 of Vāsiṣṭhiputra Pulomā (ca. 130-159).

Saṃmatīya

1. Sammitiya (Lüders, 923) : Buddhist Pillar of Sarnath of the Gupta epoch (4th cent.).

Sinhalese Theravāda

1. Taṃbapa(ṃ)ṇaka (*EI*, XX, p. 22) : Temple of Nāgārjunikoṇḍa of the year 14 of Māṭharīputra Vīrapuruṣadatta of the Ikṣvāku dynasty (ca. 250-275).

CHAPTER V

THE MAHĀSAṄGHIKAS

History of Schools of Groups I & II

The first two groups in our scheme included the Mahāsaṅghikas and their sub-sects. Scanning the various traditions about the appearance of the sub-sects, it is found that Vasumitra and Bhavya agree with the *Kathāvatthu* as far as the three sub-divisions are concerned if the name Cetiya be regarded as alternative to Lokottaravāda. In the *Mahāvastu* which is an avowed text of Lokottaravāda, a branch of the Mahāsaṅghikas, worship of Caityas is given prominence. It will not, therefore, be wrong to say that the Lokottaravādins were also called Caityakas.

Sometime after the appearance of these three sub-sects, there came into existence two more sub-sects, viz., Bahuśrutīya and Prajñaptivāda. According to Vasumitra and Bhavya, these issued out of the Mahāsaṅghikas direct, while in the *Kathāvatthu* and the Ceylonese traditions, they are made subdivisions of the Gokulikas, though the latter did not appear to have been an important sect at any time. The doctrines of these two later sub-sects are allied to those of the Mahāsaṅghikas and of the Sarvāstivādins.

The Mahāsaṅghikas have gained in importance and popularity not so much by the sub-sects mentioned above but by the sects which came into existence at a later period, i.e., the Śaila schools of Vasumitra and Bhavya and the Andhakas of the Pali tradition. The two writers mentioned above speak of three Śaila schools, viz., Caitya, Uttara and Apara, while in the Pali tradition appear five names; Hemavatika, Rājagirika, Siddhatthika, Pubbaseliya and Aparaseliya. Though the Pali tradition is partially corroborated by Vinītadeva's list, it has been fully borne out by the inscriptions discovered at Nāgārjunikoṇḍa and Amarāvatī (Dhanakaṭaka)[1]

1 See infra.

The Śaila schools of later days threw the Mahāsaṅghikas into the shade. It seems that the earlier Mahāsaṅghikas were not concentrated in one centre as were the Śailas. The former were scattered all over N. W. India, Bihar and Western India, while the latter were concentrated at Śrīparvata and Dhanakaṭaka (in Guntur district). The inscriptions indicate that a magnificent Caitya was erected here and its grandeur and sanctity attracted devotees from places all over India and Ceylon. According to the inscriptions, mentioning the names of the ruling kings, the date of erection of the Caitya should be placed about the 3rd or 4th century A.D.

The first group of sects, viz., the Mahāsaṅghikas, Ekavyavahārikas and the Caityakas (or Lokottaravādins) had generally common doctrines with minor differences, which have not been minutely distinguished by Vasumitra. As regards the second group of sects, viz., the Śailas or the Andhakas, the Bahuśrutīyas and Prajñaptivādins, Vasumitra has equally been silent. It is in the *Kathāvatthu* that we find that a large number of doctrines have been attributed to this group, and after analysing the doctrines, it appears that this group accepted some of the doctrines of Sarvāstivāda. It is proposed to discuss the doctrines of the first and second groups separately.

Literature

In the *Dīpavaṃsa*[1] it is stated that the Mahāsaṅghikas not only introduced the ten new Vinaya rules but also propounded new doctrines contrary to the established ones. At the *Mahāsaṅgīti* held by them at Pāṭaliputra they made alterations in the *Sūtra* and *Vinaya Piṭakas*, as also in their arrangement and interpretation. They did not include, in the Piṭaka collection,[2] *Parivāra, Abhidhammappakaraṇa, Paṭisambhidāmagga, Niddesa* and the *Jātakas*. The importance and accuracy of their decision are supported by the modern critical writers.[3] The *Parivāra* (*pāṭha*), intended as a manual for the bhikkhus, was no doubt a

1 *Dīpavaṃsa*, ch. iv.

2 *Ibid.*, v. 32-38.

3 Rhys Davids, *Hibbert Lectures*, p. 42; Oldenberg's Intro. to the *Vinaya Texts*, I, p. xxxiv.

composition of a much later date. The *Abhidhamma* texts also developed after the council of Veśāli and obtained their final shape in the third Synod held during Aśoka's reign.[1] Lastly, the three works, the *Paṭisambhidāmmaga*, *Niddesa* and the *Jātakas*, were added to the Canon long after its close. In view of the contents of the *Paṭisambhidāmagga*, it should have been included in the *Abhidhamma Piṭaka*, while the *Niddesa* which is an old commentary on the *Sutta-nipāta* along with the *Jātakas*, which is also a commentary on the canonical *Jātaka* book, were excluded from the Piṭaka collection.

From all these testimonies, as mentioned above, it is apparent that like the Theravādins and the Sarvāstivādins, the Mahāsaṅghikas had a complete canon of their own in its three divisions. References to the canon of the Mahāsaṅghikas are found in the inscriptions discovered at Amarāvatī and Nāgārjunikoṇḍa. On the pillar of an outer railing of the Amarāvatī stūpa there are two inscriptions, one of which speaks of certain nuns as *Vinayadhara*[2] and the other of the monks of Mahāvanaseliya as *Mahāvinayadhara*.[3] These distinctly imply the existence, about the beginning of the Christian era, of a *Vinaya Piṭaka* in that region.

There are similar references to the *Sūtra Piṭaka* also, and in greater details. In an inscription[4] on one of the slabs found near the central stūpa of Amarāvatī, there is a reference to a monk of Mahāvanasālā as *Saṃyuta-bhāṇaka* (not *Saṃyuta-bhātuka*, as read by Burgess). In Nāgārjunikoṇḍa appear the following inscriptions in the Āyaka pillars C_1 and C_2: *Dīgha-Majhima-paṃcamātuka-osaka-vācakānam*, *Dīgha-Majhima-nikāyadharena*, *Dīgha-Majhima-paṃḍa-mātuka-desakavācakānam* and *Dīgha-Manigaya-dharena*. These leave no room for doubt about the existence of a *Sutta-Piṭaka* in at least three Nikāyas : *Dīgha*, *Majjhima* and *Saṃyutta*.

There also occurs the expression *Pañca-mātuka*, which is an irregular form of *Pañca-mātṛikā* (Pali : *mātikā*). The term

1 Oldenberg, *op. cit.*, p. xxxiv.

2 Burgess, *Buddhist Stūpas of Amarāvatī and Jaggayyapeṭa* (Arch. Sur. of S. India), p. 37.

3 *Ibid.*, p. 102

4 *Ibid.*, p. 91 (Plate xlviii, 35) see also p. 105.

"mātikā" denotes the detailed contents of an *Abhidhamma* text. It is used also to indicate a complete *Abhidhamma* text. Hence, it may be surmised that the term "Paṃcamātukā" refers to five and not seven, of the *Abhidhamma* texts. Perhaps the two texts omitted are the *Paṭṭhāna* and the *Kathāvatthu*, which were later added to the *Abhidhamma* texts. Among the Vinaya texts enlisted in Nanjio's *Catalogue* there are four works with *mātṛkā* as a part of their titles, though none of them belong to the Mahāsaṅghikas.[1] Prof. Przyluski writes[2] that the Mahāsaṅghikas had a particular fancy for the number "five", especially in connection with the Vinaya texts. Mātṛkā was used by the ancient compilers to denote the *Vinaya Piṭaka* as much as the *Abhidhamma Piṭaka*, hence the word "Paṃca-mātuka" of the inscriptions may well mean the *Vinaya Piṭaka* of the Mahāsaṅghikas, whose text also had five divisions like that of the other schools.

Fa-hien (414 A.D.) came across a complete transcript of the Mahāsaṅghika Vinaya at Pāṭaliputra and translated it into Chinese two years later.[3] In Nanjio's Catalogue are mentioned two Vinaya texts of this school, viz., Mahāsaṅghika-vinaya and Mahāsaṅgha-bhikṣuṇī-vinaya (No. 543). Fortunately there is the original *Mahāvastu*,[4] which is the first volume of the *Vinaya Piṭaka* of the Lokottaravādins, a branch of the Mahāsaṅghikas. It corresponds to that part of the Pali *Vinaya Piṭaka,* which gives an account of Buddha's life and his formation of the first Saṅgha. By Buddha's life the compiler of the *Mahāvastu* meant not merely his present life but also the events of his past lives, by recounting which he showed that a particular event in this life was only a repetition or result of the past. The account is divided into three sections like the Nidāna-kathā of the Jātakas, the first dealing with his existences at the time of Dīpaṅkara and other Buddhas, the second with his life in Tuṣita heaven, and the third with his present life, agreeing mostly with the contents

1 Przyluski, *Le Concile de Rājagṛha*, p. 212.

2 *Ibid.*, pp. 353, 357, 359.

3 M. Hofinger in his *Etude sur le concile de Vaiśāli*, chapter IV, pp. 145-48 has translated the Mahāsaṅghika Vinaya into French, reproduced in English by me in the account of the Second Buddhist Council. See above. Takakusu, *Records of the Buddhist Religion by I-tsing* p. xx.

4 Senart's edition, p. 2.

of the Pāli *Mahāvagga*. Apart from a few rules relating to ordination, it has nothing to do with the disciplinary matters. It contains a few Prakrit versions of the sūtras of the *Nikāyas*, *Sutta-nipāta*, *Dhammapada* and a few other texts. It is more a collection of Jātakas than a text on Vinaya. Winternitz thinks that its date of composition should be placed between the 2nd century B.C. and the 4th century A.D.[1]

Language of the Mahāsaṅghika-Piṭaka

Bu-ston[2] tells us that the Mahāsaṅghikas claimed Mahākāśyapa as their founder, and that the language of their Piṭaka was Prākrit. The language of the *Mahāvastu*,[3] especially of its poetry portion, is mixed Sanskrit and which may well be called Prākrit or quasi-Sanskrit and pure Sanskrit, and the Sūtra-piṭaka was divided into *Āgamas* instead of Nikāyas. The southern group preferred to divide the Sūtra-piṭaka into Nikāyas and adopted the Prākrit language instead of Pali.

Principal seats of the Schools

Yuan Chwang[4] states that the majority of inferior brethren at Pāṭaliputra established the Mahāsaṅghika school. Fa-hien, as stated above, found the Vinaya of this school at Pāṭaliputra, so it may be concluded that the chief centre of this school was at Pāṭaliputra. I-tsing (671-695 A.D.) tells us that the Mahāsaṅghikas were found iṇ his time mostly in Magadha, and a few in Lāṭa and Sindhu (Western India) and some in a few places in Northern, Southern and Eastern India.[5] Before I-tsing, both Fa-hien and Yuan Chwang had in these localities come

1 See Winternitz, *History of Indian Literature*, II, p. 239; B. C. Law, *A Study of the Mahāvastu*, 1930.

2 Besides their own language, Bu-ston adds, their robes had 23 to 27 fringes, and their badge was a conch-shell. Bu-ston, II, p. 100. *Cf.* Csoma Körösi, *JASB.*, 1838, p. 134; Wassiljew, *Der Buddhismus*, p. 294-95; Eitel's *Handbook of Chinese Buddhism*, p. 88.

3 See Keith, Foreword to B. C. Law's *Study of the Mahāvastu*.

4 Watters, *op. cit.*, II, pp. 267, 269.

5 Takakusu, *op. cit.*, p. xxxiii.

across the adherents of this school though not so frequently as those of the others. The earliest epigraphical notice of this school is found in the inscription on the Mathura Lion Capital (about 120 B.C.),[1] mentioning that it had a very strong opponent in Buddhila, an adherent of the Sarvāstivāda school.

At Andarab in Afghanistan and its neighbouring places there were also some followers of this school. During the reign of Huviṣka, one Kamagulya deposited some relics of Buddha in the Wardak vase and presented the same to the teachers of the Mahāsaṅghika school. The vault which contained the relic-vase was built by the father of Kamagulya.[2] At Andarab, which was three days journey from the country of the Wardaks, Yuan Chwang found the adherents of this school in three monasteries.

There was another centre of the school at Karle, in the Bombay Presidency, famous for the largest and finest cave-temple, which still stands as a memorial of its past glory.[3] In this cave-temple there are two inscriptions, one recording the gift of the village Karajaka by Gautamīputra Sātakarṇi to the monks of the Vāluraka caves for the support of the monks of the Mahāsaṅghika sect,[4] and the other of the time of Vāśiṣṭiputra Siri Pulumāyi recording the gift of a nine-celled Hall to the same sect by an inhabitant of Abulama.[5] Though the Mahāsaṅghikas did not receive much attention from the Buddhist writers and donors, the Karle caves show that the sect won a great popularity in that part of the Bombay Presidency where the caves exist; for otherwise, the cave-temples could not have been so richly decorated with such fine specimens of sculptural and architectural beauty. Its richness and existence prove that there was a series of donors through centuries anxious to express their religious zeal and devotion to the Mahāsaṅghikas in the best way that their resources could provide.[6]

1 *E. I.*, IX, pp. 139, 141, 146.
2 *E. I.*, XI, p. 211.
3 See for its description Fergusson's *Indian and Eastern Architecture*, pp. 117f; Fergusson and Burgess, *Cave Temples of India*, pp. 232f.
4 *Ep. Ind.*, VII, pp. 64f.
5 *Ibid.*, pp. 71f.
6 Burgess, *Buddhist Stūpas of Amarāvatī and Jaggayapeṭa* (Arch. Sur. of S. India), p. 112-13.

The above inscriptional evidences relate to the Mahāsaṅghikas alone, who, it appears from the evidences, were scattered probably in small groups in a few localities of North-western and Eastern India, and had their main centre at Pāṭaliputra or Kusumapura.

Just as Bodh-Gaya grew up on the bank of the Nerañjarā as an early centre of Theravāda and a place of pilgrimage for the Buddhists, so also did Amarāvatī (extending to Jaggayapeṭa) and Nāgārjunikoṇḍa on the bank of the Kṛṣṇā (including its tributary Paler) become a flourishing centre of the off-shoots of the Mahāsaṅghikas in the first century B.C. or A.D. and turned into a place of pilgrimage for the Buddhists of later days.

On the basis of the style of sculptures and paleographic data, Burgess agreeing with Fergusson held that the construction of the Amarāvatī stūpa was commenced in the 2nd century B.C. and later enlarged and decorated with additional sculptures, the latest of which was the great railing erected a little before 200 A.D.[1] It was some time after the completion of the Amarāvatī stūpa that the stūpas at Jaggayapeṭa and Nāgārjunikoṇḍa came into existence, their dates being, according to Burgess and Vogel, the 3rd or 4th century A.D.[2] respectively. This estimate of date and the mention of the king called Māḍharīputa Siri Vīrapuriṣadata (=Srī Māṭharī-putra Srī Vīrapuruṣa-datta) of the Ikṣvāku dynasty[3] are based on paleographic evidences. The inscriptions on the *Āyaka*-pillars at Nāgārjunikoṇḍa contain not only the name of the king but also of his father Vāseṭhiputa Siri Ehuvuḷa Cāṃtamūla.[4] It appears from the inscription that the principal donor of the subsidiary structures of the stūpa was Cāṃtasiri, sister of king Cāṃtamūla, and the paternal aunt (*pituchā*), later on, probably mother-in-law, of the king Siri Vīrapurisadata.[5] Hence, the time of the inscriptions, mentioning the name of the kings Cāṃtasiri and Vīrapuriṣadata, is 3rd or 4th century A.D.

---

1 *E. I.*, XX, p. 2

2 Bühler assigns 3rd century A. D. to the reign of king Puriṣadata, *EI.*, XX. p. 2 quoting *Ind. Ant.*, XI (1882), pp. 256f

3 *E. I.* XX, p. 3

4 *Ibid.*

5 *Asia Major*, II. pp. 18-34,

It should be remembered that the period mentioned here relates to the subsidiary structures of the main stūpa, and not to the stūpa itself—the Mahācaitya, which must be assigned to an earlier period.

It is evident therefore that the off-shoots of the Mahāsaṅghikas viz., the Caitya and Śaila schools, migrated to the Guntur district from Pāṭaliputra through Orissa and made their settlement in that region in the 2nd century B. C. During the course of four or five centuries of their residence there, they gradually extended their monasteries to the neighbouring hills.

The offshoots of this school, the Lokottaravādins and Caityakas, in other words, the Śaila schools, as we know from the inscriptions of Amarāvatī and Nāgārjunikoṇḍa, established themselves along the banks of the Kṛṣṇā with several monasteries located on the different hills all around.

In short, the earlier schools (i.e. the first group) were located at Pāṭaliputra with adherents scattered all over Northern and North-western India, while the later schools (i.e. the second group) were concentrated in the south, having their chief centre in the Guntur district on the banks of the Kṛṣṇā.

Two branches of the Mahāsaṅghikas

The Mahāsaṅghikas migrated from Magadha in two streams, one towards the north and the other towards the south. The northern, rather, the north-western section later became subdivided into five. viz., Ekavyavahārikas, Kaukulikas or Kaurukullukas, Bahuśrutīyas, Prajñaptivādins and Lokottaravādins, on account of minor doctrinal differences among them. Their offshoot, the Lokottaravādins, developed leanings towards Mahāyānism, and in fact prepared the ground for the advent of the Mahāyāna school. Buddhaghoṣa, in his commentary on the *Kathāvatthu*, distinguished Mahāsaṅghikas by the words "*ekacce Mahāsaṅghikā*" implying thereby that all Mahāsaṅghikas did not subscribe to the same doctrines, or it might be that he referred by "ekacce" either to the north-western or to the southern branch of the Mahāsaṅghikas. In the *Kathāvatthu*, the views discussed are mostly of the Mahāsaṅghikas, who migrated to the south, settled down in the Andhra Pradesh around Amarāvatī and Dhānyakaṭaka. Their sub-branches concentrated at Nāgārjunikoṇḍa, dwelling on the mountains around. These were the Pubbaseliyas or Uttaraseliyas, Aparaseliyas, Siddhatthikas, Rājagirikas, and Caityikas, collectively designated as the Andhakas by Buddhaghoṣa in the introduction to his commentary on the *Kathāvatthu.* Of the northern Mahāsaṅghikas he mentioned the names of Ekabbohārikas, Gokulikas, Paññattivādins and Bahussutika, but in the *Kathāvatthu* their views have not been referred to specifically, perhaps they originated after the composition of the *Kathāvatthu.*

In the *Kathāvatthu* there is a discussion of the views of the Vetulyakas, who were in favour of the Mahāyānic doctrines. Of the two branches of the Mahāsaṅghikas, the north-western branch deified and universalised Buddha and held that the Absolute (Reality) was indescribable (*anirvacanīya*). It neither exists nor non-exists. It is devoid of all attributes (*suññatā*). It is without origin and decay. The Andhra group was more Hīnayānic in its views with a slight trace of Mahāyānism. This distinction of the two groups will be apparent from their doctrinal views as well as from their geographical location, discussed hereafter.

GEOGRAPHICAL DISTRIBUTION OF THE TWO GROUPS OF MAHĀSAṄGHIKAS

(*a*) *North-western or the Earlier Group*

Fa-hien (5th century A.D.)[1] found the Mahāsaṅghikas at Pāṭaliputra. Hiuen Tsang (7th century A.D.)[2] remarks that "the majority of inferior brethren at Pāṭaliputra began the Mahāsaṅghika school". I-tsing (671-695 A.D.)[3] tells us that the Mahāsaṅghikas were found at his time mostly in Magadha, a few in Lāṭa and Sindhu (Western India) and some in a few places in northern, eastern and southern India.[3] In these localities both Fa-hien and Hiuen Tsang came across the adherents

1 Legge, *Fa-hein*, in *IHQ.*, VII, p. 644-45

2 Watters, *Yuan Chwang*, I, p. 269

3 Takakusu, I-tsing, p. xxxiii

of this school though not so frequently as those of others. In the *Śāriputra-paripṛcchā-sūtra* (Chinese transl.) it is stated that they resided at Uḍḍiyāna along with the Sarvāstivādins, Mahīśāsakas, Dharmaguptas and Kāśyapīyas (see Bareau, *op. cit.*).[1]

The earliest epigraphical notice of this school is found in the inscriptions of the Mathura Lion Capital (about 120 B.C.),[2] mentioning that it had a very strong opponent in Buddhila, an adherent of the Sarvāstivāda school. At Andarab in Afghanistan and its neibhouring places there were some followers of the Mahāsaṅghikas. During the reign of Huviṣka, one Kamagulya deposited some relics of Buddha in the Wardak vase and dedicated the same to the care of the teachers of this school. The vault which contained the relic vase was built by the father of Kamagulya.[3] At Andarab, which was three days' journey from the country of Wardaks, Hiuen Tsang found the adherents of this school in three monasteries.

Of the three writers, Vasumitra, Bhavya and Vinītadeva, Vasumitra has been identified by Prof. Masuda[4] with the author of the *Mahāvibhāṣā* during the reign of Kaṇiṣka. Vasumitra has devoted more attention to the doctrinal views of the northern group of the Mahāsaṅghikas than to those of the southern group. He put together the views of the Mahāsaṅghikas, Ekavyavahārikas, Lokottaravādins, and Kaukkuṭikas, and attributed to them as many as forty-eight views with additional nine as later differentiated doctrines. The next two schools which received his attention were the Bahuśrutīyas and Prajñaptivādins, who also belonged to the northern group, attributing to them nine doctrines while he dismissed the southern schools (Caitya, Uttara and Aparaśailas) with three views.

Just the reverse was the attitude taken by the compiler of the *Kathāvatthu.* In this text, sixteen doctrinal views are attributed

1 Bareau, *op. cit.*, p. 56 quoting the opinion of Lin Li Kouang, who writes that there were two sects of the Mahāsaṅghikas: (i) The Mahāsaṅghikas proper unreformed representing the old liberal Mahāyānic leanings, claiming origin from the Sthaviras or Vātsīputrīyas. But such clear cut division is not approved by Bareau. *E. I.*, IX, pp. 130, 141, 146

2 *E. I.*, XI, p. 211

3 Watters, *op. cit.*, II, pp. 267, 269

4 *Asia Major*, II, p. 7f.

to the Mahāsaṅghikas in general while forty-one views to the Andhakas, comprising Pubbaseliya, Aparaseliya, Rājagirika, Siddhatthika with additional thirty-three special doctrines of Pubbaseliya and thirteen of other schools.

The career of the off-shoots of this school, however, took a different course. They were mainly located in one country, Andhra Pradesh, for which they were given the collective name of the Andhakas in the Ceylonese chronicles. We have seen above that their names appeared more than once in the Amarāvatī and Nāgārjunikoṇḍa inscriptions.

In the Pali tradition appear five names : Hemavatika, Rājagirika, Siddhatthika, Pubbaseliya and Aparaseliya. Though the Pali tradition is partially corroborated in Vinītadeva's list it has been fully borne out by the inscriptions unearthed at Nāgārjunikoṇḍa and Amarāvatī (Dhanakaṭaka), making exception of the Mahīśāsaka, a branch of Sarvāstivāda.

Out of the twelve names of the Pali tradition, we come across seven in the Nāgārjunikoṇḍa inscription. This testimony confirms the authenticity of the Pāli tradition. Vinītadeva replaced Bahuśrutīya by Prajñaptivāda; otherwise, he agreed with the traditions preserved in the Pali texts and the inscriptions. The Śaila schools in later days surpassed the Mahāsaṅghikas in popularity. It appears that the earlier Mahāsaṅghikas were not concentrated at Śrīparvata and Dhanakaṭaka (in Guntur district). In the inscriptions is mentioned that a magnificent Caitya was erected here and its grandeur and sanctity attracted devotees from places all over India and Ceylon. According to the inscriptions, the Caitya was erected some time about the 3rd or 4th century A.D.

(*b*) *Southern or Later Group*

The southern group of the Mahāsaṅghikas migrated from Pāṭaliputra to the Andhra country through Kaliṅga, where Hiuen Tsang saw the monasteries of the Mahāyānist Sthaviras. Perhaps he refers by this nomenclature to a sect adhering to the disciplinary rules of the Sthaviras but having Mahāyānic leanings — a characteristic which may be attributed to the Śaila schools. Unlike the northern group of the Mahāsaṅghikas, the southern group was concentrated in the Guntur district around Amarāvatī, Jaggayapeṭa and Nāgārjunikoṇḍa. The inscriptions

(3rd or 4th century A.D.) at Amarāvatī and Nāgārjunikoṇḍa furnish us with the names of the following sects :

(i) Hamghi (Burgess, *op. cit.*, p. 105)
Ayira-haghāna (*EI.*, XX, pp. 17, 20)
(ii) Caityika (Burgess, *op. cit.*, pp. 100, 102)
(iii) Aparamahāvanaseliya (*EI.*, XX, p. 41)
Mahāvanaseliyāna (Burgess, *op. cit.*, p. 105)
(iv) Puvasele (*EI.*, XX, p. 22)
(v) Rājagiri-nivāsika (Burgess, *op. cit.*, p. 53)
Rājaśaila (*Ibid.*, p. 104)
(vi) Sidhathikā (*Ibid.*, p. 110)
(vii) Bahusutiya (*EI.*, XX, p. 24)
(viii) Mahīśāsaka (*Ibid.*)

Except the last two, the rest are all sub-branches of the Mahāsaṅghika school.

All these evidences are obvious pointers to the cleavage between the two groups of the Mahāsaṅghikas, i.e., (i) the Mahāsaṅghikas of the north being the earlier ones with liberal disciplinary views and Mahāyānic leanings and (ii) the Mahāsaṅghikas of the south, i.e., of Andhra, claiming their origin from the Sthaviras and Vātsīputrīyas. Lin Li Kouang is also of this view though Dr. Bareau does not fully approve of the same.

Doctrines of the Northern Group of the Mahāsaṅghikas

Vasumitra has put together all the common views of the Mahāsaṅghikas, Lokottaravādins and Kaukkuṭikas. Paramārtha (557-569 A.D.),[1] a follower of the Vijñānavāda school was one of the most learned translators of Vasumitra's treatise on sects viz., *Samayabhedoparacana-cakra*. The literal meanings of the names of the sects, as given by Paramārtha are :

(i) *Mahāsaṅghikas* = Those who did not distinguish Arhats from non-Arhats, i.e., Aśaikṣas from Śaikṣas, in the deliberations of an ecclesiastical assembly, the members of which, as a matter of course, were large in number.

1 *L'origine des sectes bouddhiques d'apres Paramārtha* by Paul Demiéville in *Mélanges chinois et bouddhiques*, I, 1931-32.

(ii) *Ekavyavahārikas* = All *dharmas* are conventional and, hence, unreal, and the Absolute is one but rare and accidental.

(iii) *Lokottaravāda* = All worldly (*laukika*) *dharmas* are unreal; the real *dharmas* are supra-mundane.

(iv) *Kaukkuṭika* = Doubt or suspicion about everything. The name is derived from *Kaukṛtya* = doubt. It believed that out of the three Piṭakas, only one was reliable. It was the Abhidhamma as it contained the actual instructions of Buddha. Logic is the only means for attaining the *summum bonum*. Observance of disciplinary rules is not obligatory as these do not fit in always with the moral ideals of a Bodhisattva.

It has been stated above (vide p. 49) on the basis of the works of Bhavya, Vinītadeva and Vasumitra, that Ekavyavahārika was another name of the Mahāsaṅghika and that Kaurukullika held almost the same views as those of the Vātsīputrīyas.

Paramārtha states that the three sub-sects of the Mahāsaṅghikas, named below, held certain special views. These are as follows :

The Ekavyavahārikas held that all composites were unreal and fictitious while the absolute was contingent (i.e., dependent on something else).

The Lokottaravadins held that while all mundane *dharmas* were unreal, the supramundane *dharmas* were real. This point was not in the ambit of Mahāyāna. Paramārtha explains it as the view that stands between Śūnyatā (the transcendental reality), Tathatā (thatness) and Amala-vijñāna (pure knowledge). Prof. Demiéville thinks that neither the text of Kitsang nor that of Paramārtha is quite clear on this point.

The Kaurukullikas held the view that of the Tripiṭaka the Abhidharma alone contained the real teaching of Buddha; the other two piṭakas dealt only with the monastic rules. This school did not consider that the attainment of the *summum bonum* along with freedom from all disciplinary obligations was the sole object of a Buddhist monk. This was in conformity with the practices of a Bodhisattva. This school also denied the importance of study and preaching as well as of the practice of meditation.

The Bahuśrutīya school preferred a syncretism of Hīnayāna and Mahāyāna. They affiliated themselves to the Satyasiddhi school[1] of Harivarman. One branch of this school established distinction between real and unreal, absolute and conventional, *paramārtha* and *saṃvṛti.* It recognized Kātyāyaṇīputra of the Sarvāstivāda school as its patron.

The Bahuśrutīyas were in favour of syncretism of the views of Hīnayāna and Mahāyāna like the Satyasiddhi school of Harivarman. It seems necessary, therefore, to state here briefly the views of the Satyasiddhi school. Harivarman was the founder of the school about 900 years after Buddha's *parinirvāṇa.* He was a Sāṅkhya teacher. He became a disciple of Ācārya Kumāralabdha of Kashmir, the propounder of the Sautrāntika school of teachings of about the 4th/5th century A.D. The Sarvāstivādins denied the real existence of soul (*ātman*) and admitted the reality of the *dharmas* (objects) in their noumenal state. Harivarman modified this view of the Sarvāstivādins as well as the extreme Śūnyatā doctrine of Nāgārjuna, the founder of the Mādhyamika school of thought, and arrived at the following conclusions:

The Sarvāstivādins taught *anātman* of a person, i.e., the doctrine of non-ego. They held that the five *skandhas* jointly or severally had provisional existence, as they were the products of causes and conditions (*hetu-pratyaya*) and on that account, essentially unreal (*śūnya*). He examined the noumenal state of *dharmas* from three standpoints :

(a) provisional or noumenal existence;

(b) existence of dharmas in reality; and

(c) absolute unreality of *dharmas* with their following corollaries :

(a) that only phenomenal existence of all objects, including the ego of an individual, is unreal;

(b) noumenal existence of objects as they appear to our senses is unreal; and

(c) all *dharmas*, i.e., four elements (earth, water, air, fire) have noumenal existence as they are combined by colour, smell, taste and touch.

Mind and mental properties (*citta, caitta-dharmas*) have only provisional or noumenal existence.

---

1 Yamakami Sogen, *System of Buddhist Thoughts*, pp. 178-80.

Again, since atom and mind can be analysed, they are unreal (*śūnya*). This is the transcendental truth of Harivarman.

Conception of Buddha

In the *Ariyapariyesanā-sutta*[1] of the Theravādins is mentioned that Buddha attained omniscience and that he did not seek *Nibbāna*. He sought *Samyak Sambuddhahood* in order to propound, preach and promulgate hitherto unknown religious and philosophical views. He became a Seer and visualized the highest Truth or the Reality — the Truth which was so deep and subtle that he was at first hesitant to preach the same to the people at large, as it would do more harm to them than good. He stated :

Sabbābhibhū sabbavidū'ham asmi,
sabbesu dhammesu anupalitto.
Ahaṃ hi arahā loke, ahaṃ satthā anuttaro,
eko'mhi sammāsambuddho sītibhūto 'smi nibbuto.

[I am the all-conqueror, I am omniscient, I am untouched by all worldly objects. I am perfect in this world; I am a Teacher incomparable; I am the only enlightened, tranquilized and have extinguished everything].

Such utterances may well be the basis of the Mahāsaṅghika conception of Buddha.

Buddha, it is said, at the intervention of Brahmā, decided to preach his doctrines in a modified form for the benefit of the mediocre searchers after Truth to enable them to achieve their desired end. This modified teaching consists of the four Aryan truths (*Ariyasaccas*), Eightfold path (*Aṭṭhaṅgika-magga*), and the Law of Causation (*Paṭiccasamuppāda*), the subject-matter of His first discourse. The Mahāyānists took the above decision of Buddha to establish their thesis that only an omniscient Buddha could realize the highest Truth and that his disciples, who heard the first discourse (*Dhammacakkappavattana-sutta*), became known as the Śrāvakas, who could attain perfection (*arhathood*) only by observing the instructions contained in the discourse; in other words, they could realize only absence of individual soul (*anattā=pudgalanairātmya*) and not the non-existence

1 *Majjhima Nikāya*, I, p. 171.

(*dharma-śūnyatā*) or sameness (*tathātva*) of all phenomenal beings and objects.

The Theravādins and Sarvāstivādins along with their offshoots conceived of Buddha as a human being, who attained perfection (*Buddhahood*) and became omniscient at Bodhgaya. Until then he was subject to all human frailties common to a pious and meritorious person. The Mahāsaṅghikas did not subscribe to this view as they contended that how could one who was the best of all divine beings in merit and knowledge in his existence just prior to his birth as Prince Siddhārtha, become an ordinary human being. Hence his appearance in the mortal world was only fictitious in order to follow the ways of the world (*lokānuarṭana*). He had achieved all the perfections in his previous existences as a Bodhisattva.

The Mahāsaṅghikas, therefore, attributed to Gautama Buddha not only supra-mundane existence but also all perfections and omniscience from his so-called birth in the womb of Queen Māyā, and not from his attainment of Bodhi at Bodh Gaya. It should be noted that the Mahāsaṅghikas had in mind Buddha Gautama of Sahā *lokadhātu*, and not the countless Buddhas of the innumerable *lokadhātus* as conceived by the Mahāyānists.

The Mahāsaṅghikas and their offshoots mention specifically that

(1) Buddha's body is entirely supra-mundane (*lokottara*). The eighteen *dhātus* are bereft of impure *dharmas*. The vocal, physical and mental actions (*karman*) are dissociated from impurities (*āsrava-visaṃyukta*). The body has nothing wordly (*laukika*); it is purity only (*anāsrava-mātra*) and indestructible.

(2) His material body (*Rūpakāya* or *Nirmāṇa-kāya*) is "unlimited" as a result of his unlimited past merits. Paramārtha explains "unlimited" as "immeasurable" and "innumerable". It can be either large or small, and it can also be of any number. In his created body (*Nirmāṇa-kāya*) he can appear anywhere in the universe.

The *Kathāvatthu* (XVII. 1 & 2) throws further light on the above. It states that, according to the Vetulyakas, the doctrine that the Buddha does not live in the world of men neither should he be located anywhere and it is his created form (*abhininimito jino*) that delivered the religious discourses. The Theravādins account for this heresy by saying that it is due to the literal but wrong interpretation of the passage : *Bhagavā loke jāto loke sambuddho lokaṃ abhibhuyya viharati anupalitto lokenā ti* (Buddha, born and enlightened in this world, overcame this world and remained untouched by the things of the world (—*Saṃ Nik.*, iii. 140). This is supplemented by further discussions in the *Kvu.*, (XVIII. 1, 2 & XXI. 6) relating to the heresies, also attributed to the Vetulyakas, viz., *Na vattabbaṃ*, "*Buddho Bhagavā manussaloke aṭṭhāsī ti* (It should not be said that Buddha lived in the world of men — XVIII. 1); *Sabbā disā Buddhā tiṭṭhantī ti*[1] (Buddhas exist in all corners of the world — XXI. 6) and *Abhinimmitena desito ti* (the discourses are delivered by created forms — XVIII. 2). These show that according to the opponents of the Theravādins the Buddha is omnipresent and, as such, beyond the possibility of location in any particular direction or sphere and that all the preachings of Buddhism have been done by the apparitional images of Buddha.

With his usual naivety Buddhaghoṣa understood the Vetulyakas as holding the opinion that Buddha remained always in the Tuṣita heaven, where he was before he came to this world. The discussions in the *Kathāvatthu* as also the terse statement of Vasumitra leave no room for doubt about the fact that the Mahāsaṅghikas (especially their offshoots, — the Vetulyakas and the Lokottaravādins regarded Buddha as transcendental. Masuda[2] suggests that the *sambhogakāya* of Buddha is referred to in the heresies but the time of emergence of the conception of *sambhogakāya* is much later. From the discussion in the *Kathāvatthu* (XXI. 5) concerning "*atthi Buddhānaṃ Buddhehi hīnātirekatā ti*" (whether Buddhas mutually differ ?), it seems that the Andhakas (another offshoot of the Mahāsaṅghikas) were still concerned with the *sambhogakāya* and had not yet arrived at the conception of the *Dharmakāya*. Buddhaghoṣa says that the Andhakas hold that Buddhas differ from one another in some qualities other than

---

1 This is the opinion of the Mahāsaṅghikas only, according to the *Kvu.*

2 Masuda's opinion, however, can be supported by the fact that in the *Mahāvastu* (I, p. 169) Buddha's *kāya* is equated with *niṣyandakāya* rendered into Chinese by *pao sheng* which is also the rendering of *sambhogakāya*, see my *Aspects*, pp. 117, 120.

attainment like *satipaṭṭhāna sammappadhāna*, etc., the orthodox school holding that Buddhas may differ in respect of *śarīra* (body), *āyu*, (length of life) and *prabhāva* (radiance) but not in regard to the attainments mentioned above. The discussion in the *Kvu.* (XXVII. 3) shows that the Uttarāpathakas held the views that Buddhas could have no *karuṇā* (compassion) and that Buddha's body was made of *anāsrava dharmas* (pure elements).

(3) Buddha's length of life (*āyu*) is unlimited on account of his past accumulated merits. He lives as long as the sentient beings live.

(4) Buddha's divine power ((*tejas, prabhāva*) is unlimited. He can appear in one moment in all the worlds of the universe.[1]

(5) Buddha is never tired of enlightening sentient beings and awakening pure faith (*viśuddha-śraddhā*) in them. The Chinese commentator explains that Buddha's compassion (*karuṇā*) is limitless and so in order to enlighten beings interminably, he never enters into *Nirvāṇa*.

(6) As his mind is always in meditation, Buddha neither sleeps nor dreams.

(7) Buddha can comprehend everything in one moment (*eka-kṣaṇikacitta*). His mind is like a mirror. He can answer any question simultaneously without reflection. In the *Kathāvatthu* (v. 9) this doctrine is attributed to the Andhakas, who contend that Buddha has knowledge of all present matters (*sabbasmiṃ paccupanne ñāṇam atthī ti*).

(8) Buddha is always aware that he has no impurities (*kṣayi-jñāna*) and that he cannot be reborn (*anutpādajñāna*).

What has been stated above finds corroboration in the *Mahā-vastu* in ornate language thus : The Bodhisattva in his last existence as Siddhārtha Gautama is self-born (*upapāduka*) and is not born of parents; he sits cross-legged in the womb and preaches therefrom to the gods, who act as his protectors; while in the womb he remains untouched by phlegm and such other matters of the womb, and he issues out of the womb by the right side without piercing it.[2] He has no lust (*kāma*) and so Rāhula was also self-born.

1 *Mahāvastu*, I, p. 168.
2 *Ibid*. p. 148.

Buddha's acquisitions are all supramundane (*lokottara*)[1] and cannot be compared to anything worldly. His spiritual practices are supramundane and so are his merits, even his bodily movements such as walking, standing, sitting and lying are also supramundane. His eating, his putting on robes and such other acts are also supramundane. It is for following the ways of the world (*lokānuvartana*) that he shows his *Īryāpathas*. His feet are clean, still washes them. His mouth smells like the lotus, still he cleanses his teeth. His body is not touched by the sun or wind or rain, still he puts on garment and lives under a roof. He cannot have any disease and still he takes medicine to cure himself.[2]

In the *Abhidharmakośa* and its *Vyākhyā*,[3] it is said that, according to the Mahāsaṅghikas, Buddhas appear at the same time in more than one world and that they are omniscient in the sense that they know all *dharmas* at the same time. The former statement appears also in the *Kathāvatthu* (XXI, 6). In the *Kathāvatthu* and the *Kośa*, no special doctrines about the Bodhisattva conception are attributed to the Mahāsāṅghikas.

Buddha follows the ways of the world just as much as he follows the transcendental ways.[4] There is nothing common between Him and the beings of the world. If the transcendence of Buddha be admitted, then it follows that the length of his life should be unlimited and that he need not be subject to sleep or dream as he could have no fatigue. As he is ever awake how can he have dreams ? In the *Mahāparinibbānasutta* it is stated by Buddha himself that if he wished he could live for a *kalpa*.[5] This shows that even the early Buddhists believed that Buddha was *lokottara*.

The *lokottara* conception appears only in the introductory

---

1 *Ibid.*, I, p. 159.

2 For the beautiful inspiring account, read the *Mahāvastu*, I, pp. 167-70.

3 *Kośa*, iii. 200; ix. 254

4 *Mahāvastu*, I, p. 168 :
Lokānuvartanāṃ Buddhā anuvartanti laukīkiṃ,
prajñaptim anuvartanti yathā lokottarām pi. Cf., I, p. 159.

5 *Dīgha*, II, p. 103: yassa kassaci cattāro iddhipādā bhāvitā sa ākaṅkhamāno kappaṃ vā tiṭṭheyya kappāvasesaṃ vā.

portion of the *Mahāvastu*, and so it is evident that the text was originally Hīnayānic and that, in course of time, the introductory chapters were added by the Lokottaravādins. In the main text, the doctrines mentioned are essentially Hīnayānic, e.g., the four truths, the eightfold path, the law of causation (*pratītyasamutpāda*), impermanence of constituents of a being (*skandhas*), non-existence of soul (*anātman*), theory of the effect of past deeds (*karma*), the thirty seven dharmas leading to Bodhi (*Bodhipakṣiyadharmas*, *bodhyaṅgas*) and so forth[1]. There is no mention of the non-existence of phenomenal objects (*dharmaśūnyatā*), of the three bodies of Buddha (*trikāya*) and the two veils (*āvaraṇas*) regarding the impurities and the Truth (*kleśa* and *jñeya*). The only Mahāyānic doctrines, viz., the four stages of the practices of Bodhisattva (*caryās*), the ten gradual spiritual stages (*daśabhūmi*), countless Buddhas and their countless spheres (*kṣetras*) appear more as later additions than as integral parts of the text.[2]

Conception of Bodhisattva

The conception of Bodhisattva found in the *Mahāvastu* has been stated above. There are some additional materials in the works of Vasumitra, Bhavya and Vinītadeva. These are stated below.

At the outset it should be noted that the various sects of the Mahāsaṅghikas knew only of one Bodhisattva — the previous existences of Siddhārtha Gautama, who had to pass through numerous existences in order to attain Buddhahood, a fact admitted by the Theravādins also. Hence the views mentioned here refer only to the Bodhisattva stages of Gautama Buddha.

(i) The Bodhisattva takes any form of lower existence (*durgati*) for enlightening the beings of the world.[3]

(ii) The Bodhisattva enters his mother's womb as a white

1 *Mahāvastu*, III, p. 331-33

2 *Ibid.*, p. 44-49

3 *Mahāvastu*, I, p. 345

elephant symbolical of his great physical strength combined with softness. It is not an intermediate existence (*antarābhava*) but may be regarded as a created (*nirmita*) form.[1] In the *Kathāvatthu* (hence-forth abbreviated as *Kvu.*) (XIV. 2) the view attributed to the Śailas is that the Bodhisattva's six organs appear simultaneously while he is in the womb. He does not pass through the embryonic stages (kalala, arbuda, peśī and ghana).

(iii) The Bodhisattva has in his mind no trace of desire, hatred and malice (kāma, vyāpāda and vihiṃsā saṃjñā).[2]

Are Bodhisattvas average beings?

If, according to the Mahāsaṅghikas, Buddhas are *lokottara* and if the Buddha (Siddhārtha Gautama) is only a created form (Nirmāṇakāya) of the real Buddha, the Bodhisattvas also cannot be average beings — they must also be supramundane.[3] In Vasumitra's treatise (Bareau *op. cit.*, p. 261) the following account of the Bodhisattvas, attributed to the Mahāsaṅghikas is given :

The Bodhisattvas do not pass through the embryonic stages. They assume the form of white elephants when they enter their mothers' wombs and come out of the same by the right side.[4] The above opinion is the natural outcome of the legendary belief that came to be woven around Gautama Buddha about a century after his demise. In the *Lalitavistara*[5] the Bodhisattva is placed not only within a crystal casket in the womb but while in that state he is said to have been preaching his *dharma* to the heavenly beings that flocked to him. The story of the white elephant seen by Queen Māyā in a dream at the time of her conception and the birth of the Bodhisattva by bursting through the right side of his mother's womb is a pure legend and needs no comment.

The only doctrine that can be described as Mahāyānic is that Bodhisattvas take birth out of their own free-will in any form

1 *Ibid.*, p. 335-37

2 *Ibid.*, II, p. 363; III, p. 65

3 *Ibid.*, I, p. 145, 153-54

4 Bareau, *op. cit.*, pp. 58f., quoting the views found in the works of Vasumitra and Vinītadeva with comments.

5 *Lalitavistara* (A. S. edition), p. 73.

of existence for imparting his dharma to the sentient beings according to the latter's form of existence. This idea is well developed in the *Jātakas, Śikṣāsamuccaya* and *Bodhicaryāvatāra*. This topic has been taken up for discussion in the *Kvu.* (XXIII-3) thus :

"*Bodhisatto issariyakāmakārikahetu vinipātaṃ gacchatī ti.*" In this discussion the views of the Mahāsaṅghikas are ignored; Bodhisattva is treated as an everage human being, who through personal exertions attained Bodhi.

In the *Niyāmokkantikathā* (*Kvu.* IV. 8; XII. 5, 6; XIII. 4) also, the views of the Mahāsaṅghikas are ignored and only the Theravāda view is presented thus: There are two *niyāmas* (guides) : (i) *sammattaniyāma* (right path or guide) and (ii) *micchattaniyāma* (wrong path or guide). The first refers to the practice of pure moral laws (*brahmacariya*) and to that of the eightfold path (*aṭṭhaṅgikamagga*) leading to sanctification (*nibbāna*); it also implies the fulfilment of the six or ten perfections (*pāramis* or *pāramitās* by the Bodhisattvas. The second, i.e. *micchattaniyāma*, means the commission of immoralities and offences including the most heinous ones (*ānantarīyakamma*) leading to existences in hells. Practices not included in either of the above two are called undetermined or unpredestined (*aniyata*). In the sense expressed above, any Śrāvaka can be a *sammattaniyāma* though he may not be a Bodhisattva. The Theravādins do not recognize the Bodhisattvas as superior in attainment to the Śrāvakas. In the matter of *brahmacariya* and practice of *ariyamagga*, they do not make any distinction between a Śrāvaka and a Bodhisattva.

In the *Laṅkāvatāra* and Asaṅga's *Sūtrālaṅkāra* and a few other Mahāyānic works, however, it is repeatedly stated that a person by the development of *Bodhicitta* becomes a predestined (*niyata*) Bodhisattva, who, by fulfilment of the *Pāramitās* and practice of the various forms of asceticism, ultimately becomes a Buddha. Siddhārtha Gautama, in one of his previous existences as Jotipāla māṇava, did, as a matter of fact, develop Bodhicitta at the time of Kassapa Buddha, and then through several existences he fulfilled the *pāramitās* and had recourse to all possible *sādhanās* (meditational practices) and attained perfection.

The Andhakas took the opposite view and asserted on the basis of the passage in the *Majjhima Nikāya* (II. p. 54) that he became a *Śrāvaka* of Kassapa Buddha: Kassapo, aham Ānanda, bhagavati brahmacariyam acariṃ sambodhāyā ti etc. (*Kvu.* p. 288).

Buddha's Teachings

After dealing with the personality of Buddha, the Mahāsaṅghikas contend that the super-divine Buddha did not deliver any discourses to his disciples. The views are as follows: (i) Though Buddha is always in *samādhi*, sentient beings think that they have heard discourses from him in well-constructed sentences. The commentator explains that words flow from Buddha's mouth spontaneously, and these have been collected as discourses.

In the *Kvu.* (XVIII. 2) this view is attributed to the Vetulyakas and is explained in these words, "Buddhena Bhagavatā na desito." In support of this contention they argue that Abhidharma was preached to Māyā in Tāvatiṃsa heaven and the gist was given to Sāriputta to develop it. They further contend that whatever Ānanda heard was from the created body (nirmāṇakāya or rūpakāya) of Buddha. (2) By one utterance or word (*śabda*) Buddha can expound all doctrines.

The two views mentioned above are, however, contradicted by the next two views :

(3) All of Buddha's preachings deal only with *Dharmacakra* (Wheel of Law), his first discourse was delivered at Sārnāth but the commentator explains that his *dharma* referred only to the eradication of desire, etc ; whatever may be stated by Him expresses the truth only (*yathārtha*).[1] All sūtras of Buddha have *nītārtha* (definite or direct meaning) as opposed to *neyārtha* (indirect or implied meaning).

In the *Kvu.* (II. 10) the discussion resting with the topic :

---

1 Cf. M. Vṛ., p. 494 : vyavalmāraṃ anāśritya paramārtho na deśyate. *Paramārtha-satya* means the highest truth while *saṃvṛti-satya* means the so-called truths as used in every-day usage by the people in general. For detailed treatment see my *Aspects*, pp. 216 ff.

"Buddhassa Bhagavato vohāro lokuttaro ti" reveals that the Andhakas, to whom the above opinion is ascribed, held that Buddha's actions (*vohāro*) are *lokuttara* (supramundane), but they are looked upon as *lokiya* (mundane) or *lokuttara* (supramundane). Mr. Shwe Zan Aung prefers to confine the sense of the word *vohāro* to speech, and we think that there is good reason for it.

In Vasumitra's treatise, an opinion of this nature is attributed to the Mahāsaṅghikas in contrast to the Sarvāstivādins, viz., the *sūtras* (or discourses) preached by Buddha are all perfect in themselves (*nītārtha*). Since Buddhas speak of nothing but *dharma* (doctrines), their teaching is concerned only with *paramārthasatya* (*paramatthasacca*), i.e., not with *saṃvṛtisatya* (*sammutisacca*). The *paramārthasatya* cannot be normally expressed by words. It can be explained only by silence or at the most by an exclamation — which idea, I think, is expressed in Vasumitra's treatise thus : "The Buddha can expound all the doctrines with a single utterance and that there is nothing which is not in conformity with the truth in what has been preached by the World-honoured one."[1] In the *Upāyakauśalyaparivarta* of the *Saddharmapuṇḍarīka* it has been shown that for training up deluded beings in his doctrines, Buddha did take recourse to various expedients which were conventional, i.e., unreal (*saṃvṛti* or *sammuti*), and that through such teachings he led the deluded beings to the truth —*paramārtha.* So it follows that all his teachings collected in the *Piṭakas* are merely *saṃvṛti* or *sammuti* (conventional), and they are therefore not his real teachings.[2]

Among the other attributes of this *lokottara* Buddha, Vasumitra's treatise speaks of his powers (*balas*)[3] as unlimited

1 *Asia Major*, II, p. 19.
2 *Aspects* etc., p. 198.
3 The ten balas are :—
  1 *Thānāṭhānaṃ jānāti . . .*
  2 *Ṡabbatthagāminipaṭipadaṃ jānāti.*
  3 *Anekadhātuṃ nānādhātuṃ lokaṃ jānāti.*
  4 *Sattānaṃ nānādhimuttikānaṃ jānāti.*
  5 *Parasattānaṃ parapuggalānaṃ indriya-paropariyattaṃ yathābhūtaṃ pajānāti.*
  6 *Atītānāgatāpaccuppannānaṃ hetuso vipākaṃ jānāti.*

while the *Mahāvastu* of his five eyes (*cakṣus*)[1] as uncommon (*asādhāraṇa*) and excelling those of *Pratyekabuddhas, Arhats* and others. This particular topic—*tathāgatabalaṃ sāvakasādhāraṇan ti* has been taken up for discussion in the *Kvu.* (III. 1), but strangely enough the position taken by the compiler of the *Kvu.* is not that of a Theravādin but that of a Lokottaravādin Mahāsaṅghika but against the Andhakas, i.e., the Śaila schools. In Vasumitra's treatise this topic appears in a slightly different form.

The Theravādins do not regard Buddha as *lokottara* but attribute to him almost all the powers and qualities of a *lokottara* Buddha, and this discussion reveals one of such instances. The ten special *balas* (powers) of a Tathāgata appear not only in the *Mahāvastu* (i, pp. 159-60) but also in old Pāli works like the *Majjhima Nikāya* (i, pp. 69 ff.). The contention of the Andhakas is that there is a certain degree of difference between the Buddhas and the Arhats regarding the acquisition of the ten *balas*, and, as such, Buddhas and Arhats are not on the same level (*asādhāraṇaṃ*). In the *Mahāvastu* and the Pāli works this view is accepted with this reservation that Buddhas are *sarvākārājña*, i.e., they possess a complete and detailed knowledge of everything, while an Arhat can at the most have sectional knowledge.[2] The Pāli school, i.e., the Theravādins, holds that as far as *vimutti* is concerned, there is no difference between a Buddha and an Arhat, and that Buddhas are superior to the Arhats only on account of the fact that the former is a promulgator of a new religion and philosophy and the latter is only a follower of the same.

7. *jhānavimokkhasamādhisamāpattīnaṃ saṅkilesaṃ vodānaṃ voṭṭhānaṃ yathābhūtaṃ pajānāti.*
8. *anekavihitaṃ pubbenivāsaṃ anussarati.*
9. *dibbena cakkhunā satte passati cavamāne upapajjamāne* etc.
10. *āsavānaṃ khayā anāsavaṃ cetovimuttiṃ diṭṭhe va dhamme sayaṃ abhiññā sacchikatva upasampajja viharati.*

1 By eyes, the text means all the five, viz , *māṃsacakṣu divyac., prajñāc, dharmac*, and *buddhac.*

2. cf. *Kvu. Cy.*, p 62: Ṭhānāṭhānādini hi sāvakā *padesena* jānanti. Tathāgatā *nippadesena* iti. Tāni uddesato sādhāraṇāni; niddesato asādhāraṇāni ... niddesato *sabbākaravisayataṃ* saṃdhāya paṭikkhipati. Cf. *Mtu.*, I. p. 158 : cf. *Aspects*, p. 106 fn. 1. See *Saṃyutta*, III, p. 66.

Conception of Arhats

In view of such opinion about the personality of Buddha, the Mahāsaṅghikas could not agree to the high spiritual status attributed by the Theravādins to the Arhats for they argued that the Arhats realised only half the Truth, viz., absence of individual soul (pudgala-śūnyatā) and not the absence of both the individual soul and the worldly objects (dharma-śūnyatā) as held by the Mahāyānists. This is also described as omniscience.

The Arhat, according to the Theravādins, is fully emancipated. He is in possession of the excellent goal (*sadattho*), is free from attachment, hatred and delusion (*vītarāgo vītadoso vītamoho*), free from all impurities (*khīṇāsavo*), relieved of his burden of *khandhas* (*ohitabhāro*). He has done all that is to be done (*katakaraṇīyo*) and he will have no more existence (*nāparam itthattāya*). He has also acquired clear vision about origin and decay of beings and objects. He has got rid of all doubts (*kaṅkhā*) about the *Triratna*, non-existence of soul and the law of causation. He has visualized the Truth without the help of others (*na paravitāraṇā*) and has attained perfect knowledge of the four stages of sanctification (*catumagga-ñāṇa*) but not omniscience or *Samyak sambuddhatva* (*Kvu. cy*. p. 67).

This point was first raised by an erudite monk Mahādeva at the subsidiary Second Buddhist Synod held at Pāṭaliputra. The five propositions were accepted by the Mahāsaṅghikas including the Andhakas, Bahuśrutīyas and the Haimavatas. The five propositions have already been discussed in Chapter II (Second Buddhist Council).

In the *Kathāvatthu-aṭṭhakathā* Buddhaghoṣa writes that a section of the Mahāsaṅghikas and their offshoots asserted on the basis of the first four propositions of Mahādeva that the Arhats or the Aśaikṣas have some imperfections. The Uttarāpathakas regarded some of the Arhats as impostors.

There is another attribute derogatory to the Arhats. The Mahāsaṅghikas and some sects of the orthodox group, like the Sarvāstivādins and the Sammitīyas, hold that Arhats are subject to retrogression (Parihāyati arahā arahattā ti : *Kvu.* i . 2).

The other section of the Mahāsaṅghikas, who oppose the above view, holds that Arhats have no chance of retrogression (B. 37;[1] V. 35[2]) and further asserts that one has done all that is to be done (kṛta-kṛtya, kṛta-karaṇīya) (B. 28; V. 26), i.e., an Arhat or Aśaikṣa, who has passed through all the stages of spiritual progress, cannot have any attachment for an object or a person.

Hence all the adherents of the Mahāsaṅghika, school were not of the same view about the status of an Arhat.

The *Kathāvatthu* (II. 1) discusses the question, "Atthi Arahato asucisukkavisaṭṭhī ti ? The opponents, i.e., the Mahāsaṅghikas state that the discharge of semen of an Arhat is a physical natural discharge like urine, excreta, etc. The Sthaviravādins consider that such a statement amounts to a calumniation of an Arhat.

Srota-āpannakas

Besides Arhathood, the Mahāsaṅghikas held particular views about the status of the Srota-āpannakas. The preparatory stage of Srota-āpannaka is called the Aṭṭhamaka. It is also described as the Gotra-bhūmi, for which the Mahāyānists also use the term "Gotrabhūmiraṣṭamaka." The preparatory stage leads to the comprehension of the four Truths, for which it is designated as Samyaktva-niyāma. This stage marks the crossing of the state of a common man (pṛthag-jana = puthujjana).

The Mahāsaṅghikas hold that

(i) a srota-āpannaka has no retrogression as he gets rid of the ten fetters (saṃyojanas) (B. 40). He comprehends mind and its nature (B. 29). He can practise meditation. He regards suffering (dukkha) as a means for acquiring knowledge (ñāṇa) leading to Nirvāṇa (B. 33, 34). He can stay in the Srota-āpanna stage for a long time (B. 35). He cannot commit any of the five deadly sins (ānantaryas) (B. 40).

---

1. B = Bareau, *Les sectes etc.*
2. V = Vasumitra in *Asia Major* II

The eight stages are

(1/2) Sotāpatti-maggaṭṭha and phalaṭṭha

(3/4) Sakadāgāmi-m. and ph. (as above)

(5/6) Anāgāmi-m. and pha. do

(7/8) Arahatta-m. and pha. do

And the ten fetters are

(a) satkāyadṛṣṭi, vicikitsā, śīla-vrata-parāmarṣa. kāmarāga and pratigha.

[Belief in the heresy of soul or individuality, lack of faith in Triratna, grasping after rites and ceremonies, strong desire for rebirth in the mortal world, and revengefulness.]

(b) rūparāga, arūparāga, māna, auddhatya, and avidyā. [Strong desire for rebirth in the heavens, or in the higher heavens (arūpa), pride, arrogance, and ignorance of Truth.]

The Mahāsaṅghikas accept that a srota-āpanna is *niyato sambodhiparāyaṇo* and hence, is not subject to retrogression, but a sakadāgāmī or an anāgāmī may retrogress but not further than the sotāpanna stage, for some of the adepts in the two stages may have dormant passion (*anusaya*), which may develop into actual (*pariyuṭṭhāna*)[1] passion and thus bring about the fall.

Regarding the srota-āpanna, Vasumitra further states :

If the sotāpannas cannot commit the deadly sins (*ānantaryas*), can they commit the sin of killing beings (*pāṇātipāta*) in these words : *Diṭṭhisampanno puggalo sañcicca pāṇaṃ jīvitā voropeyyā ti ?* A sotāpanna is a person with right view (*diṭṭhisampanno*), hence, according to the Theravādins, he cannot commit the sin of killing (*pāṇātipāta*) or such other offences, not to speak of the five extreme offences like matricide or parricide.

Anuśayas and Paryavasthanas of Srota-āpatti maggaṭṭha (dormant and pervading passion of a person in the eighth stage) are now being dealt with.

1 *Anuśaya* means that which lies in the mind in a latent state with the possibility of its coming into appearance, if it receives an effective impulse, while *pariyuṭṭhāna* means its actual appearance in the mind without however a corresponding response in the outer world. For further details, see *infra*.

In the *Kvu.* (III. 5): *Aṭṭhamakassa*[1] *puggalassa diṭṭhipariyuṭṭhānaṃ pahīnan ti ?*

[Has a person in the eighth stage put an end to pervading wrong views.]

According to the *Andhakas*, an adept, who is in the eighth stage i.e., sotāpatti-maggaṭṭha and not yet sotāpanna, gets rid of the appearance of wrong views, belief in rites and ceremonies and lack of faith in Triratna (diṭṭhipariyuṭṭhāna, sīlabbata-p. and vicikicchā-p.) but not of the dormant passions (anusayas), which may become active (uppajjissati) if they receive an impulse. The Andhakas by drawing this distinction between pariyuṭṭhāna and anusaya hold that an Aṭṭhamaka may not get rid of the three *anusayas* and consequently remain away from the sotāpanna stage for a long time.[2]

The *Kathāvatthu* also discusses the following two allied views attributed to the Pubbaseliyas and the Uttarāpathakas :

(i) *Diṭṭhisampanno puggalo sañcicca pāṇaṃ jīvitā voropeyyā ti* ? (XII.7 — Pubbaseliyas).

[Can a person, possessing the right view, commit the sin of killing ?]

(ii) *Diṭṭhisampannassa puggalassa pahīnā duggatī ti* ? (XII. 8 — Uttarāpathakas).

[Is a person, possessing the right view, free from birth in a lower form of existence ?]

By the first view the Pubbaseliyas mean that a person by having *sammādiṭṭhi* does not get rid of hatred (*dosa*), hence he can commit the sin of killing—a view asserted by the Uttarāpathakas that a person with right view (*sammādiṭṭhi*) cannot be reborn in a lower form of existence; the Theravādins point out that it may be so, but he may have desire (*taṇhā*) for objects and beings belonging to the lower forms of existence.

There are, in Vasumitra, two statements relating to *anuśaya*

---

1. The *aṭṭhamakas* are those who have just stepped into the Sotāpannahood, which is the eighth or the lowest stage in the fruits of sanctification.

For the meaning of the term and its distinction from *pariyuṭṭhāna* see above.

2. Aṭṭhamaka-puggalas have saddhā but not saddhindriya—Andhaka.

and *paryavasthāna* which will clear up the above problem further :

(i) *Anuśayas* (dormant passions or latent bias) are neither mind (*citta*) nor mental (*caitasika*) dharmas, and again they never become the object of thought (*anālambana*). (B. 45; V. 2.)

(ii) *Anuśaya* is different from *paryavasthāna* (pervading passion) and vice versa. It must be said that *anuśaya* does not combine (*samprayujati*) with *citta* whereas *paryavasthāna* does.

Relating to the above topics, the *Kvu.* has,

(i) *Anusayā anārammaṇā ti ?* (IX. 4) and *cittavippayuttā.*[1]

(Dormant passions are without any basis and are dissociated from mind.)

(ii) *Anusayā avyākatā ti* (XI.1)

(Are dormant passions neutral, i.e., neither good nor bad?)

(iii) *Añño kāmarāgānusayo aññaṁ kāmarāgapariyuṭṭhānan ti ?* (XIV. 5)

(Is the dormant passion of attachment different from the pervading passion of attachment ?)

(iv) *Pariyuṭṭhānaṃ cittavippayuttan ti?* (XIV. 6)

(Is pervading passion dissociated from mind?)

Masuda offers the following interpretation from the '*Shuchi:* The *anuśayas* are really *bījas* (germs inborn in the mind) of *rāga* and other passions. They remain dormant unless excited by the corresponding impluse. They remain always in the mind even in kuśalacitta, so they are dissociated from the mind and do not require any object (*ālambana*) for support. When the anuśaya is excited by a suitable impulse, it becomes paryavasthāna (pariyuṭṭhāna) and as such becomes a mental function (caitasika), and then only it becomes an impurity and clogs the way to spiritual growth. The interpretation, given above is corroborated by the *Kvu. A.*[1] The Theravādins, however, do not distinguish between kāmarāgānusaya and kāmarāgapariyuṭṭhāna and maintain that as the anusayas are included in the

1. *Kvu. A.*, p. 117 : Tattha yesāṃ anusayā nāma cittavippayuttā ahetukā avyākatā ten eva anārammaṇā ti laddhi seyyathā pi Andhakānañ c' eva ekaccānañ ca Uttarāpathakānaṃ (*Kvu.* X. 1)

saṃkhārakkhandha, they are all sārammaṇā. But according to the Andhakas some mental dispositions (saṃkhāras) are sārammaṇa (with basis) and some are anārammaṇa (without basis),[1] but not so are the remaining four khandhas.

From the above discussion it is apparent that the anusayas, according to the Andhakas, are avyākata,[2] i.e., neither good nor bad, and consequently they are dissociated from mind (citta-vippayutta), and also causeless (ahetuka). The Andhakas in the third discussion assert that anusayas are different from pariyuṭṭhānas, but in the fourth, the *Kvu.* makes the Andhakas contend that pariyuṭṭhānas are also cittavippayuttas, which, however, appear to be contradictory. Vasumitra says that the pariyuṭṭhānas according to these schools are cittasamprayuttas, so we must dismiss the statement of the *Kvu.* as unwarranted.

"The world in its variety originates out of actions (*karma*), which accumulate on account of *anuśayas*. In the absence *anuśayas*, karma, is not capable of producing a new existence (*punarbhava*). Consequently the root of *bhava* or rebirth is *karma*, in other words, *anuśaya*. With these words Vasubandhu opens the fifth book of *Kośa*." (See *Kośa*, V, p. 1).

The Sarvāstivādins like the Theravādins regard *anuśaya*, *paryavasthāna* and *kleśa* as same, the only distinction being that *anuśaya* is subtle, while *paryavasthāna* is manifest, state of *rāga*, *dosa*, *moha*, etc.

The *Kośa* too deals with the problem under discussion, viz., whether or not *anuśaya* (e.g. *kāmarāgānuśaya*) is a dharma by itself dissociated from mind, the *prāpti* of kāmarāga, etc.? The answer of the Sarvāstivādins is in the negative like that of the Theravādins. The former quote as their authority the *Jñānaprasthāna-sūtra*, in which *anuśaya* is shown to be associated with mind (*cittasamprayukta*). They assert that *anuśayas* are *kleśas*, and hence they cannot but be citta-samprayuktas.

In this connection the *Kośa* refers to the opinion of the Sautrāntikas, who hold that *anuśaya* is different from *kleśa* inasmuch as

1. *Kvu.*, p. 407: Saṃkhārakkhandho ekadeso sārammaṇo, ekadeso anārammaṇo.

2. The Andhakas, it seems, looked upon the anusayas as acit and treated the same as avyākata. Cf. *Dhammasaṅgaṇi*.

it is neither associated with, nor dissociated from, mind because it is not a *dravya* apart; it is a *śakti* left in certain individuals by the previously existing *kleśas* and has the power of reproducing further *kleśas*. According to the Sautrāntikas, *kleśa*, when non-manifest, is *anuśaya* and when manifest, an act, it is *paryavasthāna* (*Kośa*, V. p. 7).[1]

The Aṭṭhamakas have Saddhindriya
(dominant faculty of faith)

Vasumitra does not mention this view among the doctrines of the Mahāsaṅghikas, but it is stated in the *Kvu.* that according to the Andhakas, *aṭṭhamakassa puggalassa natthi saddhindriyan ti* (III. 6), [Does a person in the eighth stage not possess dominant faculty of faith ?], i. e., the aṭṭhamakas may develop *saddhā*, *viriya*, etc. but do not acquire *saddhindriya*, *viriyindriya* etc., a distinction which the Theravādins are not prepared to admit. The Andhakas mean that saddhindriya or viriyindriya, etc. is a faculty forming a part of the mind while saddhā or viriya etc. is only a passing phase of the mind.

Abhisamaya or Realization of the Four Truths

Like the Theravādins the Mahāsanghikas hold that the realization of the four truths (*ariyasaccas*) takes place simultaneously in a moment (*ekakṣaṇika* B. 23; V.21) and not gradually, as held by the Sarvāstivādins.[2] They argue that the moment one realizes the nature of suffering (*duḥkha*), one comprehends also its origin and decay (*samudaya*, *nirodha*) as also the path leading to suffering (*mārga*). The four truths are sub-divided into fifteen thus:

(i) duḥkha (suffering), (ii) anitya (impermanence), (iii) śūnya (absence of phenomenal objects), (iv) anātmaka (nonexistence of soul), (v) samudaya (aggregated origin), (vi) prabhava (origin), (vii) hetu (cause), (viii) pratyaya (condition), (ix) nirodha (cessation), (x) śānta (quietude), (xi) praṇīta (excellent), (xii) niḥsaraṇa (liberation), (xiii) mārga (path to

---

1. For exhaustive treatment of Anuśayas, see La Vallée Poussin's *Abhidharmakośa*, V.

2. *Asia Major*, II, p. 22 fn. (Masuda's Origin and Doctrines of Early Indian Buddhist Schools. See also *Abhidharmakośa*, Chap. VI. The Sarvāstivādins have a different list of the sixteen aspects. See *Infra*.

liberation), (xiv) nyāya (logical reason), (xv) pratipatti (proceeding), (xvi) nairyāṇika (final emancipation).

Realization of Duḥkha leads to Abhisamaya

In the *Kathāvatthu* (xi. 4) "Idaṃ dukkhan ti" vācaṃ bhāsato

(1) "Idaṃ dukkhan ti" ñāṇaṃ pavattatī ti and in Vasumitra's treatise the exclamation of "Aho vata duḥkham iti" is recognized by the Andhakas as a means to the realization of the Four Truths. The exclamation of the words "this is suffering" leads to the realization that existence in this world is misery.

(2) Dukkhāhāro maggaṅgaṃ maggapariyantan ti (*Kvu.* ii, 6). (Suffering is a food or a means leading to perfection in the eightfold path).

(3) Samāpannassa atthi vacībhedo ti (*Kvu.* ii. 5) (Can a meditator utter an exclamation ?).

(4) Samāpanno saddaṃ suṇātī ti (Does a meditator hear sound ?).

All these four views are mentioned in Vasumitra's treatise (B. 31-34=V. 29-32).

The Theravādins agree to (1)/(2) but oppose (3)/(4).

The four truths are based on the keyword "dukkha", the watchword of the Teacher. The three other truths refer to its origin, decay and their causes. Buddha laid the utmost emphasis on the realization that worldly existence, being evanescent and substanceless, is misery, as it undergoes change every moment and ends in death, hence one should seek exit from the cycle of births and attain Nirvāṇa, the eternal reality. Without the realization of the basic fact that existence in the mortal world, even in heaven, is undesirable, one cannot but take resort to renunciation of the worldly life in order to practise moral precepts, meditational exercises and various other means leading to the attainment of perfect knowledge (prajñā). Hence the above two views are acceptable to the Theravādins also.

The other two views raise the question whether a meditator, practising any one of the four jhānas (dhyānas), particularly the first, which is not free from discursive thoughts (*vitakka*) and determination (*vicāra*), can utter an exclamation like "Aho dukkham iti"[1] or hear sound, say, of a lightning.[2] The Andhakas contend that meditators in the first dhyāna do not reach the stage when all the organs of sense become wholly inactive and cannot perceive anything. The Theravādins do not intend to make such a distinction.

Abhisamaya by magga-bhāvanā
(Realization of the Four Truths through spiritual progress in the four stages of sanctification)

In the Buddhist texts Magga (= mārga) bears two different meanings. These are :

(1) Magga = eightfold path of the Dhammacakkappavattana-sutta.

(2) Magga = Four stages of sanctification leading to Nibbāna, viz., Sotāpatti, Sakadāgāmi, Anāgāmi and Arahatta.

In the present discussion of the Mahāsaṅghika view, the different kinds of maggas have been used indiscriminately, because these were meant for monks highly advanced spiritually.

The Mahāsaṅghikas and a few other sects state that matter (rūpa) is an associate of the magga (i.e. Sotāpatti, etc.) (B. 55).

In the *Kvu.* (X.2) "Maggasamaṅgissa rūpaṃ maggo" is explained thus:

Right speech, right action and right means of livelihood are according to the above-mentioned sects, matter (rūpa). Hence rūpa is also a basis for progress in a magga (i.e. Sotāpatti etc.).

The Mahāsaṅghikas also contend that observance of five or ten moral precepts (sīla) is also an aid to the spiritual progress.

---

1. cf. *Kvu.*, IX, 9 : Opinion of the Pubbaseliyas : Sabbaso vitakkayato vicārayato vitakkavipphāro saddo ti? The Cy. on it is: Yasmā 'vitakkavicārā vacisaṃkhārā' ti vuttā tasmā sabbaso vitakkayato vicārayato antamaso manodhātuppavattikāle pi vitakkavipphāro saddo yevā ti. Cf. *Majjhima*, I, p. 301.

2. cf. *Kvu.*, XVIII, 8: Samāpanno saddaṃ suṇātī ti. As it has been said by Buddha that sound is a hindrance to the first jhāna and that one rises from the first Jhāna by an external sound, the Pubbaseliyas inferred therefrom that one in meditation hears sound.

In the *Kvu.* (X.6) it is stated that "maggasamaṅgī dvīhi sīlehi samannāgato", i.e., a monk spiritually advanced is associated with moral observances, which may be distinguished as worldly (lokiya) and supra-mundane or spiritual (lokottara).

Both the views are opposed by the Theravādins, who do not recognize that the first three items of the eightfold path are lokiya and not lokottara.

The Mahāsaṅghikas further contend that an adept, in spite of his five sense-perceptions, can progress along the spiritual path (B. 24, 25). In the *Kvu.* this view has been discussed :

(i) *Pañcaviññāṇasamaṅgissa atthi maggabhāvanā ti* (X. 3). (In spite of the five sense-perceptions, can a person progress along the spiritual path ?).

(ii) *Pañcaviññāṇā kusalā ti akusalā pī ti* (X. 4), and

(iii) *Pañcaviññāṇā sābhogā* (X. 5) (The five sense-perceptions may be good or bad and are associated with mental enjoyment (sābhogā).

The Mahāsaṅghikas on the basis of the statement of Bhagavān, "*Idha, bhikkhave, bhikkhu cakkhunā rūpaṃ disvā nimittaggāhī hoti na nimittaggāhī hotī ti sotena saddaṃ sutvā* etc.," contend that a person using the five sense-organs may undertake spiritual practices (*maggabhāvanā*) by grasping or not grasping the characteristics of the object seen or heard and directing his mind towards *nibbāna.* The Theravādins argue that, if through *pañcaviññāṇā* one attains sotāpatti and other maggas, then the *pañcaviññāṇā* and *magga* should be of the same category, but the former is pre-sotāpanna (*lokiya*) and the latter post-sotāpanna (*lokuttara*), the former has an object as basis (*savatthuka*) and the latter is without any basis (*avatthuka*). In this way, the Theravādins argue that on account of the function of the five viññāṇas one does not attain *nibbāna.*

The Mahāsaṅghikas argue further that the five or six perceptions (viññāṇas) may be productive of either attachment (sarāga) or detachment (virāga) (B.24; V. 22). Mind (citta) by its nature always remains pure and refulgent (pabhassara). It becomes impure by the advent of impurities (kilesas) (B. 44; V. 41).

In the *Kvu* (III. 3), it is argued as against the Andhakas that if an individual has a citta free from impurities (vītarāga), he needs not exert further for attaining emancipation.

There are two other views (B. 78, 79), which speak of root-consciousness (mūla-vijñāna) as the basis of the five or six sense-organic vijñānas (i.e. cakṣu, śrotra, etc.). This mūlavijñāna corresponding to subliminal consciousness (bhavaṅga-citta) before it becomes actual consciousness like desire, hatred, etc., is called pravṛtti-vijñāna. It is to be distinguished from desires (vāsanā) which pervade the mind. These two views anticipate Yogācāra doctrines.[1]

The Mahāsaṅghikas also contend that a spiritually advanced adept attaining the power of controlling thoughts (balapatto vasībhūto) can also control the thoughts of others (B. 74). In the *Kathāvatthu* (XVI. I), in its "Paro parassa cittaṃ niggahātī ti", it is pointed out that the interpretation is wrong. The adept acquires the power of self-control and does not or cannot control others' thoughts. In support of this, the following statement of Buddha is relied upon :

Attanā vā kataṃ pāpaṃ attanā saṃkilissati,
attanā akataṃ pāpaṃ attanā va visujjhati,
Suddhi asuddhi paccattaṃ nāñño aññaṃ visodhaye ti.

(Evils committed by oneself cause suffering to one's own self. Evils not committed by oneself make one's own self pure. Purity and impurity are one's own; none else can purify another.)

The Mahāsaṅghikas further hold that the five or six sense-perceptions (vijñānas) exist together both in the material and non-material spheres (Rūpa and Arūpa dhātus) (B. 25; V.23).

Right view & Faculty of faith

In Vasumitra's treatise it is stated that the Mahāsaṅghikas hold the views that

(i) There is neither laukika-samyagdṛṣṭi (right view) nor laukikaśraddhendriya (faculty of faith) in a common man.

The corresponding passages of the *Kvu.* are,

(i) *Natthi puthujjanassa ñāṇan ti?* (XX, 2);[2] and

1. cf. L. de la V. Poussin, *Vijñapatimātratā-siddhi*, pp. 178-79, 184n., 186.
2. Attributed to the Hetuvādins only.

(ii) *Natthi lokiyaṃ saddhindriyan ti?* (XIX, 8).[1]

The argument of the Theravādins is that a layman may have knowledge (*paññā*) and faith (*saddhā*) of a kind which may be different from those of an ārya, but *paññā* and *saddhā*, which the common man possesses, are developed into *paññindriya* and *saddhindriya* by an ārya. It may be that the common man's *paññā* or *ñāṇaṃ* is confined to gifts, precepts, sacrifice (*dāna, sīla, cāga*), etc., i.e., worldly affairs, and does not extend to the comprehension of the higher (lokuttara) subjects like truths, paths (maggas) and fruits (phalas), hence, according to the Theravādins, there may be *lokiya paññindriya* and *saddhindriya*.

Re. Indriyas (Organs of sense) :

Cakkhunā rūpaṃ passatī ti (*Kvu.* XVIII. 9). (Sentient surfaces of the eyes see).[2]

In the *Kathāvatthu* (XVIII. 9), the Mahāsaṅghikas are said to have held the view that the organs of sense perceive directly and not by their perceptive faculty (*vijñāna*). This is also the view of the Vaibhāṣikas (vide *Kośa*, transl., i. p. 81-82). The Śaila schools and the Theravādins hold the opposite view (see *infra*).

Re. Apratisaṃkhyā-nirodha (Emancipation without knowledge) : (*Kośa*, transl, ii, p. 280).

The Buddhists admit that there are two kinds of *nirodha*: one attained by means of knowledge (*pratisaṃkhyā*) and the other by complete removal of all impurities which cause rebirth, and not by knowledge (*apratisaṃkhyā*). The Mahāsaṅghikas hold that the latter is *paścād abhāva* (subsequent absence) of *dharmas*. One is not reborn by virtue of the spontaneous destruction of *dharmas*.[3]

Re. Kleśa-bīja (Germ of impurities) :

The Mahāsaṅghikas state that *kleśa-bīja* is a *dharma* distinct from *kleśa* (*Kośa*, V, p. 7).

---

1. In the Cy. it is attributed to the Hetuvādins and Mahīśāsakas, and they mean all the five indriyas : saddhā, viriya, sati, samādhi and paññā.

2. That the eyes see and not the cakṣu-vijñāna is also the opinion of the Vaibhāṣikas (*Kośa*. i. 81-82).

3. *Kośa* (transl.), vi, p. 185 fn.

Re. Asti-vāda :

The Mahāsaṅghikas maintain as against the Sarvāstivādins that the present exists but not the past and the future.

Re. Vijñapti (Signs of intimation) :

The Mahāsaṅghikas hold that *vijñapti* is also an act (*Kośa*, iv, p. 3).

Other Doctrines

Some of the doctrines attributed to the Mahāsaṅghikas in the *Kathāvatthu* only are as follows :

(i) Restraint (*saṃvara*) or unrestraint (*asaṃvara*) of the organs of sense should be treated as action (*kamma*).[1] The Theravādins regard it as non-action; their contention is that an action should be defined as actual functioning of the five organs of sense initiated by mind (*cetanā*). *Kvu* XII. 1.

(ii) All actions (*sabbaṃ kammaṃ*) are accompained by results (*savipāka*). The Theravādins contend that as *cetanā* is the source of all actions,[2] and as there are *avyākata* (neither good nor bad) and *avipāka* (unaccompained by any result) *cittas*,[3] there must also be avyākata and avipāka kammas. Hence all actions are not necessarily accompanied by results. *Kvu.* XII. 2.

(iii) Sound and other āyatanas (spheres of the organs of sense) are also results of actions (*kammassa katattā uppannaṃ*). In short, all non materials (*arūpadhammā*) are products of actions (*kammasamuṭṭhānā*).—*Kvu.*, XII. 3 & 4.[4]

(iv) Acquisition of moral purity is not mental (*sīlam acetasikan ti*; *sīlaṁ na cittānuparīvattī ti*). *Kvu.* X. 7, 8.

The Mahāsaṅghikas imply by the above opinion that purity in speech (sammā vācā), in actions (sammā kammanta) and in means of livelihood (sammā ājīva) is a corporeal property and as such, non-mental and requires no ārammaṇa (basis).[5] The M. mean that the observance of sīlas transforms the bodily

---

1. cf. *Kośā*, (tranl.), iv, p. 52.
2. Cetanāhaṃ kammaṃ vadāmi—*Atthas.*, p. 135.
3. See *Dhammasaṅgaṇi*, pp. 87 ff.
4. cf. *Kośa*, (transl.), i. p. 69-70.
5. *Kvu.*, I, p. 422.

constituents of a being in such a way that it can no longer commit any wrong, i.e., cannot be *dussīla*.

(v) The collection of sīlas (moral observances) is not associated with mind (*cittavippayuttaṃ sīlopacayaṃ*). *Kvu.* X. 9.

Buddhaghoṣa explains this as due to misapprehension of the sense of the passage in the *Saṁyutta Nikāya* (I. p. 33): *Ārāmaropā vanaropā ye janā, tesaṃ sadā puññaṃ pavaḍḍhati* (the merits of those who plant parks and woods increase at all times).

(vi) *Maggasamaṅgissa rūpaṃ maggo ti.*[1] *Kvu.* X. 2.

(In the person practising the eightfold path, the body is included).

(vii) *Maggasamaṅgī dvīhi sīlehi samannāgato ti.*[2] *Kvu.* X. 6. (A person practising the eightfold path is endowed with double morality (i.e. worldly and unworldly).

(viii) *Viññatti sīlan ti. Kvu.* X. 10 (Acts of intimation are virtues).

(ix) *Aviññatti dussīlan ti. Kvu.* X. 11. (Acts not intimating a moral purpose are immoral).[3]

Since sīla, according to the M., must be a positive action, and not mere restraint (saṃvara), so any *viññatti* (intimation) by means of body or speech is sīla. Salutation, rising to welcome, folding hands, etc. are sīlas. The M., in view of their opinion that there may be accumulation of demerits without the association of mind (*cittavippayuttaṃ apuññopacayaṃ*), contend "that acts not intimating a moral purpose are immoral."

(x) *Ñāṇaṃ cittavippayuttaṃ. Kvu.* XI, 3. (Insight is dissociated from mind).

(xi) *Aññāṇe vigate ñāṇavippayutte citte vattamāne na vattabbiṃ 'ñāṇī' ti. Kvu.* XI. 2. (One should not be called 'ñāṇī'

---

1. Transl. "That the physical frame of one who is practising the eightfold path and has attained one of the four *maggas* (i. e. Sotāpatti, etc.) is included in that path." *Points of Controversy*, p. 244.

2. Transl. "That one who is engaged in the path is practising a double morality." *ibid.*, p. 248. *Vism.*, p. 6 : Sīlena sotāpanna-sakadāgāmibhāvassa kāraṇaṃ pakāsitaṃ hoti. Sotāpanno hi sīlesu paripūrakārī ti vutto, tathā sakadāgāmī.

3. See *Dhammasaṅgaṇi*, p. 60.

(possessed of insight) though his *aññāṇa* (spiritual ignorance) is gone but his thoughts are not conjoined with insight).

In this controversy *ñāṇa* means maggañāṇa (insight of the adepts, who are in one of the four maggas). The M. contend that at the moment when an adept has cakkhuviññāṇa, etc. he cannot have maggañāṇa. In other words, they mean to say that it is only when an adept develops maggañāṇa and arrests his sense-perceptions (viññāṇa) that he may be described as 'ñāṇī,, hence ñāṇa is not associated with mind (citta = viññāṇa).

(xii) *Akusalamūlaṃ paṭisandahati kusalamūlan ti.*[1] *Kvu.* XIV. 1 (A basis of impure thoughts is consecutive to a basis that is pure, and conversely).[1]

The M. contend that as the same object may be the cause of both *rāga* (attachment) and *virāga* (detachment) and as one may follow the other immediately, it may be stated that kusala is the *anantarapaccaya* (contiguous cause) of akusala and *vice versa.* The Th. point out that cultivation of kusalamūla must be made deliberately (yoniso manasikārato) while that of akusalamūla does not require any such deliberation (ayoniso manasikārato), and also that *nekkhammasaññā* (renunciating thought) does not always follow *kāmasaññā* (worldly thought) and *vice versa*, and so kusalamūla cannot be regarded generally as the contiguous cause of akusalamūla and *vice versa.*

(xiii) *Paccayatā vavatthitā ti. Kvu.* XV. 1. (One phenomenon can be related to another in one way only).

The M. now enter into the problem of *paccayas.* There are twenty-four kinds of paccayas, viz., hetu, ārammaṇa, adhipati, sahajāta, anantara. etc.[2] They raise the question whether one object can be placed under two or more kinds of paccayas, or whether one can be related to another by one relation only. The Th. hold that one subject may be two kinds of paccayas, e.g., *viriya* may be both *adhipati* and *sahajāta; vimaṃsā* may be both *hetu* and *adhipati.* The M. do not subscribe to this view.[3]

---

1. "That a basis of bad thought is consecutive to a basis of good thought and conversely. *Points of Controversy*, p. 282.

2. cf. *Tikapaṭṭhāna*, pp. 168 ff.

3. See *Atthas.*, p. 9 ; *Dukapaṭṭhāna* p. 3; *Points of Controversy*, pp. 390-92; *Buddhist Psychology*, pp. 194 ff.

(xiv) *Avijjā paccayā pi saṃkhārā, na vattabbaṃ "saṃkhārā paccayā pi avijjā ti"*.[1] *Kvu.* XV. 2.

This view of the M. is only a corollary to the previous one. The M. hold that avijjā is the *hetu* (cause) of saṃkhārā and as such there cannot be any other relation between the two. The Th., however, argue that avijjā and saṃkhārā are related to each other both as hetu (cause) and sahajāta (co-existent) or aññamañña (reciprocal) cause, hence it may be stated that saṃkhārā are sahajātapaccayā of avijjā, and *vice versa*.[2] In the *Vibhaṅga* (pp. 156 ff.) the sampayutta (associated) and aññamañña (reciprocal) relations between any two consecutive links of the chain of causation have been exhaustively dealt with, showing clearly the attitude of the Theravādins to the problem.

(xv) *Lokuttarānaṃ dhammānaṃ jarāmaraṇaṃ lokuttaraṃ. Kvu.*, XV. 6 (Decay and death of supramundane beings or objects are also supramundane).

(xvi) *Paro parassa cittaṃ niggaṇhāti. Kvu.*, XVI. 1.

The Mahāsaṅghikas hold that the spiritually advanced monks develop the power of controlling others' thoughts.[3]

(xvii) *Iddhibalena samannāgato kappaṃ tiṭṭheyya. Kvu.*, XI. 5.

On the basis of Buddha's statement, those who have mastered *iddhipāda* (higher powers) may live for an aeon if they so wish. The Mahāsaṅghikas state that by means of higher attainments, one can extend his life up to a kalpa.[4]

---

1. "That whereas aggregates are conditioned by ignorance, it should not be said that ignorance is conditioned by aggregates." *Points of Controversy*, p. 294.

2. cf. *Majjhima Nikāya*, I. 54-55 : avijjā samudayā āsavā, āsavasamudayā avijjā; also *Dīgha Nikāya*, II, p. 56-57: viññāṇapaccayā nāmarūpam, nāmarūpapaccayā viññāṇan ti.

3. cf. above, p. 99.

4. cf. *Mahāparinibbānasutta*, p. 117.

Chapter VI

DOCTRINES OF GROUP II SCHOOLS

THE ŚAILA SCHOOLS, PRAJÑAPTIVĀDINS, BAHUŚRUTĪYAS AND VETULYAKAS

In discussing the doctrines of the Śaila and other schools, Vasumitra has mixed them up with the Mahāsaṅghikas, probably with that section of the Mahāsaṅghikas that is distinguished in the *Kathāvatthu-aṭṭhakathā* as *ekacce Mahāsaṅghikā*. It is on the basis of the *Kathāvatthu* that we have distinguished the doctrines of the later Mahāsaṅghikas, whose views may be taken as identical with those of the Śaila and other schools, and put them together in the following pages.

I. *Is Buddha human ?*

In Vasumitra's treatise, Buddhas are described as *lokottara* (supramundane), and as such they are made of *anāsrava dharmas*[1] (pure objects), and are without sleep or dream, which is a concomitant of *sāsrava dharmas*. Buddhas have unlimited *rūpakāyas* (material bodies), powers (*balas*), length of life (*āyu*), etc.

In the *Kathāvatthu* (xvii. 1, 2) the above doctrines are attributed to the Vetulyakas, according to whom Buddha does not live in the mortal world. Nor should he be located anywhere; it is his created form (*nirmāṇa-kāya* = *rūpa-kāya* i.e., *abhinimmito jino*) that delivered the religious discourses. The Theravādins account for this heresy by saying that it is due to the literal but incorrect comprehension of the passage; *Bhagavā loke jāto loke sambuddho lokam abhibhuyya viharati anupalitto lokenā ti* (Buddha,

---

1. Masuda renders it as "no sāsrava dharmas." The rendering should be "anāsrava dharmas," i.e., Buddhas are embodiment of pure dharmas viz., sīlaskandha, samādhisk., prajñāsk., vimuktisk., and vimuktijñānadarśanask., not of rūpa, vedanā, saññā., saṅkhārā and viññāṇa, which are sāsrava dharmas. See my *Aspects of Mahāyāna Buddhism and its Relation to Hīnayāna* (henceforth indicated as *Aspects*), p. 108.

born and enlightened in this world, overcomes this world and remains untouched by the things of the world, *Saṃ. Nik.* iii. 140). This is supplemented by further discussions in the *Kathāvatthu* (xviii. 1, 2; xxi. 6) relating to the heresies, which are also attributed to the Vetulyakas, viz., "*na vattabbaṃ Buddho Bhagavā manussaloke aṭṭhāsī ti*" (it should not be said that Buddha lived in the mortal world—*Kvu.*, xviii. 1); *sabbā disā Buddhā tiṭṭhantī ti*"[1] (Buddhas exist in all corners of the world—*Kvu.*, xxi. 6) and *abhinimmittena desito ti* (the discourses are delivered by created forms—*Kvu.*, xviii. 2). These show that, according to the opponents of the Theravādins, Buddha is omnipresent and beyond the possibility of location in any particular corner or sphere, and that all the discourses were delivered by the apparitional body of Buddha.

Buddhaghoṣa with his usual naïvety understood the Vetulyakas as holding the opinion that Buddha always remained in the Tuṣita heaven, where he dwelt before he came to this world. The discussions in the *Kathāvatthu* as well as the terse statements of Vasumitra leave no room for doubt about the fact that the Mahāsaṅghikas (especially their offshoots, the Vetulyakas and the Lokottaravādins) regarded Buddha as transcendental. Masuda suggests that the refulgent body (*sambhoga-kāya*) of Buddha is referred to in the heresies but the time of emergence of the conception of *sambhogakāya* is a matter of controversy.[2] From the discussion in the Kathāvatthu (xxi. 5) "atthi Buddhānaṃ Buddhehi hīnātirekatā ti" (whether Buddhas mutually differ?), it seems that the Andhakas were concerned with the Sambhogakāya and had not then arrived at the conception of the Dharmakāya. Buddhaghosa states that the Andhakas hold that Buddhas differ from one another in certain qualities other than the attainments like satipaṭṭhāna (alert mindfulness), sammappadhāna (right exertion) etc., the orthodox holding that Buddhas

1. This is the opinion of the Mahāsaṅghikas only, according to the *Kathāvatthu*.

2. Masuda's opinion can be supported by the fact that in the *Mahāvastu* (i. p. 169) Buddha's *kāya* is equated to *niṣyanda-kāya* (resultant body) rendered into Chinese by *pao sheng*, which is also the rendering of *Sambhogakāya;* see my *Aspects* etc., p. 117, 120.

may differ in respect of body, length of life and radiance (kāya, āyu, pabhāva) but not in regard to the attainments mentioned above. The discussion in the Kathāvatthu (xviii. 3) shows that the Uttarāpathakas hold the view that Buddhas can have no compassion (karuṇā) and that Buddha's body is made of pure objects (anāsrava-dharmas). In the Mahāvastu (i. pp. 167-68) the conception of supramundane (lokottara) Buddha appears thus :

Transcendental are the practices of Bhagavān, and so are his merits (kuśala-mūlas), his eating, drinking and other daily activities. He follows the ways of the world just as much as he follows the transcendental ways.[1] He makes a show of standing, walking, sitting and lying (iriyāpathas), but he never gets tired. He washes his feet or body, though there is no dirt; he cleanses his mouth, though it smells like a lotus. He eats though he has no hunger, and so forth. These are all due to his being an embodiment of the effects of good actions.[2] There is nothing in common between Him and the beings of the world. Everything of the great *ṛṣi* is transcendental, including his advent into the world.[3]

If the transcendence of Buddha be admitted, then it follows as a matter of course that his length of life would be unlimited and that he would not be subject to sleep or dream, as he would have no fatigue, and one who is without sleep and ever awake has nothing to do with dream. It is worth noting here that even in the Pāli *suttas* such as the *Mahāparinibbānasutta*, there are hints to the effect that Buddha, if he wishes, can extend his life-limit up to a *kalpa* or the end of a *kalpa*,[4] thus revealing that the transcendental conception took roots in the minds of the Buddhists at a very early date.

In the *Kathāvatthu*,[5] the discussion of the topic *Buddhassa Bhagavato vohāro lokuttaro ti* reveals that the Andhakas, to

1. cf. *Kvu.*, XVIII. 4; Buddhassa Bhagavato uccārapassāvo ativiya aññe gandhajāte adhigaṇhātī ti—opinion of some Andhakas and Uttarāpathakas.

2. *Mtu.*, I, p. 169. cf. *Laṅkā*, pp. 28, 34.

3. *Mtu.*, I, p. 159.

4. *Dīgha*, II, p. 103: yassa kassaci cattāro iddhipādā—so ākaṅkhamāno kappaṃ vā tiṭṭheyya kappāvasesaṃ vā.

5. *Kvu.*, II, 10.

whom the above opinion is ascribed, hold that Buddha's actions (*vohāro*) are *lokottara* and that they are treated as *lokiya* (mundane) and *lokottara* (supramundane) according as the object of the action is *lokiya* or *lokottara*. Mr. Shwe Zen Aung prefers to confine the sense of the word '*vohāro*'[1] to "speech', and we think that it means "conventional teaching".[2] In Vasumitra's treatise an opinion of this nature is attributed to the Mahāsaṅghikas in contrast to the Sarvāstivādins, viz., the *sūtras* (or discourses) preached by Buddha are all perfect in themselves (*nītārtha*). Buddhas speak of nothing but *dharma* (doctrines); as such their teaching is concerned only with *paramārtha-satya* (*paramattha-sacca*), i.e., not with *saṃvṛtisatya* (*sammutisacca*).[3] The *paramārthasatya* cannot be normally expressed by words. It can be explained only by silence or at the most by an exclamation—which idea, I think, is expressed in Vasumitra's treatise thus : Buddha can expound all the doctrines with a single utterance and there is nothing which is not in conformity with the truth in what has been preached by the World-honoured One."[4] In the *Upāyakauśalyaparivarta* of the *Saddharmapuṇḍarīka* it has been shown that for training up deluded beings in his doctrines, Buddha had recourse to various expedients which were false, i.e., unreal (*saṃvṛti* or *sammuti*), and that through such teachings he led the deluded beings to the truth—*paramārtha*. So it follows that all his teachings collected in the *Piṭakas* are merely *saṃvṛti* or *sammuti* (conventional) and that they are not therefore his real teachings.[5]

According to the Mahāsaṅghikas, Vasumitra says; Buddhas have both *kṣayajñāna* and *anutpādajñāna*[6] always present in

1. Sans. *Vyavahāra*.
2. cf. *M. Vṛ*., p. 494.
3. *Paramārtha-satya* means the highest truth while *saṃvṛti-satya* means the conventional truths as used in everyday usage by the people in general. For detailed treatment see my *Aspects*, pp. 216 ff.
4. *Asia Major*, II. p. 19.
5. *See Aspects*, p. 198.
6. (a) *Kṣayajñāna* means cognizance of the fact that all the *āsavas* are destroyed;
   (b) *Anutpādajñāna* means cognizance of the fact that one will not be reborn again. cf. *Kośa*, VI, 67; *Atthasālini*, p. 54. cf. *Aspects*, p. 106 fn. 1.

their minds, the Sarvāstivādins holding that all Arhats may have *kṣayajñāna*, but a few only have *anutpādajñāna*; the Theravādins, however, do not make any such distinction.

Among the other attributes of this *lokottara* Buddha, Vasumitra's treatise speaks of his powers (*balas*)[1] as unlimited while the *Mahāvastu* speaks of his five eyes (*cakṣus*)[2] as uncommon (*asādhāraṇa*) and excelling those of *Pratyekabuddhas*, *Arhats* and others. This particular topic — *tathāgatabalaṃ sāvakasādhāraṇan ti*—has been taken up for discussion in the *Kathāvatthu* (iii. 1), but strangely enough the position taken by the compiler of the *Kathāvatthu* is not that of a Theravādin but that of a Lokottaravādin Mahāsaṅghika as against the Andhakas, i.e., the Śaila schools. In Vasumitra's treatise, this topic appears in a slightly different form.

The Theravādins do not regard Buddha as *lokottara* but attribute to him almost all the powers and qualities of a *lokottara* Buddha, and this discussion reveals one of such instances. The ten special *balas* (powers) of a Tathāgata appear not only in the *Mahāvastu* (i. pp. 150-60) but also in old Pāli works like the *Majjhima Nikāya* (i. pp. 60 ff.). The contention of the Andhakas is that there is a certain degree of difference between Buddhas and Arahats regarding the acquisition of the ten *balas*, and that Buddhas and Arahats are not therefore on the same level

1. The ten balas are :
(*Mahāvastu*, pp. 159-60; *Kathāvatthu* and *Majjhima Nikāya*).

1. *Thānāṭhānaṃ jānāti . . . .*
2. *Sabbatthagāminipaṭipadaṃ jānāti.*
3. *Anekadhātuṃ nānādhātuṃ lokaṃ jānāti.*
4. *Sattānaṃ nānādhimuttikataṃ jānāti.*
5. *Parasattānaṃ parapuggalānaṃ indriya-paropariyattaṃ yathābhūtaṃ pajānāti.*
6. *Atītānāgatapaccuppannānaṃ hetuso vipākaṃ jānāti.*
7. *Jhānavimokkhasamādhisamāpattīnaṃ saṅkilesaṃ vodānaṃ voṭṭhānaṃ yathābhūtaṃ pajānāti.*
8. *Anekavihitaṃ pubbenivāsaṃ anussarati.*
9. *Dibbena cakkhunā satte passati cavamāne upapajjamāne etc.*
10. *Āsavānaṃ khayā anāsavaṃ cetovimuttiṃ paññāvimuttiṃ diṭṭhe va dhamme sayaṃ abhiññā sacchikatvā upasampajja viharati.*

2. By eyes, the text means all the five, viz., *māṃsacakṣu*, *divyac.*, *prajñāc.*, *dharmac.*, and *buddhac.*

(*asādhāraṇaṃ*). In the *Mahāvastu* and the Pāli works, this view is accepted with this reservation that Buddhas are *sarvākārajña*, i.e., they possess a complete and detailed knowledge of everything, while an Arhat can at the most have sectional knowledge.[1] The Pāli school, i.e., the Theravādins hold that as far as *vimutti* is concerned there is no difference between a Buddha and an Arhat, and that Buddhas are superior to the Arhats only on account of the fact that the former are promulgators of a new *Dharma* while the Arhats are only followers of the same.[2]

II. *Are Bodhisattvas average beings?*

If, according to the Mahāsaṅghikas, Buddhas are *lokottara*, and if the Buddhas that we *puthujjanas* know of are only the created forms of the real Buddha, the Bodhisattvas also cannot be average human beings — they must also be supramundane. In Vasumitra's treatise is given the following account of the Bodhisattvas. The Bodhisattvas do not pass through the embryonic stages. They assume the form of white elephants when they enter their mothers' wombs and come out of the same by the right side. The above opinion is the natural outcome of the lengendary belief that came to be woven around the person of the great Teacher about a century after his actual existence. In the *Lalitavistara*,[3] the Bodhisattva is placed not only in a crystal casket put within the womb but while in that state he is said to have been preaching *dharma* to the heavenly beings that flocked around him. The story of the white elephant seen by Māyā in a dream at the time of her conception and the birth of the Bodhisattva by bursting through the right side of the mother's womb is too well known to need any comment. The incorporation of these legends in the doctrines of the Mahāsaṅghikas and of their offshoots shows that the Bodhisattva conception of the Mahāyānists was yet in the process of development.

1. cf. *Kvu. Cy.*, p. 62: Ṭhānāṭhānādini hi sāvakā *padesena* jānanti. Tathāgatā *nippadesena* iti. Tāni uddesato sādhāraṇāni; niddesato asādhāraṇāni — niddesato *sabbākāravisayatāṃ* sandhāya paṭikkhipati. cf. *Mtu.*, I, p. 158: cf. *Aspects*, p. 106 fn. 1.

2. This argument is adduced in the *Kvu*. See also *Sam. Nik.*, III, p. 66.

3. *Lalitavistara*, Ch. VI, p. 73 (of A.S.B. edition).

The only doctrine that can be described as Mahāyānic is that Bodhisattvas take birth out of their own free will in any form of existence for imparting their teachings to the sentient beings of that particular form of existence.[1] It is well illustrated in the *Jātakas* and developed in later Mahāyāna works like the *Śikṣāsamuccaya* and the *Bodhicaryāvatāra*. This topic has been taken up for discussion in the *Kathāvatthu* (xxiii. 3) : *Bodhisatto issariyakāmakārikā-hetu vinipātaṃ gacchatī ti*—but the arguments put forward completely ignore the standpoint of the Mahāsaṅghikas and attempt to show the untenability of the opponent's proposition by treating the Bodhisattva as nothing but an average human adept, toiling along the path towards the attainment of *bodhi*.

In the *niyāmokkantikathā*[2] (*Kvu*., vi. 8; xii, 5, 6; xiii. 4) the same attitude is revealed by the Theravādins. By *niyāma*, the Theravādins understand *sammattaniyāma* and *micchattaniyāma*, the former being the practice of *brahmacariya*, (purity of conduct) and *ariyamagga* (path of sanctification) including, for the Bodhisattvas, the fulfilment of *pāramis*, leading to emancipation (i.e. *samyaktva* or *sammatta*, and the latter the commission of heinous crimes (*ānantarīyakamma*), leading to hell (i.e. *mithyātva* or *micchatta*).[3] In the sense as expressed above any Śrāvaka can be a *sammattaniyāma*, and he need not be a Bodhisattva. The Theravādins do not recognize the Bodhisattvas as superior in attainments to the Śrāvakas, and in the matter of *brahmacariya* and practice of *ariyamagga*, they do not want to make any distinction between a Śrāvaka and a Bodhisattva.

In the *Laṅkāvatāra* and Asaṅga's *Sūtrālaṅkāra* and similar other Mahāyāna works, however, it is repeatedly stated that a person by the development of *bodhicitta* becomes a *niyata* Bodhisattva, i.e., through the fulfilment of *pāramis* and practice of the various forms of asceticism, he ultimately becomes a Buddha. Siddhārtha Gautama, in one of his previous births as Jotipāla-māṇava, did, as a matter of fact, develop *bodhicitta* at the time of Kassapa Buddha and then through several

1. Masuda, p. 21.
2. Stepping into the path destined to reach Nibbāna
3. *Kvu*., pp. 78, 143: *Ime dve niyāme ṭhapetvā añño niyāmo nāma natthi*.

existences, he fulfilled the pāramis and had recourse to all possible *sādhanās*, whether Buddhistic or non-Buddhistic and ultimately attained perfection. He even became disciple of Āḷāra Kālāma and Rudraka Rāmaputra, whose doctrines are treated as heresies in the *Brahmajāla* and other *suttas*. In Mahāyāna texts emphasis is laid more on *bodhicitta* than on *brahmacariya* and *ariyamagga*. In the *Kathāvatthu* discussion, the Mahāyānic sense of *niyata* is ignored and the Theravāda sense of *sammattaniyāma* is kept in view. In the *Kathāvatthu* (xiii. 4), it is argued that to speak of a *niyata śrāvaka* or *bodhisattva* as having become a *sammatta* is illogical.[1] The difference of opinion rests really on the interpretation given to the word *niyata* in Mahāyāna texts as against that given by the compiler and commentator of the *Kathāvatthu.* In spite of the above interpretation of *niyāma* and attitude of the Theravādins, the Mahāyānists contended that Gautama Buddha in his bodhisattva existence did not become a disciple of Kassapa Buddha. In support of their contention they cited the passage *na me ācariyo atthi, sadiso me na vijjati* etc. The Andhakas, strangely enough, took the opposite view and asserted that he did become a Śrāvaka of Kassapa Buddha, and cited the passage from the *Majjhima Nikāya* (ii, p. 54): *Kassapo, ahaṃ Ānanda, bhagavati brahmacariyaṃ acariṃ sambodhāyā ti* etc.[2]

According to the Theravādins, the Bodhisattvas as a class of beings as envisaged in the *Sūtrālaṅkāra* and *Laṅkāvatāra*, do not exist. The individual, who happens to become Buddha, is called a Bodhisattva in his previous existences just to distinguish him as a being superior to an average one; by calling him a Bodhisattva the Theravādins do not attribute to him any special virtues unattainable by a śrāvaka. The Mahāsaṅghikas or the Andhakas do not subscribe to the above view. According to them, an individual, from the moment he develops *bodhicitta,* becomes a *Bodhisattva* and is destined (*niyata*) to become a Buddha and follow a career which is quite different from that of a *śrāvaka.* The career of the former is marked more by love and compassion for the suffering beings than by path-culture

1. *Na niyatassa niyāmokkamanaṃ tasmā asādhakan ti. Kvu.* p. 143.
2. *Kvu.*, p. 288.

while that of the latter has more of path-culture and *sādhanā* than exercise of *mettā* and *karuṇā*.

III. *Are Arhats fully emancipated ?*

According to Vasumitra, Bhavya and Vinītadeva, the secession of the Mahāsaṅghikas from the Theravādins happened on account of the five points of Mahādeva. Four of these points relate to the qualities attainable by an Arhat. According to the Theravādins only, one who is fully emancipated is called an Arhat,— he is *anupatto sadattho vītarāgo vītadoso vītamoho khīṇāsavo ohitabhāro katakaraṇīyo nāparam itthattāyā ti* (in possession of the excellent goal, free from attachment, hatred and delusion, in short, all impurities, relieved of the burden of khandhas, accomplished all that is to be done and freed from further existence). He has also acquired clear vision of the origin and destruction of beings, got rid of all doubts (*kaṅkhā*) about the Buddha, Dhamma and Saṅgha, non-existence of soul and the law of causation, and realized the truth without the help of others (*na paravitāraṇā*)[1] and attained *bodhi* which, however, is *catumagga-ñāṇa*[2] and not *sabbaññutañāṇa* — the *bodhi* of the Buddhas.[3] The Theravādins do not admit the failings[4] which are attributed to the Arhats by the Bahu śrutīyas, the Śaila schools and the Haimavatas. The failings are thus enumerated in Vasumitra's treatise :

(1) Arhats can be tempted by others;
(2) They still have ignorance;
(3) They still have doubt;
(4) They gain knowledge with other's (help).[5]

IV. *Can there be retrogression of Arhats, Srotāpannas and other Phalasthas?*

The following views regarding the possibility of retrogression of Arhats, Srotāpannas and other phalasthas are attributed in

1. See *supra*, p. 23.
2. The catumaggas are : sotāpatti, sakadāgāmi, anāgāmi and arahatta.
3. See *Kvu.*, *A.*, p. 76.
4. For the discussion "Parihāyati arahā arahattā ti" see *supra*, p. 27.
5. Masuda, pp. 24, 36, 38, 53; cf. *JRAS.*, 1910, pp. 413-23. For exposition and discussion of the four failings, see above, Ch. II, pp. 24 ff.

Vasumitra's treatise[1] to a section of the Mahāsaṅghikas and some of their sub-sects :

(i) From the gotrabhūmidharma there is in all stages the possibility of retrogression.

(ii) A Srotāpanna has a chance of retrogression while an Arhat has not.

The above two views are discussed in the *Kathāvatthu* under the topic: *Parihāyati arahā arahattā ti ?* (I. 2).

It will be observed that the *Kvu.* does not attribute to the Mahāsaṅghikas the above views about the retrogression of Arhats and Srotāpannas. According to the Mahāsaṅghikas, the *Kvu.* says an Arhat has retrogression while a Srotāpanna has not, while Vasumitra takes a contrary view, as above (ii). Vasumitra says that the former opinion is held by the Sarvāstivādins and other schools. Buddhaghoṣa points out that this opinion is held by one section of the Mahāsaṅghikas and not by all, and so Vasumitra may have referred to the views "of that section, according to whom, the Arhats may retrogress but not the Srotāpannas."[2]

All the schools advocating the view that arhats retrogress hold, as stated in the *Kvu.*, that the Sotāpannas have no retrogression. This, however, contradicts the statement of Vasumitra.[3] All these schools accept that a sotāpanno is *niyato sambodhiparāyaṇo* and hence is not subject to retrogression, but a sakadāgāmī or an anāgāmī may retrogress but not further than the sotāpanna stage, for some of the adepts in these stages may have *anusaya*, which may develop into *pariyuṭṭhāna*[4] and thereby bring about their fall — an argument which will be discussed next in connection with the Aṭṭhamakas. In regard to these two stages the *Kvu* corroborates Vasumitra's statement (no. ii).

Regarding the srotāpannas, Vasumitra[5] further states that,

(i) they are capable of knowing their own nature (*svabhāva*) through their *citta* and *caitasika dharmas*;

---

1. Masuda, p. 22.

2. *Kvu. A.*, p. 35: Sammitīyā Vajjiputtīyā Sabbatthivādino c'ekacce ca Mahāsaṅghikā arahato parihāniṃ icchati.

3. See Masuda, p. 27.

4. See p. 84 fn. 1

5. See above, pp. 85 f.

(ii) they can also attain perfection in the *dhyānas*;

(iii) they are liable to commit all sorts of offences except the five *ānantarīkas* (i.e. matricide, parricide etc.)

In the *Kvu.* we do not come across any controversy relating to the first two topics. This silence may be interpreted as acceptance of the two views by the Theravādins. As regards the third topic, we may take into consideration the controversy: *Diṭṭhisampanno puggalo sañcicca pāṇaṃ jīvitā voropeyyā ti ?* (see p. 18). A sotāpanna is a person with right view (*diṭṭhisampanna*), hence, according to the Theravādins, he cannot commit killing (*pāṇātipāta*) or similar other offences, not to speak of the five extreme offences like matricide or parricide. Vasumitra perhaps speaks of the opinion of that section of the Mahāsaṅghikas, i.e., the Andhakas, which contemplates the retrogression of the Sotāpannas, while the *Kvu.* very likely speaks of the other section, according to which the Sotāpannas do not retrogress.

There are in Vasumitra's treatise two other statements, which also relate to the Srotāpannas. They are:

(i) When one enters into the *samyaktva-nyāma*, one may be said to destroy all *saṃyojanas*.[1]

(ii) None of the *dharmāyatanas*[2] can be known or understood: they can be attained (only by those Ārya *pudgalas* above the *darśanamārga*).

The *Kvu.* contributes no discussion on the above two points. The Theravādins also cannot but subscribe to these views.

V. *Are there worldly samyagdṛṣṭi and samyak-śraddhendriya?*

Along with the above we may discuss the allied topic worded thus in Vasumitra's treatise:

(i) There is neither laukika-samyagdṛṣṭi (worldly right view) nor laukika-śraddhendriya (worldly faculty of faith).

The corresponding passages of the *Kvu.* are:

(i) *Natthi puthujjanassa ñāṇan ti ?* (XX, 2);[3] *and*

---

1. The three saṃyojanas are : *sīlabbataparāmāsa*, *vicikicchā*, and *micchādiṭṭhi*.

2. The Dharmāyatanas are *vedanā*, *saṃjñā*, and *saṃskāra*. These are spheres of *mana*. cf. *Abhi. Kośa*, p. 46. Also the field of objects of ideation. *Dhammasaṅgaṇi*, 58, 66 etc.

3. Attributed to the Hetuvādins only.

(ii) *Natthi lokiyaṃ saddhindriyan ti?* (XIX. 8).[1]

The argument of the Theravādins is that a layman may have *paññā* and *saddhā* of a kind which may be different from those of an adept, but *paññā* and *saddhā* that he possesses develop into *paññindriya* and *saddhindriya.* It may be that the layman's *paññā* or *ñāṇaṃ* is confined to dāna, sīla, cāga, etc., i.e. lokiya affairs and does not extend to the comprehension of lokuttara subjects like truths, maggas and phalas. According to the Theravādins, therefore, there may be lokiya paññindriya and saddhindriya.

VI. *Is utterance of dukkha possible in meditation and does it help realization of truths?*

To the two statements of Vasumitra, namely, (i) The path is realized by utterances and (ii) Even in the state of samāhita one can utter words, corresponds "*samāpannassa atthi vacībhedo ti*" of the *Kathāvatthu.* It is explained by Buddhaghoṣa thus: According to the Śaila schools, an adept, while he is in the first jhāna (meditation) and on the point of attainment of the Sotāpattimagga, gives out in some cases an exclamation like "aho dukkhan ti."[2] The adherents of the Śaila schools account for this by saying that in the first jhāna, there is *vitakkavicāra*, and because of *vitakkavicāra* there is *vacīsaṃkhāra*,[3] i.e., discursive and discriminating thoughts cause vocal activity, hence there is the possibility of a meditator in the first jhāna uttering the word 'dukkha'. The Theravādins contend that as all physical activities of a meditator are set at complete rest, his giving out an exclamation is an impossibility.[4]

Along with the above we should take into consideration the other three doctrines of the Mahāsaṅghikas presented thus in

---

1. Attributed in the Cy. to the Hetuvādins and Mahīśāsakas and they mean all the five indriyas, saddhā, viriya, sati, samadhi and paññā.

2. cf. *Vinaya*, I, p. 15, in Yasapabbajjā, 'upaddutaṃ vata bho upassaṭṭhaṃ vata bho.'

3. cf. *Kvu.*, IX, 9: Opinion of the Pubbaseliyas: See p. 90. fn. 1.

4. cf. *Kvu.*, XVIII, 8 : See p. 90. fn. 2.

Vasumitra's treatise:

(i) The words of suffering can help (the process of realization of the path);

(ii) Suffering leads a man to the path;

(iii) Suffering also is (a kind of) food (*āhāra*); and

(iv) Through *prajñā* suffering is destroyed and final beatitude is attained.

The corresponding expressions in the *Kathāvatthu* are as follows:

(i) "*Idaṃ dukkhan ti*" *vācaṃ bhāsato* "*idaṃ dukkhan ti*" *ñāṇaṃ pavattati?* (XI. 4).[1]

(ii) *Dukkhāhāro maggaṅgaṃ maggapariyāpannan ti?* (II.6).

(Repeated utterance of 'dukkha' induces insight and is a factor of, and included in, the Path).

Both these statements appear in slightly different terms from what has been stated by Vasumitra. The Andhakas and the Śailas hold that when a meditator realizes within his innermost heart that the world is full of suffering and is not worth living in, he exclaims, "aho vata dukkhaṃ!" Then and there his insight (ñāṇa) penetrates into the first truth, "idaṃ dukkhan ti," as a result of which he attains (*pariyāpuṇāti*) the Sotāpattimagga. So "dukkha" may be called an "āhāra" (food) in respect of the realization of the path as also an "aṅga" (limb) of the Sotāpattimagga.

According to the fourth doctrine mentioned above, as Masuda explains *dukkha* can be removed not by means of the observance of moral precepts (śīlas) and practice of meditation (samādhi) but by knowledge of the truth, causal law, and *anattā* of beings and things of the world. It is the basic teaching of Theravāda, and so no reference is made to it in the *Kvu.*

VII. *How Vijñānas function?*

The following opinions are attributed by Vasumitra to the Mahāsaṅghikas :

(i) Beings of the Rūpa and Arūpa dhātus possess all the six sense-perceptions (ṣaḍvijñānas).[2]

1. See also p. 89.
2. Or ṣaḍvijñānakāya or the group of six sense-perceptions.

(ii) The five vijñānas conduce both to attachment (*sarāga*) and freedom from attachment (*virāga*).

(iii) The rūpendriyas (organs of sense) are nothing but lumps of flesh; the eyes do not see colours, the ears do not hear sounds, the nose does not smell odours, the tongue does not taste flavour, and the body does not feel touch.

The *Kvu.* deals with these topics thus:

(i) *Saḷāyataniko attabhāvo rūpadhātuyā ti?* (VIII. 7).

(ii) *Pañc' evāyatanā kāmā ti?* (VIII. 4).

(iii) *Cakkhunā rūpaṃ passatī ti?...pe...kāyena phoṭṭhabbaṃ phusatī ti?* (XVIII. 9).

In the discussion relating to the six āyatanas (spheres of the organs of sense), the *Kvu.* states that the Andhakas take the expression *rūpī manomayo sabbaṅgapaccaṅgī ahīnindriyo ti* literally and assert that there are in the Rūpadhātu all the six indriyas and āyatanas with this difference from the Kāmadhātu, that out of the six āyatanas three, viz., ghāna, rasa and phoṭṭhabba do not exist but their *nimittas*, i.e., the subtlest forms, exist.[1] In the Abhidhamma texts it is stated that the beings of the Rūpadhātu have five khandhas and six (and not twelve) āyatanas, while those in the Arūpadhātu have four khandhas and two āyatanas (manāyatana and dhammāyatana only).[2]

Relating to the third point, the *Kvu.* contradicts Vasumitra and says that it is the Mahāsaṅghikas who hold the opposite view, viz., the eyes see colours, ears hear sounds, etc. by conceiving a pasādacakkhu, a subtle eye, which has not got the power of āvajjana (reflection) like cakkhuviññāṇa but possesses merely the power of knowing (paṭijānāti) objects. In this case also, shall we account for the contradictions by saying that the opinion of 'ekacce mahāsaṅghikā' is represented by Vasumitra while the opinion of the 'aññe mahāsaṅghikā' is noticed in the *Kathāvatthu*.[3] The Theravādins and a section of the

1. *Vibhaṅga*, p. 405 : In Kāmadhātu there are cakkhāyatana and rūpāyatana, sotāyatana and saddāyatana, etc., in all, twelve āyatanas.

. *Vibhaṅga*, pp. 405-07.

3. See *infra*.

Mahāsaṅghikas hold that the eyes, ears etc. are mere material conveyers of perception, the cakkhuviññāṇa, sotaviññāṇa, etc. are the actual percipients, in other words, eyes, ears etc. belong to the rūpakhandha, which is material, while cakkhuviññāṇa, etc. belong to the viññāṇakhandha, which makes a being aware of the things around it.

VIII. *How many avyākatas are there?*

The opinion of the Andhakas that "there is nothing which is indeterminable" (avyākṛta) has been explained by Masuda as that the Andhakas admitted only two natures of things, good or bad and not a third, i.e. neither good nor bad. This interpretation does not appear to be sound as in the Buddhist texts the three natures of things are accepted generally. The avyākatas also refer to those problems which Buddha left unanswered as any answer to them whether in the affirmative or in the negative would mislead the enquirer, or he treated the question as absurd and unanswerable. These avyākata problems are always mentioned in a stereotyped form in all Buddhist texts, whether Hīnayāna or Mahāyāna.[1] Nāgārjuna has utilised these problems in his *Madhyamaka-kārikā* to establish the Mahāyānic conception of Śūnyatā. If we accept Vasumitra's statement as correct, we shall have to say that the Śūnyatā conception was known to the Mahāsaṅghikas, and so to them the so-called avyākata problems were not avyākata (inexplicable), but this way of looking at the statement of Vasumitra seems to be too far-fetched and so, it may be regarded that Vasumitra's statement is not complete. Perhaps it refers to the problem discussed in the *Kvu: diṭṭhigataṃ avyākatan ti*? (XIV. 8),— whether a person holding one of the erroneous views can be regarded as avyākata i.e., neither good nor bad. The answer of the Theravādins is that the holder of any one of the views is wrong, hence akusala, and cannot be avyākata as supposed by the Andhakas and Uttarāpathakas.

1. Sassato loko, asassato loko; antavā loko, anantavā loko; taṃ jīvaṃ, taṃ sarīraṃ, aññaṃ jīvaṃ aññaṃ sarīraṃ; hoti Tathāgato paraṃ maraṇā, na hoti Tathāgato paraṃ maraṇā; hoti ca na hoti Tathāgato paraṃ maraṇā n'eva hoti na na hoti Tathāgato paraṃ maraṇā.

IX. *How many Asaṃskṛtadharmas are there?*

In the Pāli texts, as also in the *Abhidharmakośa* (of the Sarvāstivādins) the three asaṃskṛtas are (i) Pratisaṃkhyānirodha, (ii) Apratisaṃkhyā-nirodha and (iii) Ākāśa. The Andhakas increase them to nine by adding the four *āruppas*[1] and *āryamārgāṅgikatva*.[2] Excepting the *nirodha* of two kinds, all other asaṃskṛtas of the Mahāsaṅghikas are not recognised as such by the Theravādins, whose argument is whether each of these asaṃskṛtas is of the same nature as Nibbāna, if not, they are saṃskṛtas. Strangely enough, the *Kvu.* goes so far as to say that ākāśa is not asaṃkhata. The attitude taken in the *Kvu.* (VI. 2, 4, 6; XIX. 3, 4) is that Nibbāna is *tāṇaṃ lenaṃ accutaṃ amataṃ* (escape, refuge, infallible and immortal) so each of the seven of asaṃkhatas, even every member of the formula of Paṭiccasamuppāda, each of the four phalas must be *tāṇaṃ lenaṃ accutaṃ amataṃ*, otherwise, they are saṃkhatas (constituted).[3] The Mahāsaṅghikas interpret, as presented in the *Kvu.*, that the asaṃkhata is that which is unchangeable (āneñja) but not tāṇaṃ lenaṃ, etc. In regard to the causal law, they rely on Buddha's statement: *avijjā paccayā bhikkhave saṃkhārā, uppādā va Tathāgatānaṃ anuppādā vā Tathāgatānaṃ ṭhitā va sā dhātu dhammaṭṭhitatā dhammaniyāmatā idappaccayatā* etc., and point out that by asaṃkhata they do not mean the links separately but the unchangeable law (a) of the origin of an object through a cause, and (b) of the unchangeable nature of dhammas, undisturbed by appearance (uppāda) or non-appearance (anuppāda) or continuity (ṭhiti). As for the *āryamārgāṅgikatva*, the *Kvu.* explains that the Pubbaseliyas regard as asaṃkhata the fact of attainment (*patti*) of a magga or phala by the removal of certain mental impurities (kilesapahānaṃ) and not the maggas or

1. The four āruppas are :
   (i) Ākāśānantāyatana;
   (ii) Vijñānānantāyatana;
   (iii) Ākiñcanyāyatana; and
   (iv) Naivasaṃjñā-nāsaṃjñāyatana.
2. Cf. *Kośa*, iii, p. 77.
3. In the *Majjhima Nikāya*, (I. p. 301) it is distinctly stated that *aṭṭhaṅgiko maggo* is *saṅkhato*.

phalas by themselves. This, Vasumitra corroborates by using the term *mārgāṅgikatva* i.e. *prāpti* of a mārga and not simply *mārga*. In the *Kvu.* there are a few other discussions relating to the asaṃkhatas, to which we shall revert while dealing with the Mahīśāsakas.

The remaining three opinions of this group of schools, viz.,

(i) There is no intermediate state of existence (*antarābhava*),

(ii) Phenomena exist neither in the past nor in the future, and

(iii) The nature of mind is pure in its origin: it becomes impure when it is stained by *āgantukarajas* and *upakleśas*,

are in accord with those of the Theravādins.[1] Both of these schools do not admit that between death and rebirth there is any intervening period, in which the subtle khandhas wait for the selection of parents of the next state of existence. The *Kvu.* says that the opinion of the opponents is formed through the miscomprehension of the meaning of the word 'antarāparinibbāyī'. We shall revert to this topic while dealing with the Sammitīyas, with whom, the commentator says, the Pubbaseliyas agree.

As regards the opinion that the past and future exist — the cardinal doctrine of the Sarvāstivādins, to be dealt with hereafter, both the Theravādins and the Mahāsaṅghikas are emphatic in their protest against it.

The third point raises an important problem, that is to say, whether the mind at the beginning was pure or not. The Theravādins are decidedly of opinion that *pubbakoṭī* (beginning) and *aparakoṭī* (end) of beings are unknowable, and as such they have not gone into the question whether the mind is pure at any time before the attainment of *vimutti*. This doctrine of the Mahāsaṅghikas had its full development in the idealistic philosophy of Yogācāra, in which the *Ālayavijñāna*, the store-house of pure consciousness, gets contaminated with worldly objects through *indriyavijñānas* and mentally creates a world around it. It is by

---

1. Cf. *Aṭṭhasālini*, p. 68 : Cittaṃ āgantukehi upakkilesehi upakiliṭṭhaṃ.

the removal of this mental creation that a person regains the *ālayavijñāna* in its pure original form and becomes an emancipated being.

Special doctrines of the Śaila Schools

Vasumitra has attributed the following doctrines specially to the three Śaila schools :

(i) Bodhisattvas are average beings and may be born in the lower states of existence.[1]

(ii) Offerings made to a caitya are not necessarily of great merit.[2]

The above doctrines are in direct contrast to those of a section of the Mahāsaṅghikas and the Pūrvaśailas or Caityakas. Vasumitra evidently had in mind only the later Śaila schools, viz., Aparaśaila, Caityaśaila and Uttaraśaila, and not the Pūrvaśaila.

Regarding the origin of Caityaśaila and Uttaraśaila schools, Paramārtha[3] writes that two hundred years after Buddha's *parinirvāṇa*, a second Mahādeva appeared with heretical views. He slipped into the church stealthily (i.e. became a *steyasaṃvāsika*) by ordaining himself. This event gave occasion to fresh controversies among all the branches of the Sthavira and Mahāsaṅghika schools, particularly on the question of the validity of ordination given by an ācarya, who is himself not regularly ordained. The Mahāsaṅghikas who were in agreement with the Sthaviras in this matter, excommunicated Mahādeva. At this, Mahādeva got enraged and retired to another mountain and started the Caityaśaila and Uttaraśaila schools.

The Caityaśailas therefore should be distinguished from the Caityakas, who were identical with the Lokottaravādins or the Pūrvaśailas, and were of earlier origin. The Caityakas and

1. See *supra*.

2. In the *Mahāvastu* and the Nāgārjunikoṇḍa inscription erection, decoration and worship of caityas find prominence, for which, it seems, the name Caityaka has been applied to the Pūrvaśaila school. Cf. *Kośa*, iv. 121.

3. Paul Demiéville, *L'origine des sectes bouddhiques* in *Mélanges chinois et bouddhiques*, vol. I, 1931-32.

Pūrvaśailas are referred to in the Nāgārjunikoṇḍa inscriptions, and not the later Śaila schools mentioned above.

Nirvāṇa in Nāgārjunikoṇḍa inscriptions

In the Nāgārjunikoṇḍa inscriptions, there are a few incidental remarks relating to Buddha and Nirvāṇa. These probably apply to the conceptions held by the Pūrvaśailas or Caityakas. Buddha is described here as *jita-rāga-dosa-moha* (one who has conquered attachment, ill-will and delusion) and *dhātuvarapari-gahita* (possessed of the excellent *dhātu*), and the donor expects as a result of his or her gifts merits which he or she can transfer (*pariṇāmetuṃ*) to his or her relatives and friends—an article of faith not recognised in the Pāli works where *attadīpa attasaraṇa* is the maxim. The fruits expected are: (i) religious merits for himself, his relatives and friends, resulting in their happiness in this world and the next (*ubhaya-loka-hita-sukhāva-hanāya*),—a merit which reminds us of the Aśokan XIIth ins-cription: *esa bāḍha dekhiye iyaṃ me hidatikāye iyaṃ me pāla-ttikāye ti* and (ii) *Nivāṇa-sampati* (nirvāṇadom) for himself or herself.[1]

The recording of the view that gifts may bring happiness to all, but *nirvāṇa* only to oneself, deserves our careful consideration. The distinction drawn in this way is rather uncommon and is not made even in the inscription recording the gifts of the Queen of Vanavāsi to the Mahīśāsakas[2] or in the long inscription of the Sinhalese donor.[3]

Then the expressions *dhātuvara-parigahita* or *nivāṇa-sampati-saṃpādaka* raise the presumption that the Andhaka conception of Nirvāṇa was different from that of the Theravādins or their sub-sect the Mahīśāsakas. In the *Kathāvatthu*, there are two controversies (ix, 2; xix, 6), relating to the conception of Nirvāṇa as prevailing among the Andhakas. The view attribut-ed to the Pubbaseliyas is that the *Amatapada* (=*Nirvāṇa*), is "an object of thought of a person not yet free from bondage,"[4]

1. *Ep. Ind.*, XX, pp. 16, 18-21 : "atano" or "apano."
2. *Ep. Ind.*, XX, p. 24.
3. *Ibid.*, p. 22.
4. Mrs. Rhys Davids, *Points of the Controversy*, pp. 231-33.

and the other attributed to the Andhakas is that "the *Nibbāna-dhātu* is *kuśala* (good)" in the sense in which mental states are spoken of as *kuśala* (good), and these are faultless states.[1] Both these statements bear the implication that the Pubbaseliyas or the Andhakas conceived of *Nirvāṇa* as a 'positive faultless state'—a conception which can hardly be accepted by the Theravādins, who speak of realizing Nibbāna within one's own self by the wise (*paccattaṃ veditabbo viññūhi*) and not of grasping the same as some object producing pure happiness.[2]

Special doctrines of the Bahuśrutīyas

Regarding the special doctrines of the Bahuśrutīyas, the *Kathāvatthu* is silent. Though this school belonged to the Mahāsaṅghika group, it accepted, according to Vasumitra, many views of the Sarvāstivādins. Vasumitra adds that it held that Buddha's teachings relating to *anityatā*, *duḥkha*, *śūnya*, *anātman* and *Nirvāṇa* (transitoriness, suffering, non-existence of objects, absence of soul, and the ultimate goal) are *lokottara* (supramundane), while his teachings on topics other than those mentioned above are *laukika*[3] (mundane).

In Pāli texts the teachings and exercises connected with *maggas* and *phalas* are usually regarded as *lokottara* and the rest *laukika*.

This school, according to Paramārtha, attempted a syncretism of Hīnayāna and Mahāyāna and attributed two meanings, probably *nītārtha*[4] (direct meaning) and *neyārtha*[4] (indirect

---

1. *Ibid.*, p. 339.
2. See *Majjhima Nikāya*, I, p. 1f : Mūlapariyāyasutta.
3. Masuda, pp. 35-36.
4. Cf. *Samādhirāja-sūtra*, p. 78 :

नीतार्थसूत्रान्तविशेष जानति यथोपदिष्टा सुगतेन शून्यता ।
यस्मिन् पुनः पुद्गलसत्त्वपुरुषो नेयार्थतो जानति सर्वधर्मान् ॥

Cf. *M. Vr.*, p. 43 : उक्तं चार्याक्षयमतिसूत्रे । कतमे सूत्रान्ता नेयार्थाः कतमे नीतार्थाः । ये सूत्रान्ताः मार्गावताराय निर्दिष्टा इम उच्यन्ते नेयार्थाः । ये सूत्रान्ताः फलावताराय निर्दिष्टा इम उच्यन्ते नीतार्थाः । यावद्ये सूत्रान्ताः शून्यता-निमित्ताप्रणिहितानभिसंस्काराजातानुत्पादाभावनिरात्मनिःसत्त्व-निर्जीवनिःपुद्गला-स्वामिक-विमोक्षमुखा निर्दिष्टाः' त उच्यन्ते नीतार्था : ।

See Prof. Vidhusekhar Sastri's *Sandhābhāṣā* in *IHQ.*, IV, p. 295.

meaning) to the teachings of Buddha. It adopted the *Satya-siddhiśāstra* of Harivarman as its main text. This school is mentioned in the Nāgārjunīkoṇḍa inscription.

Special Doctrines of the Prajñaptivādins

Regarding the special doctrines of the *Prajñaptivādins*,[1] Vasumitra remarks that they agreed mainly with the Mahāsaṅghikas (i.e. later Mahāsaṅghikas). They held in addition the following opinions:

(i) *Skandhas* and *duḥkha* are not concomitant;

(ii) The twelve *āyatanas* are not real;

(iii) Either attainment of *ārya-mārga* or death is dependent on *karma*.

The Prajñaptivādins, as Paramārtha tells us, appeared some time after the Bahuśrutīyas, and distinguished themselves as Bahuśrutīya-vibhajyavādins. The main difference between the Prajñaptivādins and Bahuśrutīyas is that the former, partly like the Mahāyānists, held the view that Buddha's teachings as embodied in the Piṭaka should be distinguished as nominal (*prajñapti*), conventional (*saṃvṛti*) and causal (*hetuphala*). This school, as against the Bahuśrutīyas, agreed more with the views of the Mahāsaṅghikas than with those of the Sarvāstivādins.[2]

Special Doctrines of the Rājagirikas and Siddhatthikas

In the *Kathāvatthu*, but not in Vasumitra's treatise, certain special doctrines have been attributed to the Rājagirikas, and Siddhatthikas. To the former are attributed the following:

(i) *Natthi keci dhammā kehici dhammehi saṅgahitā* or *sampayuttā* (VII. 1. & 2).

There is no such thing as a quality attached or adhering to another, e.g., oil in mustard seed, feeling in perception, and so forth.[3]

(ii) *Natthi cetasiko dhammo* (VII. 3).

This is a corollary to the previous view. It says that *citta* (mind) only functions, and there are no other mental states associated with it.

---

1. This school came into existence 200 years after the Mahāsaṅghikas (*Kośa*, v, p 24).
2. See Demiéville, *op. cit.*, p. 49-50.
3. Cf. The topics of the *Dhātu-kathā*, (P.T.S.).

(iii) *Cetasiko dhammo dānan ti* (VII. 4).

(iv) *Ito dinnena tattha yāpenti* (VII. 6).

By the former it means that gift is not material; the mind for making a gift is really giving. By the latter it holds that merits are accumulated, and that a person enjoys its fruits in after-life on account of such accumulation.

(v) *Paribhogamayaṃ puññaṃ vaḍḍhati* (VII. 5).

The accumulating merits can go on increasing (by renewal of gifts of robes and other articles to monks, and so forth).

(vi) *Natthi arahato akālamaccu* (XVII. 2).

Arhats cannot die untimely, i.e., their death is also subject to the influence of *karma*.[1]

(vii) *Sabbaṃ idaṃ kammato* (XVII. 3).

Everything is subject to *karma*.

(viii) *Kappaṭṭho kappaṃ tiṭṭheyya* (XIII. 1).

A being destined to live for an aeon lives for an aeon as one consigned to purgatory for committing saṅghabheda.

Special Doctrines of the Vetulyakas

In the *Kathāvatthu*, the following doctrines are attributed to the Vetulyakas only :

(i) *Na vattabbaṃ "Buddho Bhagavā manussaloke aṭṭhāsi"* (XVIII. 1).

This point has been discussed above.

(ii) *Na vattabbaṃ "Buddhassa dinnaṃ mahapphalaṃ hoti"* (XVII. 10).

As Buddha does not exist as a person, it is meaningless to say that gifts to Buddha produce great merit.

(iii) *Na vattabbaṃ "saṃgho dakkhiṇaṃ paṭigaṇhāti"*.

(iv) *Na vattabbaṃ "saṃgho dakkhiṇaṃ visodheti"*.

(v) *Na vattabbaṃ "saṃgho bhuñjati pivati khādati sāyati"*.

(vi) *Na vattabbaṃ "saṃghassa dinnaṃ mahapphalaṃ hoti"* (XVII. 6-9).

All the four opinions are of the same import. The question raised here whether Saṅgha is a body of individuals, who have

1. Based on the statement : *kammunā vattati loko. Kvu.*, p. 546.

attained *magga* and *phala* (fruits of sanctification) or Saṅgha is identical with *maggaphala.* This school holds that Saṅgha does not exist apart from *maggaphala* and so it is not proper to say that Saṅgha receives gifts, or purifies them, or enjoys them, or a gift made to a Saṅgha is productive of great merits.[1]

1. Cf. *Milindapañha* p. 95 f.; *Kośa*, iv. 32; also see L. de La Vallée Poussin's paper on *La doctrine des refuges* in the *Mélanges chinois et bouddhiques*, vol. I, p. 64 f.

CHAPTER VII

DOCTRINES OF GROUP III SCHOOLS

THE MAHĪŚĀSAKAS, SARVĀSTIVĀDINS, DHARMAGUPTAKAS, AND OTHER SCHOOLS

The third group of schools, according to the Pāli tradition comprised the Mahiṃsāsakas and their offshoots, viz., Dhammaguttikas, Sabbatthivādins, Kassapikas, Saṅkantikas, and Suttavādins. According to this tradition, the Mahiṃsāsakas were the earliest to secede from the Theravāda among its sub-sects. Out of the Mahiṃsāsakas developed the Sabbatthivādins and gradually the other schools.

Vasumitra puts the appearance of sub-sects of this group a little differently. According to him, Sarvāstivāda branched off first from the Sthaviravāda, and from the latter appeared the Mahīśāsakas, Kāśyapīyas and Saṃkrāntivādins, one after another at the interval of a century. Out of the Mahīśāsakas developed the Dharmaguptakas.

Comparing the two traditions, it will be observed that the two lists agree, excepting the first appearance of the Mahıṃsāsaka, as stated in the Pāli texts. This anomaly may be explained thus : A reference to the doctrines of this school reveals that there were two Mahīśāsaka schools, one earlier and the other later. Vasumitra missed the earlier Mahīśāsakas while enumerating the sub-sects.[1] He, however, points out that the earlier Mahīśāsakas agreed more with the Theravādins while the later with the Sarvāstivādins. It may be that the Pāli tradition was aware of the earlier division only of the Mahīśāsakas, and so naturally placed their origin before the Sarvāstivādins.

The Earlier Mahīśāsakas

The antiquity of the Mahīśāsakas goes back to the time of the first Buddhist Council, hence its origin is anterior to that of the

1. See *infra*.

Mahasaṅghikas. The Vinaya texts of the Theravādins (in Pāli) record the differences of opinion of the Mahīśāsakas and the Dharmaguptakas — relating to seven rules according to the Mahīśāsakas, and eight rules according to the Dharmaguptakas — between Mahākassapa and Purāṇa of Dakkhiṇāgiri (near Rājagṛha). The Mahīśāsaka Vinaya attached special importance to the person of Purāṇa, who insisted on a second rehearsal, which, according to this school, was complied with by Mahākassapa, by the incorporation in the Vinaya of the seven rules relating to food. This shows clearly that Purāṇa and his followers formed a group by themselves, though probably not yet known by the designation, Mahīśāsaka. Prof. Przyluski has discussed this in his work *Le Concile de Rājagṛha* (pp. 319 ff.) on the basis of the Mahīśāsaka and Dharmagupta Vinaya texts in Chinese.

He writes that the episode of Purāṇa of Dakkhiṇāgiri[1] in the account of the first Council notices the difference between the Theravādins and the Mahīśāsakas. In course of time, that group of monks, which held Purāṇa in high esteem, formed the Mahīśāsaka school by including his seven rules not accepted by Mahākassapa in his Vinaya code.[2] In the Mahīśāsaka Vinaya, the second place of seniority is accorded to Purāṇa, the first being given to Kauṇḍinya. The Mahīśāsakas assert that after the deliberations of the First Council were finished, the texts were once more recited for the approval of Purāṇa, who accepted the same after adding his seven rules.

Regarding the geographical expansion of the school, Prof. Przyluski points out that (i) Purāṇa refers to the people of Mahīsaka; (ii) that the alternative name of this school is Mahāvantaka;[3] and (iii) that the Vinaya text of this school was found by Fa-hien in Ceylon.

On the basis of these facts, he states that the line of expansion of this school was the same as that of the Theravāda, i.e., along the Kauśāmbi-Bharukaccha axis and that it gradually extended

1. "Purāṇa demeure dans le sud." Here by "sud", he means Dakkhiṇāgiri, which is really not in the south.

2. See above, Ch. III, p. 39, fn. 3.

3. Tāranātha in his *Geschichte* (pp. 175, 273) speaks of the Avantakas as an offshoot of the Sāmmitīyas.

up to the sea-borne countries, and that it became particularly popular in Mahiṣamaṇḍala and Avantī, and ultimately reached Ceylon.

Prof. Przyluski's suggestions are supported by the Nāgārjunikoṇḍa inscriptions, in which it is stated that the queen of Vanavāsī erected a pillar and a monastery at Nāgārjunikoṇḍa for the benefit of the ācāryas of the Mahīśāsaka sect.[1] Vanavāsī corresponds to North Kanara. There is also a village called Vanavāsī in the Shimoga District of the Mysore State and lies on the border of Mysore territory and North Kanara. Vanavāsī is also one of the countries, which the mission of Aśoka's reign visited, and it was from this country that a *mahāthera* called Candagutta went to Ceylon at the invitation of Duṭṭhagāmaṇi to take part in the celebrations for erecting the *mahāthūpa*. Hence, it may be concluded that the Mahīśāsakas became popular in Vanavāsī, i.e., in North Kanara and Mysore, and probably had some followers in Ceylon, as this school agreed with the Theravādins in fundamental doctrines and disciplinary rules. In short, this school had its sphere of influence in south-western India and Ceylon.[2]

The *Kathavatthu* has not a word to say about the doctrines of this school. This silence, though a negative evidence, confirms our supposition that the Theravādins had little or no difference with the Mahīśāsakas as far as their doctrines were concerned. Vasumitra furnishes us with the following information regarding the doctrines of this school.

Doctrines of the earlier Mahīsāśakas

The Mahīśāsakas rejected the "Sabbam atthi" thesis of the Sarvāstivādins[3] and held that the present only exists. They made it more emphatic by stating that all *saṃskāras* perish at every

1. *EI.*, XX, p. 36; cf. *EI.* vol. III, p. 117; *Vikramāṅkadevacarita*, V, 23; *Mahāvaṃsa*, XII, 31; XXIX, 42; B. C. Law, *Geography of Early Buddhism*, p. 66.

2. Cf. Przylusky, *op. cit.*, pp. 325, 327—Mahīṣamaṇḍala, Avantī and other sea-borne countries on the west.

3. For Sarvāstivāda views, see *infra*.

moment and that entrance into the womb is the beginning, and death is the end, of human life. The material constituents of the sense-organs as also *citta* and *caitasikas* are subject to change. In other words, there are no real elements.

They do not enter into the question of Buddha's attributes and probably like the Theravādins held Buddha as an average human being.

Regarding *Arhats*, they state that (i) a srotāpanna has a chance of retrogression while an arhat has not, and that (ii) *arhats* do not perform meritorious deeds. Both of these opinions are directly opposed to those of the Sarvāstivādins and are partly in agreement with those of the Theravādins.

Re. *Samyaktvanyāma*, the Mahīśāsakas have nothing to say. They state against the opinion of the Sarvāstivādins that there is no *deva* who leads a holy life.

Re. *Anupubbābhisamaya*, the Mahīśāsakas hold views contrary to those of the Sarvāstivādins. They state that the four truths are to be meditated upon at one and the same time.

Re. *Jhāna*, they hold, as against the opinion of the Theravādins, that transition from one jhāna to another is immediate (*Kvu.*, XVIII. 6).

Re. *Puthujjana*, etc., the Mahīśāsakas held the following views in agreement with the Sarvāstivādins excepting the last :

(i) An average man is able to destroy *rāga* and *pratigha* in the Kāmadhātu.

(ii) There is *laukikasamyagdṛṣṭi* (right view of a worldly man).

(iii) There is no *laukikaśraddhendrīya* (faculty of faith obtained by a worldly man). This is discussed in the *Kvu.*, XIX. 8 (see above, p. 108).

Re. *Anuśaya* and *Paryavasthāna*, the opinions of the Mahīśāsakas are directly opposed to those of the Sarvāstivādins and the Theravādins and are in agreement with those of the Mahāsaṅghikas:

(i) *Anuśaya* (dormant passion) is neither *citta* (mind) nor *caitasika* (mental).

(ii) *Anuśaya* is different from pervading passion (*paryavasthāna*).

(iii) *Anuśaya* is never an object of thought (*anālambana*).

(iv) *Anuśaya* is dissociated from mind (*citta-visamprayukta*).

(v) *Paryavasthāna* is associated with mind (*citta-samprayukta*).

All these have been discussed in the *Kathāvatthu* in connection with the doctrines of the schools of Group II (see above).

Re. *Meditation* & *Smṛtyupasthāna*, the only difference between the Mahīśāsakas and the Sarvāstivādins is that the former do not recognize any *lokottaradhyāna*. They agree with the Sarvāstivādins in holding that all *dharmas* (mārgāṅgas) are included in the four *smṛtyupasthānas* (application of mindfulness).

Re. *Vijñāna*, the Sarvāstivādins state that the five *vijñānas* (perception derived by the organs of sense) engender *rāga* (attachment) but not *virāga* (detachment). The Mahīśāsakas consider this unreasonable and hold that these conduce both to *sarāga* and *virāga*. Both the schools agree in holding that the six *vijñānas* combine with *vitarka* and *vicāra*.

Re. *Asaṃskṛta* & *Antarābhava*, the views of the Mahīśāsakas are all opposed to those of the Sarvāstivādins:

(i) There are nine unconstituted (*asaṃskṛta*) *dharmas*, but the list is different from that of the Mahāsaṅghikas.[1]

(ii) There is no intermediate state of existence (*antarābhava*).

(iii) There is nothing which can transmigrate from one existence to another.

There are a few other opinions, which are also contrary to those of the Sarvāstivādins, viz.,

(i) No heretic can gain the five supernatural powers.

(ii) Good *karma* cannot become the cause of existence.

In addition to the above, the Mahīśāsakas hold the following two views:

(i) Though Buddha is included in the Saṅgha, a gift made to Buddha is more meritorious than that to the Saṅgha.

(ii) *Buddhayāna* and *Śrāvakayāna* have the same emancipation (*vimukti*).

---

1. Pratisaṃkhyā nirodha, Apratisaṃkhyā nirodha, Ākāśa, Anātman, Kuśala-dharma-tathatā, Akuśala-dh.ta, Avyākṛta-dh.ta, Mārgāṅga-ta., Pratītya-samutpāda-ta.

The Later Mahīśāsakas

It has already been pointed out that there were two schools of Mahīśāsakas, one earlier and the other later. The views stated above were held by the earlier school. The later Mahīśāsakas accept the cardinal doctrines of the Sarvāstivādins that past and future exist, and assert that *skandhas*, *dhātus* and *āyatanas* in their subtlest state are always present, so also are the *anuśayas* (dormant passions). They add that the earth lasts for aeons. They agree with the Sarvāstivādins in upholding that there is *antarābhava* (intermediate state between two existences). The later Mahīśāsakas, therefore, were as much in agreement with the Sarvāstivādins as the earlier Mahīśāsakas were with the Theravādins.

Sarvāstivāda

In the introductory note (p. 122 f.) appearance, geographical distribution, language and literature, and doctrines of Sarvāstivāda have been dealt with. The group of Theravādins (Sthaviravādins) was subdivided into eleven or more sects, of which the Sarvāstivādins and the Sammitīyas became prominent, the remaining sects were the Mūla-sarvāstivādins, Kāśyapīyas, etc.

Sarvāstivāda was a Hīnayāna school with its piṭakas in Sanskrit. The European scholars dubbed it as a school upholding 'Realism'. The doctrines of this school were subjected to vehement criticism by Mahāyāna philosophers like Nāgārjuna, Asaṅga, Āryadeva and others, who upheld 'Nonrealism' (*śūnyatā*) or 'Idealism' (*vijñaptimātratā*).

The Sarvāstivādins selected Mathura as the venue of their early activities and it was from this place that they fanned out to Gandhāra and Kashmir and ultimately to Central Asia and China.

The legend about the selection of Mathura as the rendezvous of the Sarvāstivādins runs as follows:

Emperor Aśoka, according to the Ceylonese chronicles, met the leading monk-saint of the time, Moggaliputta Tissa, an orthodox Theravādin. The third Buddhist Synod was held under his chairmanship. Those monks, who did not subscribe to the doctrines of Theravāda, were compelled to leave Pāṭaliputra, the scene of the Synod. They went first to Mathura. About the introduction of Buddhism, the tradition, preserved in the *Mūlasarvāstivāda Vinaya*[1] as also in the Chinese version of the *Aśokāvadāna*,[2] is as follows:

Bhagavān Buddha while traversing the Śūrasena country, reached Mathura where he noticed a green forest on a hill called Urumuṇḍa. He predicted that a hundred years after his demise, two rich brothers Naṭa and Bhaṭa would build there the Naṭabhaṭavihāra, which would become a congenial place for meditation of monks, seeking quietude (*śamatha*) and insight (*vipaśyanā*). At that time there would be a spice-dealer, whose son Upagupta would be as great a preacher as He himself was, without however the physical signs of a Buddha. He would be ordained by Madhyāndina, a disciple of Ānanda and would be the last of the dharma-preachers. In the *Divyāvadāna* (p. 348) it is stated that Buddha made the forecast about the advent of Upagupta. Śānakavāsī would be his spiritual preceptor but there is also the tradition that Madhyāndina (Madhyāntika, Majjhantika) ordained Upagupta. The episode of Vāsavadattā is given a prominent place in all the biographies of Upagupta.

Upagupta occupied a very high place in the hierarchy of the Sarvāstivāda school. In the *Abhidharmakośavyākhyā* (II. 44) Upagupta is said to have composed the *Netṛpadaśāstra*. His opinions were valued as those of the Sarvāstivādins or the Vaibhāṣikas of Mathura. In conclusion, it may be stated that Upagupta was not only a versatile preacher but also an important writer of the Vaibhāṣika school of Mathura.

The wide popularity of the Sarvāstivāda put into shade all other schools, and that, particularly, for its propagation all over Northern India and in countries outside India, like Central Asia and China. Its origin should be placed some time

---

1. Gilgit MSS., III, pt. i.

2. *A-yu-wang-tchuan* translated by Saṅghabhadra in 506 A.D. Fr. tranl. Przyluski, *Légende de l'émpereur Aśoka*.

after the Mahīśāsakas and the Mahāsaṅghikas. There is no doubt that it branched off from the Mahīśāsakas and not from the Theravādins directly as stated by Vasumitra and other writers of later days. The Sarvāstivādins should be distinguished from the Mūlasarvāstivādins,[1] who probably modified certain doctrines of the Sarvāstivādins, as also from the Vaibhāṣikas, in which name this school was later known from the time of Kaniṣka.[2]

Vasubandhu in his *Abhidharmakośa*, has the Kashmir Vaibhāṣikas more in view than the early Sarvāstivādins. This is due to the fact that the Vaibhāṣikas became more popular from the time of Kaniṣka and became predominant in Kashmir and Gandhāra.[3] The popularity of the early Sarvāstivādins was confined to Northern India around Mathurā, where it had its origin.

Prof. Przyluski[4] traces the origin of the Sarvāstivāda school in the grouping of monks, shown in the account of the Second Council. He says that the monks collected by Yaśa hailed mainly from two centres, of which one was Kauśāmbi-Avanti and the other Mathurā. The former developed into Theravāda and Mahīśāsaka schools while the latter into Sarvāstivāda, and both were opposed to the Mahāsaṅghikas, whose centre was at Pāṭaliputra and Vaisāli and at a later date in the Andhra province.

Succession of Teachers

If we turn to the succession of teachers (*ācāryaparamparā*), as given in almost all Sanskrit traditions, preserved in Tibetan, it will be observed that after Sambhūta Śāṇavāsi, the succession

---

1. I-tsing speaks of the Mūlasarvāstivādins. See Takakusu, pp. xxiii-xxiv, 7-14, 20.

2. In Kashmir there were both Vaibhāṣikas and Sautrāntikas (ye vinaya-vidādayaḥ Sautrāntikā bhadantādayaḥ). The latter are described in the *Kośa-Vyākhyā* (VIII. 32) as Vinaya-vid. There were also Vaibhāṣikas, who lived outside Kashmir referred to in the *Kośa* as "bahirdeśakā Vaibhāṣikā".

3. Prof. Takakusu writes (*JPTS.*, 1904-05, p. 119) that the Sarvāstivādins were also distinguished in the *Vibhāṣā* as Kashmirian and Gandharian, but after compilation of the *Mahāvibhāṣā* the former eclipsed the latter and became known as Kāśmīra-vaibhāṣikas, or simply Vaibhāṣikas.

4. Przyluski, *op. cit.*, p. 308.

is recorded differently from that in Pāli. Bu-ston[1] and Tāranātha[2] tell us that Mahākassapa entrusted the guardianship of the Saṅgha to Ānanda, who in turn entrusted the same to Sambhūta Śāṇavāsi. The latter gave over the guardianship to Upagupta of Mathurā.[2] It is well known that in the Sanskrit Avadānas, Upagupta is made the spiritual adviser of Aśoka as against Moggaliputta Tissa of the Pāli texts. This also lends support to the view that Mathurā became the first centre of the Sarvāstivādins soon after the Second Council, and that it was from Mathurā that the influence of the Sarvāstivādins radiated all over Northern India, particularly over Gandhāra and Kashmir.

The propagation of Buddhism in Gandhāra and Kashmir has an independent history of its own. Both the Pāli and Sanskrit traditions state that *Madhyāntika* (*Majjhantika*) was responsible for the propagation of the religion in these two countries. Madhyāntika was a disciple of Ānanda and so he was a contemporary of Sambhūta Śāṇavāsi and senior to Upagupta. Madhyāntika is recognized as a teacher by the Sarvāstivādins. That Madhyāntika preached Sarvāstivāda Buddhism in Kashmir is corroborated by the testimony of Hiuen Tsang, who tells us that Aśoka not only sent Buddhist monks to Kashmir but also built monasteries at that place.[3] He writes that during Aśoka's reign there was in Magadha 'a subtle investigator of *nāma-rūpa* (mind and matter), who put his extraordinary thoughts in a treatise which taught heresy'. An attempt was made to drown these monks into the Ganges, but they saved themselves by fleeing to Kashmir where they settled on the hills and in the valleys. On hearing this, Aśoka felt remorse and requested them to return, and on their refusal, built for them 500 monasteries and "gave up all Kashmir for the benefit of the Buddhist church."[4] The fact underlying this story is that the "investigators of *mind* and *matter*" were none other than the Sarvāstivādins, whose principal tenet is that *nāma* and *rūpa* are real and are divisible into 64 elements, which exist for ever (*sarvam asti*),

1. See Bu-ston, II, p. 108. He derived his information from the *Vinaya-kṣudraka* of the Mūlasarvāstivādins.
2. Tāranātha, Upagupta was followed by Dhitika.
3. Watters, I, p. 269.
4. Watters, I, p. 267.

and it is for this view that they had the appellation of Sarvāsti-vāda. Then the statement that they resorted to the hills and valleys of Kashmir corroborates the flight of the Sarvāstivādin monks to the north in Kashmir.

Hiuen Tsang must have fallen into confusion in regard to the name Mahādeva. There were in all likelihood two persons of this name, "one an influential abbot of Pāṭaliputra"[1] who preached the *Devadūta-sūtra*, and the other a monk who introduced the tenets relating to the imperfections of an Arhat.[2] Mahādeva the investigator of *mind* and *matter* must have been a Sarvāstivādin while the other Mahādeva, who attributed imperfections to an Arhat, was a Mahāsaṅghika.[3] Hiuen Tsang further confused the Theravādins with the Mahāsaṅghikas when he wrote that Aśoka supported the Mahāsaṅghikas against the Theravādins, and that 500 Arhats left Pāṭaliputra and propagated the Sthavira school in Kashmir, while the majority of the inferior brethren at Pāṭaliputra began the Mahāsaṅghika school.[4] The Mahāsaṅghikas, as we know, lived originally at Vaisāli and later on passed on to the south, making their principal centre in the Andhra country at Dhanakaṭaka (present Guntur District).

The statement that Aśoka became repentant later on and that he wanted the monks who fled to Kashmir to return to Magadha may be an indirect reference to the fact recorded in the *Divyāvadāna*[4] and *Aśokāvadāna*[5] that Aśoka made an attempt towards the end of his life to reconcile the monks of the different schools of Buddhist thought by convening a council to which he particularly invited the monks living at Tamasā-vana in Kashmir. The Ceylonese chronicles maintain a discreet silence over this incident, and this is not unusual in view of the sectarian spirit permeating the chronicles.

The Sarvāstivādins also claim Aśoka as their patron. They ignore the name of Moggaliputta Tissa and put in its stead the name of Upagupta as the spiritual adviser of Aśoka. The

1. *Majjhima*, III, 179.
2. Watters, I, p. 268.
3. See above, p. 22.
4. Watters, I, p. 269.
5. *Divyā.*, p. 399. *IA.*, 1895, pp. 241 ff.

Avadāna literature[1] of the Sarvāstivādins is full of episodes dealing with the life and munificence of Aśoka. Tāranātha also speaks of his lavish gifts to the Sarvāstivāda monks of Aparāntaka Kashmir and Tukhāra.[2] Kalhaṇa[3] writes that Aśoka not only built Śrīnagarī but also covered Śuṣkaletra and Vitastrā with numerous stūpas, one of which was so high that its pinnacle could not be seen. Yuan Chwang noticed four Aśoka topes, each of which contained relics of Buddha's body. The Avadānas record that towards the end of his life Aśoka's liberality to the Buddhist monks was carried to such an extent that his grandson Sampadi,[4] who was in charge of his treasury, refused to carry out his commands and even reduced his food to a myrobalan, half of which was the last gift made by him to the Buddhist Saṅgha.

Through the activities of the Sarvāstivādins, Kashmir became a centre of Buddhist philosophical studies[5] and was, according to Tāranātha, also the scene of the activities of Vatsa, the propounder of the Ātmaka theory (*pudgalavāda*) and the founder of the Vātsiputrīya or Sammitīya school.[6]

Geographical Expansion of Sarvāstivāda

During the reign of Aśoka the Sarvāstivādins did not find a congenial home at Pāṭaliputra, i. e. in Magadha and migrated to the north. They founded two centres, one in Kashmir under the leadership of Venerable Madhyāntika and the other at Mathura under that of Venerable Upagupta. Madhyāntika was the direct disciple of Ānanda while Upagupta was the disciple of Śāṇavāsika, who was also a disciple of Ānanda. The Sarvā-

1. Prof. Przyluski writes in his *Legende de l'Empereur Aśoka*, pp. 101, 117 that a council of 30,000 monks was held by Aśoka, his sources of information being the *Aśokāvadāna* and Tāranātha.
2. Schiefner, p. 38.
3. Stein, I, p. 19.
4. It has been restored by Schiefner as Vāsavadatta, but it may also be Dhanadā or Sampadi.
5. See *Gilgit Ms.*, vol. I, Intro.
6. Schiefner, p. 44. See *Infra*.

stivādins can therefore claim Ānanda as their patriarch, but Bu-ston[1] states that they claimed as their founder Venerable Rāhulabhadra "renowned for his devotion to discipline." In the *Abhidharma-kośa-vyākhyā*[2] Rāhulabhadra is mentioned as a teacher. The Theravādins were first divided into two sects, Mahīṃsāsaka and Vajjiputtaka (Vātsīputrīya). From the former appeared the Sarvāstivādins. Śāṇavāsika was very old when he ordained Upagupta at Mathura. The time of the origin of the Sarvāstivādins should therefore be placed about 150 years after Buddha's demise. According to Vasumitra's *Samayabhedopa-racanacakra*, the Sarvāstivādins branched off from the Sthaviras in the 3rd century after Buddha's demise. This date is corroborated by Bhavya, Vinītadeva and I-tsing. I-tsing speaks of four main divisions of the Saṅgha, viz., Sarvāstivāda, Sthavira, Sammitīya and Mahāsaṅghika. The *Jñānaprasthānasūtra* of Kātyāyaṇīputra contended that the objects in present have their pastness and futurity. It was refuted by Moggaliputta Tissa in the *Kathāvatthu*. It was for this reason perhaps that Aśoka supported the cause of the Sthaviravādins, and consequently the Sarvāstivādins left Magadha and went northwards to Mathura and Kashmir.

There are a few inscriptions dating from the 2nd to the 4th century A. D., attesting to the presence of the Sarvāstivādins in Mathura, Peshawar, Kashmir and Baluchistan. There were a few Sarvāstivādins at Śrāvasti[3] and Benaras (Sarnath).[4] The earliest of the three inscriptions (1st century B. C.) was found at Mathura (Mathura Lion Capital) of the time of Rañjuvula and Soḍāsa. It runs as follows :

(a) The chief queen of Mahākṣatrapa Rājula, daughter of Prince Kharoasta, mother of Nanda Diaka along with others established at this site, which was just outside the consecrated boundary (*niḥsīmā*), the relic of Bhagavān Śākyamuni the Buddha, erected a stone-pillar crowned with a lion, and built a

1. Bu-ston, II, p. 100.
2. *Abhidharmakośavyākhyā*, pp. 714, 719.
3. Among the donees the names of the Sarvāstivādins do not appear in the Set Mahat Image inscription (see *E. I.*, VIII, p. 111; IX, p. 29).
4. *ASR.*, 1907-08, p. 73.

monastery (*saṅghārāma*) for the acceptance of the monks of the four quarters, particularly, the Sarvāstivādins.

(b) In the reign of Kṣatrapa Soḍāsa, son of Mahākṣatrapa Rājula, Udaya, a disciple of Ācārya Buddhadeva, along with Prince Khalamasa and Maja as assenting parties (*anumodakā*) made the gift of a cave-dwelling (*guhā-vihāra*) to Buddhila of Nagaraka for the acceptance of the Sarvāstivādin monks.

(c) In the reign of Kṣatrapa Soḍāsa, the gift of land was made to Ācārya Buddhila of Nagaraka, who refuted the arguments of the Mahāsaṅghikas. (Ending with the words) Adoration to all Buddhas, Dharma, Saṅgha, and to the Śakas of the Śaka country, etc.

The above-mentioned inscriptions distinctly prove that the early Śaka rulers were supporters of Buddhism, particularly of the Sarvāstivādins, one of whose centres of activity was then at Mathura. Buddhila, a Sarvāstivāda teacher, must have earned a great reputation as a disputant for defeating some Mahāsaṅghika teachers in philosophical controversies, and was the recipient of gifts from distinguished personages. There is also the mention of another great teacher called Ācārya Buddhadeva. At Śrāvastī (Set Mahet) has been found an elliptic clay sealing inscribed with the name of "Buddhadeva" in the late Gupta script (*ASR*, 1907-08, p. 128). Yaśomitra in his *Abhidharmakośavyākhyā* (V. 26; IX.12) refers to Sthavira Buddhadeva as an authority on Sarvāstivāda doctrines and states that one of his preceding teachers was Sthavira Nāgasena, who was a contemporary of King Menander. Buddhadeva interpreted the Sarvāstivāda doctrines as implying that "all exists (*sarvāstitva*) as relative existence (*anyathānyathātva*, *Kośavyākhyā*, p, 470)." It is rather risky to identify this Buddhadeva with Buddhadeva of the inscription, for it was a common practice among the Buddhist monks to have identical appellations.

There is another inscription at Mathura (Buddhist Image Inscription) of the time of Huviṣka (111 A. D.), in which the installation of a Bodhisattva image is attributed to two nuns, both of whom were disciples of Bhikṣu Bala, a master of Tripiṭaka, and one of the nuns, Dhanavatī, was a sister's daughter of Bhikṣu Buddhamitra, also a master of Tripiṭaka. This inscription evidently refers to an image of Śiddhārtha Gautama before his attainment of *bodhi*, i. e., a Hīnayānic image. The preceptor of the nun is described as a student of the Tripiṭaka, attributed only to the Hīnayānists. That Bala was a Sarvāstivādin is established by two other inscriptions discovered at Śrāvastī, viz., (a) Set Mahet Stone Umbrella Staff, and (b) Image inscriptions of Kaṇiṣka I, which bear the same text. During the reign of Kaṇiṣka (78-101 A. D.) the gift of an umbrella and a staff, with a Bodhisattva (image) was made by Bhikṣu Bala and a disciple of Puṣpabuddhi, and these two were installed in the promenade (*caṅkrama*) around the Kauśāmbī-kūṭī, which was a part of the Jetavanārāma and where probably Buddha was staying when he admonished the monks of Kauśāmbī. A similar gift was made at Sarnath by Bhikṣu Bala (Sarnath Buddhist Image inscription of Kaṇiṣka I), and these were also installed in the *caṅkrama* used by Buddha for his meditation. The gift was made by Bala, wishing to share his merits with his parents, his disciples, with another monk called Buddhamitra as also with Kṣatrapas Vanaspara and Kharapallana. Both Bala and Buddhamitra were Sarvāstivādins, hence it can be inferred that at Sarnath also resided a few Sarvāstivādins during the reign of Kaṇiṣka. On the south side of the Jagat Singh Stūpa, the following inscription was discovered on the topmost step of the stone-stairs "ācāryyānāṃ Sarvāstivādināṃ parigrahe." Dr. Vogel assigns this inscription to the 2nd century A. D.[1] This inscription is repeated on a "rail surrounding the old *stūpa* in the south chapel of the main shrine." The second inscription on the Aśokan pillar at Sarnath, mentioning the name of Aśvaghoṣa, was probably dedicated to the Sarvāstivādins, which appellation was unfortunately obliterated. The third inscription on the same pillar reads as follows : "ācāryyānāṃ Sammitīyānāṃ parigrahe Vātsīputrīyāṇāṃ."[2] From these citations of the two sects, Sarvāstivāda and Sammitīya, it may be inferred that the Sarvāstivādins occupied a strong position at Sarnath up to the 2nd century A. D. and that thereafter the Sammitīyas attained greater popularity. The two sects might have lived together for some time, but in any case by Hiuen Tsang's time

1. *ASR.*, 1907-68, p, 73.
2. Sahni, *Catalogue of Sarnath Museum*, p. 30-31.

the Sarvāstivādins left the place, leaving there the monks of the Sammitīya school only.

The find of an inscription of the Kushan period in pure Pāli[1] leads us to conclude that the Sthaviravādins also resided there at a very early date, perhaps before the Sarvāstivādins attained prominence.

Very likely the progressive career of the Sarvāstivādins had a setback for some time during the reign of Puṣyamitra (187-151 B.C.) as is evident from the *Divyāvadāna*, a text of this school. But the several donations made during this period by the devotees prove that it was professed by a large section of the people. Its revival came with the invasions of the Graeco-Bactrians, Śakas, Pahlavas, Parthians and Yavanas. The *Milindapañha*, the original of which was in Sanskrit, very likely belonged to this school.[2] The existence of this text shows that the Graeco-Bactrian kings like Menander were interested in this religion. Its complete revival took place during the reign of the Śakas, and the popularity of this sect reached its climax in the reign of Kaṇiṣka.

Fa-hien (319-414 A.D.) noticed the existence of this school at Pāṭaliputra while Yuan Chwang (629-645 A.D.) found it "chiefly in Kashgar, Udyana, and several other places in the Northern Frontier, in Matipur, Kanauj, and a place near Rājagṛha and also in Persia."[3] I-tsing came across the adherents of this school in Lāṭa, Sindhu, Southern and Eastern India, Sumatra, Java, China, Central Asia and Cochin China.[4] From the above evidences it is apparent how widely popular was this school all over Northern India and outside India, but little known in Southern and Western India.

1. The Pali inscription reads as follows :
   Cattāri imāni bhikkhave ariyasaccāni
   Katamāni cattāri—dukkhaṃ bhikkhave ariyasaccaṃ
   dukkhasamudayaṃ ariyasaccaṃ dukkhanirodhaṃ ariyasaccaṃ
   dukkhanirodhagāmini ca paṭipadā ariyasaccaṃ

2. *Abhidharmakośa-vyākhyā*, ix, 12 (Jap. ed.). p. 708 refers to Nāgasena as *pūrvaka-sthavira*.

3. *JPTS*., (Prof. Takakusu), 1904-05, p. 71; Legge's *Fa-hien*, p. 99; *JRAS*., 1891, p. 420; Takakusu, *I-tsing*, pp. xxii-xxiv.

4. I-tsing, Intro.

Bu-ston's information about the School

According to Bu-ston, the founder of this school was Rāhula-bhadra of the Kṣatriya caste "renowned for his devotion to discipline." The mantle worn by the members of this school had 25 to 29 fringes, and their badge had an *utpala* (a lotus), a jewel, and the leaf of a tree.[1]

He further writes, "Just as the higher classes establish the mundane laws and customs of a country or race, in a similar manner the Sarvāstivādins, as they spoke in Sanskrit, the language of the higher classes, represent the foundation of the other sects."[2]

It cannot be definitely stated whether Bu-ston had in mind the Sarvāstivādins or the Mūlasarvāstivādins.[3]

Language and Literature

The Tibetan traditions corroborated by the recent finds of manuscripts in Eastern Turkestan and Gilgit leave no room for doubt about the fact that the Sarvāstivādins adopted grammatical Sanskrit (and not mixed Sanskrit) as the medium of their literature and that they possessed a complete canon of their own in three divisions *Sūtra, Vinaya* and *Abhidharma*. The sub-divisions of these three Piṭakas were also substantially the same as those in Pāli.

Our main source of information regarding the literature of this school is Chinese and, occasionally, Tibetan versions of the Tripiṭaka, supplemented by the find of manuscripts in Central Asia, Eastern Turkestan, Gilgit and Nepal, and by quotations found in works like the *Lalitavistara*, *Mahāvastu*, *Mādhyamika-vṛtti*, *Sūtrālaṅkāra* of Asaṅga, *Divyavadāna*, *Abhidharmakośa* with its *Bhāṣya* and *Vyākhyā*. It may be questioned whether the information available about the literature of this school are of the Sarvāstivādins or of the Mūlasarvāstivādins. For the present it is not

1. Bu-ston, II, p. 100. For further information, see Watters, *Yuan Chwang*, 1, p. 149-50.

2. Bu-ston, II, pp. 99-100.

3. Hiuen Tsang states that the Sarvāstivādins had a peculiar mode of wearing and colouring their robes not approved by the followers of several schools (Watters, I, pp. 150 ff. Takakusu, *I-tsing*).

possible to distinguish between the two, but it seems that the Āgamas were common to both, so also were the Abhidharma texts. It is only in regard to Vinaya and few Avadāna texts that there might have been some differences.

Āgama

Sūtras: The Sūtra-Piṭaka of the Sarvāstivādins was divided into Āgamas corresponding to Nikāyas of the Pāli school. There were four Āgamas called *Dīrgha*, *Madhyama*, *Saṃyukta* and *Ekottara*. In the *Kośa* there are references to the *Kṣudraka*, which implies by the existence of a *Kṣudrakāgama* too. Prof. Akanuma has compared the Āgamas in Chinese with the Pāli Nikāyas[1] in detail and has come to the following conclusions: The *Dīrghāgama* contains 30 sūtras as against 34 of the *Dīgha Nikāya*. Of the 13 suttas in the first volume of the Pāli *Dīgha Nikāya*, 3 only are omitted in the *Dīrghāgama* viz., *Mahālī* (no. 6), *Jāliya* (no. 7) and *Subha* (no. 10). All the suttas of the other two volumes are contained in this Āgama and a few in the Madhyamāgama. The order of arrangement of the sūtras in the Āgamas and Nikāyas differs widely, e.g., *Mahāpadāna* is the first sūtra in the Āgama in place of *Brahmajāla* of the Nikāya. In the Āgama the series of sūtras is as follows: *Mahāpadāna*, *Mahāparinibbāna*, *Mahāgovinda*, *Janavasabha*, *Aggañña*, *Cakkavatti*, *Sīhanāda*, *Pāyāsi*, *Udumbarika-Sīhanāda*, *Saṅgīti*, *Dasuttara*, *Mahānidāna*, *Sakka-pañha*, *Pāṭika*, *Siṅgālovāda*, *Pāsādika*, *Sampasādanīya*, *Mahāsamaya*, *Ambaṭṭha*, *Brahmajāla*, *Soṇadaṇḍa*, *Kūṭadanta*, *Kevaṭṭa*, *Kassapa-sīhanāda*, *Tevijja*, *Sāmaññphala*, *Poṭṭhapāda*, *Lohicca*. The Āgama contains two other suttas.

Of these sūtras, fragments of the *Āṭānāṭīya* and *Saṅgīti* have been discovered in Eastern Turkestan,[2] and quotations from the *Brahmajāla* and *Saṅgīti* appear in the *Abhidharmakośa*.

The relation of the sūtras of the *Madhyamāgama* to those of the *Majjhima Nikāya* is as follows: Of the 152 suttas in the

1. *The Comparative Catalogue of Chinese Āgamas & Pāli Nikāyas*, Japan (1929).

2. Hoernle, *Manuscript Remains of Buddhist Literature found in Eastern Turkestan*.

three volumes of the *Majjhima*, only 19 are omitted in the Āgama, *viz.*, *Cūḷasāropama* (no. 30), *Mahāsaccaka* (no. 36), *Sāleyyaka* (no 41), *Verañjaka* (no. 42), *Kandaraka* (no. 51), *Jīvaka* (no. 55), *Kukkuravatika* (no. 57), *Abhayarājakumāra* (no. 58), *Apaṇṇaka* (no. 60), *Tevijja-Vacchagotta* (no. 71), *Ghoṭamukha* (no. 94), *Cañkī* (no. 95), *Vāseṭṭha* (no. 98), *Saṅgārava* (no. 100), *Pañcattaya* (no. 102), *Kintī* (no. 103), *Sunakkhatta* (no. 105), *Anupada* (no. 111), and *Bhaddekaratta* (no. 131). In the *Madhyamāgama*, there are in all 222 sūtras, 82 of which correspond to the suttas in the *Aṅguttara*, 10 to the suttas in the *Saṃyutta*, 9 to those in the *Dīgha* and the rest to the suttas in the *Majjhima*. There are a few of these suttas in Pāli not found in the Āgama, while a few stray suttas correspond to passage in the *Suttanipāta*, *Thera-therīgāthā* and *Vinaya* (*Mahāvagga*). In view of the mixture of the suttas from two or three Nikāyas in this Āgama, we can hardly expect much agreement in the order of the arrangement of the sūtras.

Fragments of two sūtras of the *Madhyamāgama*, viz., *Upālī* and *Suka*, have been discovered in Eastern Turkestan.[1]

The agreement between the *Saṃyukta Āgama* and *Saṃyutta Nikāya* is similar to that of the *Madhyamāgama* and *Majjhima Nikāya*. The *Sagāthavagga* (Sec. I) of the two Piṭakas has much in common but not the *Nidānavagga* (Sec. II); the 8th and 9th chapters of *Nidāna*, viz., *Samaṇabrāhmaṇa* and *Antarapeyyāla* are wanting in the Āgama, while the 1st and 5th chapter (*Buddha* and *Gahapati*) show marked differences. In the same section, *Abhisamaya*, *Dhātu* and other *Saṃyuttas* are almost passed over in the Āgama, but there is much that is common in the following five *Saṃyuttas*: *Anamatagga*, *Kassapa*, *Lakkhaṇa*, *Opammaka* and *Bhikkhu*. In the *Khandha-vagga* (Section III) of the Āgama, the following *saṃyuttas* are wanting: *Okkantika*, *Uppāda*, *Klesa*, *Sāriputta*, *Nāga*, *Gandhabbakāya*, *Valāha*, *Vacchagotta* and *Jhāna*. In the *Saḷāyatna-vagga* (Section IV), the following are absent: *Mātugama*, *Moggallāna*, *Asaṅkhata*, *Sammappadhāna*, *Bāla* and *Iddhipāda*, while major portions of the *Magga*, *Indriya*, and *Sacca* are omitted.

The *Samyuktāgama*, as it exists in Chinese, is divided into 50

1. Hoernle, *op. cit.*

sections and incorporates a large number of suttas of the *Aṅguttara Nikāya* and a few of the other texts. There are also a few sūtras which have no parallels in Pāli.

A fragment of the *Śroṇasūtra* of this Āgama has been discovered in Eastern Turkestan, while Prof. Sylvain Levi traced a few quotations from this Āgama in the *Sūtrālaṅkāra* of Asaṅga,[1] and identified the following fragments in the collection of Grünwedel: *Kokanada-sūtra* (= *Aṅguttara*, V, pp. 196-98); *Anāthapiṇḍada* (= *Anguttara*. V. pp. 185-89); *Dīrghanakha sūtra* (= *Majjhima*, I, pp. 497-501); *Śarabha-sūtra* (= *Aṅguttara*, I, pp. 185-88); *Parivrājaka-Sthavirasūtra* and *Brāhmaṇasatyāni sūtra* (= *Aṅguttara*, II, p. 185)—are all included in the Chinese translation of the *Saṃyuktāgama*.[2]

The *Ekottarāgama* and the *Aṅguttara Nikāya* have very little in common. This is partly due to the fact that a large number of the suttas of the *Aṅguttara* is included in the *Madhyama* and *Saṃyukta Āgamas*. The Pāli text is much more extensive than the Sanskrit, and it seems that the growth of this part of the Piṭaka took place independently of each other. From Akanuma's comparative studies, the following sūtras may be pointed out as being more or less common in the two Piṭakas: *Samacitta* (I, pp. 61-9), *Devadūta* (I, pp. 132-50), *Brāhmaṇa* to *Loṇaphala* (I, pp. 155-258), *Cakka* (II, pp. 32-44), *Muṇḍarāja* (III, pp. 45-62), *Nīvaraṇa* (III, pp. 63-79), *Āghāta* (III, pp. 185-202), *Devatā* to *Mahā* (III, pp. 329-420) *Avyākata* to *Mahā* (IV, pp. 67-139), *Gahapati* (IV, pp. 208-35), *Sacitta* (V, pp. 92-112), *Upāsaka* (V, pp. 176-210), *Jānussoṇi* (V, pp. 249-73), and *Anussati* (V, pp. 328-58). This is not an exhaustive list, for there are stray agreements in other sections as well.

A fifth Āgama was not recognized by the schools other than the Theravāda. In the *Divyāvadāna* (pp. 17, 331, 333) and elsewhere the Āgamas are referred to as *Āgamacatuṣṭayaṃ*. In the Nāgārjunikoṇḍa inscriptions also, four Nikāyas are mentioned and not five. The Pāli *Khuddaka Nikāya* is really a collection not of discourses, short or long, but of a number of independent treatises, which could not be included in any of the four Nikāyas.

1. See Winternitz, *op. cit.* p. 234 fn.
2. *Toung Pao*, V, p. 209.

By *Khuddaka*, the Pālists probably meant "other works" or "miscellaneous works." Though the Sarvāstivādins did not have a fifth Nikāya, they had a few texts like the *Udānavarga*, *Sūtranipāta* (*Aṭṭhaka* and *Pārāyana vaggas*), *Sthavira-gāthā*, *Dharmapada*, *Vimānavastu*, and *Buddhavaṃsa*, which came later on to be collectively called *Kṣudraśkāgama* (see above).

Vinaya

Vinaya texts : Our information about the Vinaya texts of the Sarvāstivādins is derived solely from the catalogues of Chinese canonical literature. In Nanjio's *Catalogue*, appear the following titles :

(i) *Sarvāstivāda-vinaya-mātṛkā*, translated by Saṅghavarman (445 A.D.): Taisho xxiii, 1441; Nanjio 1132.

(ii) *Sarvāstivāda-vinaya-vibhāṣā*, translator unknown (350-431 A.D.): Taisho xxiii, 1440; Nanjio 1135, 1136.

(iii) *Sarvāstivāda-vinaya-saṅgraha*, compiled by Jinamitra, translated by I-tsing (700 A.D.) ; Nanjio 1127.

(iv) *Daśādhyāya-vinaya-nidāna*, translated by Vimalākṣa (being the preface to the *Daśādhyāya-vinaya*), Nanjio 1144.

(v) *Daśādhyāya-vinaya-bhikṣu-prātimokṣa*, translated by Kumārajīva (404 A.D.): Taisho xxiii, 1436; Nanjio 1160.

(vi) *Daśādhyāya-vinaya-bhikṣunī-prātimokṣa*, compiled by Fa-yin (420-479 A.D.) : Taisho xxiii, 1437; Nanjio 1161.

(vii) *Daśādhyāya-vinaya* or the Sarvāstivāda Vinaya, translated by Puṇyatara together with Kumārajīva (404 A.D.) : Taisho xxiii, 1435; Nanjio 1115.

The principal text of the Sarvāstivādins was the *Daśādhyāya-vinaya*. Fa-hien writes that he came across a Sarvāstivāda-vinaya in verses, but the Chinese translation of the *Daśādhyāya-vinaya* attributed to the Sarvāstivādins is in prose. The *Daśādhyāya* (Taisho ed., xxiii, 1435) is divided into 14 sections. It opens with the eight sections of the Prātimokṣasūtra. The ninth section deals with "seven dharmas", *viz*., *śikṣāpada*, *poṣadha*, *pāpadeśanā*, *varṣāvāsa*, *carmavastu*, *bhaiṣajyavastu* and *cīvara* (moral precepts, fortnightly ceremonies, confession, dwelling in the rainy season, use of leather-shoes, use of medicines, and robes). The tenth section contains "eight dharmas," viz., *Kaṭhina*, *Kauśāmbī*, *Campā*,

Pāṇḍulohitaka, *Saṅghāvaśeṣa-parivāsa*, *Paṭicchādana*, *Śayanāsana* and *Āsamudācārika-dharma* (rules re. making of Kaṭhina-robes, dispute at Kauśāmbī, events at Campā, deeds of Pāṇḍulohitaka monks, atonement for Saṅghāvaśesa-offences, concealment of irreligious acts, rules regarding bed and seat and proper conduct of monks).[1] The eleventh section entitled "saṃyutta," i.e., miscellaneous rules, deals with *dhūta* and other extraordinary precepts observed by some monks. The twelfth section is devoted to *Bhikṣuṇī prātimokṣa* containing, as it does, 8 *Pārājikā*, 17 *Saṅghāvaśeṣā*, 30 *Naiḥsargikā*, 78 *Pāyantika*, 8 *Prātideśanīyā* and *Aṣṭa-dharmā*. The thirteenth section re-arranges the preceding rules in the *Ekottara* style, from one to eleven dharmas. The concluding section, the fourteenth, contains *Upāli-paripṛcchā*, a well-known text on disciplinary rules.[2]

The text contains almost all the chapters of the Vinaya of the Theravādins and the Mūlasarvāstivādins, and appears to be a much shorter version of the text of the latter. From the title, one expects ten chapters, but actually there are fourteen, and so we have to assume that four of the fourteen chapters were later additions or were originally treated as supplements. The 11th, 13th and 14th chapters are no doubt later additions, but it is difficult to ascertain the fourth additional chapter. A close study of the Chinese translation along with Sanskrit text of the Mūlasarvāstivādins will reveal the actual position.

Mūlasarvāstivāda Vinaya

As stated above, we rely on the Chinese versions of the Sarvāstivāda literature including the Vinaya Piṭaka. In this connection, it may be mentioned that a large portion of the original Mūlasarvāstivāda Vinaya was discovered at Gilgit and edited by me after collating it with its Tibetan version. It may be assumed that the Vinaya texts of Sarvāstivāda and Mūlasarvāstivāda were not very different from each other. From the Mūlasarvāstivāda text, it appears that the Mūlasarvāstivādins also,

---

1. See *Bodhisattva-prātimokṣa-sūtra*, Intro., p. 3 (IHQ., VII. 2).
2. For further details, see introduction to the Mūlasarvāstivāda-vinaya, *Gilgit Mss*, vol. III, pt. ii.

like the Lokottarvādins, whose first Vinaya text is the *Mahāvastu*, introduced many episodes relating to the past and present lives of Gautama Buddha. The chapters of this Piṭaka that have been published (Gilgit Manuscripts, Vol. III) are as follows:—

i. Pravrajyā-vastu (fragmentary)
ii. Poṣadha-vastu (do)
iii. Pravāraṇā-vastu (do)
iv. Varṣā-vastu (do)
v. Carma-vastu (including the Śroṇa-Koṭikarṇa avadāna)
vi. Bhaiṣajya-vastu (also in fragments)
vii. Cīvara-vastu (complete)
viii. Kaṭhina-vastu (do)
ix. Kośāmbaka-vastu (do)
x. Karma-vastu (do)
xi. Pāṇḍulohitaka-vastu (do)
xii. Pudgala-vastu (do)
xiii. Pārivāsika-vastu (do)
xiv. Poṣadhasthāpana-vastu (do)
xv. Other unidentified vastus, in fragments, the last of which is Saṃghabhedaka-vastu.

Abhidharma

The Abhidharma literature of the Sarvāstivādins is fairly extensive. Apart from the well-known seven texts and the famous Vibhāṣā śāstras of the Vaibhāṣikas, this school had to its credit a few other philosophical works written by Vasubandhu, Saṃghabhadra, Dharmatrāta and Dharmottara. None of these valuable works are available in original Sanskrit except the *Abhidharmakośa,* its *bhāṣya* and *vyākhyā* of Yaśomitra. The *Vyākhyā* is no doubt a mine of information and contains most of the philosophical topics discussed in the Abhidharma literature of the Sarvāstivādins. It may also be regarded as a quintessence of the seven Abhidharma texts. For a general idea of the several texts at the present moment, we shall have to depend on the valuable analysis of the Chinese translations of the texts made by Prof. Takakusu in the *JPTS*, 1904-05, and the notes given by Prof. Louis de la Vallée Poussin in his introduction to the French translation of the *Abhidharmakośa.* With the publication of the *Vyākhyā* it has become possible to comprehend the terms and nomenclatures suggested by Takakusu on the basis of the Chinese renderings and form a better idea of the contents of the texts. The seven texts claimed by the Sarvāstivādins as constituting their original Abhidharmapiṭaka are as follows:[1]—

(i) *Jñānaprasthānasūtra* of Ārya Kātyāyaṇī-putra with its six supplements (*ṣaṭ pādāḥ*), viz.
(ii) *Prakaraṇapāda* of Sthavira Vasumitra
(iii) *Vijñānakāya* of Sthavira Devaśarmā
(iv) *Dharmaskandha* of Ārya Śāriputra
(v) *Prajñaptiśāstra* of Ārya Maudgalyāyana
(vi) *Dhātukāya* of Pūrṇa and
(vii) *Saṅgīti-paryāya* of Mahākausṭhila.

(i) The *Jñānaprasthāna-sūtra* is attributed to Ārya Kātyāyaṇīputra. In the *Kośa* it is stated that the actual author of the work was Buddha but the arrangement of chapters and topics were made by Kātyāyaṇīputra and so its authorship is attributed to him. It was translated twice into Chinese, by Gotama Saṃghadeva of Kashmir and Chu Fo-nien, in the 4th century A.D., and by Hiuen-tsang in the 7th century. It is divided into eight sections. The first section contains exposition of *laukikāgradharmas, jñāna, pudgala, śraddhā, ahrīkatā, rūpa* and its *lakṣaṇa, anarthaka* (?), and *caitasika* (=best mundane topics,[2] knowledge, individuality, faith and reverence, lack of modesty, material constituents of the body and their characteristics, *anarthaka* (?) and mental states). The second section details the *saṃyojanas* or defilements, which hinder the spiritual progress of an adept, and the causes of defilements. The third section is devoted to the acquisition of knowledge (*jñāna*) (a) of doctrinal matters by which a *sekha* becomes an *asekha*, (b) of right and wrong views, (c) of the means of attaining six *abhijñās*, (d) of the four truths and of the acquisitions to be made in the four stages of sanctification. The fourth section details what may be called evil works and acts with their consequences and also

1. *Kośa*, 1, 9 & 11.
2. *Kośa* (Fr. transl.), intro., p. xxx. See *Infra*, p. 144.

explains *vijñapti* and *avijñapti.*[1] The fifth section gives an exposition of *rūpaskandha*, i.e., the four constituents, and of those originating out of them, both internal and external. The sixth section analyses the 22 *indriyas* (predominant faculties) and the three spheres of existence viz., *kāma, rūpā* and *arūpa*, and explains in detail the *sparśendriya, mūla-citta*, etc. The seventh section is devoted to the mental states developed by an adept while he is in *samādhi*, and gradually advances from Sakadāgāmi to Anāgāmi stage. The last, the eighth section explains the four *smṛtyupasthānas*, the various wrong views, and similar other matters.

The alternative title of the *Jñāna-prasthāna-sūtra* is *Aṣṭa-grantha*, as it contains eight chapters, relating to *Laukikāgra-dharma* (=mind and mental states) which are considered to be the best of worldly (*kāma* and *rūpa dhātu*) matters. It seems that this book corresponds to the *Dhammasaṅgaṇi* in Pali. It contains eight chapters : These are :

(i) *Laukikāgradharma*=the best world-conditions;
(ii) *Jñānaṃ*=knowledge of the nature of all worldly objects;
(iii) *Pudgalāḥ*=of individualities;
(iv) *Sneha-gauravaṃ*=Śraddhā=Regard and firm faith in the Triratna, i.e., Buddha, Dharma and Saṅgha;
(v) *Āhrīkyaṃ*=immodesty;
(vi) *Lakṣaṇaṃ*=characteristics of the body, i.e., *anityatā* (=impermanence, i.e., birth, old age and death);
(vii) *Cetanā, saṃcetanā, adhicetanā*=idea, thinking, and deep thinking;
(viii) *Anarthakam*=Perhaps, it means "indifferent, i. e., neither good nor evil"[2]

The second chapter deals with

(i) *Akuśala* (evil actions and thoughts in general);

(ii) *Saṃyojanāni*=fetters of human life. These are the same as *Saṃyojanāni* in Pāli;

1. *Kośa*, 1, 11.
2. The above enumeration and interpretation are based on the Sanskrit translation of the relevant Chinese text by Śrī Śānti Bhikṣu of Śānti Niketan Viśvabhāratī.

(iii) *Sahacaritam* = fetters relating to the beings of the three dhātus : Kāma, Rūpa and Arūpa;

(iv) *Sattvāḥ* = the ways and methods to be adopted by the denizens of the three dhātus to get rid of the *saṃyojanas* (fetters);

(v) *Daśa Dvārāṇi* = it enumerates all the conceivable impurities of the denizens of the three dhātus.

The remaining six chapters have not yet been published by Śānti Bhikṣu Śastrī.

Dr. Barua suggests that the work (*Jñānaprasthāna-sūtra*) may be paralleled to the Pāli text *Paṭisambhidāmagga.*[1] There may be a verbal resemblance between the two texts, but the *Jñānaprasthāna* is written more on the lines of *Dhamma-saṅgaṇi* than on those of *Paṭisambhidāmagga.* The title also suggests that the work is expected to contain topics leading to the highest knowledge, which, in other words, is purity or emancipation.

The second book is entitled *Prakaraṇapāda*. Its authorship is attributed to Sthavira Vasumitra, who, according to the Chinese tradition, composed it in a monastery at Puṣkalāvatī. It was translated into Chinese by Guṇabhadra and Bodhiyaśas of Central India (435-443 A. D.) and also by Hiuen-tsang (659 A.D.). The work is divided into eight chapters. The first defines *rūpa, citta, caitasikas, cittaviprayuktas* and *asaṃskṛtas*[2] (material constituents, mind, mental states, non-mental states, and the unconstituted). The second deals with the same topics as those discussed in the last two chapters of the fourth section of the *Jñānaprasthānasūtra.* The third explains the sense-organs and their spheres of action, while the fourth defines several terms, such as *dhātu*, *āyatana*, *skandha*, *mahābhūmika*[3] (cf. *Kośa*, II, 23; III, 32), etc. The fifth chapter analyses the *anuśayas* (dormant passions), while the sixth explains *vijñeya*, *anumeya* and *anāsrava dharmas* (things to be known, to be inferred, and pure dharmas). The concluding chapter, the seventh, appears to be an index, containing all the technical terms with their meanings in short.

---

1. Law, *History of Pāli Lit.*, I, p. 337.
2. See *Infra.*
3. *Kośa*, ii, 61-62.

The third book, *Vijñāna-kāya* is attributed to Devaśarmā, who, according to Hiuen-tsang, compiled it at Viśoka near Śrāvastī, about a century after Buddha's death. It was translated into Chinese by Hiuen-tsang (649 A.D.). It is divided into six chapters. It contains an exposition of *pudgala*, *indriya*, *citta*, *kleśa*, *vijñāna*, etc. as given by Maudgalyāyana, enumerates the different classes of beings, persons, etc., defines the function of mental states as *hetu* (cause) and *ālambana* (basis) of spiritual progress and also of mental states of a perfect (i.e., Arhat) and an imperfect adept.[1] Prof. Poussin remarks in his *Études Asiatiques*, 1925 (i. 343-76) that the first two chapters contain the controversies relating to the existence of past and future, and of *pudgala* (soul).[2]

The fourth book is entitled *Dharmaskandha*. Its authorship is attributed to Śāriputra. It was translated into Chinese by Hiuen-tsang (659 A.D.), In the colophon of the Chinese translation this text is described as "the most important of the Abhidharma works, and the fountain-head of the Sarvāstivāda system." This book, it seems, appealed to the Chinese not for its subtlety and depth of philosophical discussions as for its comprehensiveness outlining the general course of spiritual training prescribed for a Buddhist monk. This work can also be paralleled to the *Visuddhimagga* of Buddhaghosa. Its 21 sections are as follows : *Śikṣāpadas* or *Śilas*; attainments leading to Srotāpatti; development of faith in the Triratna; the fruits of the four stages of sanctification, four *ārya-pudgalas samyak-saṃkalpa* of the eightfold path; attainment of *ṛddhipādas*; practice of *smṛtyupasthānas*: exposition of the *āryasatyas*; four *dhyānas*; four *apramāṇas*; four higher *samāpattis* (*ārūpyas*), practice of *bhāvanā*; exposition of *bodhyaṅgas*, and then an exposition of *indriyas*, *āyatanas*, *skandhas* and *dhātus*. Its concluding chapter explains the twelve terms of the formula of causation (*pratītyasamutpāda*).

The fifth book, *Dhātukāya*, is attributed to Pūrṇa in the Sanskrit and Tibetan texts, and to Vasumitra by the Chinese writers. Prof. Takakusu remarks that the original Sanskrit had

1. *Kośa*, vii, 12.
2. Cf. *Kośā* (Transl), ii, p. 150 fn. See *Infra*.

probably more than one recension. It was translated into Chinese by Hiuen-tsang (663 A. D.). The object of the treatise is to enumerate the dharmas, considered as 'reals' by the Sarvāstivādins. The dharmas are classified under the heads : 10 *mahābhūmikas*, 10 *kleśa-mahābhūmikas*, 10 *parittakleśas*, 5 *kleśas*, 5 *dṛṣṭis*, etc. This classification differs slightly from that found in Pāli texts and the *Abhidharmakośa*.[1] Prof. La Vallêe Poussin thinks that this must be a very old text, which may be regarded as the source of the Pāli *Dhātukathā* also, as it discusses the *sampayutta* and *vippayutta* relations of the dharmas as has been done in the *Dhātukathā*.

The sixth book *Prajñaptiśāstra* is attributed to Maudgalyāyana. It was translated into Chinese at a very late date (1004-1055 A. D.) by Fa-nu (=Dharmapāla) of Magadha. The Chinese text is incomplete. In the Tibetan version this treatise is divided into three parts, viz.. *lokaprajñapti*, *kāraṇaprajñapti* and *karmaprajñapti*. The *lokaprajñapti* appears in a well-digested form in the *Abhidharmakośa* (III). Prof. La Vallêe Poussin has analysed the first two *Prajñaptis* in the *Cosmologie bouddhique* (pp. 275-350).[2] In the *lokaprajñapti* the cosmological ideas of the Buddhists are given, in the *kāraṇaprajñapti* the characteristics that make a Bodhisattva are discussed, while in the *karmaprajñapti* there are enumeration and classification of different kinds of deeds.

The seventh book *Saṅgītiparyāya* is attributed to Mahākauṣṭhila by Yaśomitra and Bu-ston, and to Śāriputra by the Chinese writers. It was translated into Chinese by Hiuen-tsang (660-663 A. D.). This text was compiled, according to the introductory remarks, immediately after Buddha's death to avert disputes among the disciples regarding the Buddhist teachings and disciplinary rules. The scene of this text is laid at Pāvā, where dissensions among the Nigaṇṭha Nāṭaputtas started after the death of their teacher. It arranges the *dharmas*, both doctrinal and disciplinary, numerically in the *Ekottra* style, i.e., gradually increasing the number of dharmas from one to ten. The contents of this text agree to a large extent with those of the *Saṅgīti* and *Dasuttara suttontas*[2] of the *Dīghanikāya*.

1. *Kośa*, Intro. p. xxxvii ff.
2. Cf. Daśottara-sūtra in *Abhidharmakośa-vyākhyā* (Jap. ed.), p. 590.

Besides these seven recognized texts of the Sarvāstivādin Abhidharmapiṭaka, there were a few other digests and commentaries dealing with the topics of the Abhidharma. The exhaustive commentary on the *Jñānaprasthāna-sūtra* was, of course, the *Mahāvibhāṣā*, compiled, according to Paramārtha, by Kātyāyanīputra himself with the assistance of Aśvaghoṣa of Sāketa. Among the digests, the most important work is Vasubandhu's *Abhidharmakośa*, which has got a *bhāṣya* written by Vasubandhu himself and a *vyākhyā* written by Yaśomitra. Then there are two other texts, viz., *Abhidharma-nyāyānusāra* and *Abhidharma-samaya-pradīpika*, attributed to Saṃghabhadra, an opponent of Vasubandhu. Saṃghabhadra wrote these works to refute some of the theses of Vasubandhu, especially those which were in support of Sautrāntika views.

There was an earlier digest called the *Abhidharmasāra* written by Dharmaśrī. It contained eight chapters, viz., *dhātu*, *saṃskāra*, *anuśaya*, *ārya*, *jñāna*, *samādhi*, miscellaneous *śāstravarga* or *vāda-varga*.[1]

Among other works of note belonging to this school, we may mention *Sāriputrābhadharma*, *Abhidharmāmṛtaśāstra* of Ghoṣa, *Abhidharmahṛdaya* of Dharmottara and *Lokaprajñapti-abhidharmaśāstra* of an unknown author.

Doctrines

In the history of the secession of schools, it has been shown that the Sarvāstivādins belonged to the orthodox group, which is why there are many points of agreement between the Theravāda and Sarvāstivāda doctrines.

I. *Sabbam atthi*

The principal point of difference between the two schools is that the Sarvāstivādins maintain the existence of 5 *dharmas* in their subtlest states at all times, whether in the past, present or future, while the Theravādins deny any such existence. The former accept the fundamental creeds of Buddhism, viz., *anattā* and *anicca* of all worldly beings and objects, and their contention

1. For details see La Vallée Poussin's Intro, to the *Kośa*, p. lxiii.

is that the beings and objects constituted out of the *dharmas* at a particular time are subject to disintegration but not the *dharmas* themselves, which always exist in their subtlest states. *Vedanā*, for instance, may be *kuśala, akuśala* or *avyākṛta* at a particular time and place but it exists at all times.[1]

The *Kathāvatthu* (I.6) presents the arguments and counter-arguments of the Sarvāstivādins and the Theravādins thus: The Sarvāstivādins maintain that all *dharamas* exist but not always and everywhere and in the same form. In reply to the question whether khandhas which are all different by nature exist uncombined (*ayogam*), they answer in the negative. This, however, gives an opportunity to the Theravādins to show the fallacy that if all exist then both *micchādiṭṭhi* and *sammādiṭṭhi* should exist together. Then again by equating the past and the future with the present, the Theravādins show that if the past and the future exist then their existence should be predicated in the same way as of the present,[2] which the S. deny, saying that the past and the future exist but not exactly in the same form as one would speak of the present.

The Th. have recourse to the second argument, saying that let the 'present material aggregate' (*paccuppanna-rūpa*) be treated as one inseparable object; now, after some time has elapsed, this material aggregate becomes the past, i.e. gives up its presentness (*paccuppannabhāva*), to which the S. agree; then in the same way can it be said that the material aggregate also gives up its materiality (*rūpa-bhāva*) ? The S. deny the latter inference, reasoning thus — let a piece of white cloth be regarded as one inseparable object; now, when this cloth is coloured, it gives up its whiteness (like *paccuppannabhāva*, as in the former case), but does it give up its clothness (like *rūpabhāva* as in the former case) ? This disarms the opponents. The Th., however, follow up this argument of the S. by *suddhikanaya* (pure logic), saying that if the material aggregate (*rūpa*) does not give up its materiality (*rūpabhāva*)[3] then *rūpa* becomes permanent, eternally existing

1. See *Points of Controversy*, Appendix, pp. 375-7.
2. This argument is repeated with each of the khandhas.
3. Cy. rūpakkhandhena saṃgahitattā.

like *nibbāna*—a conclusion not accepted by the S., as according to the latter, *rūpabhāva* is different from *nibbānabhāva*.

The next question put by the Th. is, whether the past (*atīta*) gives up its pastness (*atītabhāva*)? The S. answer in the negative but take care to note that when they say that *attīabhāva* exists, they mean that *anāgatabhāva* (futurity) and *paccuppannābhāva* (presentness) do not exist like the *atītabhāva*, and similarly when they predicate existence of *anāgatabhāva*, they mean *atītabhāva* and *paccuppannabhāva* do not exist like *anāgatabhāva*. This general statement is then applied to each of the khandhas. The Th. round up the discussion by their usual *suddhikanaya* saying that *atīta* or *atītabhāva* would then be the same as *nibbāna* or *nibbāna-bhāva*, a conclusion rejected by the S. The Th. then take to *vacanasodhana* (clearing up of verbal errors), saying that (i) if the existence of the past (*atīta*) and the non-past (*nātīta*) as also of the future (*anāgata*) and the non-future (*na anāgata*) is denied, then the S. should not say that the past and the future exist; so also (ii) if they do not accept the identity of *atīta*, *paccuppanna* and *anāgata*,[1] they cannot say that *atīta* and *anāgata* exist.

The next argument of the Th. is that if the S. admit that *paccuppannañāṇa* (present cognition) exists and it has the function of knowing things (*paccupannaṃ ñāṇaṃ atthi, tena ñāṇena ñāṇakaraṇīyaṃ karoti*) and then why not should the *atītañāṇa* and *anāgatañāṇa*, the existence of which is affirmed by the S., have the function of knowing past and future things in analogy to that of *paccuppanna-ñāṇa*?[2] The Th. consider this as illogical and reject the contention of the S. that *atītaṃ ñāṇam atthi*.

The Th. now take up the instances of Arhats, Anāgāmis, etc., and show that according to the S.'s statement that *atīta rāga* exists in an Arhat, that *atīta byāpāda* exists in an Anāgāmi, and so forth, an Arhat should be *sarāga*, an Anāgāmi should be

1. By having recourse to the discussion whether *hutvā hoti*, *hutvā hotīti* and *na hutvā na hoti*, *na hutvā na hotīti*, the Th. show logically the untenability of this assertion of the S. (*Kvu*. p. 125).

2. In the text, this argument is elaborated by the application of this general statement to each of the sense-organs (paras 23-28) as also to *hattha pāda*, *pabba*, *kāya*, *āpo*, *tejo* and *vāyu* (paras 47-49).

byāpanna-citta, and so on, but this inference is not accepted by the S.

The last argument resorted to by the Th. is that if the existence of *atīta, paccuppanna* and *anāgata khandhas, dhātus, āyatanas* be admitted, then the S. should say that there are (3×5) or 15 khandhas, (3×18) or 54 dhātus, (3×12) or 36 āyatanas, which the S. reject saying that they may accept the position that *atīta* or *anāgata* exists from one standpoint and does not exist from another standpoint (*atthi siyā atītaṃ* or *siyā na atītaṃ* or *na anāgatan ti*). The Th. then bring in their *suddhikanaya* by citing the instance of *nībbāna* and establish the futility of the assertion of the S. that the past and the future exist. Both the Th. and S. then quote passages from the Sutta Piṭaka in support of their contentions, one however remaining unconvinced by the other. The following may be taken as the opinion of the S. :

1. The past and the future, as usually understood, do not exist though they are perceptible in the present.[1] In the same sense, the non-past-future should also be taken as non-existent.

2. It is *bhāva* of each of the five khandhas, and not the khandhas, that persists in the past, present and future.

3. An object (*vastu*) may lose its pastness, presentness, or futurity but not its objectness (*vastutva*), but that objectness is not identical with *nibbāna* or *nibbānabhāva*.

4. An Arhat, e.g., has *atīta rāga* but he is not therefore to be regarded as '*sarāga*'.[2]

The S. admit impermanence (*anityatā*) of the constituents but they contend that the "dharmas" (or bhāvas) of the past are transmitted into the present and likewise the "dharmas" of the future are latent in the present. This we may illustrate, by citing the example of a sweet mango — the past mango seed transmits into the present its 'mangoness', if not the 'sweetness'; and, similarly, the 'future mango' receives its 'mangoness'.from the present : the mango seed can never produce any other fruit though there may be a change in the quality, shape and colour

1. E.g. *anāgataṃ hutvā paccuppannaṃ hoti* but *anāgata* is not identical with *paccuppanna* in the ordinary sense, though in *paccuppanna* there is (the dharma of) *anāgata* so in that sense *paccuppanna* is *anāgata*.

2. Cf. the views of Śaila schools re, *anusaya*, pp. 84f., 124ff.

of the mango. The S. speak of a being in the same way. According to them, a being is composed of five *dharmas* (not five khandhas), viz., (i) *citta* (mind), (ii) *caitasika* (mental states), (iii) *rūpa* (matter), (iv) *visaṃprayukta-saṃskārās* (states independent of the mind),[1] and (v) *asaṃskṛtas* (the unconstituted).[2] The

---

1. In Vasumitra this appears also as a separate opinion of the S. : The phenomena *jāti, jarā, sthiti, anityatā* are *citta-visamprayuktas* but included in *saṃskāraskandha*. One of these four items, *viz., jarā* is discussed in the *Kvu.* (VII. 8) under the topic "jarāmaranaṃ vipāko ti" an opinion of the Andhakas, the *Kvu.*, supporting the opposite view that "jarāmaranaṃ" is not *vipāka*.

2. These five are sub-divided into seventy-five thus :

I. Rūpa (11): (*a*) *viṣaya* (5) (*b*) *indriya* (5) (*c*) *avijñapti* (1)

(*a*) *viṣaya* (5)	(*b*) *indriya* (5)
(i) rūpa	(i) cakṣurindriya
(ii) śabda	(ii) śrotrendriya
(iii) gandha	(iii) ghrāṇendriya
(iv) rasa	(iv) jihvendṛiya
(v) sparśa	(v) kāyendriya

II. Citta (1)

III. Caitasikas (46) :

(*a*) *Mahābhūmika* (10)
(sarvacitta-bhavatvāt, *Kośa*, II, p. 42)

(i) vedanā	(vi) mati or prajñā
(ii) saṃjñā	(vii) smṛti
(iii) cetanā	(viii) manaskāra
(iv) sparśa	(ix) adhimokṣa
(v) chanda	(x) samādhi

(*b*) *Kuśalamahābhūmika* (10)

(i) śraddhā	(vi) alobha
(ii) vīrya	(vii) adveśa
(iii) upekṣā	(viii) ahiṃsā
(iv) hrī	(ix) praśrabdhi
(v) apatrāpya	(x) apramāda

(c) *Kleśa-mahābhūmika* (6)	(*d*) *Akuśala-mahābhūmika* (2)
(i) moha	(i) ahrīkatā
(ii) pramāda	(ii) anapatrāpya
(iii) kauśīdya	
(iv) aśrāddhya	
(v) styāna	
(vi) auddhatya	

(*e*) *Upakleśa-bhūmika* (10)	(*f*) *Aniyata-bhūmika* (8)
(i) krodha	(i) kaukṛtya
(ii) mrakṣa	(ii) middha
(iii) mātsarya	(iii) vitarka

five dharmas (not elements as usually understood) persist in a being, the present being the resultant of the past, and potential of the future. An adept after becoming a *sotāpanna* remains so in his following existence, proving thereby that his past *dharmas* continue and the three *saṃyojanas*[1] remain ineffective. It may be argued by the Th. that the three *saṃyojanas* have altogether disappeared ; then the Sarvāstivādins may cite the instance of Sakadāgāmin as a better illustration. A Sakadāgāmin reduces *raga, dosa* and *moha* to the minimum, and in his following births that state continues, proving the continuity of past 'dharmas'. Now we may pass on to the case of the Arhats. The Arhats, it will be seen, become completely free from *rāga, dosa* and *moha,* but according to the Th., these are destroyed for ever, but according to the S., these *rāga, dosa* and *moha* persist though in an ineffective form, and these may reappear and cause an Arhat fall from Arhathood—a topic discussed in the *Kvu.* (I. 2) and attributed by Buddhaghoṣa to the S., viz., *Parihāyati arahā arahattā ti* ?[2]

(iv) Īrṣyā	(iv) vicāra
(v) pradāśa	(v) rāga
(vi) vihiṃsā	(vi) pratigha
(vii) upanāha	(vii) māna
(viii) māyā	(viii) vicikitsā
(ix) śāṭhya	
(x) mada	

IV. Citta-viprayukta (14):

(i) prāpti	(viii) jāti
(ii) aprāpti	(ix) sthiti
(iii) sabhāgatā	(x) jarā
(iv) asaṃjñika	(xi) anityatā
(v) asaṃjñi-samāpatti	(xii) nāmakāya
(vi) nirodha-samāpatti	(xiii) padakāya
(vii) jīvita	(xiv) vyañjana-kāya

V. Asaṃskṛta (3): (i) ākāśa
(ii) pratisaṃkhyā-nirodha
(iii) apratisaṃkhyā-nirodha.

See Rosenberg, *Die probleme der buddhistischen philosophie*, pp. 128-9. Rāhula Sāṅkṛtyāyana, *Abhidharma-kośa.* Table III.

1. *Viz., sakkāyadiṭṭhii sīlabbataparāmāsa, vicikicchā.*
2. For its exposition, see ante, p. 107.

In Kārikas 25-7 of the fifth Kośasthāna of the *Abhidharmakośa*,[1] there is a detailed exposition of the main thesis of the Sarvāstivādins, viz., *Sarvam asti*. The contention of the S. that the dharmas exist in the past, present and future rests on certain statements found in the Āgamas, one of which is as follows :

रूपमनित्यमतीतमनागतम् । कः पुनर्वादः प्रत्युत्पन्नस्य । एवंदर्शी श्रुतवान् आर्यंशावकोऽतीते रूपेऽनपेक्षो भवति । अनागतं रूपं नाभिनन्दति । प्रत्युत्पन्नस्य रूपस्य निर्विदे विरागाय निरोधाय प्रतिपन्नो भवति ।

[*Rūpa* (material constituents of a being), whether past or future is impermanent, not to speak of the present. A learned Śrāvaka, who realizes this, remains unconcerned with the past *rūpa*, does not rejoice at his future *rūpa* and exerts to rid his mind of the present *rūpa*].[2]

On the authority of this statement taken literally (*kaṇṭhataḥ*), the S. contend that if the past *rūpa* does not exist, there was no necessity of instructing an adept to remain unconcerned with the same. In the same way, it may be said of the future and the present.[3]

The same statement when interpreted (*arthataḥ*) yields a further argument, viz., every *vijñāna* (perception, cognition) requires the combination of two things, the sense-organ and its object. Now, one speaks of *manovijñāna* (mental perception, cognition) of past acts or things. This also implies the existence of past acts or objects, otherwise how could there be *manovijñāna* of the same. The same argument is applicable to future acts or objects.[4]

Then again, if there be no past, how can one speak of an effect due to past good or bad deeds. At the moment when the effect is produced there is the *vipāka-hetu*, which is past.[5]

For the reasons stated above the S. affirm the existence of

1. See Stcherbatsky, *Central Conception of Buddhism*, Appendix, pp. 76-91; La Vallée Poussin's Fr. transl. of *Kośa* V. 25-27; Rāhula Sāṅkrityāyana *Abhidharmakośa*.

The exposition given in the *Kathāvatthu* speaks of "*bhāvānyathātva*" of Dharmatrāta.

2. Cf. *M. Vṛ*., p. 444; Bhaddekaratta-sutta in *Majjhima*, iii, p. 187 :
Atītaṃ nānvāgameyya, nappaṭikaṅkhe anāgataṃ,
Yad atītaṃ pahīnaṃ taṃ, appattañ ca anāgataṃ,
Paccuppannaṃ ca yo dhammaṃ tattha tattha vipassati
Asaṃhīraṃ asaṃkuppaṃ taṃ vidvā mānubrūhaye.
3. *Kośa-vyākhyā* (Jap. ed.), p. 468.
4. *Ibid*., p. 469.
5. *Ibid*., p. 469.

past and future of *dravyas* only, and not of *bhāva*, *lakṣaṇa* or *avasthā*.

The Sarvāstivāda exponents, however, differed among themselves and interpreted the existence of beings and objects in the past, present and future in diverse ways, thus:

(i) Dharmatrāta states that the objects remain the same and undergo only modal changes (*bhāvānyathātva*), i.e. in form and quality, giving rise to different notions, such as, past, present and future. A thing originates when it takes new modes or form and quality and is destroyed when it abandons them. He cites the instance of gold and ornaments made out of it, as also of milk and curd, pointing out that the gold and the substance of milk remain the same, though both undergo changes in form and quality by the addition or subtraction of something else. The modal changes are described as past, present and future, decay and origin, and so forth. A certain object gives up its future mode or form and quality and reaches the present mode. Similarly it abandons its present mode and attains the past mode. If it not be so, the future, present and past objects would be entirely different from one another.

Vasubandhu has criticized this view as similar to the Sāṃkhya doctrine of evolution (*pariṇāma*), admitting, however, the fundamental difference between Sāṃkhya and Dharmatrāta's view that the former upholds the existence of an eternal reality (*prakṛti*) while Dharmatrāta adheres to the impermanent nature of worldly objects.

(ii) Ghoṣaka states that every phenomenal object has three characteristics, viz., birth, old age and death, and these exist with the object at all times. When a baby is born, milk is drawn from the udder, or a gold ornament is made, it carries with it the other two characteristics, viz., old age and death, which were existing in the baby, in milk or in gold ornament in a latent form.

The presentness (*pratyutpanna*) is distinguished by Ghoṣaka as actual use or application (*samudācāra*) while the other two, the past and the future, are distinguished as attainable (*prāpti*). The inception of an object is called birth or present, while the other two, old age and death, which will be forthcoming, are future. When the baby grows old, or milk turns into curd, or the gold ornament is worn out, its old age becomes present while its inception becomes past and its ultimate decay future. By this argument, Ghoṣaka established change in characteristics (*lakṣaṇānyathātva*). Dharmatrāta deals with the object and its form and quality (*dravya* and *bhāva*) separately, while Ghoṣaka takes the two as inseparable.

Ghoṣaka argues that if the three characteristics (*lakṣaṇas*) do not exist together and be completely separated (*viyuktaṃ syāt*), then present cannot become past nor future can become present, and so he concludes that the three time-characteristics exist together. He gives the following illustration : Suppose a man is attached to a woman; he is not thereby wholly detached from other women. The attachment is distinguished by him as actual application (*samudācāra*) and the possibility of his attachment to other women as attainability (*prāpti*).[1]

Vasubandhu criticizes the above view as a cross-mixture or blending of time (*adhvasaṃkara*). He contends that a past object or characteristic should not be regarded as possessing the characteristics of present and future. In other words, Ghoṣaka attributed three time-characteristics to one object, which is illogical, because one object can have one time-characteristic.

Again, in the case of living beings (*sattvākhya*), the question of attainability (*prāpti*) may arise but it is not applicable to material objects (*asattvākhya*), as a pitcher does not take up its hardness.

(iii) Vasumitra (1st century A.D.), author of *Paripṛcchā*, *Pañcavastuka* and other treatises,[2] states that objects exist at all the three times : past, present and future, and do not undergo any change either in substance or in their form and quality or in their characteristics as contended by Dharmatrāta and Ghoṣaka.[3] He holds that it is the activity or function (*kāritra*) that determines the pastness, presentness and futurity of an object (*avasthānyathātva*). When activity is taking place, e.g., when eyes function and see an object as it is in substance, in

1. *Kośa-vyākhyā* (Jap. ed.), p. 470.

2. This, according to Fa-pao, is the opinion of Saṃghabhadra. According to P'ou-koung this opinion is also expressed in the *Vibhāṣā*. Cf. *Kośavyākhyā*, p. 470.

3. *Abhidharmakośa* (Jap. ed.), p. 167.

form and quality or in characteristics, it is called present: likewise, when the activity ceases, i.e., when eyes have completed seeing an object, the object is regarded as past. Similarly, when the activity will take place with regard to any object, the object is described as future. In other words, in all objects, all the three time-factors are co-existent, and it is the activity or function that determines the time or nature of an object (*adhvānaḥ kāritreṇa vyavasthitāḥ*). Had there been no co-existence of the time-factors, the past and the future would be non-existent like the horns of a hare. Pastness or futurity, according to Vasumitra, is neither an error nor absolutely non-existent. Hence, all phenomenal objects exist in the past, present and future. He cites the instance of a cipher and its position in a mathematical figure. Just as a cipher placed before the figure 1 has no value, and when placed after the figure 1, it carries the value of 10, so also an object by its activity is determined as past, present and future.

Of the three interpretations stated above, Vasubandhu gives preference to Vasumitra's view, but criticises it also as faulty. Vasubandhu argues that, according to the doctrine of "all exists", "*kāritra*" should also be existent along with the object at all times, for it is not separable from the object. Being an inseparable property, *kāritra* should not be distinguished as past, present and future. *Kāritra*, again, cannot be different from an object (*dharma*), for according to the Sarvāstivādins, there is nothing beside *dharma*. Again, if *kāritra* be identical with the object, it cannot be the determinant of pastness, presentness and futurity.

Vasubandhu does not support the Sarvāstivāda view wholeheartedly. He takes here the Sautrāntika view in his criticism of Vasumitra.

(iv) There is a fourth view expressed by Buddhadeva, who is mentioned in an inscription (see above, p. 132.). He states that the phenomenal objects exist at all times; they are denoted as past, present or future relatively (*anyathānyathikatva*). Like Vasumitra, he does not agree with the contention of Dharmatrāta and Ghoṣaka that objects undergo change in form and quality or in time-characteristics. He says that an object remains the same at all times, but it is denoted as future with reference to its existence in the past and present, likewise the present is denoted with reference to its existence in the present and future. The use of past, present and future depends on the relative existence of an object. He cites the instance of a woman who is described both as a daughter and mother with reference to her father and son. Buddhadeva contends that while every object possesses all the three time-factors at the same time, only one time-factor is pointed out in relation to another. It is something like saying that a certain object is curd in its presentness, milk in its pastness and cream in its futurity. An object, the anterior existence of which is known and not its posterior, is denoted as future; again an object, the anterior and posterior existences of which are known, is denoted as present: then, again, an object, the posterior existence of which is known and not its anterior, is denoted as past. In this manner, Buddhadeva established the existence of an object at all times (*tri-kāla-sat*).[1]

Vasubandhu criticizes this view, saying that, according to Buddhadeva, three time-factors become one (*ekasmim evādhvani trayo prāpnuvanti*), which is untenable.

II. *Maitrī* (amity) and *Karuṇā* (compassion)

The S. in consonance with the Th. regard Buddha as a human being but they attribute to him divine, sometimes superdivine, powers. They look upon the Bodhisattvas as *puthujjanas* who must destroy the worldly fetters like an average adept in order to step into the *samyaktvanyāma* or *sotāpannahood.*

According to the S., "sentient conscious beings are not objects of *maitrī* and *karuṇā* and so forth on the part of the Buddha," and, further, "if anyone adheres to the view that there are sentient beings he cannot realize emancipation."

The first opinion is opposed in the *Kvu.* (XVIII. 3 : *Natthi Buddhasa Bhagavato karuṇā ti*) on the ground that the Buddha is described in the texts as 'kāruṇiko' and that he sometimes enters into *mahākaruṇāsamāpatti* and so he has *karuṇā* for sentient beings.[2] In the Pāli texts, the practice of four *brahmavihāras*, *maitrī, karuṇā, muditā* and *upekṣā,* form an essential part of the Theravāda code of spiritual practice. It is by means of

1. *Kośa-vyākhyā*, (Jap edi.), 470-71.
2. All these views have been discussed earlier, see pp. 73f. above.

brahmavihāras that an adept is able to look upon all beings as one and the same. In other words, he develops *samatājñāna*.

Regarding the second opinion, the S. state only the axiomatic truth that in Buddha's eye, no individual beings exist and as such they cannot be the object of his *maitrī* and *karuṇā*.

There are three other views relating to Buddha's teachings, which are opposed to those of the Mahāsaṅghikas[1] but are in keeping with the human conception of Buddha. These are:

(i) The Buddhas cannot expound all doctrines with a single utterance.

(ii) The world-honoured One utters words which are not always in conformity with the truth.

(iii) The *sūtras* delivered by Buddha have *nītārtha*,[2] and there are even some *anitārtha-sūtras*.

III. *Arhats*

According to the Sarvāstivādins, Vasumitra says:

(i) A srota-āpanna has no chance of retrogression while an arhat has.

(ii) All arhats do not gain *anutpāda-jñāna*.

(iii) An arhat is governed by *pratītyasamutpādāṅga* (limbs of the causal law).

(iv) Certain arhats perform meritorious deeds.

(v) Arhats are not free from the influence of their past *karma*.

(vi) Arhats gain *naivaśaikṣa-nāśaikṣa-jñāna*.

(vii) Arhats gain the four fundamental dhyānas : they cannot realize the fruits of dhyānas.

The first opinion that arhats may have retrogression is the same as that of the Mahāsaṅghikas and their sub-sects (discussed above, p. 23f., 82f., 106f.). The S., like the M., assume the existence of two classes of arhats with different degrees of attainments.[3] According to the S., all arhats are not completely

1. All these views have been discussed earlier, see pp. 73f above.

2. The word *nītārtha* means 'literal or direct meaning' and does not convey the real and inferred sense as the *neyyārtha* does.

3. See *Kośa*, vi. 64 : The Ubhayatobhāgavimutta-arhats realise nirodhasamāpatti and remove both kleśāvaraṇa (obstacle of passions) and vimokṣāvaraṇa (obstacle to the knowledge of *akarmaṇyatā* of *nāma* and *rūpa*) while the Prajñāvimukta-arhats are those who remove only kleśāvaraṇa by means of prajñā. For the six kinds of arhats, see *Kośa*, vi. 56ff.

perfect — an opinion not accepted by the Theravādins, though the latter have no objection whatever to distinguishing arhats as *Sa(=sva)-dhammakusala* and *Para-dhammakusala*. It is interesting to find this opinion discussed also in the *Milindapañha*,[1] where it is said that there are arhats who may not be aware of the name and gotra of any and every person, the various roads and so forth, but there may be some conversant with the *vimuttis*.[2]

The second opinion reiterates the first in another form. The S. hold that some and not all arhats gain the *anutpādajñāna* (lit. knowledge of the cessation of rebirth), but all may have *kṣayajñāna* (lit. knowledge of the extinction of all impurities in oneself). The M. assert that only Buddhas and not Arhats can have both *kṣayajñāna* and *anutpādajñāna*.[3]

Regarding the third opinion, Mr. Masuda on the basis of *Shu-chi* says that of the twelve items of the causal law, four, viz., nāmarūpa, ṣaḍāyatana, phassa and vedanā — (or, according to another interpretation, only vedanā) remain active in the case of arhats, the other items, i.e., avijjā, saṃkhārā, taṇhā, upādāna bhava, jāti, and jarā-maraṇa, becoming ineffective. The Chinese interpretation can be accepted only if 'vedanā' is limited to 'adukkha-asukha-vedanā', for an arhat is *chaḷupekkho*[4] (endowed with indifference to the six *indriyas*, i.e., the organs of sense) come into contact with the respective objects of the sense organs which do not evoke any feeling, good or bad, in him.

The fourth opinion speaks of *puññopacaya* of an Arhat. The Th. and Mahīśāsakas reject it, so also do the Mahāsaṅghikas.[5] The Arhats are said to have done all that is to be done (*katakarṇīya*) and are beyond merit and demerit, good or bad; hence to speak of some of them as collecting merits shows that the

1. *Milindapañha*, p. 267 : Avisayo mahārāja ekaccassa arahato sabbaṃ jānituṃ na hi tassa balaṃ atthi sabbaṃ jānituṃ. Cf. *Kvu.*, II, 2 above p.82f.

2. The five *vimuttis* are—(1) tadaṅgavimutti or vippassanā-ñāṇa attained by removing the misconceptions of nicca, nimitta etc., (2) vikkhambhanavimutti or paccavekkhaṇa-ñāṇa, (3) samucchedavimutti or magga-ñāṇa, (4) paṭipassadhivimutti or phala-ñāṇa, and (5) nissaraṇavimutti.

3. See above, p. 82f.

4. *Dīgha*, iii, p. 245; *Majjhima*, 1, p. 219; *Kvu.*, p 280.

5. *Majjhima*, II, p. 105.

S., like the Andhakas, do not look upon all arhats as completely perfect.

The fifth opinion that arhats are subject to the influence of past *karma* is perhaps based upon some instances found in the Piṭakan stories that Arhats like Aṅgulimāla and Mahāmoggallāna[1] suffered pain on account of their past *karma.*[2]

In the sixth opinion, the word *naivaśaikṣa-nāśaikṣa*, as translated by Mr. Masuda, appears to be ambiguous,[3] and preference should be given to the meaning "nirvāṇa" as assigned to it by the *Mahāvyutpatti.* The sense would then be that, according to the S., some, and not all, arhats attain Nirvāṇa (full emancipation).

The seventh opinion has not been taken up for discussion in the *Kvu.* The *Kośa* (viii. 6) tells us that there are eight fundamental *dhyānas* (*maula-samāpatti-dravyāṇi*) i.e., four *dhyānas* and four *ārūpyas* (higher dhyānas). The contention of the S, is that all arhats complete the four dhyānas but all do not necessarily attain the fruits of the four dhyānas,[4] which are detailed in the *Kośa* (viii. 27-28), thus: by the first dhyāna, one obtains *dṛṣṭa-dharma-sukhavihāra*,[5] by the second *jñāna-darśana* (or *divya-cakṣurabhijñā*),[6] by the third *prajñā-prabheda*,[7] and by the fourth *anāsravatā.*[8]

IV. *Samyaktvanyāma*[9] (destined to attain nirvāṇa)

Vasumitra attributes the following opinions to the Sarvāstivādins:—

---

1. *Milindapañha*, p. 188.
2. *Milindapañha*, p. 134 : Na hi mahārāja sabbantaṃ vedayitaṃ kammamūlakaṃ. See also *Kvu.*, viii, kammahetu arahattā parihāvatīti?
3. "For arhats there are things which are no longer to be learnt and things which are still to be learnt." *Asia Major*, p. 49.
4. *Dīgha* iii. 222; *Aṅg.*, ii. 4 : Atth' āvuso samādhibhāvanā bhāvitā bahulīkatā diṭṭhadhammasukhavihārāya saṃvattati ñāṇadassanapaṭilābhāya satisampajaññāya āsavānaṃ khayāya saṃvattati.
5. lit. enjoyment of happiness in the present body (Pāli: diṭṭhadhammasukhavihāra).
6. lit. insight into the real state of things i.e. free from any *vikalpa.* (= Pāli : ñāṇadassana).
7. lit. special or detailed knowledge of the things of the world—the corresponding Pāli expression is paṭisambhidā.
8. lit. purity (Pāli : āsavānaṃ khaya).
9. For references see *Kośa*, vi, p. 181 fn.

(i) A person can acquire *samyaktvanyāma* through the meditation of *śūnyatā* and *apraṇihitatā*; a person in *samyaktvanyāma* is called *pratipannaka* up to the fifteenth (or the last) moment of the *darśanamārga.* In the sixteenth moment he is called *phalastha* when he is in *bhāvanāmārga.*

(ii) A person can acquire *samyaktvanyāma* and can also gain arhathood independently of the four dhyānas.

(iii) A being (in Rūpa or Arūpa dhātu) can gain arhathood but not *samyaktvanyāma.* It is only when he is in Kāmadhātu that he can have *samyaktvanyāma* as also arhathood.

Allied to the above three, there are two other views attributed to the S., viz.,

(iv) There are certain devas who lead a holy life.

(v) There is no one who is free from passion in the Uttarakuru. No saint is born there or in the *Asaññi-sattvaloka.*

The first three views raise the question of *samyaktvanyāma,* i.e., of persons who are destined to attain Nirvāṇa, and have no chance of being diverted from the Aryan path and going to lower states or joining heretical sects. An adept in *samyaktvanyāma* is the same as *sotāpattimaggapaṭipanna,* i.e., one after destroying the three *saṃyojanas* (impurities), viz., *sakkāyadiṭṭhi* (belief in a self), *sīlabbataparāmāsa* (belief in the efficacy of rituals) and *vicikicchā* (lack of faith in the Triratna) is on the way to *sotāpattiphala.* According to the scheme of the S., an adept remains *srotāpattiphala-pratipannaka* for the first fifteen moments, i.e., up to the development of *mārge anvayajñānakṣānti,*[1] when he completes the *darśanamārga*; from the 16th moment he is in *srotāpattiphalastha* or *srotāpanna.*

The first opinion raises the question whether one can become a *srotāpattiphala-pratipannaka* by the meditation of *śūnyatā* (i.e. *anātmatā*) and *apraṇihitatā* (i.e. *duḥkhatā*) and *anityatā*[2]

1. See *infra.*

2. Cf. *Asia Major,* II. p. 40, n. 9.

and not of *animittatā*;[1] the answer given by the S. is in the affirmative.

The second deals with the problem whether *samyaktvanyāma* followed by arhathood can be attained without the practice of the four dhyānas, the S. asserting that it is possible to attain arhathood by means of certain practices other than those necessary for dhyānas, e. g., by means of *smṛtyupasthānas* or *brahmavihāras* and so forth.

The third is concerned with the problem: whether gods in the Rūpa or Arūpadhātu can gain *samyaktvanyāma* as also arhathood. The S. hold that they can attain the latter but not the former, as it can only be attained by a being while in the Kāmadhātu. This problem is discussed in the *Kvu.* (I.3): *Natthidevesu brahmacariyāvāso ti* ?—an opinion held by the Sammitīyas. The opinion of the S. is upheld by the Th. In the *Kvu.* it is contended that 'brahma-cariyāvāsa' does not mean merely pravrajyā (ordination), muṇḍiyaṃ (shaven-headedness) and so forth as held by the Sammitīyas, but also includes 'maggabhāvanā.' The Th. and S. hold that the Anāgāmis do not come to the Kāmadhātu but they remain in Rūpa or Arūpadhātu and by *maggabhāvanā* there, they become Arhats, without becoming a *samyaktvanyāma.*

The fourth opinion of the S. is that the gods except the Asaññisattās can have *maggabhāvanā*, though not *pabbajjā, muṇḍiyaṃ* etc.

The fifth opinion is based on a passage of the *Aṅg. Nik.* (iv. 396) and cited in the *Kvu.* (I. 8, p. 99), in which it is stated that the inhabitants of Jambudvīpa surpass those of Uttarakuru and Tāvatiṃsa heaven in energy, mindfulness and in religious life (*brahmacariyāvāsa*);[2] from this it has been inferred that there cannot be any saint in Uttarakuru.[3] It has been mentioned above that the S. as well as the Th. exclude the Asaññisattās

1. Mr. Masuda on the basis of Fa-jen states that Dharmagupta held that one cannot attain *samyaktvanyāma* without *animittasamādhi*, *Asia Major*, p. 40, n. 9.

2. *Points of Controversy*, p. 73.

3. The S. are making an anomaly in drawing the inferences. If Uttarakuru cannot have any saint how can the Tāvatiṃsa have any ?

from the gods who follow a religious life, and so, among the Asaññisattās also there cannot be any saint.[1]

V. *Anupubbābbisamaya*
(gradual realisation of the truth)

Vasumitra attributes the following views to the Sarvāstivādins :—

(i) The four truths are to be meditated upon gradually.

(ii) The *catur-śrāmaṇyaphalas* are not necessarily attained gradually.

(iii) If one is in *samyaktvanyāma*, he can attain (at once) the fruits of sakṛdāgāmi and anāgāmi on account of (the completion of) the *laukikamārga*.

An adept, according to the S., develops insight into the four truths in a gradual order[2] in 15 moments, thus : —

Darśana-mārga

(i) Duḥkhe (or in five skandhas, i,e., nāma·rūpe) dharmajñāna-kṣānti[3] (faith, conviction) (ii) Duḥkhe dharmajñāna	confined to Kāmadhātu.
(iii) Duḥkhe anvayajñāna-kṣānti[4] (iv) Duḥkhe anvayajñāna	extended to Rūpa and Arūpadhātus.

Srotāpatti-pratipannaka-darśanamārga

(v) Samudaye (sāsrvadharmānāṃ hetu i.e., karmakleśe) dharmajñāna-kṣānti[4] (vi) Samudaye dharmajñāna	confined to Kāmadhātu.

1. Mr. Masuda points out (in the fn. *Asia Major*, p. 46) that Uttarakuru is regarded as a land of pure happiness and the Asaññisattās as the highest devaloka with long life and happiness; hence the beings of these two abodes need not take to religious life.

2. Cf. *Kośa*. vi. 2.

3. Kṣānti means "faith (kṣamate=rocate, *Kośa*. vi. 18). An adept in the first moment thinks that he has realized (though actually he has not realized) the fact that the objects of the Kāmadhātu, i.e. the skandhas, are undesirable. It is in the second moment that he realizes that the skandhas are undesirable. He acquires now dharmajñāna.

4. After the realization of the actual state of skandhas of the Kāmadhātu, the adept extends his inner vision to the skandhas of Rūpa and Arūpa dhātus to realize in the next two moments that skandhas of the higher worlds are also undesirable, and hence, existence in any of the worlds is to be avoided. In the same way, the other three truths are to be comprehended.

(vii)	„ anvayajñāna-kṣānti	extended to Rūpa and Arūpadhātus.
(viii)	„ anvayajñāna	
(ix)	Nirodhe (pratisaṃkhyā-nirodhe or karmakleśa-kṣaye) dharmajñana-kṣānti.	confined to Kāmadhātu.
(x)	Nirodhe dharmajñāna	
(xi)	Nirodhe anvayajñānakṣānti	extended to Rūpa and Arūpadhātus
(xii)	„ anvayajñāna	
(xiii)	Mārge (śaikṣa aśaikṣa dharma or samatha-vipaśyanyāṃ) dharma-jñānakṣānti	confined to Kāmadhātu
(xiv)	Mārge dharmajñāna	
(xv)	Mārge anvayajñānakṣānti	extended to Rūpa and Arūpadhātus.
(xvi)	Mārge anvayajñāna[1]	

From the above table it is evident how the S. mark the gradual stages of the development of insight into the four truths. In the *Kvu.* the controversies: *Anupubbābhisamayo ti* ? (II. 9) and *Odhisodhiso kilese jahātī ti* ? (I.4) and also *Vimuttaṃ vimuccamānan ti* ? (III. 4) support the view of the S. about the gradual realization of the truths. The problem discussed is whether an adept realizes the four *sāmaññaphalas*, including *vimutti*, gradually or not ? The Th. contend that there is no bar to the realization of all the *phalas* at one and the same time. The S. subscribe to this view as will be apparent from the second opinion of the S. quoted above, except that they do not include the fourth phala, viz., *arhathood* or *vimutti*.[2] Buddhaghosa should have pointed out this discrepancy as far as the S. are concerned. According to him, the opinion that the realization of the *phalas* is attained gradually is held by the Sammitīyas.

In the third point, it is stated that, according to the S. those adepts only who have completed the *laukikamārga*[3] attain the second and third *phalas* at one and the same time. The Th. hold that *bhāvanāmārga*, which commences from the *srotāpattiphala* stage is *lokottara* and cannot be *laukika*; the S., however,

1. Cf. *Vibhaṅga* pp. 225, 315, 329.

2. There may be ascetics who obtain the four fruits gradually (anupūrveṇa catuḥphalaprāpti). *Kośa*, vi. 45.

3. *Kośa*, vi, 45 : The *bhāvanā-mārga* is of two kinds : laukika or sāsrava and lokottara or anāsrava.

contend that it may be either *laukika* or *lokottara*. A topic allied to this is discussed in the *Kvu.* (I. 5), which will be dealt with hereafter.

VI. *Puthujjana, Laukikamārga* or *Laukikāgradharma*

The S., as pointed out by Vasumitra, hold :—

(i) A *puthujjana* (average man) is able to destroy *rāga* and *pratigha* in the Kāmadhātu.

(ii) A *puthujjana* can die with a good state of mind.

(iii) There is *laukika-samyagdṛṣṭi* and *laukika-śraddhendriya*.

(iv) The *laukikāgradharma* is a stage lasting only for one moment (*ekakṣaṇikacitta*).

In the Buddhist texts a puthujjana (an average man), whether a householder or a recluse, who has not yet destroyed the three *saṃyojanas*, viz., *sakkāyadiṭṭhi*, *vicikicchā* and *sīlabbataparāmāsa*[1] in order to become a sotāpanna, can hardly be expected to destroy *rāga*, *dosa* and *moha*, which impurities are normally removed when an adept reaches the anāgāmi stage. The S. hold that a puthujjana is able to remove from his mind *rāga* and *pratigha*, which is the same as *dosa* or *vyāpāda*. The Th. discuss this view in the *Kvu.* in these words: *Jahāti puthujjano kāmarāga-byāpādan ti* ? (I. 5) concluding that a puthujjana cannot completely eradicate from his mind *rāga* (attachment) and *byāpāda* (hatred), gross and subtle. In course of this discussion, the Th. raise the other question: *Puthujjano kāmesu vītarāgo saha dhammābhisamayā anāgāmiphale saṇṭhātī ti* ? (*Kvu.* I. 5, p. 112), i.e. whether an average man, who is free from *kāma*, attains with the realization of the truth the anagāmi stage or not ? The S., as we have seen above, answer the question in the affirmative, but they do not think that such a puthujjana can attain arhathood, but he can attain all the other *phalas* at one and the same time. In other words, the contention of the S. is that a puthujjana's attainments through *laukika-mārga* may be of so high an order that the moment the truth flashes in his mind he becomes an anāgāmi, when he completes all the necessary conditions for anāgāmihood, including those of the lower two *phalas*.[2]

1. See above, p. 162.
2. See *Kvu.*, p. 113-4.

The second opinion that an average man dies with a *kusala-citta* is based on many instances of upāsakas dying with a good mental state. The Th. also subscribe to this view, and hence there is no discussion in the *Kvu.*

The third opinion is the same as that of the Th. and is opposed to that of the Śaila schools (see above, p. 109).

The fourth opinion is not touched upon in the *Kvu.* but has been dealt with fully in the *Kośa* (VI. 19) thus : —

If the conviction (*kṣānti*) concerning *duḥkha* (=skandhas) of the Kāmadhātu be the strongest, it lasts only for a moment, so also are the *agradharmas*, i.e. *laukikāgradharmas*,[1] which though *sāsrava* (impure) are the highest of the mundane dharmas and lead one to the *darśana-mārga* (way to the realization of the truths).

The point is that a puthujjana, according to the S., may attain spiritual progress up to the anāgāmi stage by practising *satipaṭṭhāna* and such other practices, which are *laukika* so long as they are practised by one who is not yet in one of the *maggas* and *phalas*.

VII. *Anuśaya* and *Paryavasthāna*

The S. are of opinion that : —

(i) All the *anuśayas* are *caitasika*; they are *cittasamprayukta* and are also objects of thought (*ālambana*).

(ii) All the *anuśayas* can be included in the *paryavasthānas* but all *paryavasthānas* are not *anuśayas.*

While the above two opinions are diametrically opposed to those of the Mahāsaṅghikas, they are in full agreement with those of the Th. The topics are dealt with in the *Kvu.* fully (see ante, pp. 84 f., 124) in which it is shown that *anuśayas* are not without *ārammana*; they are not *avyākata* (neither good nor bad); they are the same as the *paryavasthānas* (=*pariyuṭṭhānas*), which again are not *cittavippayutta.* The S. distinguish the *anuśayas* from *paryavasthānas*, saying that all *paryavasthānas* are not *anuśayas*, is true.

1. Cf. *Sūtrālaṅkāra*, xiv. 23 : laukikāgradharmāvasthā=ānantarya-samādhi. *Kośa*, vi. p. 166, n. agradharma=dharma-smṛtyupasthāna.

VIII. *Meditation*

The Sarvāstivādins hold that

(i) In the state of *samāhita* one can utter words.

(ii) No man ever dies in the state of *samāhita.*

(iii) It may be said that four *smṛtyupasthānas* can include all dharmas.

(iv) All *dhyānas* are included in the *smṛtyupasthānas.*

(v) There are four *lokottara-dhyānas.*

(vi) The *bodhyaṅgas* are acquired in seven *samāpattis* and not in others.

The first opinion is in agreement with that of Śaila schools, and as such, has been refuted by the Th. in the *Kvu.* (see ante, p. 89.

The second is opposed by the Rājagirikas and the Th. and as such, is discussed in the *Kvu.* (XV. 9) : *Saññāvedayita-nirodhaṃ samāpanno kālaṃ kareyyā ti* ? The Th. contend that a meditator while in the *saññāvediyita-nirodha-samāpatti* cannot have any death-like (*maraṇantika*) contact, feeling, perception, etc. or is not affected by poison, weapon-stroke, or fire; hence to speak of him as dying while in the meditation is wrong. The opponents contend that there is no such law (*niyāma*) that a meditator while in *saññāvedayita-nirodha* will not die.

The third topic discussed in the *Kvu.* (1. 9) is : *sabbe dhammā satipaṭṭhāna ti* ?—an opinion attributed by Buddhaghosa to the Andhakas. The interpretation of Buddhaghosa is that the opponents meant by *satipaṭṭhāna* the objects which form the basis of *sati* (*satiyā paṭṭhāna, satigocara, satiyā patiṭṭhāna*).[1] In this sense the second opinion may be explained as that the *satipaṭṭhānas* include all forms of meditation, i.e., an adept practising *satipaṭṭhāna* need not have recourse to other meditational practices. The S. may well point to the well-known statement found in many passages of the Nikāyas (vide *Majjhima*, I, pp. 55-6), that there is only one way to the attainment of purity and that is the

1. *Kośa*, vi. 14 : Le smṛtyupasthāna est triple : *smṛtyupasthāna* en soi (*svabhāva*), par connexion (*saṁsarga*), en qualité d'object (*ālambanasmṛtyupasthāna*).

practice of *satipaṭṭhāna* (*ekāyano ayaṃ maggo sattānaṃ visuddhiyā......yadidaṃ cattāro satipaṭṭhānā*).[1]

The fourth opinion hardly needs any comment. It refers to the first four dhyānas when they are practised by adepts, who are in one of the *maggas* and *phalas*. The *dhyāna* of a *maggaṭṭha* or *phalaṭṭha* is regarded as *lokottara* (supramundane).

The fifth opinion evidently refers to the contention discussed in the *Kośa* (VIII. 6) that of the eight *dhyānas* or *somāpattis*, the first seven are capable of elevating the mind of an adept to the purest state but not the eighth, in which *saṃjñā* is the feeblest and as such, the meditation of *naivasaṃjñā-nāsaṃjñāyatana* is ineffective. Consequently, the attainment of *bodhyaṅgas* takes place while the adept rises from one dhyāna to the next up to the seventh, leaving nothing for the eighth.

IX. *Vijñāna*

The S. assert, as stated by Vasumitra, that

> The five sense-perceptions (*pañcavijñānakāya*) conduce to attachment (*sarāga*) and not to detachment (*virāga*), because these only perceive the characteristics (*lakṣaṇas*) of objects and have no independent thinking faculty of their own.

If the reason adduced by the S. that the *vijñānakāyas* by themselves cannot produce *virāga*, how can they induce *sarāga*? Hence, the reasoning of the Sarvāstivādins is not quite clear, and it would be better to accept what the *Kvu.* says on the point (see above, p. 111).

X. *Avyākṛta*, *Asaṃskṛta*, and *Antarābhava*

The following opinions are attributed to the Sarvāstivādins:—

(i) There are indeterminable problems (*avyākṛta-dharmas*).

(ii) The law of causality (*pratītyasamutpādāṅgikatva*) is undoubtedly constituted (*saṃskṛta*).

(iii) The *saṃskṛta-vastus* are of three kinds; the *asaṃskṛta-vastus* are also of three kinds.

---

1. Cf. *Kośa*, vi. p. 158, n. 1 :

(iv) Only in Kāma and Rūpa-dhātus there is an intermediate state of existence (*antarābhava*).

The first two opinions are opposed to those of the Mahāsaṅghikas but agree with those of the Th. (see above, p. 112).

The third also is not accepted by the Mahāsaṅghikas but is agreed to by the Th. The difference between the Th. and the S. lies in the fact that the latter make the modification in accordance with their doctrine "sabbaṃ atthi" (discussed before pp. 148f.) according to which, the constituted things (*saṃskṛta-vastu*) should be classified as three, viz., those of the past, those of the present and those of the future (see Masuda, p. 40, n. 2).

The fourth opinion of the S. that there is *antarābhava* in the Kāmadhātu and Rūpadhātu is neither accepted by the Mahāsaṅghikas nor by the Th. (see ante, p. 114). It has some agreement with the opinion of the Sammitīyas.

XI. *Other opinions*

There are a few other opinions held by the S. These are,—

(i) All the *dharmāyatanas* (i.e. the fields of objects of ideation)[1] incomprehensible but they are attainable by the Āryas.

(ii) Even heretics can gain five supernatural powers (see above, p. 125) Wassilljew, *Der Buddhismus*, p. 272, n. 3).

(iii) Good *karma* can also become the cause of existence—an opinion objected to by the Mahīśāsakas[2]

DHARMAGUPTA

The third in importance among the schools of this group is Dharmagupta. In the First Council, certain supporters of Purāṇa and Gavampati did not accept *in toto* the Vinaya rules as adopted by Mahākassapa.[2] In the *Abhidharmakośa* (iv. 39) there is a reference to the Dharmagupta's mentioning that they would not accept the Prātimokṣa rules of the Sarvāstivādins as

1. Masuda, p. 31 : asaṃskṛta-dharmas, caitasika-dharmas and ajñāptirūpas.

2. See above, p. 39 fn. 3.

authoritative on the ground that the original teachings of Buddha were lost.

About the literature of this school, the only information we have is that there was a Vinaya text of its own (Nanjio, 1117) and that the *Abhiniṣkramaṇa-sūtra* belonged to this school. This sūtra was translated into Chinese between 280 and 312 A.D.[1] Prof. Przyluski furnishes us with the information that the canon of this school had the following divisions :

Vinaya-piṭaka	Bhikṣu-prātimokṣa Bhikṣuṇī-prātimokṣa Khandhaka Ekottara
Sūtra-piṭaka	Dīrgha-āgama Madhyama-āgama Ekottara-āgama Saṃyukta-āgama Kṣudraka-āgama
Abhidharma-piṭaka	Difficult (texts) Not difficult (texts) Saṃgraha Saṃyukta

Prof. Przyluski, on the basis of the commentary of K'oueiki on Vasumitra's treatise, remarks that this school was noted for its popularity in Central Asia and China. De Groot remarks in his *Code du Mahāyāna en Chine* (p. 3) that the Prātimokṣa of the Dharmaguptas was actually in use as the disciplinary rules in all the centres of China. The first text was translated into Chinese in 152 A.D. by K'aung-seng-kai, a Sogdian, belonging to this school, so also was the other text (*Kie-mo*) translated in 254 A.D. by T'an-tai, a Parthian. Hence, it is inferred that this school was established in the Iranian countries in the third century A.D. Buddhayaśas, a native of Kipin (mod. Kashmir), introduced the Vinaya of this school into China and from this

1. Translated into English by Beal under the title "*The Romantic Legend of Śākya Buddha.*"

Prof. Przyluski concludes that this school had its centre in the north-west.[1] He also identifies Dharmagupta with Yonaka Dhammarakkhita, mentioned in the Ceylonese chronicles as the apostle sent to Aparāntaka. The reason adduced by him for this identification is that the region between the North-west and Avanti was traversed by the Yavanas, Śakas, and Pallavas about the beginning of the Christian era, and the preacher is described as a Yonaka and then again Dhammarakkhita and Dharmagupta are identical in meaning (i.e. *rakkhita*=*gupta*).

Doctrines

About the doctrines of this school, Vasumitra writes that these were mainly the same as those of the Mahāsaṅghikas, though it was a branch of the Sarvāstivādins. The doctrines specially attributed to them are as follows :—

(i) Gifts made to the Saṅgha are more meritorious than those made to the Buddha, though Buddha is included in the Saṅgha.[1] This is a view contrary to that of the Mahīśāsakas and also to that expressed in the *Dakkhiṇāvibhaṅgasutta*,[2] in spite of the fact that Buddha asked Mahāpajāpati Gotamī to offer the robe meant for him to the Saṅgha.

(ii) Gifts made to a *stūpa* are meritorious. This opinion is opposed to that of the Śaila schools.

(iii) *Vimukti* (emancipation) of *Śrāvakayāna* and *Buddhayāna* is same, though there may be difference in the paths leading to it. This opinion is in agreement with that of the Sarvāstivādins.[3]

(iv) Heretics cannot gain the five supernatural powers.[4]

(v) The body of an *arhat* is pure (*anāsrava*).

(vi) Realization of the truths (*abisamaya*) takes place not gradually but all at a time. This is contrary to the opinion of the Sarvāstivādins (discussed above) but is in agreement with that of the Theravādins.[5]

---

1. *Le Concile de Rājagṛha*, pp. 325-6.
2. See *Kośa* (Fr. Transl.), iv. 117; *Majjhima*, iii, p. 253.
3. See above, p. 125.
4. See above, p. 125, for opinions of other schools on this point see Masuda, p. 42 n.
5. This doctrine is not mentioned by Vasumitra. It is found in the *Kośa*, vi. 27, see *Vyākhyā* (Jap. ed.), p. 542

KĀŚYAPĪYA

The Kāśyapīya school was known by three other names, Sthāvirīya, Saddharmavarṣaka, or Suvarsaka. It issued from the Sarvāstivādins on account of certain opinions, which were more in agreement with those of the Sthaviravādins or Vibhajyavādins than with those of the Sarvāstivādins. This seems to be the cause of their being called a Sthāvirīya. Its third name, Suvarṣaka appears in the works of Tāranātha and Ch'en lun, while Saddharmavarṣaka in Bhavya's treatise.[1]

About the literature of the Kāśyapīyas, Prof. Przyluski writes that it had a canon similar to that of the Dharmaguptas, and had the following divisions :

Vinaya-piṭaka	Bhiksu-prātimoksa Bhikṣuṇī-prātimokṣa Kaṭhina Mātṛkā Ekottara
Sūtra-piṭaka	Dīrgha-āgama Madhyama-āgama Ekottara-āgama Saṃyukta-āgama Kṣudraka-āgama
Abhidrama-piṭaka	Sapraśnaka-vibhaṅga Apraśnaka-vibhaṅga Saṃgraha Comparative tables

Doctrines

To the Kāśyapīyas Vasumitra attributes the following doctrines :—

(i) Arhats have both *kṣayajñāna* and *anutpādajñāna*, and are not subject to passions.

1. Prof. Przyluski identifies the Kāśyapīyas with the Haimavatas, see *infra*.

(ii) *Saṃskāras* perish every moment.

(iii) The past which has not produced its fruit exists, the present exists, and some of the future exists. This opinion is discussed in the *Kathāvatthu* (I. 8) and is the only doctrine attributed in this text to the Kassapikas.[1]

Samkantika or Sautrāntika

In the Pāli tradition the Saṃkantikas are described as an offshoot of the Kassapikas, and from the Saṃkantikas branched off the Suttavādīs. Vasumitra writes[2] that at the beginning of the 4th century (i.e. after Buddha's death), there was one school named Sautrāntika, otherwise called Saṃkrāntivāda, which issued from Sarvāstivāda. The founder of this school declares: "I take Ānanda as my preceptor." From these two traditions, it seems that the Suttavādīs are identical with the Sautrāntikas, having branched off from the earlier school, the Saṃkantikas, who may also be equated with the Dārsṭāntikas of Vasubandhu.

Doctrines

Vasumitra characterizes the Sautrāntikas as the school which admits the transference of *skandhamātras* from one existence to another as distinguished from the Sammitīyas, who maintain the transference of *pudgala* only. Both of these views are wholly opposed to the cardinal doctrine of the early Buddhists, viz., *kṣaṇika* (momentary) existence of skandhas (constituents of a being), i.e., the *skandhas* disintegrate every moment to give rise to another. The Sautrāntikas, in deference to this old *kṣaṇika* theory, add that the *skandhas* in their gross form do not pass from one existence to another; the *mūlāntika* (original or the subtlest form of) skandhas, all the five of which are of one nature (*ekarasa*), in other words, which are in reality one substance and not five different substances passing from one existence to another. Bhāvaviveka in his *Tarkajvāla* (see Obermiller,

1. *Kvu.* 1. 1 : Avipakkavipākaṃ atthi, vipakkavipākaṃ natthīti anāgatam atthīti ādīsu ekaccam atthīti uppādinnadhamme sandhāya vadatīti.
2. Masuda, p. 17.

Analysis of the Abhisamayālaṅkāra, pt. iii, p. 380) states that the school admitted the reality of the individual (i.e. *pudgala*) which, is something inexpressible but neither identical with, nor different from, the *skandhas*.

The second doctrine attributed by Vasumitra to this school is that "apart from the aryan paths (i.e. *aṣṭāngika-mārga*) there can be no eternal destruction happening every moment." This shows that, according to the Sautrāntikas, the *skandhas*, gross or subtle, end in *nirvāṇa*. This view is also allied to the doctrine of the Sammitīyas that the *pudgala* ceases in *nirvāṇa*. Hence, it may be stated that, according to the Sautrāntikas, the subtle *skandhas*, like the *pudgala* of the Sammitīyas, may continue through several existences but totally cease in Nirvāṇa.

For this doctrine of transference of *skandhamātras* through several existences, the Sautrāntikas are also called Saṃkrānti-vādins or Samkrāntikas.

Kośa on the Sautrāntika doctrines

Though Vasubandhu belonged to the Sarvāstivāda school, occasionally he gave preference in his writings to the Sautrāntika views. For this, he was severely criticized by Samghabhadra, who was a staunch Sarvāstivādin. In the *Kośa*, Vasubandhu has referred to the Sautrāntika doctrines on several occasions and pointed out the differences between the Sarvāstivāda and Sautrāntika views. Prof. La Vallée Poussin has summed up these references in his introduction to the French translation of the *Kośa*. As these throw welcome light on the Sautrāntika doctrines a gist of the same is given here :—

(i) The Sautrāntikas do not accept the *Abhidharmapiṭaka* of the Sarvāstivādins as authoritative (*Kośa,* i. 3). On this point Vasubandhu supports the Sautrāntikas.[1]

(ii) The *asaṃskṛtas* have no real existence. There is a long drawn controversy in the *Kośa* (ii. 55) between the Sarvāstivādins and the Sautrāntikas as to whether the *asaṃskṛtas* have any cause or fruits.

1. Acc. to the Sautrāntikas, *buddhavacana* is vāg-vijñapti, see *Kośa,* i. 25; iv. 2.

(iii) The Sautrāntikas deny the *citta-viprayuktas* (i.e. *saṃskāras* not associated with mind, e.g. *prāpti*, *sabhāgatā*, *jīvitendriya*, etc.) as real as contended by the Sarvāstivādins (*Kośa*, ii. 35-36).

(iv) Like all other schools, the Sautrāntikas reject the Sarvāstivāda view that past and future exist (*Kośa*, v. 25).

(v) By admitting the existence of the past and of *prāpti*, the Sarvāstivādins explain the function of causality. The Sautrāntikas deny both of these and assert instead the existence of the subtle *citta* or *bīja* or *vāsanā* and explain thereby the working of the formula of causation (*Kośa*, ii. 36, 50).

(vi) The Sautrāntikas carry the *kṣaṇikatva* doctrine to the extreme, asserting that it almost verges on zero, and as such objects can have no duration (*sthiti*). It further asserts that as destruction of objects takes place almost immediately, there is no necessity of any effective cause.[1]

(vii) The Sautrāntikas deny the existence of *avijñapti* (non-communicating corporeal and vocal acts)[2] as a real *dravya*. They hold in agreement with the Theravādins that an *avijñapti* act is mental (*cetanā, kāyasamcetanā*).

(viii) According to the commentary of the *Vijñaptimātratā-śāstra*, the Sautrāntikas are divided in their opinion relating to the conception of *citta* (mind) and *caittas* (mental states). According to the Dārṣṭāntika-Sautrāntikas *citta* only exists but not the *caittas*, but according to other Sautrāntikas, *caittas* also exist and their number according to some is three, viz., *vedanā*, *saṃjñā* and *cetanā*, while according to others, it is four, ten or fourteen. Some Sautrāntikas admit the existence of all the *caittas* of the Sarvāstivādins (for details, see *Kośa*, transl., ii. 23, fn,).

(ix) The Sautrāntikas hold that the body of an arhat is pure, as it is produced by knowedge.

(x) There may be many Buddhas simultaneously.

---

1. See *Kośa*, iv. 2-3. The *Ṣaḍdarśanasamuccaya* cites this passage from a sūtra of the Sautrāntikas : Pañcemāni bhikṣavaḥ saṃjñāmātraṃ saṃvṛtimātraṃ vyavahāramātraṃ Katamāni pañca, Atīto'dhvā anāgato'dhvā sahetuko vināśaḥ ākāsaṃ pudgala iti.

Cf. *Vedāntasūtra*, ii. 2, 23;

Nyāyavārttikatātparyaṭīkā 383. See also *Kośa*, ii. 46; *Mādhyamikavṛtti*, pp. 29, n. 5; 173, n. 8; 222, 413.

2. For details, see *Kośa*, iv. 3.

Haimavata

Bhavya and Vinītadeva enlist the Haimavatas as a branch of the Mahāsaṅghikas (Group I Schools) while Vasumitra remarks that the principal doctrines of this School were the same as those of the Sarvāstivādins.[1] He adds that the original (*mūla*) Sthaviravāda changed its name to Haimavata.[2] In the Ceylonese chronicles, however, the Hemavatikas are counted as one of the later sects, which came into existence some time after the appearance of the first eighteen schools. In view of these conflicting statements, and the acceptance of some doctrines of the Mahāsaṅghikas, it seems that this school might have branched out of the Sarvāstivādins or Sthaviravādins but doctrinally it was inclined more towards the Mahāsaṅghikas than towards the Sarvāstivādins.

Prof. Przyluski, however, identifies the Haimavatas with the Kāśyapīyas on the following grounds :—

(i) In the Ceylonese chronicles, the apostles sent to Himavanta are Majjhima and Dundubhissara of the Kassapagotta.

(ii) On the relic caskets discovered in the stūpa of Sonari and Sāñci are inscribed (a) *sapurisasa Kāsapagotasa savahemavatācariyasa* and (b) *sapurisasa Kotiputasa Kāsapagotasa savahemavatācariyasa.*

(iii) There are other inscriptions which mention Majjhima and Dundubhissara.

He adds that there can be no doubt about the fact that the monks of Kassapa-gotta were responsible for the propagation of Buddhism in the Himavanta. This school also claims Kassapa as its founder. So the same school was known by two names, one, after the region, as Haimavata and the other after its founder, Kassapa as Kassapīya (=Kāśyapīya). Since the former name was not used, the Chinese pilgrims refer to it by the other name only, *viz.*, the Kāśyapīyas.[3]

The conclusion drawn by Prof. Przyluski from the inscriptional evidences does not appear to be logical. In the inscrip-

1. Masuda, p. 53.
2. Masuda, p. 16; *Points of Controversy*, p. xxxvii.
3. *Le Concile de Rājagṛha*, pp. 317-18.

tions it is stated that some monks of the Kassapagotta propagated Buddhism in Himavanta, but there is nothing to show that the Kassapagotta monks necessarily belonged to the Kāśyapīya school. Hence the identification of Kāśyapīyas with the Haimavatas is not tenable.

Doctrines

Vasumitra treats the Kāśyapīyas and the Haimavatas as separate schools upholding different doctrines. He attributes to the Haimavatas a few doctrines which are in close agreement with those of the Sarvāstivādins, e.g.,

(i) Bodhisattvas are average beings (*pṛthagjanas*);

(ii) Bodhisattvas have neither *rāga* nor *kāma* when they enter their mother's wombs;

(iii) Heretics cannot gain the five supernatural powers;

(iv) There is no *brahmacariyāvāsa* among the gods; and

(v) Arhats have ignorance and doubt; they are subject to temptation; they gain spiritual perception with the help of others; and the path is attained by an exclamation.[1]

UTTARĀPATHAKA

From the geographical evidences collected by Dr. B. C. Law[2] about Uttarāpatha, it appears to have originally indicated the high road running north from Magadha to the north-west. Later, however, it denoted the area west of Pṛthūdaka (Pehoa, about 14 miles west of Thaneswar) and "comprised the Punjab, including Kashmir and the adjoining hillstates with the whole of eastern Afghanistan beyond the Indus, and the present Cis-Sutlej States to the west of the Sarasvatī."[3]

The name 'Uttarāpathaka' appears only in the *Kathāvatthu-aṭṭhakathā* and not in any other text, not even in the Ceylonese chronicles. Evidently Buddhaghosa had in mind some monks who could not be classed as adherents of the doctrines of a

1. The last two views (iv & v) are in agreement with those of the Mahāsaṅghikas. See above, pp. 22-23.

2. *Geogr. of Early Buddhism*, pp. 48-9.

3. Cunningham's *Ancient Geogr. of India*, p. 13.

particular school, or probably he meant, like the Andhakas, a group of schools popular in the north. From the several doctrines attributed by Buddhaghosa to the Uttarāpathakas, it appears that it was an eclectic school having doctrines taken from both the Mahāsaṅghika and Theravāda groups and occupying an intermediate stage between Hīnayāna and Mahāyāna.[1] The following are some of these doctrines regarding :—

Buddha. It is the attainment of *bodhi* or perfect knowledge and omniscience alone that make a Buddha (*Kvu.* iv. 6); Buddhas are above *maitrī* and *karuṇā*[2] (*Kvu.* xviii. 3, 4).

Bodhisattvas. On the basis of the stories of the previous existences of Gautama Buddha, the U. remark that the Buddhas are always endowed with the *mahāpuruṣa-lakṣaṇas* (*Kvu.* iv.7).

Arhats. All *Dharmas* possessed by an arhat are pure (*anāsrava*) (*Kvu.* iv. 3). The arhats are able to end their lives in the same way as Buddha did (*Kvu.* xxii. 3), as described in the *Mahāparinibbāna-sutta.* They admit that there may be persons claiming arhathood falsely (*Kvu.* xxiii. 2). Citing the example of Yaśa's attainment of arhathood they hold that a householder (*gihī*) can attain arhathood without giving up the householder's life. The Th. point out that Yaśa may have the *gihī* signs externally but his mind was free from the fetters of a householder (*Kvu.* iv. 1). Then on the basis of the existence of *Upahacca* (*Uppajja-parinibbāyī*) arhats, the Uttarāpathakas hold that a being, usually a god, at the very moment of his birth, can attain arhathood. They also hold that beings while in the womb or beings just born may attain arhathood on account of their acquisition of sotāpannahood in their previous lives.

Samyaktvanyāma : The puthujjanas, who are *aniyata* (not destined to attain Nibbāna) or who are doers of evil acts, may ultimately become *niyata* and realize the truth. This they state on the basis of some statements of Buddha himself, who foretold to certain puthujjanas that they would realize the truth ultimately, e.g., in the case of Aṅgulimāla (*Kvu.* v. 4; xix. 7: MN. II, p. 105).

---

1. Cf. Satyasiddhiśāstra of Harivarman, translated by Yamakami Sogen (C. U.).
2. See above, p. 158.

Allied to the above are two other views of the Uttarāpathakas: one is that the persons who have to take seven more births to attain Nibbāna (*sattakkhattuparama*) can reach the goal after seven births and not earlier or later. The Th. are not prepared to accept this view on the ground that such persons may quicken their pace by greater exertion or retard their progress by committing evil deeds (*Kvu.* xii. 5). The second is that an adept may attain the four fruits of sanctification by one *magga*. The Th. contend that an adept can attain the *phalas* of the corresponding *maggas* only, i.e., a sotāpanna gets rid of *sakkāyadiṭṭhi*, etc. and he cannot attain the *phalas* of the *sakadāgami* or *anāgami magga* i.e., by elimination of *rāga*, *doṣa* and *moha*. The Uttarāpathakas do not subscribe to the latter view (*Kvu.* xviii. 5).

Anuśayas. According to the U., *anuśayas* are *anārammaṇa* and *cittavippayutta* (see above, pp. 87f., 124, *Kvu.* ix. 4); the Th. contend that past *dharmas* may be *sārammaṇa* (ix.6).

Asaṃkhatas:

(i) *nirodhasamāpatti* is unconstituted (vi. 5).

(ii) space of all kinds is unconstituted (vi. 6).

Immutability (*niyata*) : All dharmas like *rūpa* and *vedanā* do not change their nature (xxi. 7); *karmaic* effects also are unalterable (xxi. 8).

Gatis (spheres of existence): The U. count the *asuragati* as one additional to the usual five, totalling in all six *gatis*.

Buddhavacana. The U. assert that the religious teachings were revised thrice in the three Councils (xxi. 1).[1]

1. All the above references are to the *Kathāvatthu*.

Chapter VIII

DOCTRINES OF GROUP IV SCHOOLS

The Vātasīputrīya-Śāṃmitīyas, Dharmottarīyas and other Schools

This group of schools comprised mainly the Vajjiputtakas or Vātsīputrīyas, Dhammuttarīyas, Bhadrayānikas, Channagarikas and Sammitīyas. Of these, the Vātsīputrīyas, later known as Vātsīputrīya-Sāṃmitīyas,[1] became the most prominent school of this group. The monks adhering to these schools were probably those Vajjiputtakas who submitted to the decisions of the Second Council and gave up their heresies, as distinguished from those who preferred to remain apart and form a distinct Saṅgha of their own. The Pāli and Sanskrit traditions place the origin of the Sammitīyas in the 3rd century B. C. We do not hear much of this school in the early history of Buddhism excepting a few criticisms of its radical doctrine of the existence of a conceptual self (*prajñapti-sat-pudgala*) apart from the five *skandhas*. This school became popular and widespread during the reign of Harṣavardhana (606-647 A. D.), and it is said that the king's sister, Rājyaśrī, joined the school as a bhikṣuṇī. The Chinese travellers also testify to its popularity in India. The earliest evidence of the existence of this school is furnished by two inscriptions of the 2nd and 4th centuries A. D., attesting to the presence of the Sammitīyas in Mathura and Sarnath. The earlier inscription is the fifth stone-slab inscription of Mathura,[2] which records the installation of an image of a Bodhisattva and its dedication to the Sammitīya monks of Sirivihāra by a monk whose teacher was Dharmaka. Besides the Sirivihāra, the stone-slab inscriptions mention three other vihāras, viz., Prāvārika-vihāra, Suvarṇakāra-vihāra and Cuttakavihāra, but the last mentioned vihāra was dedicated to the Mahāsaṅghikas. There are

1. *ERE* XI, p. 168; *Kośa-vyākhyā*, IX. 3 (Jap. ed., p. 699) Vātsīputrīyā Āryasammatīyāḥ.

2. *EI.*, VIII, p. 172; Sahni, *Catalogue of the Museum at Sarnath* p 30.

Brahmī inscriptions of the Kushan period, very likely of the reign of Huviṣka (111 A. D.), inscribed in mixed Prākrit and Sanskrit. The later inscription, mentioning this sect was found at Sarnath, is inscribed on the Asokan pillar below the Asokan edict and another inscription. It records a gift to the teachers of the Sammitīyas, who were otherwise known as the Vātsīputrikas (ācāryanaṃ parigrahe Vatsīputrikanaṃ).[1] It belongs very likely to the 3rd or 4th century A. D. when the Sammitīyas became more popular than the Sarvāstivādins at Sarnath by propagating their views and recruiting a large number of monks and nuns.

This inscription shows that Sarnath was at first a centre of the Theravāda group, the earliest popular school, which gradually yielded its place to the next popular school, Sarvāstivāda. Though Sarvāstivāda retained its popularity and influence all over Northern India, it had, at least at Sarnath, given place to the Sammitīyas.

The Sammitīyas ascribed the origin of their school to Mahākaccāyana, the famous monk of Avantī. This established their close connection not only with the Pāli school but also with Avantī, for which their alternative name given in some sources is Avantaka.[2] Their robes had 21 to 25 fringes and their badge was Sorcika flower like those of the Theravādins.[3]

Yuan Chwang writes that he carried to China 15 treatises of this school[4] while I-tsing speaks of its separate Vinaya text.[5] The latter tells us further that this Vinaya had rules regulating the use of undergarment, girdle, medicines, and beds for the members of the sect in a way peculiar to itself. The only treatise that is expressly mentioned as belonging to this school in Nanjio's *Catalogue*, and extant in Chinese translation is the *Sāṃmitīyaśāstra* or *Sāṃmitīyanikāyaśāstra* containing the tenets of this sect. Most of the passages cited in the *Kathāvatthu* as giving the views of the Sāṃmitīya school are traced to the Pāli Piṭaka.

1. See *Infra*.
2. According to Vinītadeva, the Sāṃmitīyas were sub-divided into three sects, Kuru-Kullakas, Avantakas and Vātsīputrīyas. See Bu-ston, II, p. 99.
3. Bu-ston, II, p. 100.
4. Watters' *Yuan Chwang*, I, pp. 20, 21.
5. Takakusu, *I-tsing*, pp. 7, 66, 140.

It is very likely that the Sutta-piṭaka of the Sammitīyas was substantially the same as that in Pāli.

According to the *Kathāvatthu* and Vasumitra's treatise, the main thesis of this group of schools is that there is a persisting soul (*pudgala*) passing from one existence to another and that it is not possible for the *skandhas* to transmigrate without the *pudgala*. In the *Tarkajvāla* of Bhāvaviveka also, a similar statement is found. It says that the Vātsīputrīyas, Bhadrayānikas, Dharmaguptas and Saṃkrāntivādins admit the reality of the individual self.[1] Among other views of this group, we may mention that they, like the Theravādins recognized the Arhats as not liable to fall from arhathood as against the opinion of the Sarvāstivādins. They, however, adhered to the doctrine that there was an *antarābhava* (intermediate state of existence), which was not agreed to by the Theravādins and the Mahāsaṅghikas. Their conceptions of Buddha and Nirvāṇa, fruits of sanctification and their attainments, various stages of *dhyānas* (meditation), and beings of the higher worlds had much in common with those of the Theravādins and the Sarvāstivādins. The doctrines attributed to the Sammitīyas in the *Kathāvatthu* and Vasumitra's treatise along with their criticisms are as follows :—

Doctrines

The cardinal doctrine of this school is that besides the elements composing a being, there is a 'pudgala' (an individuality, a personality, a self) which is indefinable and which persists through all the existences.[2] It is neither identical with, not different from, the skandhas as *anātman* forms the keynote of Buddhist philosophy. This theory has brought forth vigorous criticisms from most of the prominent Buddhist philosophers, including Nāgārjuna[3] and Vasubandbhu.[4] It has also been

1. See Obermiller, *Analysis* III, pp. 380. For detailed discussion see *infra*.
2. *Kośa-vyākhyā* (Jap. ed.), pp. 697-713.
3. *Mādhyamikavṛtti*, p. 275 quoting *Ratnāvalī*, p. 267, 283: *Bodhicaryāvatāra* ix 60.
4. *Abhidharmakośa*, ch. IX.

mooted whether, on account of this thesis, the Sammitīyas (=Vātsīputrīyas) should be regarded as being within or outside the pale of Buddhism. According to some thinkers, they should be treated as heretical while according to others, they are Buddhists though their *pudgalavāda,* being a form of sakkāya-diṭṭhi, acts as a hindrance to the attainment of Nirvāṇa.[1]

It is necessary now to state what the *Pudgalavāda* of the Sammitīyas actually was. It is given here *in extenso.*

Pudgalavāda

Like the Sarvāstivādins, the Sammitīyas also differed on many doctrinal points from the Theravādins and other sects. These have been discussed in the *Kathāvatthu* and mentioned in the treatises on sects written by Bhavya, Vasumitra and Vinītadeva. The *pudgalavāda* gave a rude shock to the other sectarian teachers, who regarded it as almost heretical and a negation of the *anātma-vāda* of Buddha, and was bitterly criticized by many writers like Vasubandhu and Śāntarakṣita.[2] We have to make out from the criticisms what the exact position taken up by the Sammitīya-Vātsīputrīyas was regarding the conception of soul and its transmigration from one existence to another. The publication of Prof. Venkataraman's translation of the *Sāmmitīya-nikāya-śāstra* in Chinese has been very helpful.

The Sammitīyas Vatsīputrīyas stated that Buddha admitted the existence of an impermanent soul quite different from the Upaniṣadic conception of an eternal and changeless soul, which continued unchanged through all the existences of a being unless and until it attained full emancipation and merged in the *paramātman* or *Brahman.* The Sammitīyas therefore preferred to name their changing soul as *pudgala*, distinguishing it from the *Anattā* doctrine of Buddha.

In the *Kathāvatthu*, the view of the Sammitīyas is given thus:—

The Pudgalavādins rely on the following words of Buddha

1. For details and references, see La Valée Poussin's preliminary notes in the *Kośa* (Fr. transl.) ix, pp. 227f.

2. Moggaliputta Tissa is the celebrated compiler of the *Kathāvatthu,* while Vasubandhu is the author of the *Abhidharmakośa* and its *Bhāṣya,* and its *Vyākhva* by Yaśomitra. Śāntarakṣita is author of *Tattvasaṃgraha* and its commentator is Kamalaśīla.

"atthi puggalo attahitāya paṭipanno" (there is a person who exerts for his own good): "ekapuggalo loke uppajjamāno uppajjati bahujanahitāya bahujanasukhāya lokānukampāya etc. (there appears a person who is reborn for the good and happiness of many, for showing compassion to the world of beings). Basing on such words of Buddhā, the Sammitīyas (henceforth abbreviated as the S.) state 'puggala' of the above-mentioned passages is something positive; it is neither a mirage nor a hearsay: it is neither the unconstituted reality like Nibbāna or Ākāśa nor a constituent material element (*rūpa*), feeling (*vedanā*), etc. The 'puggala' is not real in the highest sense (*parmārtha*). On the one hand, it is not something apart from the constituents (*khandhas*) of a being, and as such it is not possible to establish a relation between the *puggala* and the *khandhas* like that between the container and the contained. On the other hand, though it possesses all the characteristics of the *khandhas*, it is neither like them caused and conditioned (*sahetu sappaccaya*) nor is it like Nibbāna uncaused and unconditionted (*ahetu appaccaya*). Again, it is neither constituted (*saṃskṛta*) nor unconstituted (*asaṃskṛta*). Though it is different (*añño*) from the constituents it possesses certain characteristics of a constituted being such as happiness and unhappiness. It has certain aspects of the unconstituted inasmuch as it is not subject to birth, old age and death. It ceases only when the individual attains final emancipation (*Nirvāṇa*).

In the *Abhidharmakośa* and its commentary, the relation between *pudgala* and *skandhas* is explained by the simile of fire and fuel. Fire exists as long as its fuel lasts, so the *pudgala* exists as long as there are the constituents, but fire is different from fuel inasmuch as it has the power of burning an object or producing light, which the fuel by itself does not possess. Fire and fuel are co-existent, and the latter is a support for the former, and just as one is not wholly different from the other because fuel is not wholly devoid of fiery element (*tejas*), in the same way stands 'pudgala' in relation to the constituents of a being. The S. quote the *Bhārahārasūtra* and explain that burden (*bhāra*) refers to the constituents (*skandha*) while their carrier (*hāra*) is the pudgala. Unloading of the burden is effected by the cessation of desires, attachment and hatred. This 'pudgala' bears a name, belongs to a family and is the enjoyer of happiness and unhappiness.[1]

In discussing the *Bhārahārasūtra*, Śāntarakṣita and Kamalaśīla state that Buddha used the word 'pudgala' as a mere concept (*prajñapti*). He did not state expressly that it was non-existent as nobody enquired of its real nature. He had in mind the aggregation of five constituents and to these collectively he referred as 'pudgala.' It is not subject to origin and decay, hence it has no past, present and future. It is neither eternal (*nitya*) nor non-eternal (*anitya*). It is inexplicable and indeterminable. It is not included in the constituents but appears only when all the constituents are present.

In the *Kathāvattu* it is stated that the S. point out that their 'pudgala' has a material form in the world of men and gods, who have got material bodies (*rūpa*), and it is without any material form in the world of higher gods, who are without material bodies (*arūpī*). They state that the 'pudgala' corresponds to the entity called a being (*sattva*) and also to the vital force (*jīva*) of a living being, but at the same time it is neither identical with, nor different from, the body (*kāya*), for Buddha rejected both the views of identity, and difference of vital force (*jīva*) and body (*sarīra*) (*taṃ jīvaṃ taṃ sarīraṃ aññaṃ jīvaṃ aññaṃ sarīraṃ*). They rely on another statement made fre-

---

1. *Saṃyutta*, III. p. 25 :
Katamo bhikkhave bhāro ?
Pañcupādānakkhandhā ti'ssa vacanīyaṃ.
Katame pañca ? Seyythīdaṃ rūpupādānakkhando, vedanupā, saññupā. saṅkhārupā., viññāṇupā. Ayaṃ vuccati, bhikkhave. bhāro
Katamo ca bhikkhave bhārahāro ?
Puggalo ti'ssa vacanīyaṃ. Yo' yaṃ
āyasmā evaṃ nāmo evaṃ gotto. Ayaṃ
vuccati bhikkhave bhārahāro.
In the *Tattvasaṅgraha* (p. 130, It. 349) Kamalaśīla quotes
Bhārahāraḥ katamaḥ pudgalaḥ ?
Yo'sāvāyuṣmānnevaṃ nāmā,
evaṃ jātiḥ, evaṃ gotra, evamāhāra,
evaṃ sukhaduḥkhaṃ pratisaṃvedī,
evaṃ dīrghāyur ityādinā pudgalo vyākhyātaḥ.

quently by Buddha that a monk while practising mindfulness (*smṛtyupasthāna*) remains always aware of what is passing within his body (*so kāye kāyānupassī viharati*). In this statement Buddha uses the word 'so' meaning 'he', i.e., 'pudgala', which watches the contents and movements of his body. This 'so' is not a mere concept (*prajñapti*), it refers to actual 'pudgala.'

The S. now take up the problem of transmigration. They hold that 'puggala' passes from one existence to another, but the 'puggaḷa' of two existences is neither the same nor different. The reason adduced by them is that a person, who has attained the *Sotāpatti* stage of sanctification, continues to be a *sotāpanna* in his future existences, whether in this mortal world or in heaven (*rūpadhātu*). A *sotāpanna* man may be reborn as a *sotāpanna* god, i.e., *sotāpannahood* remains unchanged though the constituents of his body have changed from those of a man to those of a god. The transition of *sotāpannahood* from one existence to another cannot take place unless the existence and continuity of 'puggala' are admitted.

In support of this contention the S. rely on the following utterances of Buddha:—

(i) There are four pairs of (saintly) persons or eight (saintly) persons (*santi cattāro purisayugā aṭṭha purisapuggalā*). This statement refers to Buddha's Saṅgha, which consists of disciples who have attained the preparatory stage and fruits (*magga, phala*) of sanctification.

(ii) A *sotāpanna* has to be reborn seven times at the most to attain full emancipation (*so sattakhattuparaṃo sandhāvitvāna puggalo dukkhassantakaro hoti*). The S. lay stress on the words *sandhāvitvāna puggala*, i.e., the transmigration of soul (*puggala*).

(iii) The cycle of existence (*saṃsāra*) of a being is without a beginning, which is not apparent to beings immersed in desires (*anamataggo ayaṃ saṃsāro pubbā koṭī na paññāyati sattānaṃ taṇhā-saṃyojanāṃ*). The S. pick up the words 'saṁsāro' and 'satta' and deduce therefrom that Buddha admitted the transmigration of soul of beings.

(iv) Lastly, Buddha very often spoke of the acquisition of higher powers or knowledge (*abhijñā*), one of which was the power of remembering one's previous existences (*pubbe-nivāsañāṇa*). He himself referred to his previous existences and often said, "When I was Sunetra, etc." This also established their contention that there must be a soul (*puggala*), continuing through several existences and Buddha is able to remember his past births. Memory of past existences is not possible for the constituents (*skandhas*), which change every moment, not to speak of the drastic change that the beings undergo when passing from death to rebirth. The S. add that admission of memory (*smṛti*) also implies the existence of 'puggala'.

The S. state that their 'puggala' is the percipient but it is different from mind (*citta*, *vijñāna*), one of the constituents of a being. It is also not momentary (*kṣaṇika*) like mind but is perceivable in every momentary thought. It is the 'seer' whether the eyes are functioning or not, because Buddha said, "I see by my divine eyes beings appearing and disappearing." Here 'I' is 'puggala' of the S.

Then S. take up the problem of capacity for effective action (*arthakriyākāritva*) of the soul. In conformity with Buddha's teaching that the world is not a creation of God (*Iśvaranirmāṇa*) they do not want to attribute to 'puggala' any function of a doer or a creator. They, however, point out that the 'puggala' of a parent or a teacher is in a sense the doer or creator (*kartā*, *kāretā*) of a being. The 'puggala' has no independent function like that of mental properties. It is not an enjoyer of fruits. 'Puggala' and 'fruits' are not two distinct entities, though 'puggala' is said to be feeling happy or unhappy, because the conglomeration of diverse elements, which make a being, cannot have the feeling of happiness or unhappiness. There may be a doer (*kāraka*) or feeler (*vedaka*), but it is not to be distinguished from deed or feeling. The doer and the deed are neither identical nor different. The S. mention this stance of theirs in refutation of the opponent's argument that a semi-permanent soul like the eternal soul cannot have any activity. It is only the impermanent, momentary (*anitya, kṣaṇika*) soul that can have any activity (*arthakriyākāritva*).

Śāntarakṣita in his *Tattvasaṅgraha* (pp. 336-349) writes that the 'puggala' of the Vātsīputrīyas is neither identical with, nor different from, the constituents (*skandhas*). In his comments, Kamalaśīla states that the 'puggala' of the Vātsīputrīyas is the doer of deeds and enjoyer of their fruits. During transmigration it leaves one group of constituents to take up another. It is not separate from the constituents, for, in that case, it would be eternal. Again, it cannot be the same as the constituents, for in that case, it would be not one but many. It is therefore inexplicable. The exposition of Kamalaśila is supported by Prajñākaramati in his commentary on the *Bodhicaryāvatāra.*

In this connection Kamalaśīla has discussed also the criticism of Uddyotakara in his *Nyāyavārttika* (III. 1. 1) that a soul must be postulated if it is not identified with one of the constituents. Candrakīrti, however, does not dismiss the *pudgalavāda* of the Sammitīyas[1] as wholly untenable. He even admits that Buddha as an expedient taught the *pudgalavāda* as he later propounded the idealistic doctrine of *vijñānavāda.*

The *Sammitīyanikāyaśāstra* (Venataraman's translation) mentions and discusses all possible views thus (p. 21):

(i) There is no real self.

(ii) The self is indeterminable (*avyākṛta*).

(iii) Five constituents and the self are identical.

(iv) Five constituents and the self are different.

(v) Self is eternal (*śāśvata*).

(vi) Self is not eternal (*aśāśvata*) and impermanent (*anitya*).

(vii) Self is actually existent though not eternal.

Of these views the last is held by the S. In this text, the non-Sammitīya views have been briefly stated without any comment or criticism while its own view has been fully dealt with thus:—

(i) The 'puggala' is the product of five constituents, and it is neither eternal nor wholly impermanent.

(ii) Buddha's denial of self was enunciated to counteract the wrong views that the self was based on mental impressions

1. *Mādhyamikavṛtti*, p. 276, see also pp. 148, 192.

(*saṃkhārās*) or that it was identical with the body or five constituents.

He admonished his disciples to remove the notion of "I-ness" and "Mine-ness", which was based on the notion of a false self, to which wordly beings bore a strong attachment, but he did not refer to that self (*puggala*) which, strictly speaking, could not be the object of passionate seeking.

Then, again, in Buddha's sayings, the term 'non-existence' was used in a different context, e.g., he said that some were absolutely non-existent like sky-flower and horns of a hare, and again some were really non-existent but existent relatively like long and short, seed and sprout. So Buddha's denial of soul does not necessarily refer to the absolute non-existence of 'puggala'. It is sometimes referred to as inexplicable because of the fact that it can neither be identified with, nor differentiated from, the constituents, which only are apparent to the unenlightened. Again, if 'puggala' be regarded as permanent or impermanent, constituted or unconstituted, it would be adhering to one of the two extreme views of existence and non-existence, both of which were discarded by Buddha. Hence, 'puggala' as relatively existent was admitted by Buddha.

The S. contend that if self be wholly non-existent there would be neither killing of beings nor a killer, neither the attainment of fruits of sanctification nor a saint, consequently, neither a Buddha nor his teachings.

In this treatise the *Bhārahāra-sutta* has been mentioned and discussed and emphasis has been laid on the word 'puggala' used in it. On the basis of the Sūtra, the S. contend that a distinction has been made by Buddha between burden (*bhāra*) and its carrier (*hāra*), the 'puggala' carrying the burden. This *sūtra* clearly establishes that the carrier of 'puggala' is not identical with the burden of the constituents (*skandhas*). Again, the carrier and the burden are inseparable; they are interdependent and hence 'puggala' is not distinguished or separated from the *skandhas*.

It has been further pointed out that the acquisition or removal of impurities like attachment (*rāga*) or thirst (*tṛṣṇā*) is effected not by the 'puggala' alone to the exclusion of the constituents. But at the same time it should be admitted that the puggala,' and the 'skandhas' are neither identical nor different, for Buddha denied the identity and difference of the vital force (*jīva*) and body (*sarīra*).

The treatise now takes up for discussion the conception of 'puggala' from three standpoints:—

(i) The Self is designated by its support (*āśraya-prajñapta-pudgala*), i.e., the self is sometimes given an appellation or description on the basis of its *āśraya* or *ālambana*, as fire is named and described by its fuel, e. g., forest-fire, coal-fire. In a living being, the impressions (*saṃskāras*) are fuel and the "puggala" is the fire, which derives its attributes and appellation in accordance with the impressions. A being is called a man, nāga or a god in accordance with the type of body possessed by him. The self is the receiver of the material form (*rūpa*) but the 'self' and '*rūpa*', being interdependent and inseparable, exist together and at the same time. It is not clear why Candrakīrti stated in the *Mādhyamikavṛtti* (p. 192) that the Sammitīyas held that the receiver of the constituents appeared prior to the constituents to receive them.

(ii) The Self in transmigration (*saṅkramaṇa-prajñapta-pudgala*) implies that the self passes from one existence to another. The 'pudgala', whose mind (*citta or vijñāna*) carries with it the effects of his moral observances (*śīla*) and meditational practices (*samādhi*), is reborn in a higher sphere. On his death his five constituents after disintegration accompany the self to a sphere of excellence. His meritorious deeds and spiritual acquisition are his treasures, which follow him in his next existence. Thus his self does not go alone. If the self be different from the constituents, it would have nothing to stand by in his future existences. Likewise, if the self be real and eternal or unreal and evanescent, the self can take nothing with it when it passes from one existence to another.

The transmigration of self is expressed in many statements of Buddha, e. g., he said, "In this world one performs good deeds and as a result enjoys happiness in the next world", "one who controls his sense-organs gains a happy state in his next life", "a dying person arises again, etc." Buddha himself often spoke of his past existences, in which he perfected himself in many *pāramitās*. He foretold Ajita that in future he would become the Maitreya Buddha. He referred also occasionally to miserly persons possessing wealth, but when death approaches them, they have to part with everything and go alone all by themselves. It is clear from such statements of Buddha that he had in mind a 'pudgala' which transmigrated from one existence to another, accompanied by the resultant impressions (*saṃskāras*) of the past life, i.e., karmaic effects.

(iii) The self in extinction (*nirodha-prajñapta-pudgala*), i.e., when it ceases and has no more rebirth. This happens in the case of an Arhat the perfect, who has removed all his impurities (*kṣīṇāsrava*) and has attained Nirvāṇa, and therefore, cannot have any more rebirth.

In the same treatise has been discussed another statement of Buddha, in which he said that the cycle of existences has no beginning (*anamataggo yaṃ saṃsāro*) and deduced therefrom that it had a beginning, which was unknowable to the unenlightened, and so also, Buddha's declaration of the non-existence of *ātman* implied that the self (*pudgala*) was unknowable to the imperfect. It has been argued by the S. exponents that the reality or unreality of an object should not be questioned because of the fact that it is unknowable by men of average intelligence. It indicates only lack of knowledge on the part of the imperfect and not existence or non-existence of the real, or even of an unreal object. It is true that the *Arūpa* sphere is unknowable by beings of the *Rūpa* sphere, and so it is not proper to infer from that unknowability that *Arūpaloka* does not exist. Similarly, self (*pudgala*) is unknowable by the unwise, but that does not establish that 'pudgala' is non-existent. Then, again, a minute speck of dust, tip of a hair, mines within the earth, shores of ocean, a handful of salt dissolved in water, a jewel hidden behind a wall, bodies of spirits or ghosts, even the eye-lids which are so close to the eyes are not seen by the common physical eyes, but that does not prove their nonexistence. They are seen by those who possess divine eyes (*divyacakṣu*). Likewise, the beginning of the cycle of existence is unknowable by the unwise but is knowable by the fully enlightened Buddha. Buddha said that the world has no beginning, mainly with a view to seeing that his disciples did not take to the beliefs of eternalism and negativism and to seeing that they might not harbour any notion like "I was, I am and I shall be." If the beginning of the world had been non-existent like the sky-flower or horns of a hare, Buddha would not have cared to state that the world had no beginning, as one does not say that there is no sky-flower or horns of a hare. A spherical object has no beginning but no one says it does not exist, so also with the world of existence (*saṃsāra*). Lastly, if the cycle of existences has no beginning or end, it would be identical with Nirvāṇa, which is also without a beginning or end. From all these arguments, the author of the *Sammitīya-nikāya śāstra* established that Buddha did not fully explain many of his deeper ideas, and the existence of self 'pudgala' is one of them. Buddha's reticence, therefore, should not be taken as the denial of the existence of a 'pudgala' as conceived by the Sammitīyas.

Profs. Stcherbatsky and La Vallée Poussin have furnished the materials of the *Abhidharmakośa* in English and French translations, and at present we have also the original Sanskrit text of its *Vyākhyā*, edited by Prof. Wogihara. On the basis of these three texts, a gist of the arguments of this school for establishing the existence of *pudgala* is presented here. This will be followed up by a summary of the arguments and counter-arguments given in the *Kathāvatthu*, which has not so far received any attention.[1]

The *Kośa* opens the controversy with the question, whether the Vātsīputrīyas can be regarded as Buddhists and whether they are entitled to emancipation (*mokṣa*)? As has been pointed out above, they were regarded by some as Buddhists while by others as non-Buddhists.

The Buddhists believe that since there is no *mokṣa* outside the pale of Buddhism, the non-Buddhists cannot have emancipation, and that is mainly because the non-Buddhist teachers like Kapila and Uluka believe in the existence of a permanent soul, which, according to them, is different from the constituents of a being and is not a term indicating the flux of

1. *Kathāvatthu* (P.T.S.), pp. 1-69, translated in *Points of Controversy* by Mrs. Rhys Davids.

elements[1] (*skandhasantāna*). The soul, the Buddhists assert, can neither be established by direct perception (*pratyakṣa*) nor by inference (*anumāna*).

Vasubandhu (henceforth abbreviated as V.) first defines the contention of the Vātsīputrīyas (henceforth abbreviated as Vā.) thus: Is the pudgala of the Vā. real (*dravya*) or nominal (*prajñapti*)? By real (*dravya*) existence he meant existence like that of *rūpa* and such other elements, and by nominal (*prajñapti*) he meant existence like that of milk, house or army, which has no separate existence of its own apart from its constituents.

If the soul of the Vā. be of the former category (*dravya*), it would be different from the *skandhas*, as *vedanā* is from *rūpa*, and is not also all the skandhas taken together. Now, in that case, it should be either *saṃskṛta* (constituted), or *asaṃskṛta* (unconstituted). It cannot be the latter, for it would make the Vā. hold the *śāśvata* view, which is heretical.

If the soul of the Vā. be of the latter category (*prajñapti*), its existence is dependent on the skandhas, and so it cannot have any independent existence of its own, i.e., it does not exist (*pudgala iti prajñaptir asat-pudgalaḥ prāpnoti*).

The Vā. contend that their soul is real (*dravya*), but it is neither identical with, nor different from, the skandhas as fire is from the fuel. Fire exists as long as the fuel lasts, so also the soul (*pudgala*) exists as long as there are skandhas, otherwise, *pudgala* would be either *asaṃskṛta* (unconstituted), *śāśvata* (eternal) or *saṃskṛta* (constituted), *aśāśvata* (=*uccheda*= annihilating).[2] Fire is different from the fuel inasmuch as it has the power of burning an object to ashes or to produce light, which the fuel does not possess.

Vasubandhu argues that, fuel and fire appear at different

1. *Vyākhyā* (Jap. ed.), p. 697 quotes this *stotra* :

    साहङ्कारे मनसि न शमं याति जन्मप्रबन्धो
    नाहङ्कारश्चलति हृदयादात्मदृष्टौ च सत्याम् ।
    अन्य: शास्ता जगति च यतो नास्ति नैरात्म्यवादी
    नान्यस्तस्मादपशमविधेस्त्वन्मतादस्ति मार्गे ॥

2. Cf. the quotation in the *Kvu*, p. 34 :—
    Khandhesu bhijjamānesu *so* ce bhijjati puggalo
    Ucchedā bhavati diṭṭhi yā Buddhena vivajjitā
    Khandhesu bhijjamānesu *no* ce bhijjati puggalo
    Puggalo sassato hoti nibbānena samasamo.

times (*bhinnakāla*) like seed and sprout. Hence fire is impermanent, and the difference between fuel and fire is one of time and characteristic (*lakṣaṇa*), and again one is the cause of the other.

He then states that according to the Vā., fuel is constituted of three *mahābhūtas*, while fire is of the fourth (*tejas*) only: then it follows that fire is different from fuel.

The Vā. reply that fire and fuel are co-existent and the latter is a support of the former (*upādāya*; *āśritya*), and that one is not wholly different from the other, for fuel is not totally devoid of the fiery element; in the same way, *pudgala* should be distinguished from *skandhas*. Vasubandhu challenges the Vā. by citing the instance of a burning log of wood and saying that it represents both fuel and fire. That is why they are identical (*ananya*).

According to the Vā., *pudgala* is neither to be described as *anitya*, which is sub-divided into past, present and future nor *nitya*, eternal. It is *avaktavya*, indeterminable, inexplicable. It is not included in the list of the constituents of a being, but is perceived when only all the constituents are present.

The question next raised is, can the pudgala of the Vā. be cognized by any sense-organ (*indriya*). If so, by which? The Vā. reply that it is perceived by all the six sense-organs. They contend that eyes do not care to see *rūpa* (object) or recognise it unless the mind (*mana-indriya*) is there. Eyes act as the dominating factor when the visual action takes place, hence it is not correct to say that eyes alone see *rūpa*, or for the matter of that each of the five sense-organs cannot function in their respective spheres independent of the mind.[1] For cognition of *pudgala*, the Vā. state that all the sense-organs point to the mind indirectly that there is a *pudgala*; e.g., eyes discern the *rūpa* (colour-figure) of a body and thereby induce the mind to cognize the presence of an individual (i.e. *pudgala* which is neither identical with, nor different from *rūpa*).[2] V. argues that if *rūpa* be the cause of cognition of *pudgala* (*rūpānāṃ kāraṇatvam adhikriyate*), one should not

1. See above; Cf. Masuda, p. 23n.
2. See *Kośa* (Fr. transl.) ix, p. 231 fn.

say that *rūpa* and *pudgala* are different (*anyaṃ*).[1] Again, if cognition of *rūpa* leads at once to the cognition of *pudgala* (*rūpānyupādāya pudgalopalabdhir iti*), one should also say that *rūpa* and *pudgala* are identical (*ananya*),[2] in other words, one is only a modification of the other (*rūpāntaratvāt*). The Vā., however, would neither identify *rūpa* (colour-figure) with *pudgala* nor treat them as different; in the same way, they would neither regard the perception of *rūpa* (colour-figure) as identical with the perception of *pudgala* nor look upon them as different.

V. asserts that if *pudgala* be an entity, it should be either material (*rūpa*) or non-material (*nāma*), but Buddha says *rūpa* or *vedanā* or *saṃjñā* or *saṃskārā* or *vijñāna* is not self—all dharmas are without self—there is no *pudgala*. He further states that *sattva, jīva, pudgala* is a *prajñapti* (designation) applied to the false notion of a self cherished by the unenlightened.

The Vā. in reply state that they were not prepared to accept the statements attributed to Buddha as authentic[3] as these were not to be found in their Piṭaka. They referred to statements, in which Buddha spoke of a person's past existence or recognised *pubbenivāsañāṇa*[4] as one of the higher acquisitions of an adept, and asked, who is it that remembers? Is it *pudgala* or the *skandhas*? They further argue that if Buddha be regarded as omniscient, i.e., he knows everything past or present, of every place, of every being etc. it also implies a continuity of something. In other words, it implies the existence of a *pudgala*. The Vā. further state that unless there were some form of *pudgala*, why the disciples should be instructed to avoid thinking of *rūpavān ahaṃ babhūvātīte 'dhvani* (in the past I possessed a body) and so forth.[5]

V. refutes this contention by saying that *pudgala* here refers

---

1. Just as light, eyes and mind, which cause the visualisation of an object, are not different from the object. *Ibid.*, p. 238n. See *Vyākhyā*, p. 701.

2. *Ibid.*, p. 239 n. See *Vyākhyā*, pp. 701-2.

3. Cf. *Vyākhyā* : mūlasaṅgītibhraṃśāt.

4. Cf. *Majjhima*, I, p. 22 : so evaṃ samāhite citte parisuddhe pariyodāte anaṅgane . . . pubbenivāsānussarati-ñāṇāya cittam abhininnāmeti.

5. Cf. *Mājjhima*, I, p. 8 : ahosin nu kho aham atītam addhānaṃ . . . kiṃ hutvā kiṃ ahosiṃ nu kho atītam addhānaṃ, etc. etc.

only to *skandha-santāna* (continuity of skandhas), not to anything else. The Vā. then cite the *Bhārahārasūtra*, and assert that by *bhāra* is meant the constituents (*skandhas*) of a being and by *hāra* the individual (*pudgala*), who is known by a name, gotra etc.[1] If *bhāra* (=*skandhas*) included *bhāra-hāra* (=*pudgala*), there was no need of distinguishing the two, and so *pudgala* exists apart from *skandhas*; it is neither identical with, nor different from, *skandhas*.

The Vā, admit the existence of *aupapādika* beings and *antarābhava*,[2] and prove thereby the existence of *pudgala*. They also cite the passage "*ekapuggalo bhikkhave loke uppajjamāno uppajjati bahujanahitāya* (*Aṅguttara*, i. 22) and lay stress on the word 'puggala', saying this 'puggala' is born (*uppajjati*) and hence there is besides the skandhas something, which may be designated as 'puggala'. V. refutes all these by appropriate quotations and arguments.

The Vā. further state that if *pudgala* be only a word meant to designate the five *skandhas*, then why Bhagavān did not identify *jīva* with *śarīra*. V. cites the discussion on the topic from the *Milindapañha*. The Vā. further argue that why 'pudgala' has been declared by Buddha as indeterminable (*avyākṛta*), if it does not exist at all. V. in reply comments on the *Vatsagotra-sūtra* (=Pāli: *Vaccha-gotta sutta*) and other sūtras dealing with the indeterminable problems.

The Vā. point out that the statement *ātmā* does not exist in reality (*satyataḥ sthititaḥ*)[3] is a wrong view, it indirectly implies the admission of the existence of *pudgala*.

The Vā. next raise the question, if 'pudgala' does not exist, who is it that transmigrates from one existence to another ? If the elements only exist, how do you explain when Buddha says, "I was at that time the master Sunetra"? In that statement why is the 'I' of the past identified with the 'I' of the present?

---

1. Cf. *Vyākhyā* (Jap. ed.), p. 706, bhāraḥ katamaḥ. pañcopādāna skandhāḥ . . . bhārahāraḥ katamaḥ. pudgala iti syād vacanīyaṃ yo 'sav āyuṣman evaṃnāmā evaṃjātyā evaṃgotra etc.

2. Cf. *Kośa*, iii, 10, 12, 18-19, quoting Sapta-sat-puruṣa-gati-sūtraṃ.

3. Cf. *Majjhima*, i, p. 8: *Atthi me attā ti* vā'ssa saccato thetato diṭṭhi uppajjati, *natti me attā* ti vā'ssa saccato thetato diṭṭhi uppajjati, etc.

Does it indicate that the elements of the past are the elements of the present ? V. refutes it by saying that just as fire passes from one wood to another, though it never remains the same, so the elements pass from one existence to another, nothing remaining identical. If, according to the Vā., Buddhas admitted the existence of 'pudgala', they would be subject to the wrong belief of *satkāyadṛṣṭi*.

The Vā. now ask, how can memory be explained without the conception of 'pudgala'? Who is it that remembers? V. answers that it is *saṃjñā* that remembers—*saṃjñā* with attention directed to the object, an idea etc. is similar to, or connected with, it, provided there is no corporeal pain to impair its capacity.

The Vā. are of the opinion that there must be an agent, a doer, a proprietor of memory. There must be a cognizing agent, an action must have a doer. 'Devadatta walks' implies the existence of an individuality. V. replies that it is not so. He states that just as when a fire traverses from one forest to another, no question of individuality arises, similarly Devadatta is a *prajñapti* (like fire) applied to a conglomeration of elements passing from one existence to another and has no individuality.[1]

Now, we shall pass on to the arguments of the Vā. and the counter-arguments of the Theravādins as presented in the *Kathāvatthu* (1. i), which is of a much earlier date than that of the medieval and modern dialectical works.

The first question put by the Theravādins to the Vātsīputrīyas known in the Pāli texts as Sammitīyas, is as follows: Can the *puggala* be known in the same way as *that* which is real and ultimate, e.g., *Nibbāna* (or *Rūpa*) is known ? (para 1).[2] In other words, the Theravādins want to ascertain whether the Sammitīyas (henceforth abbreviated as Sam.) admit the existence of *puggala* either as the unchangeable, ever-existing reality like *Nibbāna*, or as a constituted (*sappaccaya*, *saṃkhata*) object like *rūpa*, or regard it as false like a mirage (*māyāmarīci viya*), or look upon it simply as a hearsay. The Sam. deny practically all

1. Kośa-vyākhyā (Jap. ed.), p. 710: yathā tu kṣaṇiko 'gnir iti, etc.

2. "Para" refers to the paragraphs marked in the P. T. S. edition of the *Kathāvatthu*.

the four possibilities, though they assert that the *puggala* is known as a real and ultimate fact (*saccikaṭṭha-paramaṭṭhena*).

The Sam. now assail the Th. with the counter-question whether they would admit that *puggala* is *not* known in the same way as *that* which is real and ultimate. The Th. answered in the affirmative, as, according to them, *puggala* is not even an object like *rūpa*; it is a mere *paññatti* (concept), a *sammuti-sacca* (conventional truth).

But when the same question is repeated by the Sam. (as in paras 2 and 6),[1] the Th. reply in the negative by saying "na h' evaṃ,"[2] because the answer is to be given to a question, which included both *sammutisacca* (conventional truth) and *paramattha-sacca* (the highest truth). The questions and answers which follow next have mixture of both *sammuti* and *paramattha* truths, and so they appear contradictory to a superficial reader.

Now the Th. give up the logical tricks and put the question straightaway (para 11) thus: whether *puggala* is a *paramattha-sacca*[3] or not, *i.e.* whether or not Puggala is known in the same way as the real and ultimate *everywhere* (*sabbattha*) in and out-side *rūpa* (material parts of the body), *always* (*sabbadā*) in this and the following existences, and in *everything* (*sabbesu*), i.e., in all *khandhas, āyatanas, dhātus,* etc. The answer of the Sam. is also definitely in the negative, i.e., they do not consider 'puggala as real in the highest sense, and as existing *everywhere, always* and in *everything* as pointed out by the Th.

The next attempt of the Th. is to find out whether the Sam. regard *puggala* as something existing like any of the 57 elements, *rūpa, vedanā, saññā etc.* The Sam. deny it saying they do not admit *puggala* as an element apart from the 57 elements,[4] and in support of their contention they quote from the Nikāyas (*Dīgha*, iii, 232; *Majjhima,* i. 341*; Aṅguttara,* ii. 95) the passage "atthi puggalo attahitāya paṭipanno," which indicates that *puggala* exists but not apart from the elements. The Th. also

1. The remaining paras 3-5 and 7-10 are mere logical rounding up of the questions and answers put in paras 1 & 2.

2. The question is, — Yo saccikaṭṭho paramaṭṭho tato so puggalo n'upalabbhati saccikaṭṭha-paramaṭṭhenātī ti ?

3. Perhaps like the *jīvātman* of the Vedānta school of philosophy.

4. Samayasuttavirodhaṃ disvā paṭikkhepo paravādissa, *Aṭṭhakathā*, p. 16.

do not clearly state that *puggala* (as a *paññatti*) is different from the elements, the reason assigned by Buddhaghosa[1] is that the questions of the opponents have a mixture of *sammuti* and *paramattha* truths, and as such the Th. have no other alternative but to leave them unanswered (*ṭhapanīya*).[2]

The next attempt of the Th. is to show that the Sam. should advocate either *Ucchedavāda* or *Sassatavāda.* With this end in view, the Th. put the questions whether *puggala* is identical with or different from *rūpa*, or *puggala* is in *rūpa* (like the container and the contained) or vice versa. The Sam. reject all the four propositions as, otherwise, they would become either an Ucchedavādin or a Sassatavādin. Though, according to the Sam., *puggala* is of the same nature (*ekadhammo*) as *rūpa* and other elements,[3] they would not treat it as an element separate from, and independent of, the 57 elements.

The Th. now assail their opponents by questioning on *lakkhaṇas* of *puggala*, and ask whether *puggala* is *sappaccaya* (caused) or *appaccaya* (uncaused) like *Nibbāna.* The Sam. deny both and ask how the Th. would explain the 'puggala' in the statement of Buddha: 'Atthi puggalo attahitāya paṭipanno ti.' Is the 'puggala' referred to in this passage *sappaccaya, saṃkhata* or *appaccayya, asaṃkhata?* The Th. deny both, as in their opinion the term *puggala* is only a *sammutisacca*, and as such it is non-existent.

The next argument put forward by the Th. is, whether the statement "*puggala* perceives" is the same as the statement, "that which perceives is *puggala*"[4] i.e. whether the two statements are identical as *citta* is with *mano* or different as *rūpa* is from *vedanā.* Buddhaghosa interprets the position of the opponents thus: the Sam. hold that *puggala* perceives, but not everything that perceives is *puggala*; e.g., *rūpa, vedanā*, etc. are not *puggala*, but *puggala* perceives and that which perceives refers only to the percepient (*puggala*), and not to *rūpādi.*[1] The opponents, however, rely on the statement "atthi puggalo

1. See his *Aṭṭhakathā*, p. 16.

2. *Kvu.*, pp. 14-17, paras 130-137 dilate on the above question, comparing 'puggala' with each of the 57 elements.

3. *Aṭṭhakathā*, p. 18.

4. Puggalo upalabbhati (yo yo) upalabbhati (so so) puggalo ti ? *Kvu.*, p. 24.

attahitāya paṭipanno ti" which again is countered by the Th. by saying that the Sam. should equally rely on the statement "suññato lokaṃ avekkhassu, etc." and admit that there is no *puggala*.

The Th. now proceed to examine the *paññatti* (description) of *puggala*. In answer to the question, whether the *puggala* of the *Rūpadhātu* is *rūpī* and likewise of the *Kāmadhātu* is *kāmī* and of the *Arūpadhātu*, *arūpī*, the Sam. affirm the first and the third but not the second. The Sam. argue that *puggala*=*satta*=*jīva* and *kāya*=*sarīra*. Though they do not admit either the identity of, or difference between, *jīva* and *sarīra*, they hold, though not logically tenable, that *kāya* must be different from *puggala* as there are such statements as 'so kāye kāyānupassī viharati and so forth,' in which *so* cannot but refer to *puggala*.

The next discussion relating to *upādā-paññatti* (rebirth) of *puggala* raises the question of transmigration. The Sam. affirm that *puggala* passes from this existence to next but it is neither the self-same puggala nor a different puggala—a statement similar to what the Th. would say about the passing of the *khandhas*—avoiding the two heretical opinions of *sassatavāda* and *ucchedavāda* as also the *ekaccasassatikavāda* and *amarāvikkhepikadiṭṭhi*.[2] In support of their contention the Sam. quote the passages in which a 'puggala' is said to pass from one existence to another (*sandhāvati saṃsarati*).

According to the opinion of the opponents that the self-same, or a different, *puggala* does not pass from one existence to another, the Th. point out that they admit that some form of *puggala* referred to in the above-mentioned passages, does pass from one existence to another. This *puggala* can then have no death, it once becomes a man and then a god and so forth, which is absurd.[3] In reply, the Sam. point out that a sotāpanna-

1. *Aṭṭhakathā*, p. 20: The opponents say : Mama puggalo, atthi puggalo 'ti satthuvacanto upalabbhati. Yo pana upalabbhati, na so sabbo puggalo. Atha kho ke hi ci na puggalo ke hi ci na puggalo 'ti. *Tattha kokāratthe kekāro hikāro co nipātamatta.* Koci puggalo koci na puggalo 'ti ayaṃ pan' ettha attho. Idaṃ vuttaṃ hoti : puggalo pi hi rūpādīsu pi yo koci dhammo upalabbhati yeva. Tattha puggalo 'va puggalo rūpādīsu pana koci pi na puggalo 'ti.

2. See my *Early Monastic Buddhism* (1941), I, pp. 63 ff.

3. See my *Early Monastic Buddhism* (1941) I, p. 63 f.

manussa is known to take rebirth as a sotāpanna-deva and question how can this sotāpanna-hood pass from one existence to another unless there exists some form of *puggala* to carry the qualities. In order to show the unsoundness of the statement, the Th. ask whether the passing *puggala* remains identical in every respect[1] and does not lose any of its qualities.[2] The opponents first negative it on the ground that a man does not continue to be a man in the *devaloka*; but on second thought they affirm it in view of the fact that the carrier of certain qualities from one existence to another is a *puggala,* an *antarābhava-puggala.*[3] The Sam. take care to keep clear of the two extreme views; *taṃ jīvaṃ taṃ sarīraṃ* and *aññaṃ jīvaṃ aññaṃ sarīraṃ*. They affirm that the transformed *khandhas* and *puggala,* and not the identical *khandhas* and *puggala*, pass from one existence to another. The *khandhas* are, however, impermanent and constituted, while the *puggala* is not so, but it is not permanent and unconstituted either. Without *khandha, āyatana, dhātu, indriya* and *citta, puggala* cannot remain alone but for that reason, the colour and other qualities of the *khandha, āyatana,* etc. do not affect the *puggala.* Again the *puggala* is not a shadow (*chāyā*) of the khandhas.

In reply to the question, whether the *puggala* is perceivable in every momentary thought, the Sam. answer in the affirmative, but they would not accept the inference drawn by the Th. that the *puggala* in that case would have momentary existence (*khaṇika-bhāvaṃ*), i.e,, would disappear and re-appear every moment like *cetasikas* (thoughts).

The Sam. now ask the Th. whether they would admit that one (*yo*) who sees something (*yaṃ*) by means of an organ of sense (*yena*) is the *puggala* or not. The Th., after assenting to it as a conventional truth (*sammuti-sacca*), put the same question in the negative form thus: One (*yo*), who[4] does not see anything (*yaṃ*) by means of an organ of sense (*yena*), is

1. Anañño=sabbākārena ekasadiso.

2. Avigato=ekena pi ākāreṇa avigato.

3. The self which exists between death and rebirth. See above pp. 114, 125.

4. E.g., a blind man, an asaññisatta.

not a *puggala*. The Sam., however, without arguing further, quote a few passages, in which Buddha said: I (i.e. the *puggala*, according to the Saṃ.) see by means of my divine eyes (*dibbena cakkhuṇā*) beings appearing and disappearing and so forth, and infer therefrom that the seer is *puggala*.

Their next discussions related to *purusakāra*. The Th. do not admit the existence of any *doer*, so they asked the Sam. whether the latter would subscribe to the same opinion. On their denial the Th. ask whether the Sam. would admit the existence of the doer, and a creator of the doer, which is negatived by the Sam. on account of the heretical doctrine of *issaranimmāṇa* (God the creator of the world) but which on second thought is affirmed by them in view of the fact that the parents, teachers etc. are also in a sense the makers (*kattā, kāretā*) of a person. The Th. without going into the implied sense of the replies, say that such a state of things (i.e., a doer having a doer and a deed which implies not just a deed but also a doer) would lead to the conclusion that so long as there is deed (*kammo*), there is its doer (*kārako puggalo*), and hence there can be no end to *puggala-paramparā* and that would falsify the fact that by the stoppage of the wheel of actions, *dukkha* can be brought to an end. Then again nibbāna, mahāpaṭhavī, etc. must also have a doer. All the inferences drawn by the Th. are rejected by the Sam. In conclusion, the Sam. deny that the deed and the doer can be distinct, just to avoid admitting that the *puggala* has mental properties.

While in the above discussion, the doer of a deed is enquired into in the following discussion it is the identity of the doer of a deed with the enjoyer of its fruit that is enquired into.

The Th. deny the existence of a feeler or enjoyer apart from *vipāka-pavatti* (that which is realized, that fructification of an effect). The Sam. hold that *patisaṃveditabba* is *vipāka* (result) but the *puggala* is not *vipāka*.[1] They further state that Nibbāna

1. But it may happen that *puggala*, who is in the enjoyment of his fruits (i.e. merits), may be again an object of enjoyment of another puggala, e.g. a son enjoying the fruits of his actions may be the object of affection of his mother, and so forth. This explanation of Buddhaghosa should be compared with the above like the *kāretā* of *kattā*.

or Mahāpaṭhavī, etc. is not *vipāka* like *divine happiness* (dibbasukha) or *human happiness* (manussasukha) so none of them is an object of enjoyment of the *puggala* but again the Sam. do not admit that *sukha* is distinct from the *sukha-enjoyer*. The Th. logically wanted to make their opponents admit that there must not only be an enjoyer of a fruit but also an enjoyer of the enjoyer of the fruit and so on like an endless chain; in other words, according to them, as shown above, *dukkha* can have no end.

The Th. now put the crucial question thus: whether the doer of a deed is identical with, or different from, the enjoyer of its fruit. The opponents first deny both to avoid contradiction in Buddha's saying; *sayaṃ kataṃ paraṃ kataṃ sukhadukkhaṃ,* etc. but on second thought, in view of their theory that there is a common element keeping the link between the present and the future life, they admit it. In short, the Sam. affirm that there is a *kāraka* (doer) and *vedaka* (feeler or enjoyer) of a deed, but the two are neither identical nor different, neither both identical and different, nor not both identical and different.

The Sam. next apply the test of *abhiññā* (supernormal powers), *ñāti* (relatives) and *phala* (attainments) and put the arguments thus:

(i) How can a person perform certain miracles keeping his organs of sense. etc. inert and inactive, unless there is something else as *puggala.*

(ii) How can one recognize the existence of parents, castes, etc. without positing that there is a *puggala,* and

(iii) How can a *phalastha* continue to be the same in more than one life, unless the existence of a *puggala* is admitted.

The Th. avoid the issues by submitting the counter-argument to the effect that one who cannot perform miracles is not a *pudgala.* In this way they refute the other two arguments.

The next question of the Th. is whether the *puggala* is constituted (*saṃkhato*) or unconstituted or neither constituted nor unconstituted (*n'eva saṃkhat nāsaṃkhato*). The Sam. affirm the last alternative but would not treat the *puggala* as something apart (*añño*) from the *saṁkhat khandhas.* They state that the *puggala* has certain aspects of *saṃkhata,* e.g., it is subject to sukha, dukkha, and so forth; again it has certain aspects of *asaṃkhata*, e. g., it is not subject to birth, old age and death (*jāti*, *jarā*, and *maraṇa*).

In reply to the Th.'s question whether a *parinibbuto puggalo* exists in Nibbāna or not, the Sam. negative both, as the affirmation of either would make them either a Sassatavādin or an Ucchedavādin.

Now the Sam. put the counter-question: Does not a person say that he is feeling happy or unhappy and so forth ? How can a person say so unless he is a *puggala* and not a mere conglomeration of separate khandhas ? In refuting this contention, the Th. put the same question in a negative form thus: Well, if a person does not feel happiness or unhappiness, then there is no *puggala*. The Th. further ask whether Sam. would treat *sukha* and *puggala* as something separate and distinct. The Sam. evade a direct answer and ask: Well, when a *puggala* (*koci* or *so*) is said to be *kāye kāyānupass viharati*, does it not affirm the existence of a puggala ?

The controversy is then closed by citations of passages from the Nikāyas, the Th. quoting only those which clearly express *anattā* of all things, while the Sam. quote those passages in which the word *puggala* or *attahito* or *so* appear.

Through these controversies, it is apparent that the Sam. are seeking to establish that the five khandhas which are distinct from one another cannot give rise to the consciousness of I-ness, a unity. The facts that a person acts or thinks as one and not as five separate objects, that in many passages Buddha does actually use the words *so*, *attā* and *puggala*, that a person's attainments like *sotāpannahood* continue to be the same in different existences, and that one speaks of his past existences, and so forth, do lead to the conclusion that, besides the five khandhas, there exists some mental property which forms the basis of I-ness, and maintains the continuity of *karma* from one existence to another. That mental property, however, is changing khandhas but in view of the fact that one can think of his past, even of the events of his past existences, the changing khandhas alone cannot be made responsible for the memory. The Sam. therefore affirm the existence of a sixth (mental) property and call it *puggala*, which can remain only along with khandhas and so must disappear when the khandhas disappear in Nibbāna. As this mental property or *puggala* is not *kṣaṇika* (constituted, momentary object) and again, as it is not also unchanging and ever existing like Nibbāna, so it is not *asaṃkhata*. Therefore the *puggala* must be admitted to be neither *saṃkhata* nor *asaṃkhata*.[1]

Referring to the *pudgala-vāda* of the Sam., Śāntarakṣita in his *Tattvasaṅgraha*, ch. vii (f) remarks jokingly that the Saugatas (*i.e.*, the Buddhists) as the upholders of the *anattā* doctrine should bother their head with identity and difference of the doer of a deed and the enjoyer of its fruit. Śāntarakṣita, of course, dismisses both *anattāvāda* and *pudgala-vāda* from the standpoint of the Vedānta school of philosophy, according to which the eternality of *ātman* is maintained.

Vasumitra summarizes the doctrines of the Sammitīyas or the Vātsīputrīyas thus:

1. The *pudgala* is neither the same as the *skandhas* nor different from the *skandhas*. The name *pudgala* is provisionally given to an aggregate of *skandhas*, *āyatanas* and *dhātus*.

2. Dharmas cannot transmigrate from one existence to another apart from the *pudgala*. These can be said to transmigrate along with the *pudgala*.

Other doctrines

Vasumitra attributes to the Vātsīputrīyas a few other views which have already been discussed. These are:

(i) The five vijñānas conduce neither to *sarāga* (desire) nor to *virāga* (removal of desires);[2]

(ii) To become free from desire (*virāga*), one must relinquish the *saṃyojanas* which can be destroyed by an adept when he

---

1. Cf. Obermiller's *Analysis of the Abhisamayālaṃkāra*, III, p. 380, referring to *Tarkajvālā* and Schayer, *Kamalaśīla's Kritik des Pudgalavāda*. Obermiller writes 'the Vātsīputrīyas, Bhadrayānikas, Sāṃmityas. Dharmaguptas and Saṃkrāntivādins are those that admit the reality of the 'individual.' They say that the 'individual' is something inexpressible, being neither identical with the five groups of elements nor different from them. It is to be cognised by the six forms of *vijñānas*, and is subject to *saṃsāra* (phenomenal existence).

2. See *ante*, pp. 110, 169.

reaches *bhāvanāmārga*, and not while he remains in *darśanamārga*.

(iii) When one has entered the *samyaktvanyāma*, one is called *pratipannaka* in the first twelve moments of the *darśanamārga* and when one is in the thirteenth moment one is called *phalastha*.[1]

(iv) There is *antarābhava*.[2] The Sammitīyas, like the Sarvāstivādins, hold that every being, whether destined for Kāmaloka or Rūpaloka by his *karma*, remains for some time in an intermediate state of existence. At that time the body takes no material form, not even the *skandhas*. It is not an independent state of existence but just a waiting stage preliminary to its existence in one of the two lokas. The Sammitīyas add that those beings, who are destined for hells, or Asaññī sphere, or Arūpaloka, have no *antarābhava*.

(v) *Parihāyati arahā arahattā ti* (*Kvu.* 1. 2).[3]

(vi) *N'atthi devesu brahmacariyāvāso ti* (*Kvu.* 1. 3).[4]

(vii) *Odhisodhiso kilese jahatīti* (*Kvu.* 1. 4).[5]

(viii) *Jahati puthujjano kāmarāga-byāpādan ti* ? (*Kvu.* 1. 5).[6]

DHAMMUTTARĪYA, BHADRAYĀNĪYA AND CHAN-NĀGARIKA

Vasumitra skips over the special doctrines of these three schools,[7] mentioning in verse only that they differed regarding the attainments of an *arhat*, and the consequent chances of his fall from arhathood. It seems that in other matters, these three schools agreed with the views of the Sammitīyas. In the *Kvu.* II 4 : To the Bhadrayānikas is attributed the doctrine of "anupubbābhisamaya" (gradual realization of the four truths). In the *Kvu. aṭṭhakathā* (p. 56), to the Chan-nagarikas is attributed the

1. Cf. Masuda's notes in the *Asia Major*, II. p. 56. In short, the *Sammitīyas* count in all the fourteen moments instead of Sarvāstivādins' sixteen; so the 13th moment of the Sammitīyas corresponds to the 15th of the Sarvāstivādins; see p. 164-5.

2. See *ante*, pp. 114, 125.

3. See *ante*, pp. 82, 108.

4. See *ante*, p. 163.

5. See *ante*, p. 165.

6. See *ante*, p. 166.

7. See *ante*, p. 30

doctrine *Dukkhāhāroti* i.e., the *utterance* of the word "dukkha" leads to knowledge (ñāṇa) (cf. above p. 110).

VIBHAJYAVĀDA

This is one of the schools enlisted by Bhavya and Vinītadeva, but not by Vasumitra. It does not appear in the list of schools of the Ceylonese chronicles. Bhavya and Vinītadeva treat it as an offshoot of the Sarvāstivāda school. Prof. La Vallée Poussin has traced in the Chinese commentary of the *Vijñaptimātratā-siddhi* a passage in which Vibhajyavādins are identified with Prajñaptivādins.[1] This apparently refers to the Bahuśrutīya-vibhajyavādins,[2] by which name the Prajñaptivādins distinguished themselves from the Bahuśrutīyas. Prof. Poussin has shown that the position of the Vibhajyavādins cannot be clearly made out as their doctrines have much in common with the doctrines of the Sarvāstivādins, Mahāsaṅghikas, Sammitīyas and others. To add to this confusion, we have the Ceylonese tradition in which the Pāli school, i.e., the Theravādins, preferred to call itself Vibhajyavādins.[3] This anomalous position of the Vibhajya-vādins, it seems, may be explained by regarding them not as an independent school, but as a term denoting those who did not accept the doctrines of a particular school in toto.[4] It may be shown that those Sarvāstivādins, who did not accept the *sarvam asti* thesis in toto and held instead the opinion that the past, which has not yet produced its fruits, and the future do not exist were known as Vibhajyavādin, i.e., Sarvāstivāda-vibhajyavādin, just as we have Bahuśrutīya-vibhajyavādin. On this analogy we may say that among the Theravādins there were perhaps some dissenting groups, who were distinguished as

1. *Kośa*, Intro., p. lv.
2. See above, p. 101.
3. *Mahāvaṃsa*, p. 54.
4. See *Kośa*, Index, p. lvi; V. p. 23-24 fn., quoting *Arthapradīpa*, 3, p. 48. "Les Vibhajyavādins ou bien sont des maitres divergents du Grand Véhicule, ou bien toutes les écoles du Petit Vehicule sont nommées Vibhajya-vādins : ceux-ci ne sont pas une école déterminée. Par conséquent, dans le *Mahāyānasaṅgraha* (Nanjio 1183), les Vibhajyavādins sont expliqués comme Mahīśāsakas; dans la Vibhāṣā, comme Sāṃmitīyas."

Theravāda-vibhajyavādins. The Ceylonese monks of Mahāvihāra probably preferred to call themselves Vibhajjavādin as we find it clearly expressed in the versified table of contents of chapter III of the Cullavagga[1] and in the colophon of the commentary on the *Tikapaṭṭhāna*,[2] as also in the *Dīpavaṃsa* (xviii. 41, 44). In the account of the Third Council, as given in the Ceylonese chronicles,[3] as also in Buddhaghoṣa's commentary,[4] the Vibhajjavādins are declared to be orthodox monks.[5]

As Vasumitra does not count the Vibhajyavādins as one of the sects, he has not mentioned any special doctrines of theirs. It is only in the *Abhidharmakośa* that we come across certain doctrines attributed to this sect. Evidently Vasubandhu had in his mind the Sarvāstivāda-vibhajyavādins. The doctrines summarized by Prof. La Vallée Poussin are in short as follows :—

i. Sound is an effect (saddo vipāko, *Kvu.* xii. 3; *Kośa*, i. 37).

ii. The faculties of faith, memory, etc. (śraddhendriya, smṛtīndriya etc.) are pure (*anāsrava*). (*Kośa*, ii. 9).

iii. There is no intermediate state of existence (*antarābhava*) (*Kośa*, *iii*. 10).

iv. Pratītyasamutpāda is unconstituted (*asaṃskṛta*) (*Kośa*, ii. 28).

v. Abhidhyā, vyāpāda, mithyādṛṣṭi are physical acts (*kāyika*).

1. See *Vinaya*, CV., pp. 72, 312 : ācariyānaṃ Vibhajjavādānaṃ Tambapaṇṇidīpapasādakānaṃ Mahāvihāravāsīnaṃ vācanā saddhammaṭṭhitiyā ti.

2. *Tika-paṭṭhāna* (Cy.), p. 366 : ācariyānaṃ vādam avihāya Vibhajjavādi-sissānaṃ etc.; p. 567 : theravaṃsappadīpānaṃ therāguaṃ Mahāvihāravāsīnaṃ vaṃsālaṇkūrabhūtena vipula-visuddha-buddhinā Buddhaghoso ti . . . therena katā.

3. *Mahāvaṃsa*, V, 271.

4. *Kathāvatthu-aṭṭhakathā*, p. 6.

5. Before Vibhajjavāda came to be regarded as a sect, it meant those who dealt with the metaphysical problems analytically, from a particular standpoint as opposed to those who solved the problems straightway (*ekaṃsavādin*) by a direct answer. See *Majjhimā*, II, pp. 99, 107; cf. *EMB.*, I, p. 124 : Vibhajjavyākaraṇīya and Ekaṃsavyākaraṇīya. In the *Majjhima* I, p. 163; *Papañcasūdanī*, II, p. 171, Buddha declared that he knew *theravāda*, which, according to Buddhaghoṣa, meant thirabhāvavāda (mental steadiness). Though these two terms, *Vibhajjavāda* and *Theravāda*, were used in the Nikāyas. they did not denote any sect, but we may take them to mean the source, from which the sectarian name issued later on.

vi. Bhagavān is always in meditation (*Kośa*, Fr. transl. iv. p. 43 n.) and has no *middha* (torpor) (*Ibid*).

vii. Vibhavatṛṣṇā is abandoned by bhāvanā (*Kośa*, vi. 10-11).

viii. Arhats have no fall from Arhathood (*Kośa*. vi. 58).

ix. There are 43 Bodhipakṣika-dharmas (*Kośa*. vi. p. 281 n.) : the six additional dharmas are anicca-saññā, dukkha-s., anattars., pahāna-s., virāga-s., and nirodha-s.

x. There is *rūpa* (matter) in the Ārūpya-dhātu (*Kośa*. viii. 3. *Kośa*, Fr. transl, p. 135 n.).

Some schools like the Andhakas, Mahāsaṅghikas, Mahīśāsakas point out that *rūpa* exists in Ārūpyadhātu but in a very subtle state. The contention of the Vibhajyavādins is possibly the same as that of the *Tāmraparṇīyas*[1] (*Kośa* i, 38) who state that *mano-dhātu* is a material organ, which they call *hadaya-vatthu* (see *Visuddhamagga*, p. 447). This basis of *mano-dhātu*, which is material, exists in the Ārūpyadhātu also.

xi. The Ārya of the 4th Ārūpya (i.e.- nevasaṃjñānāsaṃjñā-yatana) dhātu obtains arhathood without the aid of the *magga*. This is a doctrine of the Mahīśāsakas.

xii. There are twelve viparyāsas, (see *Kośa-vyākhyā* p. 454), of which eight are removed in *darśanamārga* and four in *bhāvanāṃārga* (*Kośa*, v. p. 23 n.).

xiii. *Jñāna* is the same as *dharmas*, which are good by nature (*svabhāvataḥ*), while *vijñāna* means those *dharmas* which are good by association (*samprayogataḥ*) with *jñāna* (*Kośa*. iv. p. 33 n.; ix. p. 248 n).

xiv. Realization of the four truths takes place all at once, and not gradually[2] (*Kośa*. vi, pp. 123, 185).

1. *Vyākhyā*, p. 39.
2. See above, p. 88.

CHAPTER IX

DOCTRINES OF GROUP V SCHOOLS

Sthavirvāda or Theravāda

(including Mahāviharavāsins and Abhayagirivāsins)

According to both Pāli and Sanskrit traditions, the original school, which the Ceylonese chronicles[1] do not count as schismatic, was called Theravāda or Sthaviravāda.

An alternative name of the Sthaviravādins is given as Vibhajyavādins. It is doubtful whether there was any independent school having the name of Vibhajyavāda. It has been shown above (p. 208) that Vibhajyavāda was sometimes affixed to the name of a school on account of certain adherents differing in minor points from the principal doctrines of a particular school and preferring to distinguish themselves as Vibhajyavādins of that particular school. In this way, we may explain the Vibhajyavāda of the Ceylonese tradition, that is, the Ceylonese did not accept in toto the doctrines of Theravāda and preferred to distinguish themselves as Sthavira-vibhajjavādī or simply as Vibhajjavādī. In the *Kathāvatthu,* the term Sakavāda is used instead of Sthaviravāda or Vibhajjavāda.[2]

Hiuen Tsang speaks of a group of monks as Mahāyānists of the Sthavira school. From his records,[3] it seems that he divided the monks of Ceylon into two groups, calling the Mahāvihāravāsins as Hīnayāna-Sthaviras and the Abhayagirivāsins as Mahāyāna-Sthaviras. He came across such Mahāyānist Sthaviras in the Mahābodhi-saṅghārāma, built at Gaya by a king of Ceylon,[4]

1. *Dīpavaṃsa*, V. 51 : Sattarasa bhinnavādā eko vādo abhinnako. See Watters, I, p, 164.
2. *Points of Controversy*, p. xli.
3. Watters, II, p. 234.
4. Watters, II, p. 138.

and also in Kaliṅga[1] and Surat.[2] In the monasteries of Samataṭa,[3] Drāviḍa,[4] he says, the monks belonged to the Sthavira school. No mention is made of Mahāyāna. He was aware of the split of the Buddhist church into two schools, Sthaviras and Mahāsaṅghikas and quite deliberately used the expression Mahāyānist Sthaviras. His remarks about the division of monks in Ceylon remind us of the Ceylonese tradition according to which the Abhayagiri monastery became for some time a centre of the Vetulyakas, the immediate forerunners of the Mahāyānists,[5] and very probably the Chinese pilgrim referred to the Vetulyakas or the monks generally living in the Abhayagiri monastery as Sthaviras of the Mahāyāna school. By Mahāyānist Sthaviras, Hiuen Tsang[6] probably meant those monks who followed Vinaya rules of the Sthaviravādins but held doctrinal views of the Mahāyānists, like *Suññatā* doctrine of the Vetulyakas.

In the *Abhidharmakoṣa* and its *bhāṣya*,[7] certain erudite monks are referred to as Sthaviras, e.g., Sthavira Saṃghabhadra, Sthavira Vasubandhu, Sthavira Śrīlāta while the Chinese commentators on the texts point out that by "nikāyāntara", the text referred to the Sthavira school. In the *Kośavyākhyā* (p. 705), there is a reference to the *Tāmraparṇīya-nikāya*. These references, however, are inadequate for drawing any conclusion.

Leaving aside for the present the Haimavatas, or the Mahāyānist Sthaviras, let us turn to the original Sthavira school, the Sthaviravādins of the Mahāvihāra of Ceylon. Vasumitra passed over the doctrines of this school while the *Kathāvatthu* referred to them by the word *sakavāda*. For the purpose of finding out the distinctive doctrines of this school, we shall elicit from the *Kathāvatthu* the views of the *Sakavādins* as against those of other schools on any particular doctrine.

Centres of popularity

The Tibetan traditions ascribe the foundation of this school to Mahākaccāyana,[8] who was a native of Ujjaini and son of the

1. *Watters*, II, p. 109.
2. *Ibid.*, II, p. 248.
3. Watters, Yuan Chwang, II, p. 188.
4. *Ibid.*, II, p. 226.
5. Watters, I, p. 164; II, p. 161.
6. See above p. 99 f.
7. See *Kośa*, index, *sv*. Sthavira.
8. See also *Mahākarmavibhaṅga*, pp. 61-2.

priest of king Caṇḍa Pajjota of Avantī. The Pāli traditions, however, give prominence to Upāli, and speak of the succession of his disciples, the chief of whom was Dāsaka. The latter's disciples were Siggava and Caṇḍavajji, who were young at the time of the Second Buddhist Council.[1]

The events of the Second Council, in which the Theravādins became separated from the main body, indicate that the monks of the west, especially of Kauśāmbī and Avantī, formed the nucleus of this sect. The biography of Mahinda, who is mainly responsible for the propagation of this school of Buddhism in Ceylon, also shows that this school was more popular in the west of India than in the east. Taking into consideration all these facts, it may be stated that the Theravādins had one centre at Pāṭaliputra along with other schools, but were chiefly concentrated in and around Ujjaini, which became its second but more important centre.

In the Sarnath inscription,[2] there is a reference to the existence of the Theravādins at that place in the early days, while in the Nāgārjunakoṇḍa inscriptions, mention is made of the activities of this sect in the propagation of Buddhism. In the *Maṇimekalai*, we find that it had its popularity in countries around Kāñcī, which became one of their principal centres in the post-Christian eras.[3] The fact that Buddhaghoṣa and Dhammapāla had their training at Kāñcī goes to show that Kāñcī became later the educational seat of the Theravādins. After Mahinda's demise, the school obtained a firm footing in Ceylon and made the Mahāvihāra its chief academic centre. Hiuen Tsang saw one hundred monasteries of the Sthavira school in Drāviḍa and also in Samataṭa. He says that Dhammapāla was born in the Drāviḍa country.[4] From this survey, it may be inferred that the

1. *Aṭṭhasālinī* (p. 32) however gives prominence to the disciples of Sāriputta, the chief of the Ābhidhammikas thus: Sāriputta-Bhaddaji-Sobhita-Piyajālī-Piyapāla-Piyadassi-Kosiyaputta-Siggava-Sandeva-Moggaliputta, etc. Moggaliputta Tissa was a disciple of Siggava and Caṇḍavajji. See *Samantapāsādikā*, I, p. 40.

2. See above p. 135n.

3. See Aiyangar, 'A Buddhist School at Kāñcī (*Proceedings of the 4th Oriental Conference*, Allahabad).

4. Watters, II, p. 226.

school originated at Pāṭaliputra, became popular in the western countries, made Ujjaini its second centre, and then it gradually made headway towards the south, settling in and around Kāñcī, and ultimately established itself in Ceylon.

Language

According to the Tibetan traditions, this school had its Piṭaka in the Paiśāci dialect. Much value is attached to this tradition. Grierson holds that Paiśāci had its home in the North-west (Kekaya and Gandhāra, i.e. near Taxila) and that it gradually made its way to the western countries as far as the Konkan coast.[1] Guṇāḍhya, who belonged to Ujjaini, it is said, wrote *Bṛhatkathā* in Paiśāci.[2] On philological ground, Sten Konow localizes Paiśāci around the Vindhya hills. He holds that Pāli is the literary form of Paiśāci. The traditions preserved in the Ceylonese chronicles also indicate that Pāli had its home somewhere in Avantī. So it is plausible that the Tibetan tradition should refer to Pāli as literary Paiśāci.

Literature

The whole of Pāli literature belongs to this school, and as such it hardly needs any comment. The only information that we should add is that Hiuen Tsang records that he carried to China fourteen volumes of the Sthavira Sūtras, Śāstras and Vinaya. No Sinologist has so far dealt with this literature, which is why we are still in the dark about the Sthaviras, whose literature the Chinese pilgrim had in view.

Doctrines

The Theravāda doctrines are fairly well-known and have been given in detail in the present author's *Early Monastic Buddhism*. Our object here will be to mention the differences which this school had with other schools as pointed out by Vasumitra and

1. *Bhandarkar Commemoration Volume*, pp. 119-20; see also *JRAS*. 1921, pp. 244-5; 424-8.

2. *ZDMG*., LXVI, (1910), pp. 114f.

Buddhaghoṣa. Since these differences have been discussed in detail in connection with the doctrines of each school, these are not repeated here. It should be noted that the doctrines of the Sarvāstivādins, Sammitīyas, Mahīśāsakas, Sautrāntikas and the Mahāsaṅghikas have been mainly kept in view.

The views of the Theravādins, as against the opinions of the above-mentioned schools are as follows :—

Re. Buddhas :

(i) Buddhas possess *rupakāya* and worldly attributes and are subject to all the physical frailties of a human being; it is the attainment of *bodhi* that makes a being Buddha.
(ii) Buddhas are above *maitrī* and *karuṇā*, but they do show *maitrī* and *karuṇā* to beings.
(iii) Buddhas cannot expound all the doctrines through a single utterance.

Re. Bodhisattvas:

(i) Bodhisattvas are average beings and are subject to *kleśas*.
(ii) They are not self-born (*upapāduka*).

Re. Reals:

Past and future *dharmas* do not exist, not even their *dharmatva*. To say that an Arhat has *atīta rāga* though ineffective is wrong.

Re. Arhat:

(i) Arhats are perfect, hence they cannot have a fall from arhathood. They possess both *kṣayajñāna* (i.e. the knowledge that they have no more *kleśas*) and *anutpādajñāna* (i.e. the knowledge that they will have no more rebirths). There are, however, two grades of Arhats, *viz.*, *svadharmakuśala and paradharmakuśala* as mentioned above, p. 24).
(ii) Arhats, having reached the stage which is beyond merit and demerit, cannot accumulate merits or be subject to the influence of the past *karman*.

(iii) All Arhats practise the four *dhyānas* and enjoy their fruits.

(ix) All Arhats attain *Nirvāṇa.*

Re. Puthujjana :

An average being does not fully eradicate from his mind attachment (*rāga*) and hatred (*dosa*) but he may die in a good state of mind.

Re. Meditation :

(i) In the state of *samāhita*, one cannot utter words.
(ii) An Arhat cannot die while in the highest *samādhi* (*saññā-vedayitanirodha*).

Re. Antarābhava :

There is no intermediate state of existence (*antārābhava*) in the *Kāma* and *Rūpa dhātus.*

Re. Pudgala :

(i) Pudgala does not exist in the highest sense.
(ii) There is nothing which can transmigrate from one existence to another.

Re. Anuśayas and *Paryavasthānas* :

Anuśayas (dormant passions) and *Paryavasthānas* (*pariyuṭṭhānas* in Pali=pervading passions) are *caitasikas* (mental states), *citta samprayuktaḥ* (associated with mind), and have objects of thought (*na anārammaṇa*).

Re. Vijñānas :

The five *vijñānas* conduce as much to attachment to the objects of the world as to detachment from the same.

Re. Asaṃskṛtas :

There are three *asaṃskṛtas* (unconstituted), viz., *pratisaṃkhyā-nirodha, apratisaṃkhyā-nirodha* and *ākāśa*, and not nine (see above, p. 125).

Re. Brahmacarya of gods :

The gods, except the *Asaññisattas*, may practise *magga-bhāvanā* though they do not have ordination according to the Vinaya rules.

Re. Anupubbābhisamaya :

(i) The adepts realize the truths gradually.
(ii) They get rid of *kleśas* (impurities) also gradually.
(iii) They may, only in exceptional cases, realize the four *sāmaññaphalas*, including *vimutti* all at once.

Re. Laukika and *Lokottara* :

All the practices and fruits after *śrota-āpattiphala* are supramundane (*lokottara*), and not worldly (*laukika*).

EPILOGUE

The First Buddhist Council, which was presided over by Mahākassapa, was held soon after Bhagavān Buddha's demise in 487 or 483 B.C. Ānanda, the constant companion of Buddha, recited the Teacher's sayings, later codified as the Sutta Piṭaka, while Upāli, the foremost Vinayist, recited the disciplinary rules prescribed for the observance of monks and nuns, later codified as the Vinaya Piṭaka. The proceedings of the Council were approved by all the monks present except by Purāṇa of Dakkhiṇāgiri, who wanted incorporation of slight changes in the seven or eight rules relating to the cooking, storage and eating of food by monks. This difference being of a minor nature, no dissension took place in the Saṅgha, though later, the earlier Mahīśāsakas included these 7 or 8 rules in their Vinaya Piṭaka (see above, p. 39, n. 3). It was little over a century after the session of the First Council that actual dissensions took place in the Saṅgha in the Second Buddhist Council held at Vesāli, in which the dissenters asserted that they would not regard all Arhats (=*Ari* (*kilesas*)+*han* (destruction) as perfect (see p. 22). Thenceforward, sects after sects appeared under the two broad divisions, viz., Theravāda and Mahāsaṅghika, the former having eleven sub-sects and the latter seven. Some of the sub-sects of the Mahāsaṅghikas, particularly the Lokottaravādins and the Śailas, who settled mostly at Amarāvatī and Nāgārjunakoṇḍa in the Andhra Province, not only confirmed the views of their parent sect, the Mahāsaṅghikas, regarding the imperfections of Arhats but also deified Buddha as a superdivine being. This conception led to the evolution of Bodhisattva-vāda, which introduced the doctrine of *Pāramitās*(=perfection in six or ten virtues by extreme sacrifice of one's ownself for the fulfilment of the six virtues, viz., *dāna* charity, *śīla* or moral observances, *kṣānti* or perseverance, *vīrya* or energy, and *prajñā* or perfect knowledge. In this connection, it should be noted that the Pāli school, i.e., the orthodox and conservative Therāvādins included in their *Khuddaka Nikāya* 550 Jātakas, depicting the previous existences of Gautama Buddha and his fulfilment of ten *pāramis*, i.e., in addition to the six mentioned above, they introduced four *pāramis*, viz., (7) *upāya-kauśalyā* (devices for imparting training to the Śrāvakas for developing their mind for the attainment of Buddhahood), (8) *jñāna* (knowledge of the ways and means for the attainment of Buddhahood) (9) *praṇidhāna* (to promise to attain Buddhahood), and (10) *bala* (to acquire enough strength to proceed to Buddhahood). The incorporation of *pāramis* by the Theravādins in the *Jātakas* reveals that they were not immune from Mahāyānic influence. This happened, of course, at a much later date. In short the conception of the Lokottaravādins, as mentioned above, forecasts the ultimate appearance of Mahāyānism.

It will be observed in the discussion recorded in the *Kathāvatthu* (see above, p. 26) that the distinctions between Arhats and Buddhas lay in the fact that Arhats got rid of only *kleśāvaraṇa* (=mental impurities) and thereby attained only cessation of further existences (*nirvāṇa*) but not of *jñeyāvaraṇa* (the veil, which covers the highest truth (*paramārtha*), i.e., the sameness of all beings and objects of the universe (*tathatā*) or the inexplicability of Truth (*anirvacanīyatā* or *śūnyatā*) devoid as it is of all conventional attributes.

How this transition from Hīnayāna to Mahāyāna took place may be indicated thus :—

The history of Buddhism for the first five or six centuries may be divided into the following three periods :—

A. Early or Pure Hīnayāna Buddhism preserved mainly in the Pāli Nikāyas, Vinaya Piṭaka and Abhidhamma Piṭaka or in their Sanskrit versions or fragments of the same so far discovered.

B. Mixed Hīnayāna Buddhism represented by the various sects, which came into existence about a century after Buddha's demise. The sources for this period are mentioned above (see pp. 11-12).

C. Appearance of Mahāyāna. The sources for this period are mainly the *Prajñāpāramitās*, the *Saddharmapuṇḍarīka, Daśabūmikasūtra*, *Gaṇḍavyūha, Laṅkāvatāra* as also the works of Nāgārjuna, Śāntideva, Aśvaghoṣa, Asaṅga, Vasubandhu and others so far as they throw light on the relative position of Hīnayāna and Mahāyāna.

First Period
(*circa* 450 *to* 350 B.C.)

A. Early or Pure Hīnayāna Buddhism

There has already appeared a fairly large amount of literature, dealing with the first period (i.e., the first century after the inception of Buddhism) and offering solutions of many problems, a result which has been made possible by the strenuous labours of the Pali Text Society, initiated by Dr. Rhys Davids in regard to the publications of the Pali Canonical texts. By early or pure Hīnayāna Buddhism, we mean only that form of Buddhism which has been described in a considerable portion of the Vinaya Piṭaka and the four Nikāyas. For the present purpose of drawing a rough sketch of the period of transition from Hīnayāna to Māhāyāna, we shall state some of the conclusions reached by scholars about Buddhism of this period in order to show how it changed in course of time and gave rise to the different schools. These conclusions are as follows :—

1. The spread of Buddhism was at first confined to a few towns and villages situated in the central belt of India from the east to the west. Of these the most noteworthy were : Kajaṅgala, Campā, Rājagaha, Gayā, Kāsi, Nālandā, Pāṭaliputta, Vaisāli, Sāvatthi; the dominion of the Licchavis, Vajjis, Videhas, Mallas, Bhaggas, and Koliyas; Kosambi, Saṅkassa, Ujjeni, Avanti, Madhurā, and Verañja. There were a few adherents, who came from the northern country of Maddaraṭṭha, and two Brāhmaṇa villages of Kuru, and also from the southern places like Patiṭṭhāna. Gandhāra and Takkhasilā were as yet unknown to them.[1]

2. The kings and clans mentioned in them are all pre-Aśokan, e.g., Bimbisāra, Ajātasattu, Pasenadi Kosala and Caṇḍa Pajjota, and the clans like the Bulis, Koliyas, and Vijjis.[2]

3. The place of the laity was not yet well defined. Laymen appeared more as supporters of the Saṅgha than as actual adherents of Buddhism. They revered Buddha and his disciples, heard their teachings and observed some of the precepts, and

1. See my *Early History etc.*, pp. 82 ff.; E.J. Thomas, *Life of the Buddha*, Map.
2. *Ibid.*

occasionally uttered the formula of *triśaraṇa*—the only mark that distinguished a devotee of Buddha from others. This, however, did not affect their social status, which in India had always been associated with caste and religion, as they continued to be the members of the society to which they belonged.[1]

4. The religion in its full form was meant exclusively for those who retired from household life, entered the order of monks and observed the *pātimokkha* rules, which was not possible for a householder. Householders could not comply even with the first five *śīlas*.

5. The *Pāramitās* were yet unknown. The account of the *Life of Buddha* usually commenced from the time of Prince Siddhārtha's retirement to his attainment of Bodhi with occasional references to his previous existences, as in the *Mahāgovinda-sutta* or *Mahāsudassana-sutta*. The conception of a Bodhisattva performing *pāramis* was hazy, if not unknown.[2]

6. The Jātakas, as one of the nine Aṅgas, referred to only some of the stories about the previous existences of Buddha as found in the *Mahāgovinda*, *Mahāsudassana*, *Makhādeva* and similar other stories traced by Dr. Rhys Davids in the *Nikāyas* and *Vinaya Piṭaka,* but they did not appear as yet as a separate collection depicting the Bodhisattva's practices of the *pāramitās*.

7. Buddha was a human being but possessed omniscience, supernatural powers, and other attainments beyond the reach of other beings.[3] The appearance of a Buddha was exceedingly rare in the world, only one occurring in several kalpas.

8. The doctrines were confined to the three essentials : *anicca*, *dukkha*, and *anattā*, and the four *ariyasaccas, paṭiccasamuppāda* and *aṭṭhaṅgika-magga* : practices were limited to the thirty-seven *Bodhipakkhika-dhammas*. The practices were usually divided under three heads ; *sīla* (observance of moral precepts), *samādhi* (meditation), and *pañña* (development of insight and knowledge, enabling one to realize the Truth).

1. N. Law, *Studies in Indian History and Culture*, ch. v, "Early Buddhism and the Laity."

2. See *E.R.E.*, II, sv. Bodhisattva.

3. See Saunders, *Epochs in Buddhist History*, pp. xviii-xix for a scheme of Buddhology.

9. The goal of life was Arhathood and rarely Pacceka-buddhahood, but never Buddhahood. The stages of progress to Arhathood were four, *viz.*, *sotāpatti*, *sakadāgami*, *anāgami*, and *arhatta*.

10. Nibbāna was a state of absolute rest and marked the end of all *kilesas* (impurities) and, consequently, of all *dukkha*. It was an extremely happy and peaceful (*sānta*, *paṇīta*, *accantasukha*) condition.

Second Period

(*circa* 350 *to* 100 B.C.)

B. Mixed Hīnayāna Buddhism

The history of the events and doctrines of Buddhism of this period—one of the most important periods in its history—is still not fully known; first, because the sources from which the reconstruction can be made are scanty,[1] and secondly, because those that are available are of a very late date. This period witnessed the breaking up of the Buddhist Saṅgha into many sections and the dispersal of these over the various parts of India, each growing in its own way. Though dissensions in the Saṅgha may be undesirable from the orthodox point of view, they were indicative of the deep interest taken by the disciples in ascertaining the real teachings of Buddha as also of the attempts to interpret the old teachings in a new way, and to adapt them to the changed circumstances brought about by the advancement of knowledge for over a century.

Growth of the Abhidhamma Literature

To keep pace with this movement of thought, the older schools had to gird up their loins in order to make their position strong and unassailable. As a result of this effort, there is the Abhidhamma literature of the Theravāda and Sarvāstivāda schools.

1. *E. g.* Sanskrit : *Mahāvastu*, *Lalitavistara*, *Divyāvadāna*, *Avadāna śataka*, *Aśokāvadāna*, Vasumitra's treatise on the Schools, fragments of the Sanskrit Canon discovered in Eastern Turkestan and the neighbouring regions and Gilgit. *Kathāvatthu*, Ceylonese chronicles, *Nikāyasaṅgraha* and the texts, enlisted in p, 48.

The agreement between the Nikāyas (Āgamas)[1] and the Vinayas[2] of the Theravāda and Sarvāstivāda schools and the disagreement in their Abhidhamma[3] literatures show clearly that while compiling their Nikāyas and the essential parts of the Vinayas, the two schools lived close to each other in Magadha or thereabouts,[4] and utilised a common source,[5] but while compiling their Abhidhammas, they lived far apart from each other and developed the Abhidhamma texts independently.[6] From the nature of the contents of the *Kathāvatthu* of the Theravādins, it is also evident that the Abhidhammas were developed not only to add strength to their respective views but also to criticize the views of their opponents and establish their own against them. Hence we can say that this period witnessed not only the appearance of the new schools but also a new development of the older ones.[7]

1. Theravāda : Suttapiṭaka : *Dīghanikāya, Majjhimanikāya Aṅguttaranikāya, Saṃyuttanikāya* and *Khuddakanikāya.*

Sarvāstivāda: *Dīrghāgama, Madhyamāgama, Ekottarāgama* and *Saṃyuktāgama.*

2. Theravāda: Vinayapiṭaka: *Pātimokkha, Mahāvagga, Cullavagga, Suttavibhaṅga* and *Parivāra.*

Sarvāstivāda: Vinayapiṭaka: *Vinayavastu, Prātimokṣasūtra, Vinayavibhāga, Vinayakṣudrakavastu* and *Vinaya-uttara-grantha.*

3. Theravāda: Abhidhamma: *Dhammasaṅgaṇi, Vibhaṅga, Dhātukathā, Puggalapaññatti, Kathāvatthu, Yamaka* and *Paṭṭhāna.*

Sarvāstivāda: Abhidhamma: *Saṅgītiparyāya. Dhātukāya. Prajñaptisāra, Dharmaskandha, Vijñānakāya* and *Prakaraṇapāda.*

For details see *Early History etc.*, pp. 277 ff.

4. *i.e.*, in the first period.

5. For a comparison of the fragments of Sarvāstivāda Āgamas with the corresponding portions of the Pāli Nikāyas, see Hoernle, *Manuscript Remains etc.*, pp. 30 ff.

For the correspondence, verbal and otherwise, between the *Prātimokṣasūtra* of the Sarvāstivādins and the *Pātimokkha* of the Theravādins, see *J. A.* 1913; see also Lévi, *J.A.*, 1912; Oldenberg, *Z.D.M.G.*, vol. lii; Watanabe, *Tables of Problems in the Saṃyukta Āgama and Saṁyutta Nikāya* (Tokyo, 1926), and also my *Early Monastic Buddhism* **II**, pp. 125f.

6. See *J.P.T.S.*, 1904—5, pp. 60 ff.

7. An evidence for the later growth of the *Abhidhamma* literature is the orthodox tradition (*Attha.*, pp. 28-32) that Buddha did not preach the *Abhidhamma in extenso* but gave only the *mātikā*, which was later developed by Sāriputta and handed down by him through his disciples to Revata. This evidence is important in view of the fact that this is a statement made by persons who believed that everything of the scriptures was Buddhavacana. The rejection of the *Abhidhamma* by the Mahāsaṅghikas as non-canonical is also an evidence in support of our contention. See *Early History etc.*, p. 235. In the *Kośa-vyākhyā* (p. 12) it is stated that the *Abhidharma* was preached in fragments by Buddha.

Appearance of the Jātakas and Avadānas

Besides the efforts of the old and the new schools to vie with one another in the field of literature, one notices also a keen competition among them for propagating the tenets of their respective schools, which, as a matter of fact, resulted in a great measure in the wide propagation of Buddhism.[1] It is a well-known fact that the *Jātakas* and *Avadānas* were meant for inspiring in the minds of common people a faith in Buddhism and thereby popularizing the religion.[2] The Jātakas were only an afterthought of the Theravādins. They originally did not form a part of their scriptures (*Buddhavacana*). The Jātaka Book[3] or the floating mass of stories, some of which found their way into the famous stone-monument of India, belongs certainly to an ancient date as is proved by scholars like Rhys Davids, Cunningham, Oldenberg, and Winternitz, but still all of them are not considered to be of the same age as the *Nikāyas*. Dr. Rhys Davids' suggestion, that the stories found both in the *Nikāyas* (*i.e.*, Suttanta Jātakas of *Cullaniddesa*) and in the *Jātaka* collection form the oldest type Jātaka stories and may therefore be called *Pre-Jātaka*, is of great value.[4]

1. The inscriptions, which speak of the gifts made to a particular school, add sometimes that the gifts were meant also for the *cāturdiśa saṅgha*, *i.e.*, members of the Buddhist Saṅgha of the four quarters.

Compare the *Ava. Ś.*, p. xxxix (*Kalpadrumāvadāna*):

Gacchata bhikṣavo yūyaṃ sattvānāṃ vinayārthataḥ,

Deśān pratyabhigacchantaḥ prakāśayata *saṃvṛtiṃ*.

(The word *saṃvṛti* in this verse is noteworthy. The Mahāyānists will not admit that the *dharmas* which were mostly propagated by the Hīnayānists at first were anything but the conventional truth. There is, of course, also the hint that *paramārtha* truth is a a matter for realisation and cannot be the subject of preaching,)

2. See Speyer, Preface to the *Ava. Ś.*, pp. v, vi.

3. In the *I.H.Q.*, vol. iv, p. 6, Prof. Winternitz draws our attention to the fact that the Mandalay and Phayre Mss, of the Jātaka-Book (*i.e.*, Verse-Jātaka) have been examined by Dr. Weller and found to be extracts made from the Jātaka commentary. He, however, still cherishes the view that there was a canonical Jātaka-Book and that it was in verses.

4. *Buddhist India*, pp. 190f.; Mr. G.D. De (*Cal. Rev.* 1929-30), however shows that versions of some of the Suttanta-Jātakas are posterior to the versions of those of the Jātaka-aṭṭhakathā; hence all Nikāya-Jātakas are not of the oldest type and cannot be regarded as pre-Jātaka.

Mention of *Jātakas* in the *Navāṅgas* (nine sections), an ancient division of the Buddhist scriptures, may lead one to think that the ancient Buddhists were not without a Jātaka literature of their own. This seems plausible at first sight, but it should be remembered that the division of the Buddhist scriptures into nine Aṅgas does not refer to nine different groups of literature but to nine types of composition to be found in the collections of the ancient Buddhists. In one Sutta or Suttanta there may be portions which can be called a *sutta, a geyya,*[1] a *gāthā,* an *udāna*, a *veyyākaraṇa*, an *abbhutadhamma,* or a *jātaka.* It was long after the navāṅga division was known that the compilations *Udāna*, *Itivuttaka*, and *Jātaka* came into existence. The explanation of navāṅgas as attempted by Buddhagoṣa[2] also shows that he did not know any particular sections of literature corresponding to navāṅgas. It is very interesting to note in his exposition that for two of the nine aṅgas, viz., *Vedalla* and *Abbhutadhammā,*[3] he could not find any work or group of works, which could be classified under these headings, and so he named some suttas which came under them. Taking these two as our clue, we may suggest that the other seven of the navāṅgas should also be explained in the same way. Instead of putting the whole Abhidhamma collection under Veyyākaran,[4] the Suttas, in which Sāriputta, Mahākaccāyana or Buddha[5] gave detailed exposition

1. *Attha.*, p. 26: Sabbaṃ pi sagāthakaṃ suttaṃ Geyyan ti veditabbaṃ.
2. *Sum. Vil.*, pp, 23, 34; *Attha.*, p, 26; *Petavatthu A.*, p. 2.
3. *Attha.*, p. 26: Sabbe pi acchariyabbhutadhammapaṭisaṃyuttā suttantā Abbhutadhamman ti veditabbaṃ. The 'Acchariyabbhutadhamma Sutta' (*Majjhima*, III, pp. 118 f.) may be treated as one of the Abbhutadhamma class. For Abbhutadhamma, see also *Mtu.*, III, p. 200.
4. As is done in the *Attha.*, pp. 27-28.
5. The Mahākaccānabhaddekaratta-sutta (*Majjhima*, III, No. 133) offers an excellent example of a sutta containing gāthā and veyyākaraṇa. The Mahākammavibhaṅga-sutta (*Majjhima*, III, No. 136) is a type of veyyākaraṇa sutta.

Buddhaghoṣa makes himself quite clear in his attempt to establish that the *Kathāvatthu* is as much Buddha-bhāṣita as were the Madhupiṇḍika and such other Suttas expounded by Mahākaccāna, Ānanda and others. His argument is that Buddha at some places gave only the mātikā (substance), which was sometimes explained by Mahākaccāna, and the whole of it was regarded as Buddhavacana. Suttas of this type, in my opinion, were meant to be included under Veyyākaraṇa-division. See *Attha.*, p. 5.

of the four truths or of the eightfold path, or of any tenet of Buddhism or of any of the pithy sayings of Buddha, should have been included. So also the Jātaka-Aṅga does not refer to the 550 Jātakas as Buddhagoṣa says, but to the few stories found in the Nikāyas, in which Buddha referred to the incidents of one of his previous existences. *Pūrvānusmṛti* is one of the *abhijñās* (superior knowledge) acquired by the Arhats, and so it is quite in keeping with the tenets of early Buddhism to speak of one's previous existences. But the idea of utilising these stories of Pūrvānusmṛti as a means of propagation of the religion came later, at least subsequent by a century and a half to the inception of Buddhism. So it is in the second period of our division that we must place the compilation or composition of the Abhidhamma and the Jātaka literatures.[1]

Like Buddhaghoṣa, the Mahāyānic expositors attempted to classify their literatures according to the twelve aṅgas — a division current among the Sarvāstivādins, Mahāsaṅghikas and others, placing the *Aṣṭasāhasrikā Prajñāpāramitā* under *Sūtra*, the *Gaṇḍavyūha*, *Samādhirāja* and *Saddharmapuṇḍarīka* under *Veyyākaraṇa*, and so forth.[2] But this division of scriptures into twelve Aṅgas was not the work of the Mahāyānists. It had been made by the Sarvāstivādins[3] and the Mahāsaṅghikas, followed by some of the other Hīnayānic schools. The three additional Aṅgas are *Nidāna*, *Avadāna* and *Upadeśa*.[4] Burnouf explains *Nidāna* as

1. In addition to what had been said in connection with the Abhidhamma (see in, ante, p. 224), it may be pointed out that the Mahāsaṅghikas also rejected that claim of the Theravādins that the Abhidhamma and the Jātakas were canonical. Compare the Yogācāra tradition that in the first part of his life, Buddha preached the four Āgamas. Dharmānusmṛtyupasthāna, *Lalitavistara*, *Karmaśataka* and *Avadānaśataka*. Wassiljew, *Buddhismus*, p. 352. According to the Sarvāstivādins, each of the Abhidharma books had a compiler. Cf. *Kośa-vyākhyā*, p. 12: śrūyante hi abhidharmaśāstrāṇāṃ kartāraḥ,

2. Burnouf, *Intro.*, pp. 51-67; Hodgson, Notices etc., in the *Asiatic Researches*, XVI; Wassiljew, *Buddhismus*. pp. 118 ff.

3. *Kośa*, VI, 29b. Professor La Vallée Poussin drew my attention to the fact that the 12 aṅgas were mentioned in Yaśomitra's *Vyākhyā* and not in the *Kośa* itself.

4. Taking *Vaipulya*=*Vedalla*, see Kern, *Manual of Buddhism*, p. 7. For a discussion about Vaipulya=Vaitulya, see *J.R.A.S.*, 1907, pp. 432 ff and 1927, pp. 268ff; but cf. Buddhaghoṣa's interprteation in the *Atthas*, p. 26.

those treatises which show the causes antecedent to events, e. g., how Śākyamuni became a Buddha. The cause was the completion of the Pāramitās by Buddha and so the treatises or portions of treatises, describing the completion of pāramitās are called Nidānas. He also points out that there is no literature which can be classified under Nidāna.[1] The explanation of Burnouf is supported by the Nidānakathā of *Jātakatthavaṇṇanā*, but in the Mahāyāna literature as well as in the *Mahāvastu*, Nidāna signifies the introductory description which sometimes contains, as in the case of the *Mahāvastu*,[2] hints of the topics to be dealt with in the treatise. The description of the preparations made by Buddha, viz., entering into samādhi and putting forth rays of light from his body, the appearance of Buddhas on lotus, and so forth before preaching the *Prajñāpāramitā*, is called Nidāna.[3] In the Tibetan versions of the *Ratnakūṭasūtras*, the place where a particular sūtra was delivered is referred to as Nidāna.[4] Considering the use of this expression, we may take it as the aṅga (portion) of a treatise, which contains the introductory matters. The sense of the term *Avadāna* is clear and needs no comment. It includes stories of previous births whether of Buddha or any of his disciples or of any prominent figure professing the Buddhist faith, and a huge literature has grown under this heading.[5] In the explanation of the term *Upadeśa*, however, there is some obscurity. There is hardly any justification for considering the Buddhist Tantras as coming under the heading Upadeśa, for these had not yet come into existence when the term *Upadeśa* came into vogue.[6] It certainly means 'instruction' and this is supported by the Tibetan rendering of the term by *bab-par-bstan paḥi-sde*. In one[7] of the Chinese texts it

1. Burnouf also points out the technical significance of the term Nidāna as 12 links of the Pratītyasamutpāda. Cf. Nidānasutta in the *Dīgha*.

2. *Mtu.*, I, pp. 2, 4.

3. *Pañca.*, p. 17.

4. M. Lalou's paper in the *J.A.*, 1928.

5. See Speyer's Intro, to the *Ava. Ś.* The Pāli collection has also an *Apadāna*. It contains accounts of the previous lives of Arhats.

6. Burnouf. *op, cit.*, pp. 55-6; *As. Res.*, XVI, p. 427; Wassiljew, *op. cit.*, p. 119: "die Upadesas eine analytische Untersuchung der Lehre."

7. On 12 Aṅgas, see Nanjio's *Catalogue*. No. 1199 (Taisho ed. of the Tripiṭaka, vol. 31, p. 586).

has been explained as those discourses which contained exposition of the profound and mystic dharmas. That the term later bore this sense is also apparent from the fact that the *Abhisamayālaṅkārakārikā* is sometimes called *Prajñāpāramitopadeśaśāstra*.[1]

Incorporation of *Pāramis* in the doctrines of the Theravādins

One can easily observe the type of literature that was intended for inclusion under at least two of these headings. It cosisted more of anecdotes, stories, parables and so forth than of actual doctrines of Buddhism. These were incorporated into the Buddhist literature in the garb of Pūrvānusmṛtis, their chief object being to popularize Buddhism and to show that they were meant as much for the benefit of the mass as for the select few, who would retire from the worldly life. This is an innovation which the earliest orthodox school, the Theravādins, had to make reluctantly under the pressure of circumstances. Their early literature did not refer to the pāramitās,[2] and much later, when they spoke of the pāramis, it was only to inspire faith in the mind of the people and not to set an example to encourage them to fulfil the pāramis. The attitude of the Sarvāstivādins and the Mahāsaṅghikas, however, was different. They did not minimise in the least the extreme difficulty of the task of fulfilling the pāramitās, but they did not discourage people from the endeavour. Not only to inspire faith, but also to encourage people in the performance of *dāna*, *śīla*, *kṣānti*, *vīrya*, *dhyāna* and *prajñā*, they invented story after story and associated them not only with the life of Buddha but also with the lives of persons, who attained prominence in the history of the Buddhist faith.

The Theravādins, it will be observed, speak, of ten pāramis mentioned above (p. 218). Throughout Sanskrit literature,

1. See my Intro. to the *Pañcaviṃśatisāhasrikā*.

2. The omission of 'Pāramitā' in the Dasuttara and Saṅgīti suttantas of the *Dīgha* is significant. The word 'pāramippatto' (*Majjhima*, III, p. 28) is sometimes found in the sense of success, perfection but not in the technical sense of six or ten pāramis.

whether Hīnayāna or Mahāyāna, earlier or later, the pāramitās are mentioned as six.[1] It is in the *Daśabhūmika-sūtra*[2] that we first find mention of ten pāramitās, the following four added to the usual six,—*Upāyakauśalya, Praṇidhāna, Bala* and *Jñāna*. If we compare the three lists, it would be evident that the conception of the six pāramitās was the oldest. The Theravādins added to it *Nekkhamma, Sacca, Adhiṭṭhāna, Mettā* and *Upekkhā*, and dropped *Dhyāna*. Apparently, this list lacks a system,[3] for the last two, Mettā and Upekkhā, are included in the four brahmavihāras and have to be practised by all Arhats to attain perfection, while Sacca may easily be included in Sīla. Of the other two, Adhiṭṭhāna is to take a resolution (which in the case of Sumedha only was to become a Buddha) and to carry it out at any cost. It corresponds to Praṇidhāna of the Mahāyānists.[4] The Nekkhamma pārami, *i.e.*, retirement from the household life, was emphasized by the Theravādins; it, in fact, formed one of the chief features of the doctrines of this school, while it was not insisted upon by the Mahāsaṅghikas and Sarvāstivādins. The Mahāyānists also gave to Nekkhamma a superior place, but they did not make it imperative upon every person to retire in order to derive the benefits of the religion.

One of the main reasons for the varying treatment of the Pāramitās by the three schools is that the Theravādins rejected the idea of any person aspiring to Buddhahood, while the other two schools regarded the probability of a person becoming Buddha as a very rare event. In the *Divyāvadāna*,[5] there are passages, in which it is stated that after the delivery of a discourse, some persons were established in the Truth, some in one of the four stages of sanctification, some developed aspiration for the attainment of Śrāvakabodhi or Pratyekabodhi, and some for Anuttarasamyaksambodhi. Remarks like these are significant and show that the Sarvāstivādins, to which school

1. *Divyā.*, pp. 95, 127, 480; *Lal. Vis.*, pp. 345, 474; *Śata.*, p. 242.
2. *Daśa.*, pp. 63, 72, 81, 94. Cf. *Mvyut.* 34.
3. Cf. Prof. La Vallée Poussin's remark in the *E.R.E.*., sv. Bodhisattva.
4. See my *Aspects etc.* ch. IV; four kinds of Adhiṭṭhāna, see *Mvyut*, 80 and *P.T.S. Dict.*; Adhiṭṭhāna in the *Mahāvaṃsa*, ch. XVII. 46.
5. *Divyā.*, pp. 226, 271, 368, 469, 476, 478, 495, 569.

the *Divyāvadāna* belonged,[1] were not as conservative as the Theravādins. The Mahāsaṅghikas, as is well known, were the first to bring about this change in the angle of vision. They were the precursors of Mahāyāna, and hence it is hardly necessary to adduce reasons why the practice of Pāramitās should form an integral part of their doctrines. So the introduction and formulation of the Pāramitās were due originally either to the Mahāsaṅghikas or the Sarvāstivādins and were adopted later in a modified form by the Theravādins.

Closely connected with the Pāramitās are the Jātakas and Avadānas, and, consequently, the Bharhut and Sanchi sculptures. All the three schools put forth their best efforts in propaganda, but it is still an open question as to which of the three schools inspired the origin of the famous stone monuments. Attempts have been made by many scholars[2] to identify the sculptural representations of the Jātakas, representations which have been traced to the *Jātakatthavaṇṇanā*, but still the identifications are not all beyond doubt, and it is not improbable that a better elucidation of these sculptures will be found in the huge literature of Avadānas.

Propagation

The efforts of the various schools to propagate their particular faith met with success, as is evidenced by the early stone-monuments of India. Every school no doubt increased the number of its adherents, and we have evidence of this in some of the inscriptions, belonging to a period a little later than that with which we are here concerned. These inscriptions are records of gifts made specially to a particular school.[3] But along with these there are some inscriptions in which no particular sect is mentioned, but gifts are made for the benefit of the saṅgha of the four regions (cāturdiśa-saṅgha).[4] This shows clearly that the devotees might have had faith in the tenets of

1. Csoma Körösi, *As. Res.*, XX; Speyer, Intro. to the *Ava. Ś.*
2. Of whom Cunningham, Oldenberg, Barua, Charpentier may be mentioned.
3. See Lüders' *List*, Nos. 1105, 1107.
4. See Lüders' *List*, Nos. 1099, 1107.

only one of the schools but they supported all the schools, *i.e.*, Buddhism in general. As the dates of these inscriptions do not help us much with regard to the period under review, we have to confine ourselves to the scanty evidence yielded by the few works, whose dates of composit on might be a little later, but which may be regarded as yielding evidence for this period.

It has been seen from the Nikāyas that early Buddhism was confined to the central belt of India from Aṅga to Avanti, though it also claimed a few adherents from the distant countries of the north and the south.[1] The account of the distribution of relics as given in the Mahāparinibbāna Sutta in its Pāli and Tibetan versions[2] gives a fairly correct idea of the spread of Buddhism towards the beginning of the first period. The people who shared the relics were the Licchavis of Vaisāli, Śākyas of Kapilavatthu, Bulis of Allakappa, Koliyas of Rāmagāma, Brāhmaṇas of Veṭhadīpa, Mallas of Pāvā and Kusinārā, Moriyas of Pipphalivana, and the inhabitants of Magadha. The places mentioned are all in eastern India. The only place mentioned outside the eastern territory is Gandhārapura, where a tooth of Buddha is said to have been enshrined.[3] This is, as the commentator points out, a later addition; in any case, the people of Gandhārapura did not share in the relics. A further hint about the spread of Buddhism in the first period is furnished by the boundaries of the Majjhima-janapada as given in the *Mahāvagga* of the *Vinaya*.[4] The boundaries are as follows: Kajaṅgala nigama in the east, next to the Mahāsāla forest, the river Sallavati on the south-east, Setakaṇṇika nigama on the south, Thūna brāhmaṇagāma on the west and Usira pabbata on the north. According to this account, Avanti-dakkhiṇāpatha was a paccantima-janapada (border country)[5] and so also the country in the east beyond Kajaṅgala, which is identified with

1. See for details, my *Early History etc.*, pp. 92. 137ff., 155, 169ff; Dr. E. J. Thomas, *Life of the Buddha*, Map.
2. *Digha*, II, p. 167; *As Res.*, XX, p. 316.
3. *Digha*, II, p. 167.
4. *Mv.*, I, p. 197; *Jāt.*, I, 49; *Divyā.*, p. 21.
5. *Mv.*, I, p. 197.

Bhagalpur.[1] The *Divyāvadāna*[2] preserves this tradition replacing only the eastern boundary Kajaṅgala by Puṇḍravardhana. If Puṇḍravardhana be identified with a place in North Bengal, the *Divyāvadāna* shows a slight extension of the eastern boundary. The only other name in this account that deserves attention is the Usīraddhaja of the *Mahāvagga* and Usīragiri of the *Divyāvadāna*. We know of an Usīra mountain situated near Mathura,[3] and Tāranātha also tells us that Upagupta, the famous monk of Mathura and spiritual adviser of Aśoka according to the Sarvāstivāda tradition, lived there for three years before going to Kashmir after leaving Vārāṇasī.[4] So it is apparent that Mathura, a stronghold of the Sarvāstivādins, was included in the Majjhima-janapada.

From the accounts of the Vaisāli Council also, as given in the *Cullavagga*[5] and the *Vinayas* of the Sarvāstivāda and Dharmagupta schools, it seems that the horizon of Buddhism, even at the beginning of the second century after its appearance, did not extend farther. The geographical information has been given above (p. 14).

Traditions of *Ācariyaparamparā*

The traditions of the Second Council as preserved by the Theravādins and the Sarvāstivādins are the same,[6] and as far as the succession of monks is concerned, there is also no disagreement. The Theravādins only refer to Sambhūta Sāṇavāsī as a member of the committee of the Second Council while the Sarvāstivādins speak of him as the patriarch, who succeeded Ānanda. The two traditions bifurcate after the Second Council,

1. For the identification of the boundaries of the Majjhima-janapada see S.N. Majumdar's Intro. to Cunningham's *Geography*, p. xliii.

2. *Divyā.*, p. 21; Puṇḍravardhana on the east; Sarāvatī on the south; Sthūṇopasthūṇaka [brāhmaṇagrāmas on the west; and Usīragiri on the north.

3. Watter's *Yuan Chwang*, I, p. 308.

4. *Tāra.*, pp. 10, 13.

5. *Cv.*, XII, i, 7f. See *Ind. Ant.*, 1908, *Council, etc.*; *Pag Sam Jon Zang*, p. viii,; for the Mahiśāsaka tradition, see Wassiljew's notes in the App. to *Tāra*, pp. 289-90.

6. *I.A.*, 1908, pp. 4 ff; 89 ff.

one speaking of the Aśokan Council under the leadership of Moggaliputta Tissa, while the other speaking of Upagupta as the religious adviser of Aśoka, and dwelling at length on the Kaṇiṣkan Council at Jalandhara instead of the Aśokan Council. This divergence of traditions is significant, and henceforth, the history of Buddhism is no longer the history of a single form of Buddhism but of many, principally of the three schools, Theravāda, Sarvāstivāda and Mahāsaṅghika.[1] The Theravāda is pre-eminently a Vinaya school,[2] and though the Tibetan tradition ascribes to Kaccāyana its leadership,[3] it may be noted that Upāli as the compiler of the Vinaya was highly venerated by the Theravādins, and his connection with the Aśokan Council is established through his disciples. It should be observed that though the Theravādins speak of lines of disciples (*ācariyaparamparā*) from Upāli or Sāriputta, there was no system of patriarchal succession. In the *Majjhima Nikāya*[4] it is expressly stated that in the Buddhist Saṅgha there was no recognized head. It had, according to the Founder's dictum, a fully democratic basis. The Tibetan and Chinese traditions gave, in fact, currency to the idea of patriarchal succession,[5] which, however, is not worth credence.[6] The *Atthasālinī* also gives us a list of ācariyas of the Ābhidhammikas, tracing it from Sāriputta. The traditions of the

1. Tāranātha (p. 44) refers also to Sthavira Vatsa who introduced the Ātmaka theory. He adds that Dhitika, who succeeded Upagupta, convened a council in the Puṣkariṇī vihāra (of Maru Land) to suppress the Ātmaka theory of Vatsa and succeeded to convince the followers of Vatsa and, ultimately, the teacher himself of the untenability of the theory. This legend evidently refers to the Vātsīputrīyas or the Vajjiputtakas, or Sammitīyas, who attained prominence during the reign of Harṣavardhana. See Appendix and *Early History etc.*, pp. 297ff.

2. *Early History etc.*, p. 211; Watters, *Yuan Chwang*, 1, p. 302 referring to the Vinayists, (*i.e.*, the Theravadins) as worshipping Upāli.

3. Wassiljew, *op cit.*, p. 295; Eitel, *Handbook etc.*

4. *Majjhima*, Sutta 108; see also Dutt, *Early Buddhist Monachism*, pp. 141 ff.

5. *Attha.*, p. 32: Ācariyaparamparā: Sāriputtatthero Bhaddaji Sobhito Piyajāli Piyapālo Piyadassī Kosiyaputto Siggavo Sandeho Moggaliputto Visudatto Dhammiyo Dāsako Soṇako Revato ti. (Then in Ceylon) Mahindo Iddhiyo Uttiyo Bhaddanāmo ca Sambalo.

6. *Tāra.*, p. 9.

Theravādins and the Sarvāstivādins about the *ācariyaparamparā* of the first two centuries may be combined thus:—

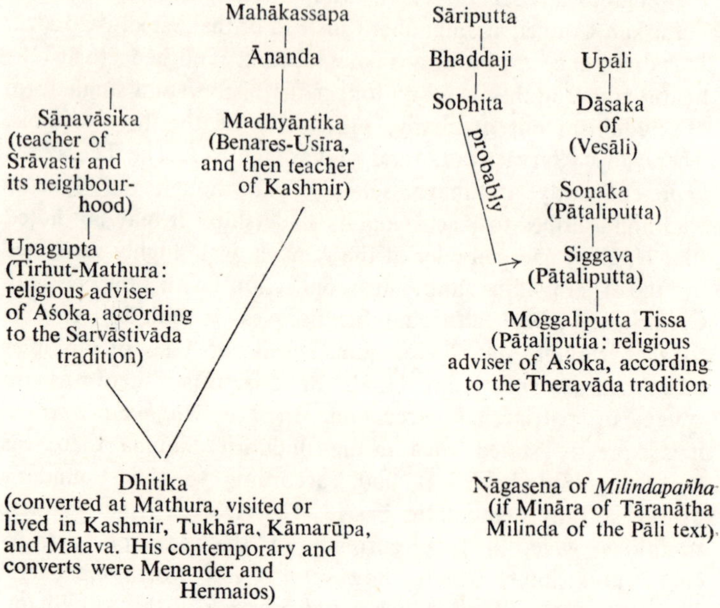

As mentioned above, there was no such *ācariyaparamparā* as patriarchal succession, nor should an attempt be made to calculate the duration of abbotship on the basis of an average period, as is usually done in connection with kings, for the Buddhist saints were generally long-lived, and there was no custom of a disciple succeeding his teacher. Moreover, the ordination of disciples could have happened in the earliest or the latest part of a teacher's life. According to Tāranātha, Madhyāntika was ordained by Ānanda shortly before his death; hence it is quite possible that he was a contemporary of both Sāṇavāsī and Upagupta, or of Dāsaka, Soṇaka, Siggava and Moggaliputta. Reading the tradition in this way, and also observing the names of places, which were the centres of activity of the various bhikkhus, it may be stated that after the Council of Vaisāli, the Sarvāstivādins attained more and more popularity and spread towards the north, having two important centres, one at Mathura with Upagupta as the chief teacher, and the other in

Kashmir with Madhyāntika as the chief, the two centres having later on coalesced under the leadership of Dhitika, who, it seems, greatly extended the horizon of influence of the Sarvāstivāda school by pushing it eastwards to Kāmarūpa, westward to Mālava, and north-westward to Tukhāra, the realm of Mināra and Imhasa. The Theravādins retained their seat in Magadha all along with a branch at Ujjayini, founded by Mahākaccāyana. Mahinda and Saṅghamittā,[1] it seems, were closely connected with the Ujjayini branch of the Theravāda school and propagated the same in Ceylon.

Aśoka's part in the propagation of Buddhism

Emperor Aśoka had no doubt Buddhistic leanings but in his exhortations, so far as they have been found in the edicts, there is not the slightest hint of his actively helping the propagation of Buddhism. His edicts refer to *dhammavijaya* as opposed to conquest by arms, but by *dhamma* he did not mean Buddhism. His *dhamma* consisted of maxims for leading an ideal life and performing meritorious deeds, which made a person happy in this world as well as in the next. The edicts do not contain any reference to Nirvāṇa or Śūnyatā, Anātma or Duḥkha, while on the other hand, these speak of heaven and happiness in a heavenly life,[2] which was never an ideal of early Buddhism, for it considered existence in any one of the three dhātus: Kāma, Rūpa and Arūpa to be misery (*duḥkha*). But it must be admitted that when an emperor like Aśoka showed a bias for a particular religion and even proclaimed himself to be a Buddhist upāsaka, and paid visits to the monasteries or sacred places of the Buddhists, the religion automatically received an impetus and its propagation by the Buddhist monks then became easy. So it may be regarded that Aśoka was a passive propagator of

1. It is noteworthy that with the ordination of Mahinda are associated the names of Majjhantika (very probably of Kashmir fame) and Mahādeva, the propagator of Buddhism in Mahiṣamaṇḍala along with Moggaliputta. See also *Early History etc.*, pp. 260 ff.

2. Hultzsch, *Corpus*, p. liii. The remark of Dr. Hultzsch that Aśoka's *dhamma*, preaching for heavenly life, represents an earlier stage of Nirvāṇa is without any basis.

Buddhism and, during his rule, the religion very probably made its way throughout his kingdom, reaching also places beyond his dominion, *viz.*, the kingdoms of the Yavanas, Kambojas, Gandhāras, Pitenikas in the west, and Coḍas, Pāṇḍyas as far as Tāmraparṇi on the south.[1] As Aśoka was an adherent of Buddhism only as a supporter, or at most as an upāsaka,[2] he cannot be expected to be interfering in the sectarian disputes that were going on at his time. Hence it is difficult to attach importance to the tradition of the *Mahāvaṃsa* according to which he supported the Vibhajjavādins (=Theravādins),[3] or to the statement in the *Avadānas* that he was a devotee of Upagupta. It may also be observed that he did not refer to the Bodhisattva conception, nor to the pāramitās, which could suitably have been incorporated into his code of moral maxims. His admonition to his subjects to choose the middle path, avoiding the two extremes, *viz.*, of retirement from worldly life on the one hand and of indulgence in envy, anger, laziness, and so forth on the other,[4] shows that he was not so much in favour of retirement from household life, upon which the early Hīnayāna Buddhists always laid emphasis. Aśoka's preference for the life of an ideal upāsaka as against that of a monk may have stimulated the Buddhist monks to devise ways and means to popularize their religion, and as a result of the efforts of the monks in this direction, appeared a large number of Jātakas and Avadānas.

The tradition of the *Mahāvaṃsa* about the part played by Aśoka in the Third Council with Moggaliputta Tissa as its president, and about the despatch of missionaries to the various parts of India, still awaits verification. It is not improbable that a sectarian council of the Theravādins was held under the leadership of Moggaliputta Tissa during Aśoka's reign and that active propaganda was set on foot to spread Buddhism in the various

1. For details, see Hultzsch, *Corpus* (1925), pp. xxxviii, xxxix.
2. *Ibid.*, pp. xliv-xlv.
3. *Mahāvaṃsa*, p. 54.
4. Hultzsch, *op. cit.*, p. 114. The rendering of Prinsep, Bhandarkar and Smith is adopted here in preference to that of Hultzsch whose rendering does not appear to be in consonance with the general tenor of the inscription. See M.N. Basu's remarks in this connection in the *I.H.Q.*, III, p. 349.

territories in and outside India,[1] which the *Mahāvaṃsa* recorded with a colouring of its own. In the same way, we can account for the religious advisers of Aśoka, viz., Upagupta and Moggaliputta Tissa. Aśoka as an impartial ruler must have offered equal treatment to the Buddhists and the non-Buddhists. In the circumstances it may be inferred that he would not support one sect of Buddhism against another. The Theravādins as well as the Sarvāstivādins associated his name with the contemporaneous leading figures of their respective sects in order to add importance to themselves. It would be fruitless therefore to attempt an identification of Moggaliputta Tissa with Upagupta—as has been done by Smith and other scholars.[2] We may with some amount of confidence accept the tradition of the *Mahāvaṃsa* that about the time of Aśoka, Buddhism made its way to the countries of Kashmira-Gandhāra, Mahiṣamaṇḍala, Vanavāsī, Yona, Mahāraṭṭha, Himavantapadesa Suvaṇṇabhūmi, and Laṅkādīpa.[3]

Career of the Mahāsaṅghikas

Further light could have been thrown on the propagation of Buddhism during this period, if the tradition about the propagation of the Mahāsaṅghikas had been available. It may be that the Chinese versions of the Mahāsaṅghika Vinaya may yield some information, but as yet we are in the dark about it. From the account of the Vaisāli Council, it can be stated that they retained their seat at Vaisāli, and from the inscriptions on the Mathura Lion Capital (120 B.C.)[4] and on the Wardak vase

1. The agreement of the tradition of the Sarvāstivādins that Madhyāntika was the propagator of Buddhism in the north with that of the *Mahāvaṃsa* that Majjhantika was despatched to convert Kāśmīra-Gandhāra, and the corroboration of the tradition by the casket containing the relics with the inscriptions (on the top of the lid) 'sapurisasa Kasapagotasa savahemavatācariyasa,' and (inside the lid) 'sapurisa(sa) Majhimasa' deserve consideration. See Cunningham, *Bhilsa Topes*, p. 287.

2. Waddell in *J.A.S.B.*, 1897, pt., i, p. 76; *Proc. A.S.B.*, 1899, p. 70; Smith, *Early History of India*, 4th ed., p. 199 fn.

3. *Mahāvaṃsa*, p. 94; *Sāsanavaṃsa*, p. 10. For detailed treatment see Smith, *Asoka* (3rd ed.), p. 44; Bhandarkar, *Aśoka*, pp. 159 ff.

4. *Ep. Ind.*, IX, pp. 139, 141, 146.

in Afghanistan,[1] it may be inferred that they made attempts to proceed towards the north, but the caves of Karle and the location of the centre of activities of their offshoots, the Pubbaseliyas and Aparaseliyas at Dhanakaṭaka[2] (i.e., Amarāvatī and Nāgārjunakoṇḍa stūpas) indicate that they were later successful in their propagation more in the south than in the north.

According to Dr. Burgess, the Amarāvatī stūpas at Dharaṇikoṭa (Dhānykaṭaka) were originally constructed as early as the 2nd century B.C.,[3] and Nāgārjuna was closely associated with the Buddhist establishment of this place. At any rate there is no doubt that Dhānyakaṭaka was the chief centre of the Caityakas, the Pūrva and Apara śaila branches of the Mahāsaṅghika school, and that the people living there and in its neighbourhood lavished gifts on this Buddhist establishment. The *Mañjuśrīmūlakalpa*[4] also mentions that it contained the relics of Buddha.[5] This is corroborated by the recent find of an inscription, recording the gift of a pillar by the sister of Mahārāja Mādhariputra Srivīrapuruṣadatta to the Caitya enshrining the dhātu of Sammāsambuddha. Among the inscriptions of this place, edited by Dr. Burgess, there is one (No. 121), which refers to the Caityakas, of which the Pūrva-and Apara-śailas were branches. Another important place near Dhānyakaṭaka was Śrīparvata (Śrīśailam), where, according to the Tibetan tradition, Nāgārjuna passed his last days.[6] The *Mañjuśrīmūlakalpa* also takes notice of this mountain as a suitable place for Buddhistic practices and one of the inscriptions, recently found, records that some devotees constructed a number of caityas and vihāras, and dug wells for pilgrims visiting the sacred place from Gandhāra, Cīna, Aparānta, Vaṅga, Tambapaṇṇidīpa, etc.[7] (See above. p. 63).

1. *Ibid.*. XI, p. 211; for other places in India where the Mahāsaṅghikas made their way, see *Early History etc.*, pp. 241ff.
2. See *Pag Sam Jon Zong*, p. 74: Dhana-srihi-gliṅ.
3. Burgess, *Amaravati and Jaggayapeta Stupas*, p. 100.
4. *Mañjuśrīmūlakalpa* (Trivandrum Sanskrit Series), p. 88.
5. *Ibid.* Śrīdhānyakaṭake caitye jinadhātudhare.
6. Burgess, *op. cit.*, p. 6; *Tāra.*, pp. 73, 81. See above, pp. 67 ff.
7. *Annual Report of S. I. Epigraphy*, 1927, pp.43,71. Dr. L. D. Barnett kindly drew my attention to the recent finds of the inscriptions.

Buddhism after Aśoka

The *Mahāvaṃsa* and the *Sāsanavaṃsa* present a connected history of Buddhism in India up to the period of Aśoka, and then turn to the history of Buddhism in Ceylon, leaving us in the dark about the career of the Theravādins in India, till we come to the *Milindapañha*. From it is learnt that king Milinda of Sāgala (Sialkot, Lahore) took great interest in Buddhism, and that Nāgasena, a native of Kajaṅgala, the easternmost boundary of the Majjhima-janapada, came to him, passing through Vattaniya and Pāṭaliputta. He stopped at the Saṅkheyya-pariveṇa at Sāgala. This account of Nāgasena's route indicates that Buddhism had already made its way as far north as Sāgala.[1]

Tāranātha, however, continues the story and gives us an account of the spread of Buddhism after Aśoka, but as his narrative is based mainly on the Sarvāstivāda tradition, we may regard this story as essentially that of the Sarvāstivādins. He tells us that Upagupta ordained Dhitika,[2] a native of Ujjayinī, at Mathura, the usual place of residence of Upagupta. The teachership was transferred from Upagupta to Dhitika, who spread the religion widely, and converted Mināra, the king of Tukhāra. Many monks of his time went thither from Kashmir and established firmly the religion at that place. They were supported by both King Mināra and his son Imhasa.[3] Dhitika then went to the east to Kāmarūpa where he converted the rich Brāhmaṇa Siddha and established the religion there. After this, he visited Mālava and converted the rich Brāhmaṇa Adarpa, laying thereby the foundation of the religion in that region. He came at length to his native place at Ujjayinī and there spent his last days. He was succeeded by Kāla or Kṛṣṇa,[4] who was followed by Sudarśana of Bharukaccha. The spheres of activity

1. *Mil.*, pp. 8, 16.

2. *Tāra.*, p. 23: All Sarvāstivāda traditions both in Chinese and Tibetan mention Dhitika as the successor of Upagupta.

3. Schiefner suggests that Mināra=Menander, and Imhasa=Hermaios, see *Tāra.*, pp. 23, 24 fn.

4. There is a reference to the spread of Buddhism in Ceylon; also Kṛṣṇa is said to have visited the place. *Tāra.*, p. 44.

of both these monks were in the west (Sindh) and the north (Kashmir) of India generally. In connection with Kṛṣṇa, it is stated that he spread the religion in the south of India, in many small islands including Ceylon, and subsequently in Mahācīna.[1] Poshadha, who came after him, spread Buddhism in Orissa during the rule of Vigatāśoka.[2] Tāranātha's history is full of legends, and as such all his statements cannot be taken as authentic. But considering the fact that he makes some statements which are not *prima facie* unreasonable and are, in many cases, corroborated by the Chinese travellers, we can attach to them some importance, though, of course, great caution should be exercised.

Doctrinal Developments

We shall now proceed to take a panoramic view of the doctrinal developments that took place during this period and heralded the advent of Mahāyānism. The Mahāsaṅghikas were evidently the earliest school of the Hīnayānists to show a tendency towards conceiving Buddha docetically, which was later on brought to completion by a branch of theirs, the Lokottaravādins.[3] But whether the conception of the Bodhisattva and the practice of the six pāramitās was introduced for the first time by the Mahāsaṅghikas or by the Sarvāstivādins is uncertain. The mention of *ṣaṭpāramitā,* the fulfilment of which is compulsory for the Bodhisattvas, is frequently found in the works of both the Sarvāstivādins and the Mahāsaṅghikas, and both are responsible for the growth of the large mass of Avadāna literature,[4] the central theme of which is the fulfilment of the pāramitās.

1. Kāla is called Kṛṣṇavarṇa in the Chinese tradition, see *Saṃyuktavastu,* II, p. 95b; *Tāra.*, p. 47. Tāranātha's statement that Sudarśana and Aśoka died at the same time cannot be accepted.

2. *Tāra.*, p. 50.

3. *E.R.E.*, sv. Docetism, for details.

4. Hüber has traced 18 Avadānas of the *Divyāvadāna* in the Chinese version of the Sarvāstivāda Vinaya (*B.E.F.E.O.*, V, pp. 1-37). See also Lévi, *T'oung Pao,* Ser. II (1907), no. I. So it is quite probable that the *Divyāvadāna* is a book of the Sarvāstivādins.

The Goal of Buddhahood

Then there remains the other conception. *viz.*, the attainment of Buddhahood as the goal to be aspired after, and the consequent lowering of the position of the Arhats.[1] The Theravādins do not definitely deny that Buddhahood is unattainable, for there is the instance of Sumedha Brāhmaṇa becoming śākyamuni and that of a certain being, who will in future become Maitreya Buddha, but such instances are so few and far between that it would not be reasonable to hold up the ideal for the generality of the human beings to follow. They assert that a Buddha is hardly expected to arise even in so many kalpas,[2] and this is echoed in the *Lalita vistara*, *Mahāvastu*, and some of the Mahāyānic texts: but still one reads in the *Divyāvadāna* that after the delivery of a discourse, some aspired to *Srāvakabodhi*, some to *Pratyekabodhi*, and some to *Samyaksambodhi*.[3] The fact mentioned last that some aspire to *Samyaksambodhi* leads us to infer that by the time of the *Divyāvadāna* the Sarvāstivādins admitted the practicability of holding up Buddhahood as an ideal. So, clearly, the Sarvāstivādins encouraged the aspiration to Buddhahood and hence to the life of a Bodhisattva, and the goal of Buddhahood was not purely Mahāsaṅghika or Mahāyānic. The Sarvāstivādins like the Theravādins conceived Buddha as an actual human being, but they magnified his attainments and powers so much that one is led to regard their conception of Buddha as that of a superhuman being.

---

1. In Vasumitra's treatise as well as in the *Kathāvatthu* it is stated that the Sarvāstivādins believed that the Arhats were liable to fall from arhathood. On this point the Theravādins hold a different opinion. They believe that the Arhats are as pure as Buddhas, and cannot fall from that position. The Mahāsaṅghikas also do not support the Sarvāstivādins in regard to this point. See above, pp. 81, 108.

2. Kadāci karahāci Tathāgatā loke uppajjanti. *Dīgha*, II. p. 139 *Mtu.*, I, p. 55.

3. *Divyā.*, pp. 226. 271, etc. The treatise of Vasumitra also says that the Sarvāstivādins were aware of the three Yānas. The date of the compilation of the *Divyāvadāna* may be later, but it contains many avadānas which are old. The mention of three Bodhis in the *Divyāvadānas* and the reference of Vasumitra in connection with the Sarvāstivādins to the three Yānas show that, to the Sarvāstivādins, the Samyaksambuddhahood was a goal as much as the other two Bodhis.

Conrtibutions of Sarvāstivāda to Mahāyāna

The Sarvāstivādins had two Kāya conceptions, *viz.*, *rūpakāya* and *dharmakāya*, but these did not bear any Mahāyānic sense, though their conception of dharmakāya helped the Yogācarins in the formulation of their conception of the same. The Sarvāstivādins were also responsible for the addition of the fourth term, *śūnya*, to the usual trio, *viz.*, duḥkha, anitya, and anātma, though the word conveyed no Mahāyānic meaning as it connoted no other sense than anātman.[1]

But the most important doctrine of the Sarvāstivādins, which contrarily led to the development of Mahāyāna, is their extreme *Astitvavāda* (the theory of the actual existence of elements composing a being). It may be said that Mahāyāna is a continuation of the Buddhological speculations of the Mahāsaṅghikas and their offshoots, and contrarily against the astitvavāda of the Sarvāstivādins — a dogma which appeared to the Mahāyānists as an utter distortion of Buddha's teachings.[2] It was this reaction, which led to the other extreme, the establishment of *dharma-śūnyātā* (non-existence of everything whatsoever) as the real teaching of Buddha.

The third contribution made by the Hīnayānists, especially by the Sarvāstivādins, is the exposition or analysis of skandhas, dhātus, āyatanas, āryasatyas, aṅgas of the pratītyasamutpāda, and so forth.[3] The Mahāyānists incorporated them in their work *in toto*, although they relegated them to the domain of Saṃvṛti or Parikaepita, Paratantra, admitting, however, their

1. *Lal. Vis.*. p. 419; *Divyā.*, pp. 266, 367: anitya, duḥkha, śūnya, anātma. See *Kośa*, VI, p. 163 and VII. pp. 31 f. where śūnya is explained as being devoid of ātman, puruṣa, and so forth.

2. It will be observed that the remarks of Nāgārjuna and other early Mahāyāna writers are mostly directed against the realism of the Sarvāstivādins. The *Madhyamakāvatāra* cannot help admitting that the Hīnayānists also teach śūnyatā as much as the Mahāyānists do (see *Le Muśeon*, Vol. VIII, p. 271) but in the general attack of the Mahāyānists against the Hīnayānists, they hold the latter as *Aśūnyavādins*, evidently keeping the Sarvāstivādins in view.

3. That the Mahāyānists incorporated mostly the Sarvāstivāda expositions and analyses may be asserted in view of the fact that *Prajñāpāramitās* mention many terms, which are not very common in Pāli suttas, *e.g.*, Paryavasthāna, Saṃgrahavastu, Dvādaśāṅga (instead of Navāṅga).

utility as being indispensable to Bodhisattvas in arriving at the Paramārtha or Parinispanna truth.[1]

Contact of the Sarvāstivādins with the Mahāyānists

TheMahāsaṅghikas may have been the forerunners of Mahāyāna but it is clear that the Sarvāstivādins contributed much to the growth of Mahāyāna in one way or the other. As a sign of close contact, it may further be pointed out that Subhūti,[2] a prominent figure in the Sarvāstivāda tradition, played an important rôle in the *Prajñāpāramitā.* It is anomalous to find a Hīnayāna monk explaining the śūnyatā doctirne, which goes directly against his own: so the *Prajñāpāramitā* offers us an explanation of the anomaly by saying that whatever was preached by Subhūti was not according to his own lights but through the inspiration of Buddhas. The adoption of the *Lalita Vistara* by the Mahāyānists as the recognized *Life of Buddha* also shows a point of contact between them and the Sarvāstivādins, for, as we learn from the Chinese translators, the *Lalita Vistara* was a biography of Buddha of the Sarvāstivāda school. Mahāyānism in all probability germinated in the south, where the offshoots of the Mahāsaṅghikas had their centres of activities, but where it appeared more developed was a place somewhere in the eastern part of India, a place where the Sarvāstivādins were predominant. Tāranātha tells us that the *Prajñāpāramitā* was first preached by Mañjuśrī at Oḍiviśa (Orissa),[3] which, if not the actual centre of Sarvāstivādins, was in the neighbourhood of the Sarvāstivāda spheres of influence, for it has already been stated that Dhitika propagated Sarvāstivāda Buddhism in Kāmrūpa and Puṇḍravardhana, which was the extended eastern limit of the Madhāyadeśa. But the most fruitful contact between the Sarvāstivādins and the Mahāyānists took place at Nālandā, which became the principal centre of Mahāyāna and the seat of Nāgārjuna.

1. See my *Aspects of Mahāyāna*, etc. chapter III.

2. See, *e.g.*, the *Ava. Ś.*, pp. 127-132 and p. xl. (*Kalpadrumāvadāna*); R. L. Mitra, *Nep. B. Lit.*, pp. 295-6. In the *Apadāna*, and in the *Aṅguttara*, and its commentary, Subhūti is mentioned as the chief of the Araṇavihārins, but he is not given much prominence in Pāli works.

3. *Tāra.*, p. 58.

The Mahāsaṅghikas were basically Hīnayānists

Thus it is apparent that the Sarvāstivādins were as much responsible for the growth of Mahāyāna as the Mahāsaṅghikas. Apart from the Buddhological speculations, the Mahāsaṅghikas cannot claim much as their contribution to the growth of Mahāyāna. It may be that the *Prajñāpāramitā* which, as the Tibetan tradition[1] tells us, was possessed by the Pūrvaśailas, contributed much to the philosophy of Mahāyāna, but as yet we are completely in the dark about this *Prajñāpāramitā*. From Vasumitra's account of the tenets of the Mahāsaṅghikas[2] or from the discussions found in the *Kathāvatthu* about the doctrines of the Mahāsaṅghikas, one hardly notices anything particularly Mahāyānic in them. For instance, the Mahāsaṅghikas speak

(i) of the pañca-(or ṣaḍ-)vijñānakāyas, differing from the Theravādins and the Sarvāstivādins as to the function of the physical organs of sense;[3]

(ii) of the four or eight Hīnayānic stages of sanctification along with the attainments appertaining thereto,[4] the *Kathāvatthu* adding that the Māhāsaṅghikas assert that the Arhats have avijjā, vicikicchā, as they cannot comprehend the things that come within the purview of (Buddhaviṣaya);[5]

(iii) of the indispensability of the application (prayoga) of prajñā, for destroying duḥkha and obtaining accanta-sukha (*i.e.*,

---

1. *Tāra.*, p. 58.
2. Masuda, *op. cit.* See also above, pp. 110, 169, 206.
3. Masuda, *op. cit.*, I, 22-4; *Kvu.*, xviii, 9; x, 3-4: Pañcaviññāṇasamaṅgissa atthi maggabhāvanā (one may practise the path while he has five-fold consciousness. The conception of Vijñāna of the Mahāsaṅghikas is a little different from that of the Theravādins and the Sarvāstivādins, specially in view of two other tenets held by them, viz., "At one and the same moment, two mental states can arise side by side" and "the nature of mind is pure in its origin, etc." Masuda, *op cit.*, A. 43, B. 3.
4. Masuda, *op. cit.*, I, 26-30, 33-5, 39, 48; *Mtu.*, I, p. 139.
5. *Kvu.*, xxi. 3; i, 2. The Theravādins hold that sabbaññutañāṇa (omniscience) is a special acquisition of Buddhas and beyond the scope of Arhats; so it is wrong to hold that Arhats have avijjā, vicikicchā. Cf. Vasumitra (Masuda, *op. cit.*, I, 35): "That according to the Mahāsaṅghikas, Arhats are liable to sink while the *Kathāvatthu* (i, 2, *Cy.*, p. 35) says that some of the Mahāsaṅghikas hold that Arhats are not so liable."

final beatitude, Nirvāṇa), one of the most important tenets of the Hīnayānic schools;[1]

(iv) of samyagdṛṣṭi, śraddhendriya as not laukika (worldly), the *Kathāvatthu*[2] adding that the Mahāsaṅghikas hold that old age and death could neither be lokiya (worldly) nor lokottara (transcendental), because they are apariniṣpanna (unmade),[3] and because the "decay and death of supramundane beings and things is supramundane and cannot be mundane";[4]

(v) of samyaktva-nyāma[5] (destined for right knowledge) and the consequent destruction of saṃyojanas (fetters);

(vi) of Buddha's preaching the Dharma in the nītārtha sense;[6]

(vii) of asaṃskṛta dharmas as being nine in contrast to three of the Sarvāstivādins;[7]

(viii) of upakleśas (impurities), anuśayas (dormant passions) and paryavasthānas (pervading passions);[8]

(ix) of the non-existence of phenomena of the past and future, as against the opinion of the Sarvāstivādins,[9] and

(x) of the non-existence of antarābhava (existence intermediate between death and re-birth) as against the opinion of the Sarvāstivādins[10] and the Sammitīyas.

In these and on a few other points of difference noticed in the work of Vasumitra and the *Kathāvatthu*, there is very little to distinguish them as distinctly Mahāyānic. In the *Mahāvastu*[11]

---

1. Masuda. *op. cit.*, I. 31: For Prajñā and Prayoga, see also *Mtu.* I, p. 270. Throughout *Mtu.* one notices that Nirvāṇa was conceived as sukha (kṣeme sthale śame nirvāṇe, *Mtu.*, I. p. 34). The Mahāyānists have nothing to do with duḥkha or sukha.
2. *Kvu.*, xv, 6. See also above, p. 92.
3. Mrs. Rhys Davids translates it as "not pre-determined."
4. *Points of the Controversy*, xv, 6.
5. i.e., one who has entered into the Darśanamārga, see Masuda, *op. cit.*, p. 27 fn.; Cf. *Pañca*, leaf 262b
6. Masuda, *op cit.*, I, 5, 40. This goes directly against the Mahāyānic view that Buddha's discourses have two senses, nītārtha and neyārtha, and also against the Sarvāstivāda view. See Masuda, *op cit.*, p. 52.
7. Masuda. *op. cit.*, I, 41; see above, pp. 113, 125.
8. Ibid., I, 44; see above, p. 92.
9. Ibid., I; 45; see above, p. 158f.
10. Ibid., I, 47; see above, pp. 114, 125.
11. It does not really belong to the Mahāsaṅghikas; so its date must be later, and it may be relegated to the third period of our division. Only those passages which corroborate the tenets of the Mahāsaṅghikas mentioned in the treatise of Vasumitra are referred to here.

also, the discourses on the Truths[1] or the Causal Law, or on anitya, duḥkha, and anātma do not go beyond the limits of Hīnayāna conceptions. The only Mahāyānic traces in the tenets of the Mahāsaṅghikas are :

(i) the Buddhological speculation, *viz.*, that Buddhas are lokottara (supramundane), without any sāsrava dharma (defiled elements), possessed of limitless rūpakāya (physical body),[2] prabhāva (power), and āyu[3] (length of life), can remain without any sleep or dream, are always in samādhi, and do not preach by name or designation, possess kṣaṇikacitta (*i.e.* understand all dharmas with a moment's thought), and so forth (see above, p. 100); and

(ii) the Bodhisattva conception, *viz.*, that the Bodhisattvas are not born and do not grow in the womb the same way as an ordinary being, are not defiled by the impurities of the womb,[4] enter the womb in full consciousness,[5] never harbour any feeling of kāma (lust),[6] dveṣa (hatred or enmity), and moha (delusion) take birth in hīna-gatis (lower forms of existence) for the benefit of the various classes of sentient beings, and so forth.[7]

These Buddhological speculations are more or less corollaries to the Mahāsaṅghika conception of the life of Śākyamuni. The Mahāsaṅghikas do not show thereby any recognition that all beings can become Bodhisattvas and ultimately Buddhas. The

1. *Mtu.*, III, pp. 334, 446.

2. Cf. *Mtu.*, I, p. 263 : Buddha appears everywhere. In the *Nikāyas* one also reads "eko pi hutvā bahudhā hoti, etc." *Dīgha*, I, p. 78. In the *Lalita Vistara* (p. 100) we read of the Bodhisattva appearing in all the houses presented to him by the Sakiyans.

3. Masuda, *op. cit.*, I, pp. 18, 19; *Kvu.*, xi, 5 : The Mahāsaṅghikas cite the passage of the *Mahāparinibbāna Sutta*, in which Buddha said to Ānanda that he could live many kalpas if he had so wished. The Theravādins without refuting this statement cite another passage which goes against this view.

4. *Mtu.*, I, p. 143; II, pp. 14-15 : Garbhāvakrānti and sthiti are all miraculous; Bodhisattvas are not touched by any impurities. *Mtu.*, II, pp. 16, 20. See above, p. 103.

5. *Mtu.*, II, p. 10.

6. *Mtu.*, I, p. 153 : Kāmā na sevanti. Rāhula was an aupapāduka. He descended from Tuṣita heaven and remained in his mother's womb for six years (*Mtu.*, III, p. 159).

7. Masuda, *op cit.*, p. 21.

conception of the four caryās and ten bhūmis of the Lokottaravādins indicates a slight leaning to Mahāyānism. Thus, there appears to be little of Mahāyāna in the tenets of the Mahāsaṅghikas.[1] The Mahāsaṅghikas, therefore, were basically Hīnayānists, only with the conception of Buddha slightly different.

Now we can state briefly the history of Buddhism in the second period thus :

1. Buddhism is no longer one. It is divided into three principal sections, *viz.*, Theravāda, Sarvāstivāda, and Mahāsaṅghika. The Theravādins remained in the central belt of India, making their position stronger in Avanti where Mahākccāyana had laid the foundation of Buddhism and from which place Mahendra was despatched to Ceylon to propagate Theravāda Buddhism there. The Sarvāstivādins were also in the central belt of India with their centres of activity in Mathura and Kashmir, the former having been founded by Upagupta and maintained by Madhyāntika, who spread it widely all over Northern India including Tukhāra on the north-west, Mālava on the west and Oḍiviśa (Orissa) and Kāmarūpa on the east. The Mahāsaṅghikas established themselves at Vaisāli and had followers sprinkled all over Northern India, but they became popular in the south. In short, Buddhism during this period spread all over Northern India and parts of Southern India.

2. Emperor Aśoka took great interest in Buddhism but did not help any particular sect. The *dhamma* preached in his edicts is mainly ethical and lacks the specific colouring of any school of Buddhism. He encouraged leading a righteous household life rather than the life of a monk or an ascetic. He, however, respected and supported the monks and recluses. The interest taken by rulers, like Mināra and Imhasa, helped greatly the propagation of Buddhism outside India.

---

1. The tenet of the Mahāsaṅghikas that "the nature of mind is pure in its origin; it becomes impure when it is stained by passions (upakleśas), the adventitious dust (āgantukarajas)" has, according to Masuda, been added by Aśvaghoṣa in his *Awakening of Faith*. See Masuda, *op. cit.*, p. 30.

3. The relation of the laity to the Buddhist Saṅgha was not materially altered as compared with the previous conditions but a greater interest was created for the laity by popularizing Buddhism through the Jātakas and Avadānas, and by holding up the Pāramitā practices before them as ideal.

4. Much stress was laid on the composition of the *Jātakas* and *Avadānas*, and great religious merit was attached to reading, writing, painting, and carving them. This caught the fancy of the laity as a means of earning religious merit, and resulted in many sculptures, some of which only are preserved at Sanchi and Bharhut. The credit for popularizing the religion through the Jātakas and Avadānas goes, at the first instance, to the Sarvāstivādins, and, later, to the Theravādins.

5. The old division of *Navāṅga* was increased to *Dvādaśāṅga* by the addition of Nidāna, Avadāna, and Upadeśa. Though the Jātakas formed one of the divisions of the Navāṅga, they did not exist as a separate literature, but were embodied in the discourses purporting to have been delivered by Buddha and his disciples.

6. The account of the *Life of Buddha* commenced not from the time of Sidhārtha's retirement but from the first resolution (praṇidhāna) made by Sumedha Brāhmaṇa, and the prophecy (veyyākaraṇa) made by Dīpaṅkara Buddha.

7. The essential doctrines are still the same as in the first period with slight changes *e.g.*, the addition of *śūnya* to the usual anitya, duḥkha, and anātman, and of the six pāramitās to the thirty-seven Bodhipakṣika dharmas.

8. Some radical changes were effected in the tenets of the schools, which developed during this period, *e.g.*, the Sarvāstivādins started their doctrine of realism, of the existence of past, present, and future, and so forth, while the Mahāsaṅghikas conceived Buddha docetically and introduced the Bodhisattva conception.

9. The goal of life remained Arhathood and Pratyekabuddhahood with the Theravādins, while the Sarvāstivādins added to them the goal of Samyaksambuddhahood.

10. The conception of *Nirvāṇa* as sukha, śānta, etc., did not change much, the Sarvāstivādins, and the Mahāsaṅghikas agreeing mainly with the Theravādins.[1] But the doctrine of realism of the Sarvāstivādins has led Prof. Stcherbatsky to interpret their Nirvāṇa as an ultimate lifeless state.[2]

11. The growth of the *Abhidhamma* literature took place during this period. As the principal schools located their centres of activity at different places, the development of the literature of each school was independent of one another. This accounts for the wide divergence between the Abhidhamma literature of the Theravādins and that of the Sarvāstivādins.

12. The conception of Bodhisattva, Pāramitā practices, and the goal of Buddhahood are the only Mahāyānic traces that appeared in the doctrines of the Mahāsaṅghikas and Sarvāstivādins, and their offshoots.

Third Period

(*circa* 100 B.C. *to* 300 A.D.)

C. The Beginning of Mahāyāna

Before proceeding to ascertain the approximate time of the emergence of Mahāyāna, the special characteristics, which distinguish Mahāyāna from Hīnayāna should be determined. Generally speaking, Mahāyānism denotes:

(i) the conception of Bodhisattva,

(ii) the practice of Pāramitiās.

---

1. The Sarvāstivādins held that the *vimukti* of the Śrāvakas, Pratyekabuddhas, and Buddhas is the same. (Masuda, *op. cit.*, p. 49.) The Mahiśāsakas held the same view (Masuda, *op. cit.*, p. 62), but not the Dharmaguptas. The *Sūtrālaṅkāra*, however, holds that with regard to *vimukti*, the Buddhas and the Śrāvakas stand on the same footing. This is also the opinion found in the other Yogācāra texts. Cf. also *Mtu.*, II, pp. 285, 345.

2. Stcherbatsky, *Conception of Nirvāṇa*, pp. 25ff.

(iii) the development of Bodhicitta,

(iv) the ten stages (*bhūmi*) of spiritual progress,

(v) the goal of Buddhahood,

(vi) the conception of Trikāya, and

(vii) the conception of Dharmaśūnyatā or Dharmasamatā or Tathatā.

The Mahāyānists distinguish themselves by saying that they seek the removal of both *kleśāvaraṇa* (veil of impurities) and *jñeyāvaraṇa* (veil covering the paramārtha truth), and this is possible by the realization of both *pudgalaśūnyatā* (absence of soul) and *dharmaśūnyatā* (non-existence of all beings and objects). The Hīnayānists realize only the former and thereby remove kleśāvaraṇa only. They, therefore, attain *vimukti* (emancipation) from *kleśas*, and as far as this is concerned, they are on the same footing as the Mahāyānists, but they lack true knowledge as conceived by the Mahāyānists, *viz*., dharmaśūnyatā, because they do not remove jñeyāvaraṇa. The Hīnayānists, however, do not admit their inferiority with regard to jñāna, for they consider that the destruction of avidyā (ignorance of truth) or, in other words, acquisition of true knowledge is the only means to emancipation, and this is effected by Arhats in the same way as by Buddhas. The Arhats are very often mentioned in the Pāli works as attaining sambodhi. They, however, admit that Buddhas on account of their superior merits (technically, *gotra*) due to their long practice of meritorious deeds, attain some powers and excellences and also omniscience, which are beyond the reach of the Arhats. This in short, is the relative position of the Hīnayānists and the Mahāyānists.

If the development of Hīnayāna in its various phases be examined, one cannot help observing that some of the distinguishing characteristics of Mahāyāna mentioned above are also found in the later phases of Hīnayāna *e.g.*,

(i) conception of Bodhisattva,

(ii) practice of six pāramitās,

(iii) development of Bodhicitta,

(iv) goal of Buddhahood, and

(v) two of the three Kāya conceptions, *viz.*, Rūpa (or Nirmāṇa-)kāya and Dharmakāya, the conception of the latter being essentially different from that of the Mahāyānists.[1] So, to be exact about the time of emergence of Mahāyāna, we should consider when the conceptions of Dharmaśūnyatā and Dharmakāya (= Tathatā) were introduced.

Semi-Mahāyāna

From what has been sta'ed above in regard to the lines of development in the preceding period, it is evident that the Hīnayānists, either to popularize their religion or to interest the laity more in it, incorporated in their doctrines the conception of Bodhisattva and the practice of pāramitās.[2] This was effected by the production of new literature: the *Jātakas* and *Avadānas*. While the Jātakas are confined to the previous lives of Buddha, the Avadānas introduced the Bodhisattva conception, and presented the same as an ideal for the laity. The object of the Avadānas is to show how the devotees sacrificed everything, even their lives, for perfection in one of the pāramitās, not for any earthly or heavenly pleasures, but for the attainment of bodhi and then for rescuing all beings from misery.[3]

---

1. In the *Mtu.*, the expression Sambhogakāya does not occur; yet the description of Buddha's body sometimes shows it to be tantamount to that conception.

2. For an interesting discussion on this point see Speyer, *Ava. Ś.*, pp. v ff.

3. *Divyā.*, p. 473 : Rūpavatī makes sacrifice for "na rājyārthaṃ na bhogārthaṃ na svargārthaṃ na śakrārthaṃ na rājñāṃ cakravartināṃ viṣayārthaṃ nānyatrāham anuttarāṃ samyaksambodhim abhisambudhyādāntān damayeyam amuktān mocayeyam anāśvastān āśvāsayeyam aparinirvṛtān parinirvāpayeyaṃ."

The *Divyāvadāna*, as stated above, refers to the aspiration after the attainment of Buddhahood; the *Mahāvastu*[1] also refers to devotees developing Bodhicitta and aspiring after Buddhahood by the simple act of worshipping a stūpa or offering some gifts to it. In connection with the Sarvāstivādins, Vasumitra speaks (i) of the sameness of *vimukti* of Buddhas, Śrāvakas and Pratyekabuddhas (ii) and also of the three Yānas; and (iii) of Bodhisattvas continuing to be pṛthagjana till they step into the samyaktva-nyāma (the path leading to right knowledge).[2] The *Mahāvastu* also speaks of the existence of the three Yānas[3] and of the paths and practices to be followed by a Bodhisattva. It mentions the four *caryās* of a Bodhisattva and the ten *bhūmis*, but the conception of the bhūmis[4] has very little in common with that of the ten bhūmis of the *Daśabhūmikasūtra* and *Bodhisattva-bhūmi*[5] except the first two. Of course, it may be assumed that the Lokottaravāda conception of the bhūmis served as the source for the later development of the Mahāyānic conception.

Thus the Avadānas, which are primarily the production of the Sarvāstivādins, clearly show a new phase of development of

---

1. *Mtu.*, pp. 364, 365, 367 : bodhāya cittaṃ nametvā; pp. 375, 377 bodhim atulyaṃ spṛśati. See above, p. 78.

2. Masuda, *op. cit.*, p. 49 : "The Buddha and the two vehicles have no differences as to emancipation (vimukti) : the Āryan paths (mārga) of the three vehicles (however) differ from one another. This is wanting in the Tibetan version," Masuda refutes Wassiljew's opinion (p. 275, n. 4) that it was an interpolation of the later Mahāyānists. For vimuktisāmānya of Śrāvakas, Pratyekabuddhas, and Buddhas, see above p. 125.

Masuda, *op. cit.*, p. 50 : The Haimavata school supported the Sarvāstivādins on this point, adding, however, that the Bodhisattvas were not subject to rāga and kāma. See Masuda, *op. cit.*, p. 52. The *Mtu.* calls a Bodhisattva in the first bhūmi a pṛthagjana, who becomes an Ārya from the second bhūmi.

3. *Mtu.*, II, p. 362.

4. Rahder's Intro. to *Daśa.*, pp. iii f.

5. Edited by the present author.

Hīnayānic Bodhisattva-yāna. The Lokottaravādins[1] of the Mahāsaṅghikas show a little more development than the Sarvāstivādins by defining the four *caryās*, *viz. prakṛticaryā, praṇidhānacaryā, anulomacaryā*, and *anivartanacaryā*,[2] the first referring to the preliminary practices of a Bodhisattva while he is a pṛthagjana, the second to the development of Bodhicitta, the third to the gradual progress made by a Bodhisattva up to the sixth bhūmi, and the fourth to the practice of the last four bhūmis,[2] from which a Bodhisattva can never retrocede but ultimately must attain Bodhi. The attainment of Bodhi, therefore, came to be regarded as one of the goals of Hīnayāna. It is for this reason that the *kośa*[3] has discussed the thirty-four moments required for the attainment of Bodhi, and other matters relating to Buddhahood, and the Hīnayānic works[4] mention some of the Bodhisattva practices as well as philosophical expressions like śūnyatā, dharmadhātu, dharmakāya, tathātva, though these are devoid of their Mahāyānic sense.

In view of these facts, it may be held that before Mahāyāna came into being with its new interpretation of Buddha's words evolving a new sense of śūnyatā, there had already been a Hīnayānic Bodhisattvayāna, which might be called semi-Mahāyāna, or Mahāyāna in the making. This semi-Mahāyānism concerned itself only with the six Pāramitā practices and the extraordinary powers and knowledge attained by Buddhas. It was as yet unaware of 'Advaya Advaidhīkāra,' Dharmaśūnyatā or Tathatā. That the six pāramitās belong to the domain of Hīnayāna is also hinted at in the *Daśabhūmikasūtra*. In this sūtra as well as in other treatises dealing with bhūmis, the ten bhūmis are divided

---

1. *Mtu*, II, p. 46; *Lal. Vis.*, p. 35.

2. Since the writer of the *Mtu.* had very vague ideas about the last four bhūmis, he dismissed them with mere enumeration of some names of Buddhas and recounting some stories.

3. *Kośa*, II, 44; VI, 21a-b; cf. *Kvu.*, i. 5. *Paṭis. M.*, I, pp. 121ff. discusses the ñāṇa of Buddhas.

4. *Mtu.*, II, p. 357 : Śūnyatāṃ śāntaṃ bhāventi, see also *Saṃyutta* II, p. 267; III, p. 167.

into two sections, the first six carrying a Bodhisattva to the realization of Pudgalaśūnyatā, or in other words, the Truth as conceived by the Hīnayānists, and the last four leading to the realization of Dharmaśūnyatā, the Truth as conceived by the Mahāyānists. So the actual Mahāyānic stages of progress commenced from the seventh, but it is stated in the *Daśabhūmika-sūtra* that the six pāramitās are completed by a Bodhisattva in the first six bhūmis. Thus it follows that the practice of Pāramitās alone does not make a person a follower of Mahāyāna, though it must be admitted that Mahāyāna takes its stand upon the pāramitās as far as the practices are concerned, for it is said in the *Prajñāpāramitās* that Buddhas deliver discourses connected with the six pāramitās,[1] and also in the *Madhyamakāvatāra*[2] that Mahāyāna teaches not only śūnyatā but also pāramitās, bhūmis, and so forth. Lastly, the fact namely, that the conceptions of *nirnimitta* and *niḥsvabhāva*, indicating the chief features of the attainments of a Bodhisattva in the last four bhūmis, were yet unknown to the compiler of the *Mahāvastu*, is evident from his non-mention of the qualities attained in the last four bhūmis. Hence, it may be concluded that Buddhism entered into its semi-Mahāyānic stage very early, if not at the time of Aśoka, at any rate, soon after him.

The time of composition of the *Prājñāpāramitā*

The new Mahāyānic conception of Śūnyatā was for the first time propounded in the *Prajñāpāramitās*. It should, therefore be ascertained when the *Prajñpāramitā* first came into existence. This is a Tibetan tradition that the Pūrvaśailas and Aparaśailas had a *Prajñāpāramitā* in Prākṛt dialect;[3] unfortunately no other

1. *Pañca.*, p. 7 : ṣaṭpāramitāpratisaṃyuktāṃ dharmadeśanāṃ karoti.
2. *M. Ava.*, (*Le Muséon*, VII, p. 271) : En effet, la doctrine du Grand Véhicule n'enseigne pas seulement le néant des éléments, mais encore les terres des Bodhisattvas, les vertus transcendantes (pāramitās), les resolutions (praṇidhāna), la grande compassion, etc., mais encore l'application du merite á illumination, les deux equipments de mérite et de savoir et la nature incomprehensible du dharma (acintya-dharmatā).
3. Wassiljew, *Buddhismus*, p. 291 quoting the Tibetan *Siddhānta*.

information about it is forthcoming. Tāranātha tells us that shortly after the time of king Mahāpadma Nanda, a king called Candragupta reigned in Oḍiviśa (Orissa)[1]. Mañjuśrī came to his house in the form of a bhikṣu and delivered the Mahāyāna teaching. The Sautrāntikas maintained that this teaching denoted the *Aṣṭasāhasrikā Prajñāpāramitā*, but the Tantric school asserted that it indicated the *Tattvasaṅgraha*.[2] It may be safely stated that the Tantric tradition was baseless in view of the subjects treated in the *Tattvasaṅgraha*,[3] and preference should be given to the Sautrāntika tradition that the *Aṣṭasāhasrikā* was the earliest text to contain Mahāyāna teaching. If the contents of the *Aṣṭasāhasrikā*, *Pañcaviṃśatisāhasrikā*, and *Śatasāhasrikā* be compared, it will be seen that the *Aṣṭasāhasrikā* is the earliest of the three and that it can be as early as the first century B.C.[4]

THE GEOGRAPHICAL DATA ABOUT THE ORIGIN OF MAHĀYĀNA

Without attaching much importance to the chronology of kings and such other information presented by Tāranātha, one may with sufficient caution utilize some of his statements with regard to the developments in the history of Buddhism, the geographical distribution of the schools, and the succession of teachers in the various centres. He states that, according to one tradition, 500 bodhisattvas[5] took part in the Jalandhara Council of Kaṇiṣka, that about this time the Mahāyāna texts appeared and were usually preached by monks who had attained

1. *Tāra.*, p. 58; *Pag Sam Jon Zang.*, p. 82 also says that Mahāyāna Buddhism had its beginning in Oḍiviśa shortly after the reign of Mahāpadma Nanda.
2. Recently published in the Gaekwad Oriental Series.
3. For a survey of its contents see my review in *I.H.Q.*, Dec., 1929.
4. For deails, see Intro, to the *Pañca*.
5. Aśvaghoṣa is called a bodhisattva in the Chinese *Saṃyukta-ratna-piṭaka-sūtra.* (No. 1329, Vol. VI). See Takakusu, *I-tsing*, p. lix. Cf. De Groot, *Le Code du Mahayana en Chine*, p. 8 : Two or three days after the first ordination, according to the Prātimokṣa rules, the monks pass through a special ordination according to the Brahmajāla sūtra and become bodhisattvas.

the *anutpattika dharmakṣānti* (faith in the non-origination of all *dharmas*)[1], a dogma characteristic of Mahāyānism. It may be a development of the Hīnayānic *Kṣayajñāna*,[2] (eradication of āsravas) and Anutpādajñāna (non-origin) and hence non-rebirth, but it bore a completely different sense in the Mahāyāna scriptures. The reference to the existence of a class of monks called Bodhisattvas at the time of Kaṇiṣka's Council is also significant, for the *Divyāvadāna* speaks of the existence of a class of monks called *Bodhisattvajātika* along with a hint that they were not looked upon with favour by the Hīnayānists.[3] Tāranātha expresses his difficulty in accounting for the existence of monks called Bodhisattvas in the Kaṇiṣkan Council. He tells us further that about the time of Kaṇiṣka, the Brāhmaṇa Kulika of Saurāṣṭra invited the Sthavira Arahanta Nanda, a native of Aṅga, who had comprehended the Mahāyāna teaching, in order to hear from him the new teaching.[4] The only point that deserves notice is the use of the appellations, Arahanta and Sthavira, indicating that Nanda was a Hīnayānist monk, who had comprehended the Mahāyāna teaching. The remark of Tāranātha that the monks who had attained anutpattikadharmakṣānti preached also Mahāyāna, shows there was a class of Hīnayāna monks, who had been propagating the Mahāyāna teaching.[5] Then the associations of Oḍiviśa with the beginning of Mahāyāna teaching and that of the monk Nanda with Aṅga suggest that the origin of Mahāyāna should be looked for somewhere in the east. A passage occurring in all the *Prajñāpāramitās*, partially lends support to the statement of Tāranātha. In this passage it is stated that Mahāyāna teaching would originate in the south (Dakṣiṇāpatha), pass to the eastern countries (Vartanyām),[6] and prosper in the north. Evidently, the

1. *Tāra.*, p. 61. See *M. Vr.*, p. 363c., *Laṅka.*, p. 81; *Aṣṭa.*, p. 331 : anutpādajñāna-kṣāntika bodhisattva.

2. For Anutpādajñāna and Kṣayajñāna, see *Kośa*, VI, 17, 71. The Kṣayajñāna with the Anutpādajñāna produces Bodhi; see also *Kośa*, vi. 50; vii, 1, 46, 7. See above, pp. 159-61.

3. *Divyā.*, p. 261.

4. *Tāra.*, p. 62.

5. Perhaps Aśvaghoṣa, author of the *Buddhacarita*, and the *Śraddhotpāda-sūtra* belonged to this class of Hīnayāna monks.

6. *Aṣṭa.*, p. 225. For Vartanyām, see *Trikāṇḍaśeṣa*, 2, 1. 12.

statement of the *Prajñāpāramitā* was written while the work was composed in the north after the Mahāyāna teaching had been effectively propagated there. This statement may be substantiated by pointing to the Tibetan tradition about the existence of a *Prajñāpāramitā* in the Prākṛt dialect belonging to the Śaila schools, the centre of which was in the south (Guntur District). Very probably, this *Prajñāpāramitā* contained the rudiments of Mahāyāna teaching. Then the shifting of the centre of Mahāyāna to the east is hinted at by Tāranātha, as mentioned above. In this connection it may also be pointed out that Nālandā was one of the earliest centres and store-houses of Mahāyāna teaching, becoming, later on, the seat of Nāgārjuna. It seems quite probable that Mahāyānism originated in the south some time before Kaṇiṣka and became a recognized form of Buddhism by the time of Kaṇiṣka, *i.e.* about the beginning of the Christian era when it established its chief centre in the east, gradually pushing its way towards the north to blossom forth in its full glory under the care of the great Nāgārjuna. In the south too, it continued to thrive, for in the *Gaṇḍavyūha* it is stated that Mañjuśrī started from Jetavana to travel in Dakṣiṇāpatha[1] and came to Tāladhvajavyūha-caitya in the great city of Dhanyākara,[2] where many devotees lived. Here he delivered a discourse and aroused aspiration for bodhi in the mind of Sudhana, son of a rich banker of the place and directed him to go to Sugrīvaparvata in the country of Rāmavartta (also in Dakṣiṇāpatha) in order to learn the Samantabhadra-bodhisattva-caryā. Sudhana travelled to many places[3] of the Dakṣiṇāpatha in search of knowledge, arriving at last at Dvāravatī. After learning all that he could in southern India, he went to Kapilavastu and visited some countries[4] of the north. In the *Mañjuśrīmūla-*

1. *Gaṇḍavyūha* edited by D. T. Suzuki and Hokei Idzumi, p. 154.

2. *Ibid.* p. 50 : Dakṣināpathe Dhanyākaran nāma mahānagaram; very likely it is the same as the famous Dhānyakaṭaka (Dharaṇikoṭa).

3. The names of places in some cases seem to be fictitious; some of the names are :—Sāgaramukha, Sāgaranāma Laṅkāpatha, Vajrapuranāma Draviḍa-paṭṭana, Vanavāsī, Milasphuranaṃ nāma Jambudvīpaśirṣam, Potalaka (the dwelling place of Avalokiteśvara), and Dvāravatī.

4. The northern countries visited by Sudhana are : Bodhimaṇḍa and Kapilavastu.

kalpa[1] also Dhānyakaṭaka, Śrīparvata, and a few other places of the Dakṣiṇāpatha are mentioned, showing the prevalence of Buddhism there. Nāgārjuna, whose birth-place was in Vidarbha (Berar),[2] also dwelt in the south, passing his last days at Śrīparvata (mod. Śrīśailam).[3] Āryadeva likewise came from Southern India, as did Nāga,[4] the other disciple of Nāgārjuna. It appears therefore that the south may claim credit for being not only the place of origin of Mahāyāna but also of some of the notable figures, who were instrumental in making Mahāyāna what it was in the 2nd and 3rd centuries A.D. The dates of Āryadeva and Nāga are placed in the early part of the 3rd century (200-225), and, Nāgārjuna precedes them by a few decades.[5] The glory of Nāgārjuna and his school of philosophy threw into shade the great figure of Maitreya, the traditional founder of the Yogācāra school, until the time of Asaṅga, who brought his works into prominence and placed this school of philosophy on a high pedestal.

Nature of the contents of early Mahāyāna works

The first two centuries of the Christian era witnessed a conflict between Hīnayāna and Mahāyāna as well as the systematization of the Mahāyāna doctrines. The works, which depict (in one-sided fashion, it must be admitted) this struggle, are, *viz.*, the *Prajñāpāramitās*, *Saddharmapuṇḍarīka*, *Laṅkāvatāra*, *Daśabhūmikasūtra* and *Gaṇḍavyūha* were very probably the products of

---

1. *Mañjuśrīmūlakalpa* (Trivandrum Sanskrit Series), p. 88.
2. Walleser, *Die Lebenszeit des Nāgārjuna* in *Z. fur Buddhismus* (Munich), I, pp. 95ff.
3. Nāgārjuna's name is closely associated with Dhānyakaṭaka, near which are Śrīparvata and Nāgārjunikoṇḍa (west of Palnad Taluk); for details see Burgess, *Stūpas of Amarāvati*, pp. 5, 6, 112; *Annual Report of South Indian Epigraphy*, 1926-7, p. 71.
4. Nāgāhvaya in *Laṅkā.*, p. 286 : see Vaidya's *Catuḥśatikā Intro.*, pp. 22, 61; Wassiljew, *op. cit.*, p. 130; Vidyābhūṣana's *Logic* (1st ed.), p. 71.
5. Prof. Walleser thinks it should be the beginning of the 2nd century. See Z. *fur Buddhismus* (6 Jahrgang, Schluss Heft), p. 242; *I-tsing*. p. lvii : Nāgārjuna, Aśvaghoṣa, and Āryadeva are regarded as contemporaries of Kaṇiṣka.

this period, but evidences are still lacking as to the exact dates of composition of these works. The only clue is supplied by the dates of their Chinese translations, but these are to be regarded as the latest limits of the time of their composition.[1] In the absence of any definite data about the earliest limit, one can take into consideration the nature of their contents, indicating a time when the Mahāyānists were trying to belittle the Hīnayānists. The *Prajñāpāramitās* are full of Hīnayānic technical expressions and phraseology and show how the position of the Hīnayānists is untenable, how they are deluded by the superficialities of their religion, and how insignificant is their knowledge in comparison with that of a Bodhisattva practising the prajñāpāramitā. The *Saddharma-puṇḍarīka* applies itself to the task of proving that the Hīnayānists are of poor intellect, but they can still make progress in religious matters, ultimately turning to Mahāyāna and comprehending the truth. The *Gaṇḍavyūha* essays to depict the great struggles of a Bodhisattva—struggles which are beyond the capacity of the Hīnayānists—in order to learn the Samantabhadra bodhisattvacaryā. Sudhana visits many Bodhisattvas, bhikṣus, bhikṣuṇīs, upāsakas and upāsikās versed in certain portion of the Caryā, and acquires the same from them. The *Daśabhūmikastūra*, as the title indicates, describes the practices connected with the bhūmis, the gradual stages of a bodhisattva's sanctification. It also never misses an opportunity to attack the Hīnayānists and to show how the last four bhūmis of the Bodhisattvas are

---

1. Dates of the Chinese translations :

(i) Of the *Prajñāpāramitās*, the earliest version translated was the *Daśasāhasrikā*, which, however, has no Sanskrit original. It was translated between 25 and 220 A.C.; the *Pañcaviṃśatisāhasrikā* between 265 and 316 A.D. and the *Śatasāhasrikā* about 659. A.D.

(ii) The *Saddharmapuṇḍarīka* was translated between 265 and 316 A.D. by Dharmarakṣa, and between 384 and 417 A.D. by Kumārajiva. For its various versions, see Hoernle, *Manuscript Remains, etc.*; *J.R.A.S.*, 1927, pp. 252ff.; Feer, *Annales du Musée Guimet*. II, p. 342; *As. Res.*, XX, p. 436; Wassiljew, *Buddhismus*, p. 151.

(iii) The *Laṅkāvatāra* was translated by Guṇabhadra (443 A.C.) and Bodhiruci (553). See *Eastern Buddhist*, IV, p. 99.

(iv) The *Daśabhūmikasūtra* was translated by Dharmarakṣa (297 A.C.) and by Kumārajīva (384-417). See Rahder's Intro. to the *Daśa*.

(v) The *Gaṇḍavyūha* was translated between 317 and 420 A.C.

wholly beyond the capacity of the śrāvakas. The *Laṅkāvatāra*, though one of the latest books of this group to be translated into Chinese, contains an exposition of the early Yogācāra system and harps throughout on the theme, viz., how the Hīnayānists are concerned only with svasāmānyalakṣaṇa (particular and generic characteristics of objects) and are ignorant of the non-existence of all objects.

The Mahāyāna works that immediately follow are those of Nāgārjuna, Asaṅga, Āryadeva, Vasubandhu, etc. Though the main object of Nāgārjuna's *Kārikā* is to establish the thesis that things are relatively existent, and that the truth is one and realizable only within one's own self, he takes up the dogma of the Hīnayānic schools and tries to prove its hollowness from the new standpoint set up by him. Asaṅga, though of a much later date, not allow the Hīnayānic doctrines to pass unnoticed. He shows in his *Sūtrālaṅkāra* the inferiority of the Hīnayānists in mental calibre and their unfitness to comprehend the truth. Vasubandhu likewise in his *Vijñaptimātratāsiddhi* pointedly indicates how the Hīnayānists labour under misconceptions, complete eradication of which is the aim of the Mahāyānists. Thus it is seen that though most of the works mentioned above belong to a time posterior to the appearance of Mahāyāna, they present materials illustrative of the conflict for ascendancy that was going on between the Hīnayānists and the Mahāyānists.

One remarkable feature, however, of the criticisms contained in these Mahāyānic works against the Hīnayānists is that they do not attempt to distort the position of the Hīnayānists in order to take advantage. The statements made in them with regard to the Hīnayānists are mostly borne out by the earlier and later Hīnayāna works. Hence, instead of distorting their real position, they throw a flood of light on the Hīnayānic doctrines. The Mahāyānists found fault with the Hīnayānists, not because they failed to comprehend the real teachings of Buddha but because they looked upon as truth that which appeared to the Mahāyānists as only partial truth.

APPENDIX

HIUEN TSANG ON THE DISPERSION OF BUDDHIST SECTS IN INDIA

(629-645 A.D.)

Hiuen Tsang (henceforth abbreviated as HT.) remarks in his introduction to the account of the state of Buddhism in India that Buddhism at his time, i.e., in the 7th century A.D., was pure or diluted according to the spiritual insight and mental capacity of its adherents. The first split in the saṅgha took place at Vaiśāli between the Sthaviras and Mahāsaṅghikas. Both recognized the three Piṭakas. The Mahāsaṅghikas, however, added the fourth Piṭaka known as the Vyākaraṇa (prophesies of Buddha) (W.I. 103-6).[1] The tenets of these sects kept them apart and became the subject-matter of controversies among the śāstra-matters of different sects. Each sect claimed to have intellectual superiority. There were "many noisy discussions," but side by side there were also monks "sitting in silent reveries" (*niṣīdana*), strolling to and fro (*caṅkrama*) usually while circumambulating a stūpa or temple, standing still (*ṭhāna*) or laying down (*śayana*). After such general remarks HT. proceeded to give an account of the state of the religion in different places, where he came across its adherents, mentioning the number of monks and monasteries, as well as the sects, to which they belonged. A brief synopsis is being presented here as per the peregrinations of the pilgrim within India.

The first country visited by HT. in India was—

Udyāna (= Ujjāna) in Swat valley, corresponding to the four districts of Panjkora, Bijawar, Swat and Buniz, situated on the north of Peshawar (Parashawar) (C. 194). The people of this

---

1. For distribution of sects on the basis of inscriptions so far discovered, see above, pp. 51ff.

2. Abbreviations used in this account are as follows :

HT.—Hiuen Tsang. The page numbers indicated are from Watters' Yuan Chwang, I and II.

place held Buddhism in high esteem and were reverential believers in Mahāyāna. There were formerly 140 monasteries with 18,000 monks. All these were in ruins and the number of monks was few. Fa-hien writes that though they were Mahāyānists, they followed the Hīnayāna Vinaya rules. HT. remarks that the monks could recite texts, but they did not comprehend the deeper meaning of the same. At this place there were 4 or 5 hamlets, one of which was known as Mang-kil. About 200 li from Mang-kil there was the Mahāvana monastery; not far from this monastery was the Rohitaka stūpa. At this place HT. came across five redactions of the Vinaya Piṭaka, belonging to the five sects, viz., Dharmaguptaka, Mahiśāsaka, Kāśyapīya, Sarvāstivāda and Mahāsaṅghika. (W.I. 226 f.).

Darel, the ancient capital of Udyāna government. It has been identified by Cunningham (p. 95) with the country of the Dards. In the valley, an image of Avalokiteśvara was erected at the instance of the missionary Madhyāntika. After the erection of this image, Buddhism became popular. Cunningham writes that the image of Buddha erected here was colossal.

Bolor, about 83 miles across the Indus. Cunningham identifies it with Balti or Little Tibet (C.96).[1] HT. records that there were several monasteries and monks, who were without learning and careless about the observance of the Saṅgha-rules.

Takṣaśilā, (modern Taxila in Pakistan). Its boundaries were as follows : in the north Urasā, in the east the Jhelum; in the south Siṃhapura, and in the west the Indus. The city has been identified by Cunningham with the ruins near Shah-dheri (=Royal Residence), 12 miles north-west of Rawalpindi (C. 120; Notes, 681). Here have been found, among other objects, traces of at least 55 stūpas, 28 monasteries, 9 temples, a copper-plate inscribed with the name 'Takṣaśilā' and a vase with Kharoṣṭhi inscription. (For further details, see Sir John Marshall's *Guide to Taxila.*) HT. refers to Śāntarakṣita and the Sautrāntika teacher Kumāralabdha, who dwelt here formerly.

HT. visited this country twice, once in 630 A.D. when he came

---

1. C. indicates Cunningham's *Ancient Geography of India* with Introduction and Notes by Prof. Surendranath Majumdar Sastri (edition 1924), and figures indicate page-numbers.

to this country and again in 645 A.D. on his return journey. He saw numerous monasteries but all in ruins. The few monks he saw were all Mahāyānists. The people were adherents of Buddhism. Emperor Aśoka sent here his son Kuṇāla for quelling disturbances and restoring peace to the region. The prince, however, was blinded through the machinations of his step-mother Tiṣyarakṣitā. His eyes were restored later by arhat Ghoṣa, who was a physician and an occultist (vide *Divyāvadāna*, XXVII).

There is a tradition that the ruler of Takṣaśilā was exceedingly rich, having nine crores of gold and silver coins (C.12). He was a contemporary of King Bimbisāra, who invited him to meet Buddha. He came and took ordination as a monk, but unfortunately on his way back, he met with an accident and lost his life (*Divyāvadāna*, XXVI). He donated his vast wealth for the construction of *stūpas* over Buddha's relics to be distributed later by Emperor Aśoka (W.I. 248).

Simhapura. From Takṣaśilā HT. travelled south-east about 117 miles to reach this place. This country was a dependency of Kashmir. Cunningham (p. 142) identifies its capital with Ketās, situated on the north side of the Salt Range. Near the south of the capital there was an Aśoka stūpa known as the Māṇikyāla stūpa, commemorating the sacrifice of his body by the Bodhisattva (i.e. in one of the previous lives of Buddha) to save the life of a tigress. Near this stūpa there was a monastery but it was deserted. HT. saw here Śvetāmbara Jaina monks. He noticed one monastery, in which there were about 100 monks, who were all Mahāyānists. From this place HT. proceeded about 8 miles eastward to an isolated hill where also was a monastery with about 200 monks, who were also Mahāyānists.

Kashmir. On his way from Siṃhapura to Kashmir HT. came across several monasteries. At Huṣkara-vihāra he spent the night. He was welcomed by the king of the place. He lodged for one night in Jayendra-vihāra (W.I. 259). The king gave him 20 clerks to copy the manuscripts. HT. remained there for two years and devoted his time to the study of the Sūtras and Śāstras.

Kashmir was variously known as Kapis, Nagar, Gandhāra, and Udyāna. Kapis (or Kipin) was formerly occupied by the Śakas.

Ṛṣi Revata or Raivataka was converted here to Buddhism (W.I. 260). HT. refers to Madhyāndina, a disciple of Ānanda, the missionary sent to this country after the Third Buddhist Council held at Pāṭaliputra. HT. saw there 100 monasteries and 5,000 monks. On his way he crossed Uṣkara and Baramula (=Varāha-mūla-pura). Along with Madhyāndina went 500 Arhats and 500 ordinary monks. Among the latter was one called Mahādeva of great learning and a subtle investigator of *nāma* and *rūpa* (=mind and matter). He was the son of a Brāhmaṇa merchant of Mathura (W.I.268). He committed the *ānantarīya* (deadly) sins. It is evident that he was mistaken for the Mahādeva who brought about the split in the Saṅgha in the Second Buddhist Council (*vide* above, p. 22). There was also another Mahādeva, who preached the *Devadūtasūtra* and was an influential abbot of Pāṭaliputra (W.I. 269).

The outstanding event that took place in Kashmir was the session of the Fourth Buddhist Council under the auspices of Emperor Kaṇiṣka in the 400th year after Buddha's mahāparinirvāṇa. The emperor was puzzled by the different interpretations given by his spiritual teachers while he was studying the Buddhist texts, and so he wanted that the main object of this Council should be to record the various interpretations given of Buddha's words by the teachers of different sects. It was at Arhat Pārśva's advice that the Emperor decided to hold the Council (W.I. 271).

HT. found in this country one monastery with 300 monks, but no mention is made of their sect. In one monastery he saw the image of Bodhisattva Avalokiteśvara. He refe red to Ācārya Saṃghabhadra, a Kashmirian Sarvāstivādin, who composed the *Kośa-kārikāśāstra* in 25,000 ślokas, and to Ācārya Skandhila, who composed the *Abhidharmāvatāraśāstra*. He found here a Mahāsaṅghika monastery also (W.I. 279).

Punach. From Kashmir HT. travelled 117 miles north-west to reach this place. According to Cunningham (pp. 147-8), it was bounded on the west by the Jhelum river, on the north by the Pir Panchal range, and on the east and south-east by Rajaori. In the 7th century it was subject to Kashmir. HT. records that there were 5 monasteries in ruins. In one monastery there were only a few monks. No sect is mentioned (W.I. 284).

Rājapura (=Rajaori, south of Kashmir). HT. travelled 67 miles south-east from Kashmir to reach this place. It was bounded on the north by the Pir Panchal range, on the west by Punach, on the south by Bhimbar and on the east by Rihan and Aknur (C. 149). HT. saw here 10 monasteries with a few monks. No sect is mentioned (W.I. 284).

Sākala (=Sangalawala Ṭiba; C.212=Sāgala of the *Milindapañha*). Cunningham traces (i) a modern town in the midst of the ruins, (ii) a *stūpa* of Aśoka, one mile to the north-west of the monastery inside the town. The low ridges of a rock have been identified by Cunningham with Mundapāpura, which is still known as the land of the Madras. HT. records that it was the capital of King Mihirakula. It was also known as the Yona country. This king wanted to study the Buddhist scriptures and requested the monks to depute a learned monk, but unfortunately the monks selected a Śramaṇa, who was an attendant of the monks. For this, the king felt insulted, got enraged and became determined to exterminate Buddhism from his realm. At this time Bālāditya, a Gupta ruler and a zealous advocate of Buddhism, rebelled against him and made him a prisoner, but at the request of his mother, he was released, but Mihirakula was later murdered by his brother, who then occupied the throne, was also a persecutor of Buddhism (W.I. 289).

From Rājapura, HT. proceeded south-east to

Takka (Cheh-na=Tāki or the Punjab between Vipāsā on the east and the Indus on the west). According to Cunningham (p. 219), it was then the capital of the Punjab. It is 19 miles in direct line from Sākala. Its antiquity is proved by the find of a large number of Indo-Scythian coins at this site. Its history therefore goes back to the 1st century A.D. HT. found here 10 monasteries with only a few believers in Buddhism (W.I. 286).

From Cheh-na (Takka) HT. proceeded to

Chinapati-Bhumi or **China-Bhukti** identified by Cunningham (p. 230) with Patti. This place was selected by Emperor Kaṇiṣka for the residence of his Chinese hostages, to whom, according to the Chinese commentator of HT.'s life, he gave good treatment. HT. records that there were 10 monasteries but he does not mention the number of monks living nor their sect. The Chinese commentator of HT.'s life therein furnishes us with the information that there was one monastery known as Toṣāsana (= pleasure-giving seat), in which dwelt the Śāstra-master Vinītaprabha, who wrote commentaries on the Abhidharma texts. HT. stayed with him for 14 months to study the Abhidharma treatises (W.I. 291).

From the capital of Chinapati-bhūmi HT. went south-east about 80 miles. In HT.'s life the distance is said to be only 8 miles and reached.

Tamasāvana. It was an isolated independent establishment. In the *Divyāvadāna* (p. 399) it is said to be the name of a monastery also. This monastery had 300 monks of the Sarvāstivāda sect. The monks observed the monastic rules strictly. The śāstra-master Kātyāyanīputra composed here the *Jñānaprasthāna-sūtra*. (W.I. 294).

From Tamasāvana monastery HT. proceeded to

Jālandhara, identified by Cunningham (p. 156) with Kangra. It was the name of a city as well as of the district. A former King of Mid-India Wu-ti (= Udita) met an Arhat and appreciated Buddhism. He gave the Arhat sole control of matters relating to monks without any distinction. He travelled all over India and erected *stūpas* and monasteries at all the sacred places. HT. found here 20 monasteries with 1,000 monks, who were either Hīnayānists or Mahāyānists but the number of Hīnayānists was few. There was one monastery called Nagaradhana where HT. studied Abhidharma with Ācārya Candravarma (W.I. 266-7). Cunningham (p. 129) adds that here an inscription, said to be of 801 A.D., has been found, mentioning the name of the king of this place as Jaya Malla Candra.

From Jālandhara, HT. proceeded to

Ku-Lo-To identified by Cunningham (p. 162) with Kullu in the upper valley of the Bias. HT. found here an Aśoka stūpa and 20 monasteries with 1,000 monks mostly Mahāyānists, a few being Hīnayānists (W.I. 298).

Śatadru (She-to-t'u-lo). From Ku-lo-to HT. travelled south over a high mountain and across a river for more than 116 miles to reach this place. Cunningham (pp. 166-7) identifies the place with Sar-hind (= Frontier of Hind) occupied later by Sairindhas of Sirind, i.e., Sar-hind. Śatadru was bounded by the Sutlez on the west and north and Tihara to Ambala on the south and from Ambala to Simla on the east. HT. found here 10 monasteries with a few monks (W.I. 299).

HT. proceeded from Śatadru to

Pāriyātra (=Bairat), the capital of Matsya. The present town is 105 miles south-east of Delhi and 41 miles to the north of Jaipur (C. 391). HT. found here 8 monasteries with a few Hīnayāna monks (W.I. 300).

HT. then proceeded from Bairat to

Mathurā. This famous city was the capital of a large kingdom, lying between the districts of Bairat and Atranji, extending beyond Agra as far as Narwar and Seopuri on the south and the Sindhu river on the west. It included the present districts of Mathura with the small states of Bharatpur, Khiraoli and Dholpur, and the northern half of the Gwalior territory (C. 427-8). HT. found here 20 monasteries of both Hīnayāna and Mahāyāna schools. Fa-hien (pp. 44, 46) saw here 30 monasteries with 3,000 monks, 4 *stūpas* of past Buddhas, and one *stūpa* each for Śāriputra, Mudgalaputra, Pūrṇa Maitrāyaṇīputra, Upāli, Ānanda and Rāhula and one hill-mound of Upagupta. The site of Upagupta monastery was Uru- or Rurumuṇḍa hill. The monastery was built by two brothers, Naṭa and Bhaṭa, which is, why it was also called Naṭa-bhaṭa-vihāra. Upagupta had a great success as a missionary (W.I. 307). Growse identified the Upagupta-vihāra with Yaśa-vihāra in the Kankāli-ṭilā.

HT. saw here 20 monasteries with 200 monks, who were all diligent students of both Hīnayāna and Mahāyāna (W.I. 301). He refers to Fa-hien's account of the stūpas of the past Buddhas and the noted disciples of Gautama Buddha. He also noticed that the worship of the stūpas was continued as it was in Fa-hien's time. He refers to the cave-monastery where a monkey offered honey to Buddha.[1]

---

1. C. (376) writes that HT. referred to the large provinces of Central India, but he did not follow the different directions systematically. Hence C. prefers to deal with all the places of Central India in the following order :

[contd.

Sthāneśvara. Its northern boundary may be taken as a straight line drawn from Hari-ka-patan to Muzaffarnagar near the Ganges, and its southern boundary is an irregular line drawn from Pak-patan on the Sutlez, via Bhatner and Narnol, to Anupshahr on the Ganges (C. 379-83). (The name Sthāneś-vara is derived from Sthānu+Īśvara=Mahādeva). It is said to be the scene of the epic battle of Kurukṣetra, also known as Dharmakṣetra.[1] HT. records that at this place there were 3 monasteries with 700 Hīnayāna monks very probably of the Sarvāstivāda school (W.I. 314-7).

Kapittha (Sen-ka-she=Sāṅkāsya) on the Ikṣumati river. Buddha, it is said, descended here from Traystriṃśa heaven, 18 yojanas south-east of Mathura midway between Piloshana and Kanauj (C.425, 705). HT. speaks of 4 monasteries with 1,000 monks of the Sammitīya school. Within the wall of the monastery there were triple stairs made of precious substances, symbolizing the descent of the Tathāgata from the trayastriṃśa heaven. There was also an Aśoka stone Pillar (W.I. 333-4, 338).

Matipura (= Madawar — C. 399, 401), a small district between the Ganges and the Rāmgaṅgā river. There were 10 monasteries with 800 Sarvāstivādins. Guṇaprabha, author of

---

1. Sthānesvara 2. Bairat 3. Srughna 4. Madāwar 5. Brahmapura 6. Govisana 7. Ahicchatra 8. Pilosana 9. Sankisa 10. Mathura 11. Kanauj 12. Ayuto 13. Hayamukha 14. Prayāga 15. Kauśāmbī 16. Kuśapura 17. Vaiśākha 18. Śrāvasti 19. Kapila 20. Kuśīnagara 21. Vārāṇasī 22. Yodhapatiputra 23. Vṛīji 24. Nepal 25. Magadha 26. Hiraṇya Parvata 27. Campā 28. Kānkjol 29. Puṇḍravardhana 30. Jajhoti 31. Maheśvarapura 32. Ujjain 33. Malwa 34. Kheda or Khaira 35. Ānandapura 36. Vadari or Eder.

(This serial list is no doubt valuable for forming a correct view of the ancient Geography of India, but as our object is to present HT.'s account of the state of Buddhism in Central India, we have to follow Watters' Yuan Chwang.

1. *Mahābhārata* Vanaparva: south of Sarasvatī and north of Dṛṣadvatī, those who dwelt in Kurukṣetra lived in paradise.

the *Tattva-siddhi-śāstra* or *Tattva-sandeśa-sūtra* which deals with Sarvāstivāda doctrines, dwelt here. He did not show reverence to Maitreya Bodhisattva (W.I. 323, 325). His contemporary was Devasena. Burnouf thinks that Guṇaprabha was also known as Guṇamati, teacher of Vasumitra of the *Abhidharma-kośavyākhyā*, who had a dispute with a Sāṅkhya teacher, Saṅghabhadra, the Kashmirian Vaibhāṣika teacher, died here. Another contemporary of Saṃghabhadra was Vasubandhu, devoted to mystic doctrines, evidently because he was also the author of the *Vijñapti-mātratā-siddhi* of the Yogācāra school (W.I. 322-4).

Brahmapura (near Matipura). Its another name was Barāṭ-paṭṭana or Lakkhaṇapura and it was situated amidst the hills, north-east of Haridvāra (C.408). There were 5 monasteries but with few monks (W.I. 329).

Ahicchatra, capital of West Pañcāla near Ramgarh in Rohilkhand (C.416). There were 10 monasteries with 1,000 Sammitīya monks. (W.I. 332).

Vīrāsana (Bhilsana) (C.417), 8 miles to the north of Etah. Buddha delivered here the Skandha-dhātu-sthāna sūtra. There were 2 monasteries with 2,000 Mahāyāna monks. (W.I. 332).

Kānyakubja (Kanauj) (C. 430-43). At the time of HT.'s visit the reigning king was Harṣavardhana with his capital at this place. He was a patron of Buddhism. There were 100 monasteries with 1,000 Hīnayāna and Mahāyāna monks. In Fa-hien's time there were only 2 monasteries. It is therefore apparent that after Fa-hien's time there was a great increase in the popularity of Buddhism. Harṣa reigned for 30 years and held quinquennial assemblies of Buddhist monks. There were 3 monasteries with 5,000 Sarvāstivāda monks (W.I. 343-8).

Govisana (or Kashipur). On its north was Brahmapura, on the west Madawar and on the south and east Ahicchatra, It corresponded to the modern districts of Kashipur, Rampur and Pilbhit. (C.411-2). There were 2 monasteries with 100 Hīnayāna monks (W.I. 330-1).

Srughna (= Sugh). It is 50 miles from Sthāneśvara, wherefrom HT. reached this place. (C.394). There were 5 monasteries and about 1,000 monks, the majority of whom were Hīnayānists. The monks were learned and lucid expounders of abstract doctrines. Many monks came to them for having their doubts resolved by them. (W.I. 318).

Navadevakula (at present Nohbatganj) on the eastern bank of the Ganges (C.438). HT. travelled about 16 miles south-east from Srughna to reach this place. There he saw 3 monasteries with 500 Sarvāstivāda monks. These were enclosed within a wall with separate gates for each vihāra(W.I. 352, 361). It was 20 miles south-east of Kanauj.

Ayodhyā. From Navadevakula HT. travelled about 100 miles and crossed the Ganges to the south to reach Ayodhyā. C. (p. 438) furnishes us with the following information:

"From Kanauj the two Chinese pilgrims followed different routes, Fa-hien having proceeded direct to Sha-chi (Ayodhyā, near Fyzabad on the Ghagra) while HT. followed the course of the Ganges and proceeded 21 miles to the south to the forest of Holi, where were several stūpas erected on spots where Buddha had taken his seat. There were 100 monasteries with 3,000 Hīnayāna and Mahāyāna monks. Here, in an old monastery resided Asaṅga, who composed the *Yogacaryābhumi-śāstra* also known as the *Saptadaśa-bhūmi-śāstra* as also the *Sūtrālaṅkāra-ṭīkā* and *Madhyāntavibhāga-ṭīkā* (edited partially by Prof. Vidhusekhar Sastri) and fully by the Japanese scholars."

Asaṅga at first was a follower of the Mahiśāsaka school; his brother Vasubandhu joined the Sarvāstivāda (later Vaibhāṣika) school. His third brother was Buddhasiṃha. Asaṅga became a Mahāyānic Yogācārin and converted Vasubandhu to that school. Vasubandhu developed the Yogācāra philosophy further and started the Vijñaptimātratā philosophy. This change took place when Vasubandhu heard the *Daśabhūmikasūtra* from a student of Asaṅga.

Hayamukha, north of Ayodhyā across the Ganges. C. (p. 444) prefers Tod's identification with Baiswāra bounded by the Ghagra river on the north and the Jumna on the south. HT. states that there were 5 monasteries with 1000 monks of the Sammitīya school. Here formerly resided Buddhadāsa, author of the *Mahā-vibhāṣā-śāstra* but the Chinese pilgrims do not mention his name (W.I. 359).

Prayāga (Allahabad) at the junction of the two rivers, Jumna and the Ganges. HT. saw here only two monasteries with few monks. He refers to Harṣavardhana and his quinquennial assemblies that were held here (W.I. 361).

Kauśāmbī (village Kosam, near Allahabad). C. (pp. 448-455) writes that it was one of the most celebrated places in ancient India. It is mentioned in the *Rāmāyaṇa*. The story of King Udayana of Kauśāmbī is referred to in Kālidāsa's *Meghadūta*. The distance from Prayāga to Kauśāmbī is 38 miles. The present ruins consist of a huge fortress with an earthen rampart. HT. saw here 10 monasteries but these were mostly in ruins. There resided, however, 300 Hīnayāna monks. Within the palace of the king there was a temple enshrining Buddha. Here in Ghoṣitārāma formerly resided Vasubandhu, who composed the *Vijñaptimātratāsiddhi*. It was translated into Chinese by Gautama-prajñāruci in 520 A.D. and then by Paramārtha in 560 and the third by HT. in 661. This treatise refuted the existence of both matter and mind. In other words, it envisages the unreality of phenomena and consequently of sense-perceptions, apart from the thinking principle, the eternal mind (*vijñaptimātra*) unmoved by changes and unsoiled by error (W.I. 371). HT. remarks that at Kauśāmbī Buddhism, as foretold by Śākyamuni, would ultimately cease to exist. Watters comments on this remark that in the *Mahāmāyā-sūtra*, Buddha predicted that at the end of 1500 years after his demise, a bhikṣu would kill an arhat and the disciples of the arhat would avenge it. This trouble would bring about the end of the religion at the time mentioned above.

Kāsapura (Kuśapura, C.456 : Kājapura, Kuśabhavanapura, named after Rāma's son, later known as Sultanpur). It is surrounded on the three sides by the river Gomatī (Gumtī) (C.459). HT. reached the place from Kauśāmbī after crossing the Ganges. Here were the ruins of an old monastery, in which resided Ācārya Dharmapāla, who defeated the heretics in disputation.

Viśoka (= Viśākhā, Sāketa). The story of Viśākhā is related in the Pali texts. She was the daughter of the rich

Dhanañjaya seṭṭhi, who had emigrated there from Rājagṛha (C.462-3). Here were 20 monasteries with 3,000 Sammitīya monks. In one monastery resided Devaśarman, who lived 10 years after Buddha's demise and wrote a treatise, denying both ego and non-ego. There was here another arhat called Gopā, who wrote a treatise on the Śāstra on the essential realities of Buddhism, affirming the existence of both ego and non-ego. The opposite views of the two teachers led to bitter controversies. This treatise formed one of the six pādas of the *Jñānaprasthāna-sūtra* of the Sarvāstivādins or the Vaibhāṣikas. The Sautrāntikas did not regard this text as canonical (W.I. 374).

Śrāvastī (Sāvatthī, at present Set Mahet). It is 85 miles from Viśoka, a sub-division of Uttar Kośala in Gonda district. The territory of Śrāvastī comprised all the countries between the Himalayas and the Ghagra river (C.474). It is one of the most celebrated centres of Buddhism, as Gautama Buddha resided here for the 14th vassā (rainy season retreat) and subsequently for all the vassās after the 19th vassāvāsa (vide my EMB. (1941) I, p.145 fn.). Buddha exhibited here the miracle of an earthquake limited to a circle defined by him. (Cf. *Gilgit Manuscripts*, vol. III, p. 163: Śrāvastyāṃ mahāprātihāryaṃ vidarśitaṃ bhavati). Here was Jetavanavihāra built by Anāthapiṇḍika Seṭṭhi (W.I. 377.401).

Kapilavastu, the birth-place of Gautama Buddha. It is situated about 85 miles south-east from Śrāvastī. C. (p. 475) identifies it with Nagar in the northern district of Oudh beyond the Ghagra river and therefore in Kośala. The monasteries were in ruins. Only in one monastery, however, there were 300 Sammitīya monks (W.II. 1).

Rāmagrāma was a famous place between Kapilavastu and Kuśīnagara, identified by C. (p. 482) with Deokali. It is now in ruins (W.II. 20f.).

Kuśīnagara (md. Kasia), the site of mahāparinibbāna of Gautama Buddha. It was a wild forest in HT.'s time (W. II. 26f).

Vārāṇasī. The people of this place were wealthy, well-behaved and esteemed in learning. The majority of the people believed in Śaivism, Vaiṣṇavism, etc. There were many ascetics practising austerities. There was an Aśoka stūpa, in front of which was a polished green stone, clear and lustrous like a mirror, in which the reflection of Buddha could be constantly seen (W.II.48).

About two miles from here, there was the Deer-park (mṛgadāya, Sarnath) with a monastery, divided into eight sections and enclosed by a wall. There was also a temple of Buddha very high with eight niches, in which were placed images of Buddha. In the monastery there were about 1500 monks of the Sammitīya school (W.II. 48).

Yuddhapati (Chan-chu) identified by C. (p. 503) with Ghazipur, which was on the Ganges, about 50 miles to the east of Banaras. Here were about 10 monasteries with 1,000 Hīnayāna monks (W.II.59).

Vaiśāli (W.II. 63). After crossing the Gandak, HT. travelled about 25 miles to reach Vaiśālī, identified by C. (p.507) with Besaḍ (Rājā Visāl-ki Garh), the reputed founder of Vaiśalī. Buddha visited the place and said, 'How beautiful, O Ānanda, is the land of Vṛjis.' The people of Vaiśālī were also known as the Licchavis. Here lived the famous danseuse, Āmrapālī, who later on became a nun. Near the site, Vimalakīrti wrote the *Vimala-kīrti-sūtra* (W.II.65).

The present name of Vaiśāli is Tirhut (Tīrabhukti, mentioned in a 12th century ms.). Tirhut is the ancient Videha (C. 718). It was the site of the Second Buddhist Council. Here HT. found only one monastery with a few Sammitīya monks. About half a mile to the north of the monastery Buddha stopped in his last journey to Kuśīnagara, identified by C. (p. 493) with Kasia near Gorakhpur.

Śvetapura. HT. travelled about 13 miles from Vaiśāli to reach this place, where he found a monastery with a few Mahāyāna monks (W.II. 79).

Vṛji (=Vajji). It is identified by C. (pp. 509, 512) with modern Tirhut. HT. travelled about 13 miles from Vaiśāli to reach this place. At the time of Buddha, the Vajjians were divided into eight clans (aṭṭha-kulas), viz., Licchavis, Vaidehīs, Tīrabhuktis, and others. HT. found here 10 monasteries with both Hīnayāna and Mahāyāna monks (W.II. 81).

Nepāl. HT. travelled about 245 miles from Vṛji over a mountain to reach this valley. There were about 2,000 monks of both the Yānas. The rulers of the country were Licchavis and some of them were eminent scholars of Buddhist literature. At HT.'s time it was a dependency of Tibet (W.II. 83-85). C. (516-7) writes that the Raja of Nepal was a Kṣatriya of the Aṃśuvarman race.

Magadha. HT. returned from Nepal to Vaiśāli and therefrom reached Kusumapura, ancient captial of Magadha. The capital was in ruins. At this time the new capital was Pāṭaliputra, 'Palibothra' of the Greeks. (C. 516-20).

While speaking of Magadha, the scene of Buddha's early activities, the pilgrim became enthusiastic and recounted several legends and episodes, many of which he must have learnt from the Chinese version of the *Divyāvadāna*. Some of these are:

(i) Legend of Aśoka's Hell. In this Hell a Śramaṇa was taken for being put to death. The Śramaṇa sought a few moments' respite, within which he became an Arhat. When he was put in the cauldron placed over blazing fire, the fire turned into a pool of cool water with lotus flowers, on one of which the Arhat was found seated in composure (cf. *Divyāvadāna*, p. 374f.).

(ii) Erection of stūpas by Aśoka on the relics of Buddha's earthly remains, in accordance with the advice of his spiritual adviser, Ven. Upagupta.

(iii) Kukkuṭārāma monastery situated in the south-west of Pāṭaliputra, in which a large number of monks, including Piṇḍola Bharadvāja, who is believed to have seen Buddha, were maintained by Aśoka.

(iv) Kapota-vihāra with 200 Sarvāstivāda monks.

(v) Tiloshaka or Tiladaka monastery, a rendezvous of scholar-monks. There was a temple with an image of Buddha, flanked by Avalokiteśvara on the right and the goddess Tārā on the left. The images were made of bronze.

(vi) A monastery built in honour of Ācārya Śīlabhadra, a scion of the royal family of Samataṭa. The Ācārya was very keen for learning and travelled over many countries throughout India. At last, he was ordained by Dharmapāla, a Mahāyānist, and received the necessary instruction from him (W.II. 109).

(vii) A temple with images of Bodhisattvas, Avalokiteśvara and Maitreya.

(viii) A monastery erected by king Bālāditya's son at

Nālandā, where dwelt Ācāryas Dharmapāla, Guṇamati, Sthiramati, Prabhāmitra, Jinamitra, Jinacandra, and Śīlabhadra.

(ix) A temple at Bodh-Gaya known as the Mahābodhi Saṅghārāma built by a king of Ceylon, in which resided 1,000 Mahāyānist Sthavira monks.

Hiraṇyaparvata (= I-lan-na-fo-to) identified by C. (p. 346) with the district of Monghyr. It was bounded on the north by the Ganges; on the south by a forest-clad mountain as far as Parasnath Hill near the junction of the rivers Burakar and Damodar. There were two monasteries with 1,000 monks of the Sarvāstivāda school. There was a stūpa of Śroṇa Viṃśatikoṭi. Here Yakṣa Bakula was overcome by Buddha (W.II. 178-9).

Campā identified by C. (p. 477) with Bhagalpur. There were 10 monasteries with Hīnayāna monks. (W.II. 181).

Kajangala (or Kajughira, Ku-chu-wen-k'i-lo) identified by C. (p. 548) with Kankjol (modern Rajmahal). There were 6 or 7 monasteries with 300 monks (W. II. 183).

Puṇḍravardhana (or Paṇḍravardhana) identified by C. (p. 549) with Pabna (Bengal). There were 20 monasteries with 8,000 monks of both Hīnayāna and Mahāyāna schools. In Po-ki-sha monasteries there 700 Mahāyāna monks. Here Digambara Jainas were numerous (W. II. 184). 20 li to the west of the capital there was a magnificent Buddhist establishment known as Po-shi-po, which had spacious halls and tall storeyed chambers. There were 700 monks of the Mahāyāna school (W. II. 184).

From Puṇḍravardhana HT. travelled 150 miles across the river Brahmaputra to reach Kamrup, an extensive valley of the river together with Kuśa-vihāra. The valley was divided into three districts: Sadiya, Assam proper and Kamrup. According to C. (p.572) Kamrup was included in Eastern India, which comprised the Delta of the Ganges, Sambalpur, Orissa and Ganjam. HT. divided the province into six kingdoms: Kāmarūpa, Samataṭa, Tāmralipti, Karṇa (or Kiraṇa)-suvarṇa, Odra (Orissa) and Ganjam. The order of HT.'s arrangement will be followed in this account.

Kāmarūpa (mod. Assam). Its enlightened ruler at HT.'s time was King Bhāskaravarman, who, though a Brāhmaṇa, took interest in Buddhism and treated the accomplished Śramaṇas with due respect (W. II. 185-6). He invited HT. to pay a visit to his country.

Samataṭa (Jessore). It comprised Gauḍadeśa (Malda), Paṇḍuā ahd Mahāsthāna, 7 miles north of Bogra (C. 724). There were 30 monasteries with 2,000 monks of the Sthavira school. The king was an enthusiastic adherent of Buddhism (W. II. 187).

Tāmralipti near an inlet of the sea. It was bounded on the west by the Hooghly river; on the north by Burdwan and Kalna up to the bank of the Kasai river (C. 577-8). There were 10 monasteries with more than 1,000 monks (no sect mentioned) (W.II. 189).

Karṇa (Kiraṇa) Suvarṇa. It lies to the north-west of Tāmralipti and the same distance to the north-east of Orissa. A number of tribes like the Santhals lived there (C. 575-7). Here were 10 monasteries with 2,000 monks of the Sammitīya school. There were also three monasteries in which the followers of Devadatta resided. They abstained from drinking milk, according to Devadatta's restrictions. There was a magnificent monastery at Raktamṛttikā (Rangamati).

Odra (Ota), identified by C. (p. 584-5) with Orissa. There were 100 monasteries with several Mahāyāna monks. The king himself copied a text entitled *Ta-fang-kuang Fo-hua-yen-ching* (= *Buddhāvataṃsaka-Mahāvaipulya-sūtra* (see my *Aspects of Mahāyāna Buddhism*, p. 42). He sent this text to the Chinese Emperor in 795 A.D. The text was translated into Chinese by Ven. Prajñā of Kipin (Kashmir) (W.II. 193-6).

Kaliṅga. According to the *Dīgha Nikāya* (II, p. 167, 235; *Jātaka* II. p. 367) its capital was Dantapura on the Godāvari river (C.593). The name was derived from a *stūpa* on Buddha's tooth-relic. Its modern capital is Rājamahendri on the Godāvari river (C. 591f.). There were a few monasteries with 500 monks of the Mahāyānist Sthavira school, but the term "Mahāyānist" does not appear in the "Life of HT." In a Tantrik sūtra, Buddha is said to have made the forecast that Kaliṅga would be one of the 12 countries where "perfection could be attained." (W.II. 198)

Dakṣiṇa Kośala, north-west of Kaliṅga, identified by C. (p. 520) with Berar (Vidarbha). The king was a Kṣatriya but a Buddhist in faith and was noted for benevolence. There were 100 monasteries with 10,000 Mahāyāna monks. Nāgārjuna resided here for some time. He was met here by Ven. Āryadeva of Siṃhala. HT. refers to Nāgārjuna's Epistle to king Sātavāhana, available in Tibetan and translated into English by Prof. Wenzel in the JPTS. 1885. (W.II. p. 200, also p. 204).

Andhra, south of Dakṣiṇa Kośala. C. (pp. 603, 605) identified it with modern Telingāṇā. There were 20 monasteries with 3,000 monks (sect not mentioned). It was the centre of the logician Diṅnāga, who was born in Siṁhavaktra, a suburb of Kāñcī in the south. He joined the Vātsiputrīya school. Expelled from the community by his teacher, he joined the Sarvāstivāda school of Vasubandhu. He resided for some time in Bhoraśaila in Orissa. Very often he resided in Ācāra monastery in Mahārāṣṭra. He was a contemporary of the famous poet Kālidāsa. He composed the *Ārya Prajñāpāramitā-vivaraṇa,* translated into Tibetan by Triratnadāsa. He gave up Hīnayānism and devoted himself to the study of Mahāyānism (W.II. 212, 214).

Dhanakaṭaka (= Dharaṇikoṭa) where are the famous Amarāvatī and Jaggayyapeṭa stūpas. Āyaka Pillars at Nāgārjunikoṇḍa were the gift of king Māḍhariputa Siri Vīrapurisadata (=Māṭharīputra Śri Vīrapuruṣadatta) of the Ikṣvāku dynasty (*Ep. Indica*, XX. p. 2-3) of the 3rd or 4th century A.D. The subsidiary structures of the stūpa were made by Cāṃtasiri, sister of king Siri Cāṃtamūla and later probably mother-in-law of king Siri Vīrapurisadata· (See above p. 63). C. (p. 596) writes that Amarāvatī was about 70 miles south of Rājamahendri. There was a high mountain called Brahmagiri, from which King Sātavāhana hewed out a pavilion of five storeys for the residence of Ācārya Nāgārjuna. Fa-hien also noticed it and called it the Pigeon monastery. HT. states that monks of this country were Mahāsaṅghikas, whose Abhidharma treatises were studied by him with two monks, whom he in turn taught the Mahāyāna scriptures. He refers to the Pūrvaśailas and Aparaśailas, who formed one establishment.

In this connection HT. refers to the Śāstra-master Bhāvaviveka, mentioned by Candrakīrti, the commentator of Nāgārjuna's *Madhyamaka-kārikā*. He was a native of South

India (Malayagiri). His disciples lived during the period between Nāgārjuna and Diṅnāga. Bhāva-viveka is said to be the author of the *Prajñā-pradīpa-śāstra* and *Tarka-jvālā*. Schiefner restores the name *Prajñāpradīpa-mālā-mādhyamika-vṛtti* (W.II. 214-24).

Culiya (=Culya or Cola country). C. (p. 626) identifies it with Karnul district, which is north-north-west of Kāñcīpura and 100 miles to the west-south-west of Dharaṇikoṭa. Tanjore was the capital of the country.

Drāviḍa. Its capital was Kāñcīpura (Conjeevaram) on the Palar river (C. 626). It was a seaport of South India often used by the boats sailing to and from Ceylon. Here were 100 monasteries with 10,000 monks of the Sthavira school. It is the birthplace of Dharmapāla, who wrote treatises on etymlogy, logic and metaphysics of Buddhism. HT. states that out of sheer curiosity for learning the Brahmanic Yoga-śāstras, he studied them but found that these were not of that high standard as he had heard them to be from Śīlabhadra. During the pilgrim's stay at Kāñcīpura, about 300 monks arrived there from Ceylon, which country they quitted on account of political disturbance consequent upon the death of the ruling king. On the basis of this information C. (p. 628) calculates that HT. must have arrived at Kāñcīpura about th 30th July, 639 A.D., as, according to Turnour's list of the kings of Ceylon, Raja Buna Mugalan was put to death in 632. (W.II. 226).

Malayakūṭa, identified by C. (p. 622) with the modern districts of Tanjore and Quilon. Madura is its present capital. This county is also known as Malayalam or Malabar (C. 629). It extends up to the Kaveri river. HT. travelled about 500 miles south from Kāñcīpura to this country. Here he saw the remains of many monasteries, one of which was built by Mahinda, son or brother of Emperor Aśoka. He found here only one monastery with a few monks. On the east there was the Potalaka mountain, said to be the favourite resort of Bodhisattva Avalokiteśvara. Near by there was a seaport from which Bodhisattva Vajrabodhi sailed to China.

From Drāviḍa HT. turned northwards and came to

Konkaṇapura, identified by C. (p. 633) with the whole coastline from Bombay to Mangalur. In the 7th century, the northern half of this territory was ruled by the powerful Cālukyas of

Mahārāṣṭra. This place was bounded by Drāviḍa on the south, Dhanakaṭaka on the east, Mahārāṣṭra on the north, and the sea on the west. The pilgrim saw here one temple with the image of Avalokiteśvara. In another temple he saw a similar image about 70 feet high. He stated that Diṅnāga stayed here for some time. There were 100 monasteries with 10,000 monks of either Hīnayāna or Mahāyāna school. There was also a temple with a sandal-wood image of Bodhisattva Maitreya, said to have been made by Śroṇa Viṃśatikoṭi, of whom also there was a *stūpa* (W.II.239).

Mahārāṣṭra, identified by C. (p. 635) with the area bounded by Malava on the north, Dakṣiṇa Kośala and Andhra on the east, Konkaṇa on the south and the sea on the west. The king was Pulakeśi. HT. travelled about 400 miles from Konkaṇapura to reach this place. Its capital was Paithan or Pratiṣṭhāna in the 7th century. The pilgrim found 100 monasteries here with about 5,000 monks of both Hīnayāna and Mahāyāna schools. In an old monastery there was an image of Avalokiteśvara. In a monastery built by Achelo (Ācāra) of Western India, there was a temple with a stone-image of Buddha, 70 feet high. Diṅnāga stayed here for some time (W.II. 239).

Broach (or **Bharukaccha**). It is about 250 miles from Paithan (C. 634). Here the pilgrim saw 10 monasteries with 300 monks of the Mahāyānist Sthavira school (W.II. 241). C. (p. 374) states that it was also called Bharoch (Bhṛgukaccha).

Mālava. According to C. (p. 562), it lies south-east of the river Mahī, about 333 miles to the north-west of Broach. In short, it is the tract of the country lying between Ujjain and Cutch; on its west and east were Gurjjara and Bairaṭ respectively, on the north was Valabhi and on the south was Mahārāṣṭra. HT. writes that the two countries, which esteemed Buddhism and encouraged the study of the Buddhist scriptures were Magadha in the north-east and Valabhi in the south-west. In Mālava there were many monasteries and no less than 20,000 monks of the Sammitīya school. Sixty years before HT.'s visit, it was ruled by a king called Śilāditya, who was a staunch Buddhist. By the side of his palace, the king had built a Buddhist temple artistic in structural and rich in ornamental works. In the temple there were seven images of Buddha. HT. refers to the legend about the controversy of Bhikṣu Bhadraruci with a Brahmin disputant, who was defeated in a disputation (W. II. 242).

Atali, 50 miles to the north-west of Malwa (C. 564). There was only one Deva-temple, but no Buddhist monastery, nor any monk (W.II. 243).

Kheda (or Kaira=Ki-ta). C. (p. 565) thinks that the district of Kaira extended from the bank of the Sabarmati on the west to the great bend of the Mahī river on the north-east, and to Baroda in the south. Dr. Fleet would identify the place with Cutch (modern Kach). The pilgrim found here 10 monasteries with more than 1,000 monks, who were followers of either Hīnayāna or Mahāyāna school (W.II. 245). HT. divided Western India into three states: Valabhi, Gurjjara, and Sindh.

Valabhi (or Balabhadra=Fa-la-pi). It is situated on the eastern side of Gujrat between Ahmedabad and Cambay. It is the extreme western division of Malwa also known as Surāṣṭra. HT. found here 100 monasteries with 6,000 monks of the Sammitīya school. Its reigning king was a Kṣatriya called Dhruvabhaṭṭa, a nephew or son-in-law of Śilāditya, the reigning kings of Kanauj (Kānyakubja). Dhruvabhaṭṭa was a believer in Buddhism. Not far from his capital was a large monastery erected by Acala, in which Ācāryas Guṇamati and Sthiramati resided some time and composed their valuable treatises. (W.II. 246).

Ānandapura. It was about 117 miles north-west of the city of Valabhi. C. (p. 565) identifies it with the triangular tract lying between the mouth of the Banas river on the west and the Sabarmati river on the east. HT. found here 10 monasteries with 1,000 Sammitīya monks (W. II. 247).

Surāṣṭra (Surat). C. (p. 372) writes that its capital was at the foot of the Ujjayanta Hill (another name of Girnar) in the city of Junagarh (=Yavana-gaḍ) 80 miles to the west of Valabhi. Here are the inscriptions of kings Rudradāman and Skandagupta. HT. found 50 monasteries here with 3,000 monks of the Mahāyānist Sthavira school (W.II.248).

Ujjeni(=Ujayana, also Ujjayinī, capital of Avanti province. According to C. (p. 560-1) it was bounded on the west by the Chambal river, on the north by the kingdoms of Mathura and Jajhoti, on the east by Maheśvarapura and on the south by the Satpura mountains running between the Narbada and the Tapti. HT. found here several monasteries but most of them were in ruins. Only 3 or 4 were in a state of preservation with about 300 monks of both Hīnayāna and Mahāyāna schools. (W.II. 250, 351).

Jajhoti (= Chi-chi-to). identified by C. 550-1) with the district of Bundelkhand. Its capital was Khajuraho. The name Jajhoti is derived from Yajur-hotā, an observance of the Yajurveda. There were many monasteries but only a few monks. The king and the people were believers in Brahmanism. The king, though a Brāhmaṇa, patronised Buddhism (W.II. 251).

Maheśvarapura. C. (p. 560) identifies it with Māhiṣmatipura on the upper Narbada. Its boundaries roughly extended from Dumoh and Leoni on the west to the sources of the Narbada on the east. The people were non-Buddhists and so was the king[1] (W.II.250).

HT. went back from Maheśvarapura to Guchala (Gurjjara, north-east of Surāṣṭra), crossed the Sindhu (Indus) river and reached (W.II. 252).

Sindh. C. (pp. 285f.) writes that Sindh comprised the whole valley of the Indus from the Punjab to the sea, including the delta and the island of Cutch. In the 7th century Sindh was divided into four principalities, viz., Upper Sindh, Middle Sindh, Lower Sindh and Cutch.

Upper Sindh comprised the present districts of Kach-Gandāva, Kāhan, Sikārpur and Larkana to the west of the Indus, and to the east the districts of Sabzalkot and Khairpur. In the 7th century its capital was Vicālapura (Pi-chen-po-pu-lo).

Middle Sindh comprised the districts of Sehwan, Hāla, the northern parts of Haidarabad, and Umarkot.

Lower Sindh or Lar district or the district of Pitasila included Patala or Nirunkot in Haidarabad. Nirunkot was situated on a hill. Pitasila was a rock, a long flat-topped hill on which was situated Haidarabad.

The fourth province was Cutch identified by C. with Alor near Bhakar on the Indus (C. 320-346). HT. writes that the people of the place were firm believers in Buddhism. There were several monasteries with 10,000 monks of the Sammitīya school. The king also had faith in Buddhism. Upagupta, it is said, often visited the place. (W.II.252-3).

Mūlasthānipura (Multan) in the north of Sindh. It was the southern province of the Punjab. To the east of Multan was the Rāvi river (C.273). HT. (W.II.224) mentions that there was a magnificent temple of Sūrya-deva. There is no mention of Buddhism.

Parvata (Po-fa-to). Prof. S. N. Majumdar Sastri (p.687) identifies it with a place about 116 miles north-east of Multan. HT. writes that there were 10 monasteries and 1,000 monks of both Hīnayāna and Mahāyāna schools. Ācārya Jinaputra composed the *Yogacaryābhūmi*-śāstra here and Ācāryas Bhadraruci and Guṇaprabha were ordained. The monasteries were in ruins. It was here that HT. studied the *Sammitīyamūla-abhidharma-śāstra* (cf. Nanjio 1272). (W.II.255).

Adhyavakila (or Audumbara = A-tien-p'o-chin-lo). C. (p.346-7) thinks it to be an alternative name for the fourth province of Sindh, i. e., Cutch (see above). HT. writes that its capital was on the Indus river near the sea. There were 80 monasteries with 5,000 monks, mostly of the Sammitīya school. (W.II.256).

Gurjjara (= Ku-che-lo). According to C. (p.357) it was 300 miles to the north of Valabhi or 467 miles to the north-west of Ujjain. Its capital was Bālmer (Pi-lo-mi-lo). HT. writes that there was only one monastery with 100 monks of the Sarvāstivāda school. The king, a scholar, was a believer in Buddhism and a patron of exceptional abilities. (W.II.249).

Avantaka (=A-fan-t'u). Watters (p. 261) suggests that it must have been a locality from which the Sammitīyas were alternatively known as Avantakas. C. thinks that it was Middle Sindh (see above). HT. writes that here were 20 monasteries with 3,000 monks, the majority of whom were Sammitīyas. (W.II.259).

HT. travelled about 150 miles from Avantaka to reach **Varaṇa.** It is identified by C. (p. 97) with the district of Banu. HT. writes that there were many monasteries, though they were mostly in ruins. There were, however, 300 monks, who were all Mahāyānists. (W.II.262).

This is the last place from which the pilgrim returned to his country across the Himalayas.

A TABULAR STATEMENT OF THE BUDDHIST SECTS IN INDIA

(on the basis of information furnished by Hiuen Tsang, 7th century A.D.)

Sthavira-(Thera-) vāda

Countries	No. of monasteries	No. of monks
Samataṭa (Jessore)	30	200
Drâviḍa (capital Kāñcīpura)	100	10,000
Total	130	10,200

Mahāyānist-Sthavira[1]

Bodh-Gaya Mahābodhi Saṅghārāma	1	1,000
Kaliṅga (south-west of Ganjam)	10	500
Bharukaccha (Broach)	10	300
Surāṣṭra (Surat)	50	3,000
Total	71	4,800

1. Lin Li-Kouang on the Chinese version of the Saddharma-smṛtyupasthāna-sūtra, being an introduction to the *Dharmasamuccaya*, a treatise like the *Mahāvyutpatti*, writes :

That the Mahāyānist Sthaviras should be interpreted literally. They actually belonged to the Sthavira shcool but held Mahāyānic views and an Arhat playing the role of a Bodhisattva, i.e. practising *maitrī* and *karuṇā* (amity and compassion) towards all beings. The Abhayagiri monastery of Ceylon, a centre of staunch Theravādins, held Mahāyānic views, for which they were criticised by the conservative monks of Mahāvihāra of Ceylon. See Lin Li-Kouang, *op. cit.*, p. 209 and Beal's *Buddhist Records of the Western World*, II, p. 247.

Mahāsaṅghikas (including Śaila sub-sect)

Countries	No. of monasteries	No. of monks
Pāṭaliputra	1	100
Dhanakaṭaka (Amarāvatī)	20	1,000
Total	21	1,100

Sarvāstivāda

Tamasāvana	1	300
Matipur	20	800
Navadevakula	3	500
Kapota Vihāra (in Magadha)	1	200
Hiraṇyaparvata	2	1,000
Gurjjara	1	100
Total	28	2,900

*Sammitīya**

Ahicchatra	10	1,000
Kapitha (Saṅkāsya)	4	1,000
Hayamukha	5	1,000
Viśoka	20	3,000
Śrāvastī	some in ruins	few
Kapilavastu	mostly in ruins	30
Vārāṇasī	30	3,000
Śarnath	1	1,500
Vaiśali	1	few
Hiraṇyaparvata	10	4,000
Karṇasuvarṇa	10	2,000
Mālava	some	20,000
Valabhi	100	6,000
Ānandapura	10	1,000
Sindh	many	10,000

* It will be observed that the Sammitīyas were the largest in number. It was due perhaps to their *Pudgala-vāda* (migrating but changing soul), which appealed to the Indian Buddhists, who accepted it along with Anatta-vāda of Buddha.

Countries	No. of monasteries	No. of monks
Aviddhakarṇa (A-tien-po-tche-lo)	80	50,000
Badakshan (Pi-to-tche-lo)	50	3,000
A-fan-tu (Middle Sindh)	20	2,000
Total	351	1,08,530

Hinayānists

Puṣkarāvati (Peshawar)	1	some
Shabazgarhi	1	50
Sāgala	1	100
Kuluto	nil	few
Pariyātra (Bairat)	nil	few
Sthāneśvara	3	700
Śrughna	5	1,000
Matipur	1	200
Govisana	2	few
Prayāga	2	few
Kauśāmbī	10	300
Ghazipur	10	1,000 (Beal's Records of the Western World)
Magadha	1	50
Campā	few dozens	200
Total	37	2,600

Mahāyānists

Udyāna	140	18,000
Takṣaśila	few	few
Siṃhapura	1	100
Kullu	20	1,000
Varaṇa	few	300
Total	161	19,400

Both Hīnayānists and Mahāyānists[1]

Countries	No. of monasteries	No. of monks
Kashmir		(sprinkling of Sarvāstivādins and Mahāyāna)
Punach	few	few
Śatadru	10	few
Mathura	20	no figure
Ayodhyā	100	300
Prayāga	2	few
Vaiśāli	3 or 4 in ruins	few
Śvetapura	10	no figure
Nepal	no figure	2,000
Kajaṅgala	6	300
Puṇḍravardhana	20	3,000
Tāmralipti	10	1,000
Malayakūṭa	1	no figure
Konkaṇapura	100	10,000
Ujjayini	3 or 4	300
Mahārāṣṭra	100	5,000
Kheda	10	1,000
Total	397	22,900

1. Very likely both Hīnayāna and Mahāyāna monks had doctrinal differences, but they lived together in the same monastery observing the same monastic rules as those of the Hīnayānists, for the Mahāyānists had no monastic code of their own.

I-tsing's Observations on the Dispersal of Buddhist Sects in India

(671-695 A.D.)

About half a century after Hiuen Tsang's departure from India, I-tsing reached Tāmralipti in 673 A.D. He studied mainly at Nālandā. His mission was to collect the Vinaya texts of the Mūlasarvāstivāda-nikāya in order to correct the malpractices of the Chinese monks.

I-tsing's account of the dispersal of the Buddhist sects in India is as follows:—

I. Ārya Mahāsaṅghika-nikāya had

1. 7 sub-sects.
2. Tripiṭaka in 3 lac ślokas.
3. It was followed in Magadha. A few of them were in Lāṭa and Sindh as also in North and South India.

II. Ārya Sthavira-nikāya had

1. 3 sub-sects.
2. Tripiṭaka in 3 lac ślokas.
3. It was followed in South India and Magadha. A few in Lāṭa and Sindh. It existed along with other sects in East India but not in North India.

III. Ārya Mūla-sarvāstivāda-nikāya had

1. 4 sub-sects, viz., (a) Mūla-sarvāstivāda, (b) Dharmagupta, (c) Mahīśāsaka and (d) Kāśyapīya.
2. Tripiṭaka in 3 lac ślokas.
3. It was flourishing most in Magadha, North and East India, a few in Lāṭa and Sindh and in South India.
4. Dharmaguptas, Mahīśāsakas and Kāśyapīyas were not found in India proper but had followers in Udyāna. A few in Campā.

IV. Ārya Sammitīya-nikāya had

1. 4 sub-sects
2. Tripiṭaka in 2 lac ślokas, Vinaya Piṭaka had 30,000 ślokas.
3. It was flourishing most in Lāṭa and Sindh and in South India; along with other sects in East India but not in North India.

V. Mahāyāna and Hīnayāna. Both of these existed in North India, and also were sprinkled over all other places in India.

I-tsing (Intro., pp. 14-15) describes Mahāyāna very simply thus :

(a) those who worshipped the Bodhisattvas were called Mahāyānists, and

(b) those who did not worship them were Hīnayānists.

He then stated that Mahāyāna was divided into two schools : Mādhyamika and Yogācāra. The former upheld that what was regarded as commonly existed was in reality non-existent, i.e., all objects were mere empty show, while the Yogācārins affirmed that no phenomenal objects existed in reality but their conception existed in mind only (i.e., Vijñaptimātratā), which, however, was real.

Lastly, he remarked that the two systems were perfectly in accordance with the noble doctrine.

Incidentally, he referred to some literary persons, who were mostly Mahāyānists. These were

(i) Mātṛceta, author of the *Śatapañcāśatka.*

(ii) Aśvaghoṣa, the poet and author of the *Buddhacarita Kāvya*, and the *Sūtrālaṅkāra-śāstra* (which, it should be noted, was different from Asaṅga's *Śūtrālaṅkāra*).

(ii) Nāgārjuna's *Suhṛllekha* to king Sātavāhana (translated by Dr. Wenzel from its Tibetan version in JPTS. 1886).

I-tsing has missed to mention several other works of Aśvaghoṣa and Nāgārjuna, (for which see Winternitz, *History of Buddhist Literature*, pp. 256ff.)

He mentions the names of the following distinguished writers: Āryadeva, Vasubandhu, Asaṅga, Bhāvaviveka, Dharmapāla, Dharmakīrti, Śīlabhadra, Guṇamati, Prajñāgupta, Guṇaprabha, and Jinaputra.

Lastly, he mentions the name of Śilāditya (Harṣavardhana) as author of the *Jīmūtavāhana-nāṭaka* (= *Nāgānanda* edited by Prof. Vidhuśekhar Śāstri). He was the patron of Hiuen Tsang.

INDEX

Abhayagirivāsin 49
Abhidhamma 59-60
Abhidhammikas 43-4, 234
Abhidharma 142 f., 222-3
Abhidharmakośa 75, 113, 128, 142, 154, 170, 185, 209, 212
Abhidharmakośavyākhyā 127, 132-3
Abhidharmapiṭaka 175, 219
Abhidharmasāra 148
Abhidharma Vibhāsā-Śāstra 28
Abhiniṣkramaṇa-Sūtra 171
Abhisamaya 89-90
Abulama 62
Acariyaparampara 233-34, traditions of, 232
Ācārya Buddhadeva 133, 157-8
Āciṇṇa 19-20
Āciṇṇa kappa 16
Adasakam nisīdanam 16
Adhi-patimokkha 36
Afghanistan 66, 238
Āgamas 61, 137, 139, 154
Āgantukarajas 114
Ahogaṅga 9, 13
Aindra school of grammarians 8
Ajātasattu 1-2, 8
Ajita 8-9
Akusalamūla 96
Ālāra Kālāma 105
Ālayavijñāna 114-5
Allahabad 9-10
Amalapada 116
Amarāvatī 50, 59, 63-5, 68, 218, 238
Amathita Kappa 16
Ānanda 2, 8, 22, 36-7, 40-3, 79, 129-32, 174-5, 234
Ānantarikas 108
Anātma-vāda 184
Andarab 62, 66
Andhakas 26, 48, 67, 81-5, 90-1, 99-102, 112, 116, 161, 168, 179
Andhra Pradesh 64, 67, 128, 130, 218
Aṅga 1, 110
Aṅguttara Nikāya 3, 37, 139, 199
Antarābhava 114, 126, 169, 183, 202, 207, 209, 216
Anumati Kappa 16, 19-20
Anuruddha 3, 8, 37, 43
Anusayas 84-8, 107, 124-5, 145, 167, 180, 216
Anutpādajñāna 101-2, 160, 173
Aparaśaila 52
Araññakas 46
Arhat 13, 23, 81, 102, 106, 124, 130, 150, 153, 159-60, 179, 215; Sanavasika, 5,—Yasa, 5
Ariyamagga 104-5
Ariyapariyeṣanā-sutta 71
Arūpadhātu 111, 163, 201, 210
Arūpaloka 192
Āryadeva 126
Aśaikṣas 21, 83
Asaṃskṛtas 113
Aśoka 3-4, 6, 33, 59, 126, 129-31, 235-8
Aśokāvadāna 3-4, 127, 130
Asti-vāda 94
Aśvaghoṣa 134, 219
Ātmaka theory 6, 131
Avadānas 129, 131, 226-7, 230, 236, 240
Avalokiteśvara 7
Avanti 4, 9-10, 13, 45, 128, 172, 182, 213
Avasa kappa 16
Avyākatas 112

Bahiyo 37
Bahuśrutīyas 48, 50, 54, 66, 69, 83, 98, 106, 118, 208
Bala 134
Balaprāptas 21
Baluchistan 132
Bareau, Dr. 27, 48, 65, 68, 77, 145
Barua, Dr. 145

Belvalkar, Prof. 7-8
Benaras 132
Bhadda 3
Bhadrasena 5, 7
Bhadrika 2
Bhadrayānika 49, 183
Bhadrayānīya 55, 207
Bhandarkar, Prof. 2
Bharadvāja 2
Bhārahārasūtra 185-6, 190, 197
Bhaṭa 127
Bhāvanāmārga 165, 207, 209
Bhavya 7, 12, 49, 132, 177
Bhikkhunī Nandā 9, 14
Bhikṣu Nāga 6
Bhīrukavana 7
Bhiṭā 9
Bihar 58
Bimbisāra 2
Bindusāra 3
Bodh-Gaya 63, 72
Bodhicaryāvatāra 104
Bodhicitta 104-5
Bodhipakkhīya dhammas 36
Bodhisattva 44, 69, 74-8, 103-4, 133, 178-9, 240
Bodhisattva-vāda 218
Bodhyaṅgas 169
Bombay 62
Brahmacariya 104-5
Brahmacariyavāsa 178
Brahmajāla 105, 137
Brāhmaṇa Vatsa 6
Brahmavihāra 158-9, 163
Brāhmī 182
Buddha, teachings of 69, 117, 171
Buddhadatta 11
Buddhaghoṣa 28-9, 48, 64, 73, 95, 99, 107, 109, 146, 153, 165, 168, 178-9, 200, 213, 215, 226
Buddhajīva 11
Buddhamitra 133-4
Buddhavacana 35, 38, 224
Buddhavisaya 26
Buddhayaśas 11, 171
Buddhila 62, 133
Buddhism, propagation of 129, 224; Spread of 220
Buddhist Council 1, 4, 7-11, 13-5, 22-3, 29, 33-4, 41, 121, 129, 170, 213, 218
Buddhist Sects, sources of 48-56; groups of, 49
Buddhist Synod 82, 126
Burgess, Dr. 63, 238
Bu-ston 2, 6-9, 11, 15, 61, 129, 136, 141

Caitasika 152
Caityakas 50, 52, 58, 64, 115, 238
Caityas 5-6, 57, 64
Cakkhuviññāṇa 112
Campā 141
Caṃtamūla 63
Cāṃtasiri 63
Candrakīrti 191
Caṅkrama 134
Cāturdiśa-saṅgha 230
Cetanā 176
Cetiya 57
Cetiyavādins 48
Ceylon 3-4, 11, 32, 123, 213-4
Ceylonese Chronicles 67, 126, 130, 172, 177, 209, 211, 214
Ceylonese traditions 57, 208
Chaṇḍa Pajjota 213
Chan-Nāgarika 207
Ch'en lun 173
Che-Song-lieu 12
China 12, 127, 135, 171, 181
Chinese 11, 20, 27, 31; traditions 8
Chu Fo-nien 143
Citta 45, 118, 152, 176, 188;-Vipra-yuktas, 176
Cochin China 135
Cullavagga 11, 13, 30, 209, 232
Cunda 36
Cunningham 224

Dabba Mallaputta 42
Dakkhiṇāgiri 35
Dānapati 20
Darśaka 2
Darśanamārga 164, 207
Daśādhyāya Vinaya 12, 140
De Groot 171

Devadatta 34-6, 55
Devaśarmā 146
Dhamma 38, 40, 106, 235
Dhammacakkhu 25
Dhammadhara 34, 35
Dhammakathikas 41-2
Dhammakusala-Arhat 24
Dhammapada 61
Dhammapāla 213
Dhammasaṅgaṇī 144
Dhammutariya 207
Dhanakaṭaka 58, 65, 67
Dhanavatī 133
Dharmaguptas 17-8, 30, 170-172, 183
Dharmaguptakas 121-2
Dharmaskandha 146
Dharmāśoka 29, 33
Dharmatrāta 155-7
Dharmottarīya 49, 55, 181
Dhātukāya 146
Dhūta 46
Dhūtāṅgas 35
Dhūtavāda 44
Dhūtavādins 36
Dhyānas 108, 161, 168-9, 183
Dīgha 199
Dīghabhāṇaka 41
Dīpaṅkara 60
Dīpavaṃsa 11, 29, 48, 58, 201
Divyāvadāna 2, 127, 130, 229-30
Droṇa 17
Dukkha 167, 203-4, 235; realization of, 89; utterance of, 110
Dul-va 11, 16
Dundubhissara 177
Dussīla 95
Dvaṅgula-kappa 16

Early History of Kauśāmbi 9
Early Monastic Buddhism 24
Easterners 10
Ekabbohārikas 48
Ekavyavahārika 49-50, 58

Fa-hien 11, 60-1, 135, 140
Fa-pao 156
Fergusson 63
French 20

Gāmakkhetta 40
Gāmantara Kappa 16
Gandhakuṭī 14
Gandhāra 126, 128-9, 237-8
Gandhāras 235
Gandhārapura 231
Ganges 9
Gautamīputra Sātakarṇi 62
Gavāṃpati 2, 39, 170
Gayāsīsa 36
Geography of Early Buddhism 9
Ghoṣaka 155-7
Gilgit 141
Gokulika 49, 57
Gotama Saṃghadeva 143
Graeco-Bactrians 135
Grierson 214
Groups of Schools 49-51
Guhā-vihāra 133
Guntur district 58, 64, 67, 130
Gupta script 133

Haimavata 53, 82, 177-8; sect, 12, 48; Vinaya, 30
Harivarman 70, 118
Harṣavardhana 181
Hemavatikas 177
Himavantapadesa 237
Hīnayāna 32, 69, 112, 117, 126, 179, 219-20, 222, 229, 236
Histoire du Bouddhisme Indien 51
History of Buddhism 11
Hiuen Tsang 9, 12, 65, 67, 129-30, 134, 143-7, 211-3
Hofinger, M. 20, 29-30
Huviṣka 62, 66, 182

Iddhipāda 138
Identification of Schools 49-50
Ikṣvāku dynasty 63
Imperial History of India 6
Indriyavijñānas 114
Īśvaranirmāṇa 188, 203
I-tsing 11, 61, 135, 182

Jagat Singh stūpa 134
Jaggayyapeṭa 63, 67
Jaina, tradition 13

Jālaka 5
Jambudvīpa 163
Jātaka 59-60, 104, 218, 224-6, 230, 236
Java 135
Jayaswal 5-6
Jetavanīya 49
Jīvitendriya 176
J. Masuda 12, 66-7, 86, 160-1
Jñānaprasthānasūtra 132, 143-5
Jñeyāvaraṇa 26

Kaccāyana 8, 45
Kākavarṇi 3, 33
Kālāśoka 4-9, 14, 29, 32-3
Kaliṅga 67, 212
Kalyāṇamitra 6
Kāmadhātu 163, 167, 170
Kamagulya 62, 66
Kāmarūpa 235, 238
Kanauj 9-10, 135
Kāñcī 213-4
Kaṅkhā 25
Kapila 193
Karuṇā 106, 158-9
Kashgar 135
Kashmir 3-4, 6, 23, 126, 128-32, 143, 232, 235, 237-8, 240
Kāśi 1,6
Kāśyapīya 54, 126, 173, 177-8
Kauṇḍinya 122
Kauśāmbi 10, 122, 128, 134, 141, 213
Keith 7
Kharoasta 132
Ki-tsang 12
Kleśāvaraṇa 26
Kosala 9-10
Kosambi 9, 13, 35
Kośasthāna 154
Kouie-ki 12, 27, 171
Kṛṣṇa 63-4
Kṣayajñāna 101-2, 160
Kṣudrakavastu 11
Kubjita 8
Kukkuṭārāma 28
Kumārajīva 12
Kuśalacitta 167
Kusalamūla 96
Kushan period 135, 182
Kusumapura 6, 14, 63

Lalitavistara 77, 103
Lamotte, Prof. 51
Laṅkādīpa 237
Laṅkāvatāra 78
Lāṭa 61, 65, 135
Laukikamārga 164, 166
Laukika-Samyagdṛṣṭi 108
Laukika-Śraddhendriya 108
Law, B.C. 9, 178
Licchavi 4, 15
Lin li Kouang 68
Lokottaravāda 57, 66
Lokottaravādins 50, 64, 142, 218

Mādhyamikavṛtti 191
Mādhyandina 127
Madhyāntika 3-4, 129, 131, 234-5
Magadha 1-2, 4, 9, 61, 64-5, 129, 131, 178
Maggañāṇa 96
Magga-phala 120
Mahābodhivaṃsa 5, 11
Mahādeva 5-7, 13, 20, 22-4, 28, 30-3, 106, 115, 130
Mahākāśyapa 2, 22, 61; Mahākassapa, 35, 38, 41, 43-4, 46, 129, 170, 218
Mahāmoggallāna 43-4
Mahāpadma Nanda 1, 6, 8, 33
Mahāparinibbānasuttanta 34, 45, 75, 100, 179
Mahāsaṅghika 10, 22, 24, 26, 29, 33, 47-8, 50, 57
Mahāvaṃsa 1, 11, 33, 49, 236-7, 239
Mahāvanavihāra 14
Mahāvastu 30, 57, 60, 76, 81, 142, 227
Mahāvihāra 209
Mahavihāravāsin 49
Mahāvinayadhara 59
Mahāvyutpatti 48
Mahāyāna 23, 26, 30, 64, 69, 112, 117, 126, 179, 212, 218, 227, 229-30
Mahīṃsāsakas 121, 132
Mahīsāsakas 17-20, 50, 55, 116, 121-3, 125-6, 128, 160, 218
Mahīsāsaka-vinaya 11, 30, 39

Majjhima-bhāṇaka 41
Majjhima-Nikāya 37, 41, 79, 102, 105, 137, 233
Malawa 10, 235
Mañjuśrīmūlakalpa 1, 4-7, 11, 238
Marshall, John, Sir 9
Mathura 3, 9-10, 28, 30, 127-9, 132-3, 181, 232, 234, 239
Mātikādharas 41
Matipur 135
Maxmüller 7
Menander 133, 135
Mettā 106
Micchattaniyama 104
Milinda 239
Milindapañha 135, 160
Moggallāna 36-7, 43
Moggaliputta 33, 126, 234
Moggaliputta-Tissa 9, 129 30, 233, 236-7
Mūlasarvāstivāda 30
Mūlasarvāstivādins 136, 141
Mūlasarvāstivāda-Vinaya 11, 16, 127, 141
Muṇḍa 3-4
Mysore 123

Nāga 6-7, 31
Nāgadāsaka 2-4
Nāgārjuna 112, 126, 183, 219, 238
Nāgārjunikonda 50, 59, 63-5, 67-8, 116, 118, 218
Nanda 2-3, 5-8, 31
Nandivardhana 5
Nanjio 60, 140, 171, 182
Nan-kin 12
Nārada 3
Naṭa-bhaṭa-vihāra 127
Neṭrpadaśāstra 127
Nibbāna 113, 150, 180, 184, 198, 200, 203-4, 222
Nibbānabhāva 150-1
Nigaṇṭha-Nātaputta 9, 36, 45, 147
Nikāyas 34, 36, 39, 57, 168, 199, 205, 223-4, 231
Nikāya-Saṅgraha 11
Nirvāṇa 46, 89, 116-7, 161-2, 175, 183-5, 192-3, 216, 235
Nirodha 113
Nītārtha 117, 159
Niyāma 104
Niyāmokkantikathā 78, 104
N. N. Ghosh 9

Obermiller 2, 11, 17-8, 174
Oldenberg 224
Orissa 64

Paccantima Janapada 45
Paccayas 96
Pācīnakā 8
Pācittiya 16
Paiśāci 214
Pāli 11, 15, 19, 41, 81, 129, 182; Grammar, 8; traditions 57, 67, 121, 129, 174, 213; school, 103; suttas 100
Paṃcamātukā 60
Pāṇini 6-8; school 9; Vyākaraṇa 7
Paññattivādins 48
Pārājikas 22
Paramārtha 23-4, 69, 117
Pāramis 104
Paravitāraṇā 25
Pataliputra 9-11, 15, 23, 28, 50, 58, 60-5, 82, 127-31, 135, 213-4
Persia 135
Peshawar 132
Phala 120
Pilindavatsa 2
Piṇḍola Bharadvāja 2
Piṭaka 41-2, 58, 80, 101, 118, 126, 151, 182, 196, 214
P'ou-koung 156
Poussin, L. de la Vallée, Prof. 16-7, 142, 146-7, 175, 193, 209
Prajñapti 194
Prajñaptivādins 50, 58, 66, 98, 118
Prakaraṇapāda 145
Prakrit 19, 118
Prasenajit 3
Przyluski 9-10, 39, 60, 122-3, 128, 171-2, 177
Pubbaseliyas 114, 116-17
Pudgala 174-5, 183-7, 192, 195-8, 206, 216

Pudgala-vāda 184, 189
Purāṇas 1, 4-5, 33, 39, 122, 170
Purāṇa of Dakkhiṇāgiri 218

Queen Māyā 72, 77, 79, 163

Rāhula 2, 43, 74
Rāhulabhadra 132, 136
Rājagaha 4
Rājagirikas 118
Rājagṛha 10, 135
Rājyaśrī 181
Raychaudhury 1, 46
Revata 9-10, 13-15
Revata khadiravanīya 43
Rockhill, W. W. 11
Rudraka Rāmaputra 205
Rūpa-bhāva 149-50
Rūpadhātu 170, 201

Sabbakāmi 8-10, 15
Sabbaññutañāṇa 25
Sahajāti 9, 14
Sailas 52, 172, 218
Saila schools 57-8, 64, 93, 98, 109, 115-6
Sambhoga-Kāya 99
Sambhūta Sāṇavāsī 8-10, 13, 15, 128-9, 132
Sambuddha 3
Saṃkrāntivādins 50, 175
Sammitīyas 56, 163, 174, 181-5, 189, 191, 207-8, 215
Sammitīya School 131
Sammitīya Nikāya Śāstra 184, 189, 193
Sāñchi 177
Saṅgha 6, 13, 20-1, 23-5, 29-41, 106, 119-20, 125, 129, 131, 172, 233
Saṅghabheda 34-5, 37-8
Sañjaya 5
Sāranāth 134, 181-2
Sarvāstivāda 12, 22, 53, 62, 70, 126-8, 131-2, 174-6, 222, 232-3
Sarvāstivādins 10, 18-20, 43, 50, 86-7, 121, 123, 126, 133, 208, 215-228
Satyasiddhi-Śāstra 118
Sautrāntikas 43, 55, 174-6, 215
Schiefner 5-6, 11
Śiśunāga 4, 32-3
Śrāvakas 21, 78-9, 105
Śrāvakabodhi 7, 229
Sthavira 10, 13, 32, 67, 115, 130, 132, 211-4
Sthaviravāda 177, 211
Sthiramati 6-7
Sumana 8-10, 15
Śūrasena 5, 7-8, 127
Surat 212
Suttantas 42-3
Suttantikas 41-2
Sūtrālaṅkāra 78

Takakusu, Prof. 142, 146
Tāmraśāṭīyas 50
Tāmravarṇiya-Nikāya 212
T'an-tai 171
Tāranātha 4-8, 11, 49, 129, 131, 173, 234, 238, 240
Tarkajvālā 174, 183
Tassho 12
Tattvasaṅgraha 189, 206
Tāvatiṃsa 163
Tchou-fu-nien 11
Thera 32; Purāṇa 35
Theravāda 16, 56, 105, 121, 127-8, 148, 179, 182, 211, 214, 222, 233
Theravādins 10, 19, 24, 26, 38, 47, 87, 93, 98, 121, 123, 126, 128, 130, 213, 218, 223, 228-9, 232, 234
Thiti 113
Tibet 7, 31
Tikapaṭṭhāṇa 209
Traividyās 21
Tripiṭaka 23, 133-4
Triratna 46
Tukhāra 131
Tu'akucī 3

Ubbāhikā 14-5
Ubhatobhāgavimutta Arhats 24
Ucchedavāda 200
Udaya 133
Udayana 135
Udāyibhadda 1-3
Ugrasena 5

Ujjaini/Ujjeni 10, 212, 214, 235, 239
Upādhyāyas 22
Urumuṇḍa 127
Uttarakuru 163
Uttarāpathakas 56, 112, 178-9
Upagupta 3, 127, 129-31, 233-4, 237-8
Upāli 22, 41-5, 213
Uttarīyas 50

Vacīsaṃkhāra 109
Vaibhāśikas 43; school 127-8
Vaiśālī 4, 9-10, 13-4, 18-21, 29, 33, 128, 132, 134, 137
Vājiriya 48
Vajjiputtakas 29, 132
Vālukārāma 14
Vālukā Saṅghārāma 20, 21
Vāluraka 62
Vanaspara 134
Vārāṇāsi 232, 237
Vararuci 6-8
Vaśībhūtas 21
Vāsiṣṭīputra siri Pulumāyi 62
Vassakara 40
Vasubandhu 128, 155-8, 174, 183-4, 195, 219
Vatsa 131
Vātsiputrīyas 6
Vatthūpamasutta 46
Vedānta 206
Vetulyakas 48, 98
Vibhajyavāda 208
Vibhajyavādins 208, 209, 211
Vibhāṣā 24, 43
Vigatāśoka 240
Vijñānas 111, 154, 169, 188, 216
Vijñānavāda 23, 189
Vijñapti 94, 144
Vimaṃsā 96
Vimutti 114, 125, 160, 165, 172
Vinaya 10, 13, 18, 20, 35, 38, 40, 52-3, 45, 140, 170, 223
Vinaya-mātṛkā-Sūtra 12
Vinaya Piṭaka 21-2, 59
Viññāṇakhandha 112
Viññatti 95
Vipassanābhinivesa 24
Vipasyanā 127
Vīrasena 5
Viśoka 4-5
Vogel, Dr. 124
Voharo 80

Watters 10, 28, 32
Weber 7
Westerners 9-10,15
Winternitz 224
Wogihara, Prof. 193

Yamunā 10
Yasa 5, 8-10, 13-5, 128, 179
Yavanas 135, 172, 236
Yogācāra 114
Yojana 17
Yonaka 172
Yuan Chwang 28, 31-2, 44, 61, 131, 135, 182